Yuto Tsukuda

It's great when it rains on days when you don't need to go out. On the other hand, if it's really nice out and you can't leave the house, it really feels like you're missing out.

Shun Saeki

At the Ueno Zoo, it's not that easy to get a full-frontal picture of a squirrel like this. However, my wife somehow managed to snap this one easily. It helped that the squirrel didn't move an inch. It was, for a moment, the picture of the unmoving divinity.

D0711830

About the authors

Yuto Tsukuda won the 34th Jump Juniketsu Newcomers' Manga Award for his one-shot story *Kiba ni Naru*. He made his *Weekly Shonen Jump* debut in 2010 with the series *Shonen Shikku*. His follow-up series, *Food Wars!: Shokugeki no Soma*, is his first English-language release.

Shun Saeki made his *Jump NEXT!* debut in 2011 with the one-shot story *Kimi to Watashi no Renai Soudan*. *Food Wars!: Shokugeki no Soma* is his first *Shonen Jump* series.

Food Wars!
SHOKUGEKI NO SOMA

Volume 4
Shonen Jump Manga Edition
Story by Yuto Tsukuda, Art by Shun Saeki
Contributor Yuki Morisaki

Translation: Adrienne Beck
Touch-Up Art & Lettering: NRP Studios
Design: Izumi Evers
Editor: Jennifer LeBlanc

Printed in the U.S.A.

Published by VIZ Media, LLC
P.O. Box 77010
San Francisco, CA 94107

10 9 8 7 6 5 4 3 2
First printing, February 2015
Second printing, July 2015

www.viz.com

THE WORLD'S MOST CUTTING-EDGE MANGA
SHONEN JUMP ADVANCED
www.shonenjump.com

RATED T+ FOR OLDER TEEN

PARENTAL ADVISORY
FOOD WARS! is rated T+ for Older Teen and is recommended for ages 16 and up. This volume contains sexual situations/humor.

ratings.viz.com

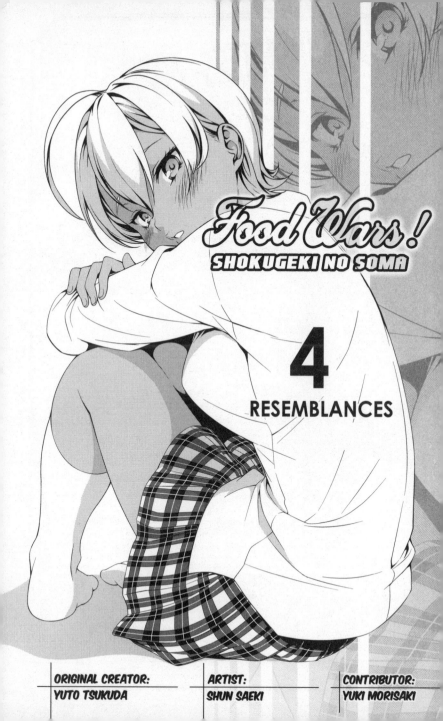

Food Wars!
SHOKUGEKI NO SOMA

4
RESEMBLANCES

ORIGINAL CREATOR:	ARTIST:	CONTRIBUTOR:
YUTO TSUKUDA	SHUN SAEKI	YUKI MORISAKI

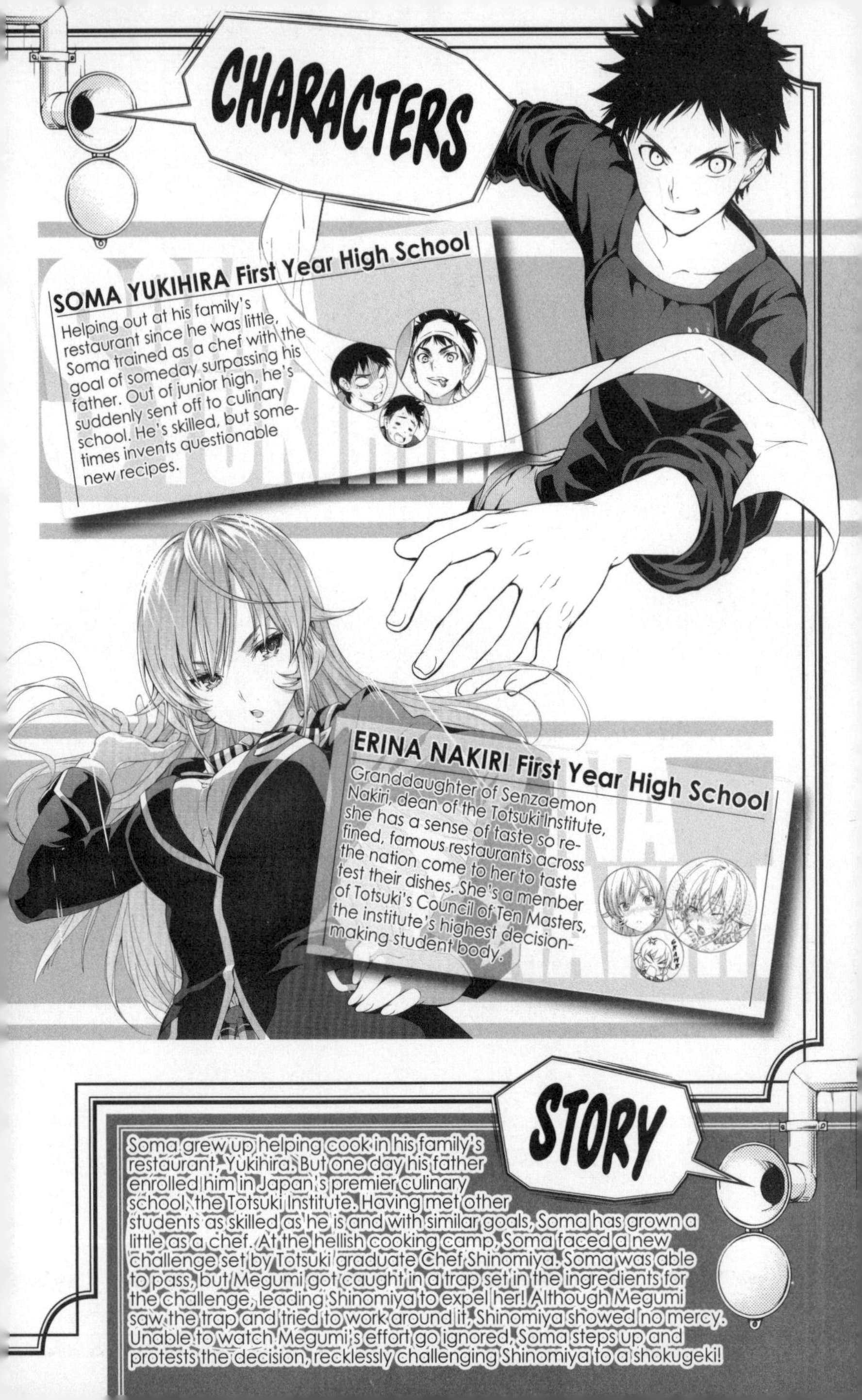

CHARACTERS

SOMA YUKIHIRA First Year High School

Helping out at his family's restaurant since he was little, Soma trained as a chef with the goal of someday surpassing his father. Out of junior high, he's suddenly sent off to culinary school. He's skilled, but sometimes invents questionable new recipes.

ERINA NAKIRI First Year High School

Granddaughter of Senzaemon Nakiri, dean of the Totsuki Institute, she has a sense of taste so refined, famous restaurants across the nation come to her to taste test their dishes. She's a member of Totsuki's Council of Ten Masters, the institute's highest decision-making student body.

STORY

Soma grew up helping cook in his family's restaurant, Yukihira. But one day his father enrolled him in Japan's premier culinary school, the Totsuki Institute. Having met other students as skilled as he is and with similar goals, Soma has grown a little as a chef. At the hellish cooking camp, Soma faced a new challenge set by Totsuki graduate Chef Shinomiya. Soma was able to pass, but Megumi got caught in a trap set in the ingredients for the challenge, leading Shinomiya to expel her! Although Megumi saw the trap and tried to work around it, Shinomiya showed no mercy. Unable to watch Megumi's effort go ignored, Soma steps up and protests the decision, recklessly challenging Shinomiya to a shokugeki!

Shokugeki no SOMA

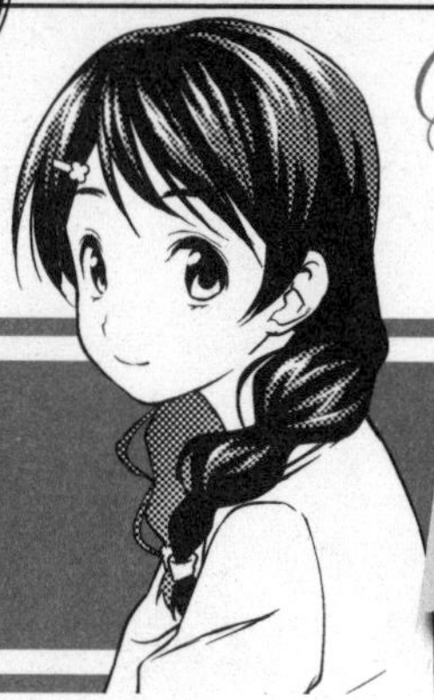

MEGUMI TADOKORO First Year High School

Coming to the big city from the countryside, Megumi made it into the Totsuki Institute at the very bottom of the rankings. Partnered with Soma in their first class, the two became friends. However, he has a tendency to inadvertently yank her around from time to time.

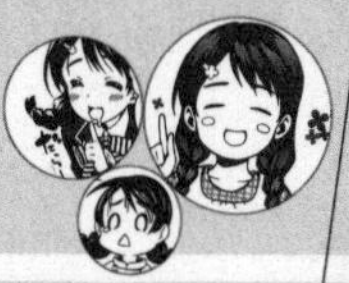

SHUN IBUSAKI
First Year High School

A resident of Polaris Dormitory, he doesn't talk much. With a talent for smoking foods, his dishes are first class.

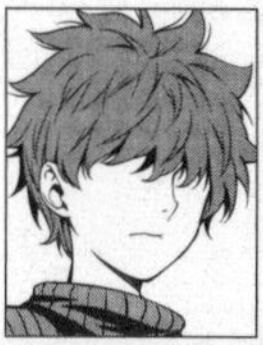

YUKI YOSHINO
First Year High School

A resident of Polaris Dormitory, she raises game animals on campus. Bright and cheerful, she is the energetic one of the Polaris bunch.

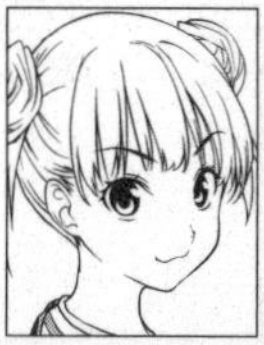

TAKUMI ALDINI
First Year High School

Working at his family's trattoria in Italy from a young age, he transferred into the Totsuki Institute in junior high. Isami is his younger twin brother.

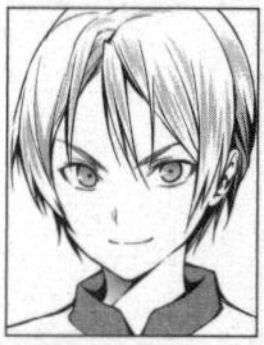

IKUMI MITO
First Year High School

Specializing in meat dishes, she is defeated by Soma in a shokugeki battle and forced to join the Donburi Bowl Society. Her nickname is "Nikumi." (Which she hates.)

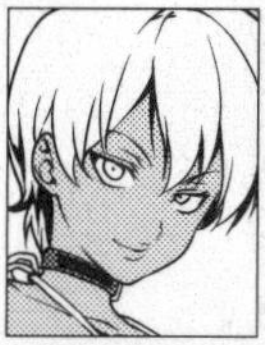

GIN DOJIMA

A Totsuki Institute graduate, he is the company director and head chef of the Totsuki Resort Hotel chain. His daily routine includes physical training.

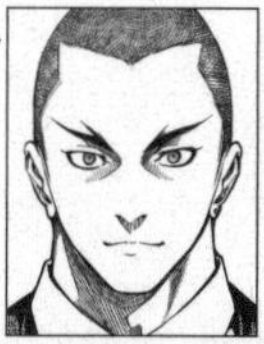

KOJIRO SHINOMIYA

A Totsuki Institute graduate, he now runs his own restaurant in France called Shino's. He is the first Japanese person to receive France's Pluspol Award.

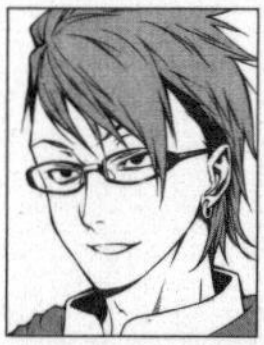

Food Wars! SHOKUGEKI NO SOMA

4

Table of Contents

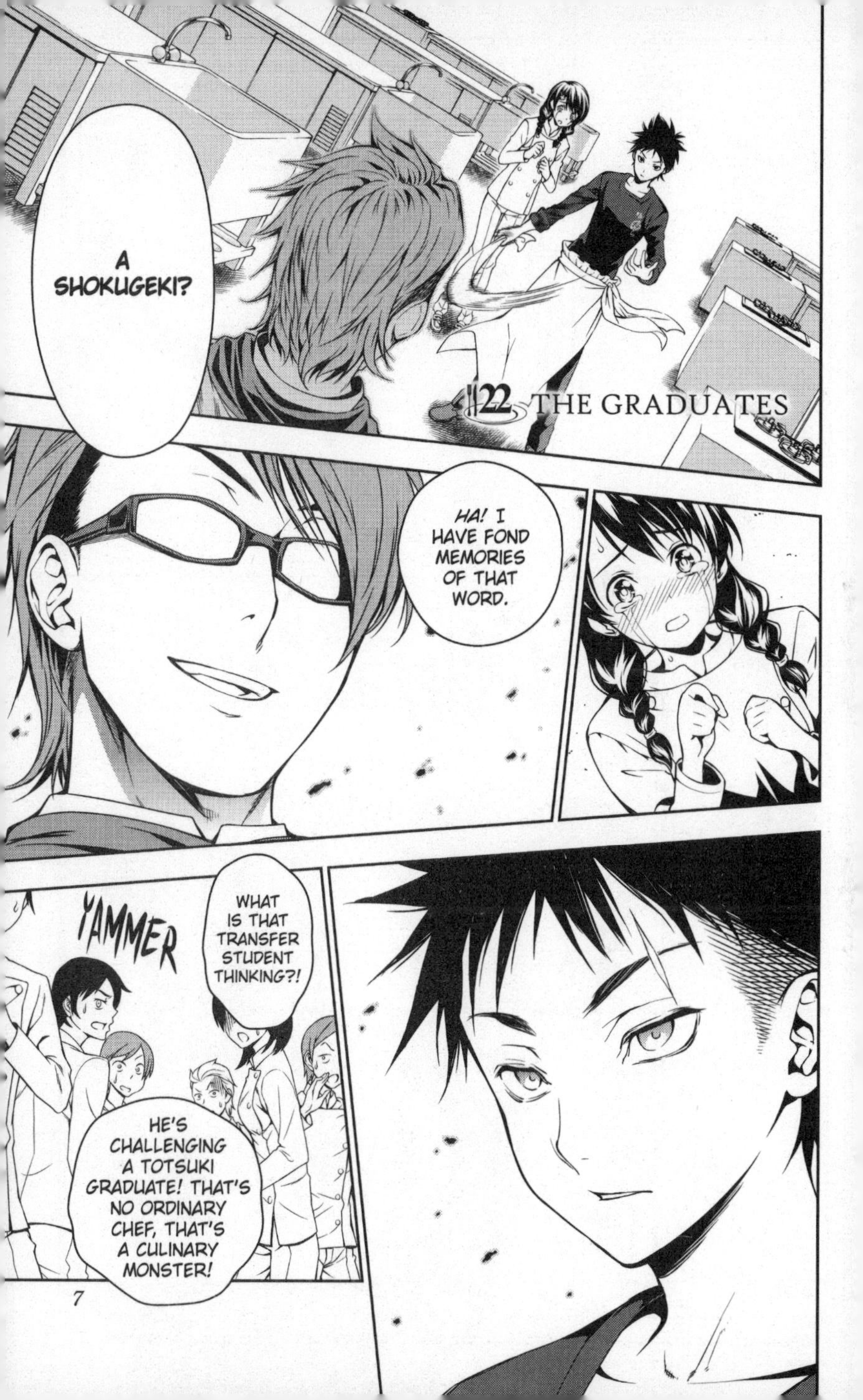
A SHOKUGEKI?
22 THE GRADUATES
HA! I HAVE FOND MEMORIES OF THAT WORD.
YAMMER
WHAT IS THAT TRANSFER STUDENT THINKING?!
HE'S CHALLENGING A TOTSUKI GRADUATE! THAT'S NO ORDINARY CHEF, THAT'S A CULINARY MONSTER!

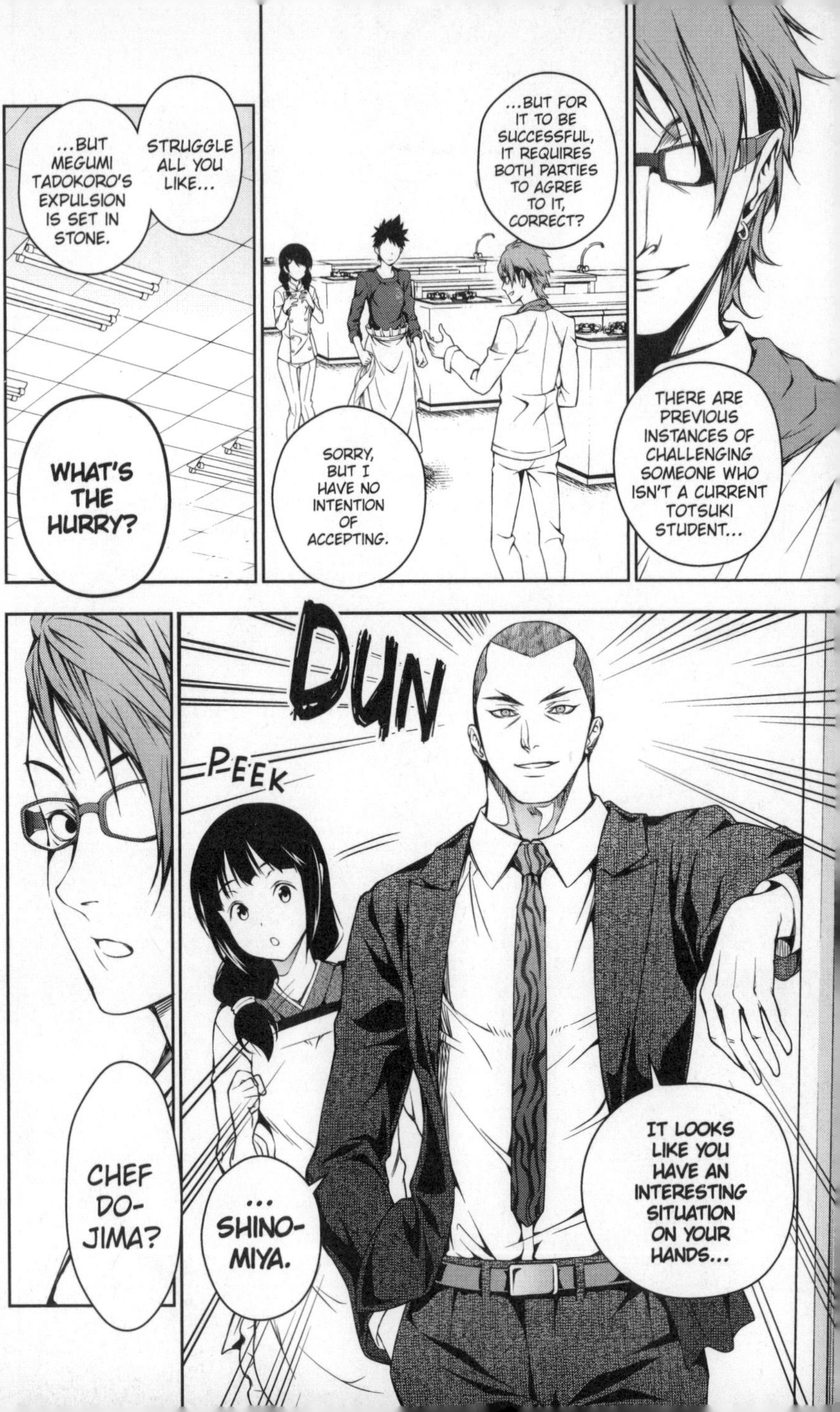
THERE ARE PREVIOUS INSTANCES OF CHALLENGING SOMEONE WHO ISN'T A CURRENT TOTSUKI STUDENT...
...BUT FOR IT TO BE SUCCESSFUL, IT REQUIRES BOTH PARTIES TO AGREE TO IT, CORRECT?
SORRY, BUT I HAVE NO INTENTION OF ACCEPTING.
STRUGGLE ALL YOU LIKE...
...BUT MEGUMI TADOKORO'S EXPULSION IS SET IN STONE.
WHAT'S THE HURRY?
DUN
IT LOOKS LIKE YOU HAVE AN INTERESTING SITUATION ON YOUR HANDS...
PEEK
... SHINO-MIYA.
CHEF DO-JIMA?

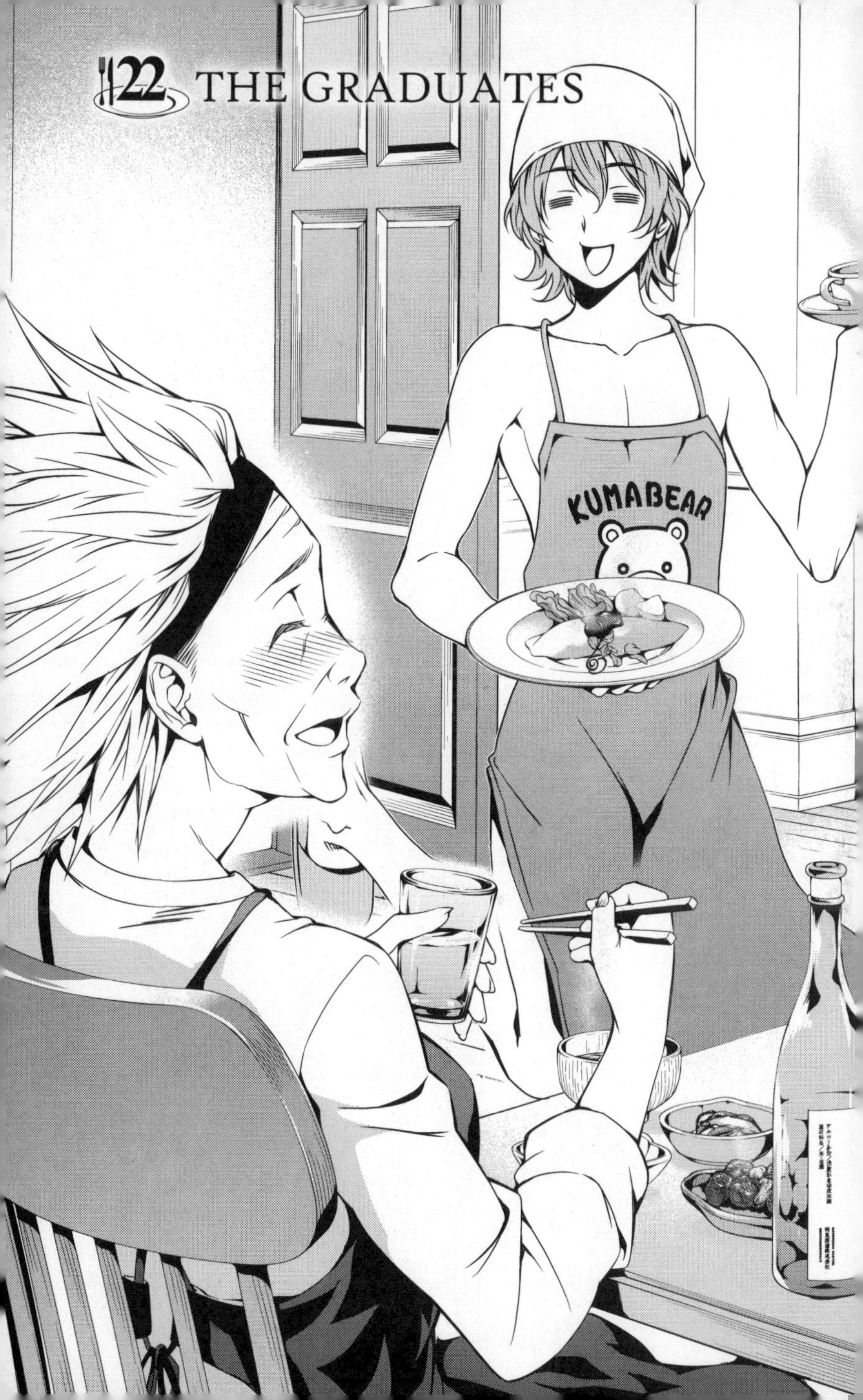
22 THE GRADUATES
KUMABEAR

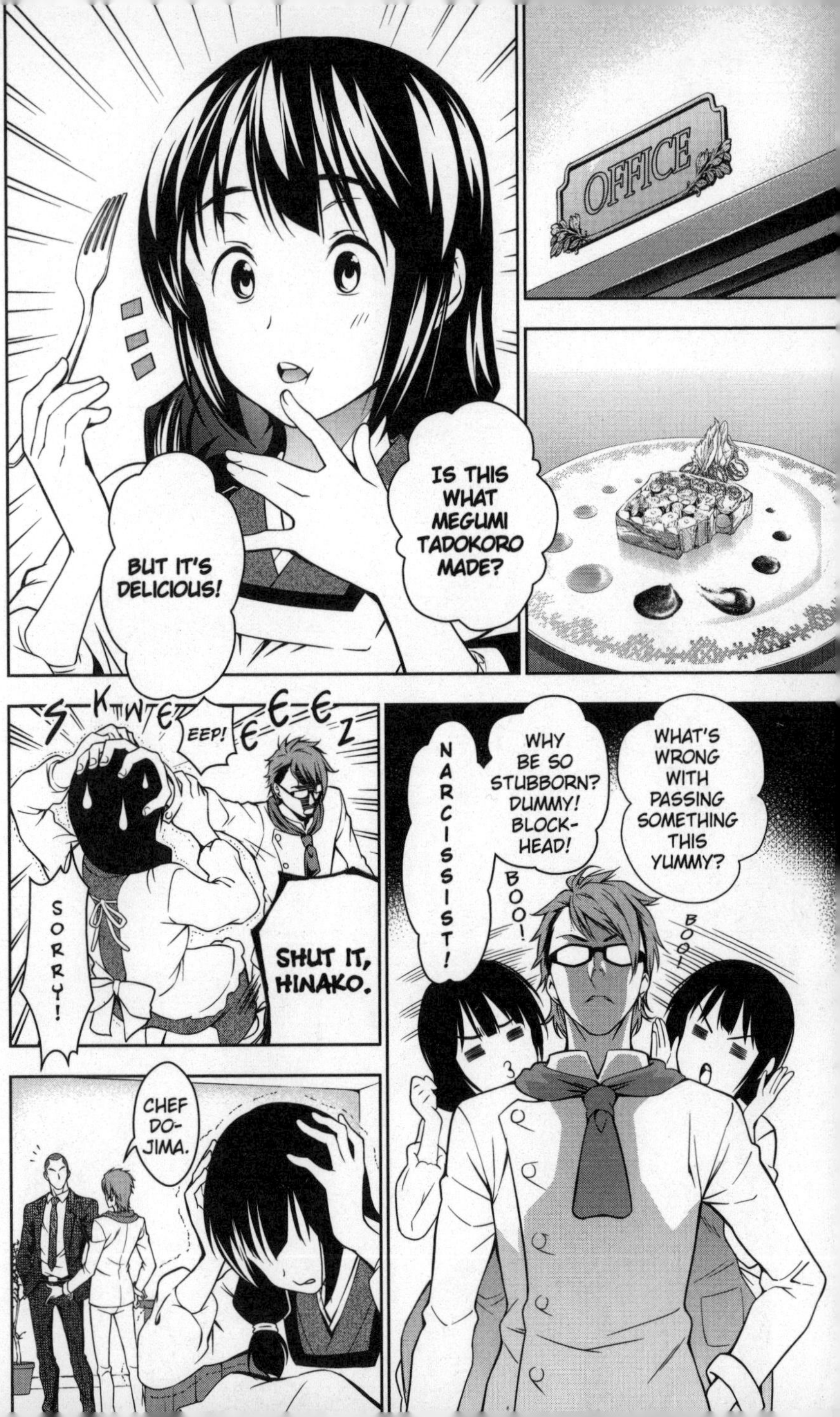
OFFICE
IS THIS WHAT MEGUMI TADOKORO MADE?
BUT IT'S DELICIOUS!
WHAT'S WRONG WITH PASSING SOMETHING THIS YUMMY?
BOO!
WHY BE SO STUBBORN? DUMMY! BLOCK-HEAD!
BOO!
NARCISSIST!
SKWEEEZ
EEP!
SHUT IT, HINAKO.
SORRY!
CHEF DO-JIMA.

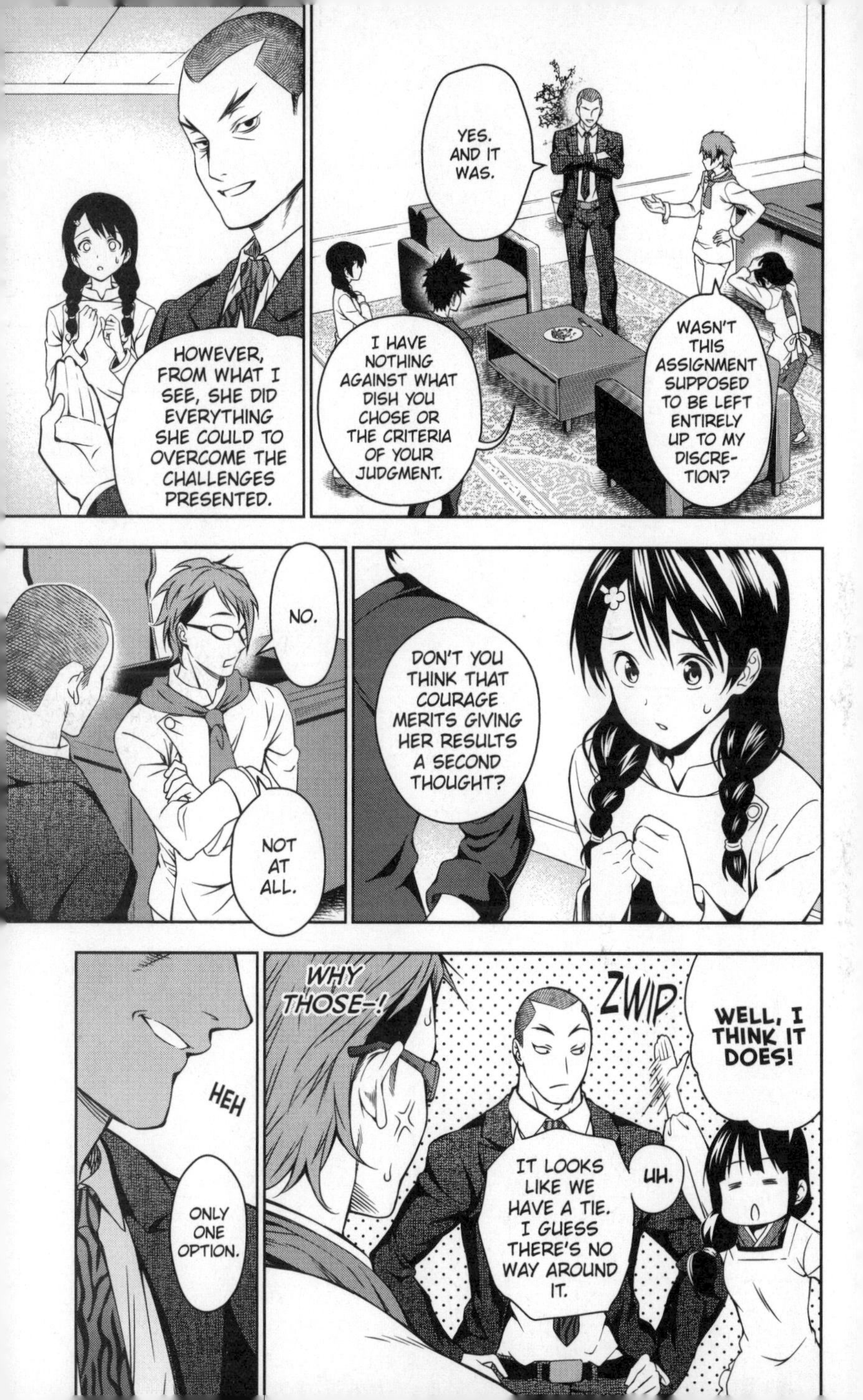
WASN'T THIS ASSIGNMENT SUPPOSED TO BE LEFT ENTIRELY UP TO MY DISCRE- TION?
YES. AND IT WAS.
I HAVE NOTHING AGAINST WHAT DISH YOU CHOSE OR THE CRITERIA OF YOUR JUDGMENT.
HOWEVER, FROM WHAT I SEE, SHE DID EVERYTHING SHE COULD TO OVERCOME THE CHALLENGES PRESENTED.
DON'T YOU THINK THAT COURAGE MERITS GIVING HER RESULTS A SECOND THOUGHT?
NO.
NOT AT ALL.
WELL, I THINK IT DOES!
ZWIP
WHY THOSE-!
UH.
IT LOOKS LIKE WE HAVE A TIE. I GUESS THERE'S NO WAY AROUND IT.
HEH
ONLY ONE OPTION.

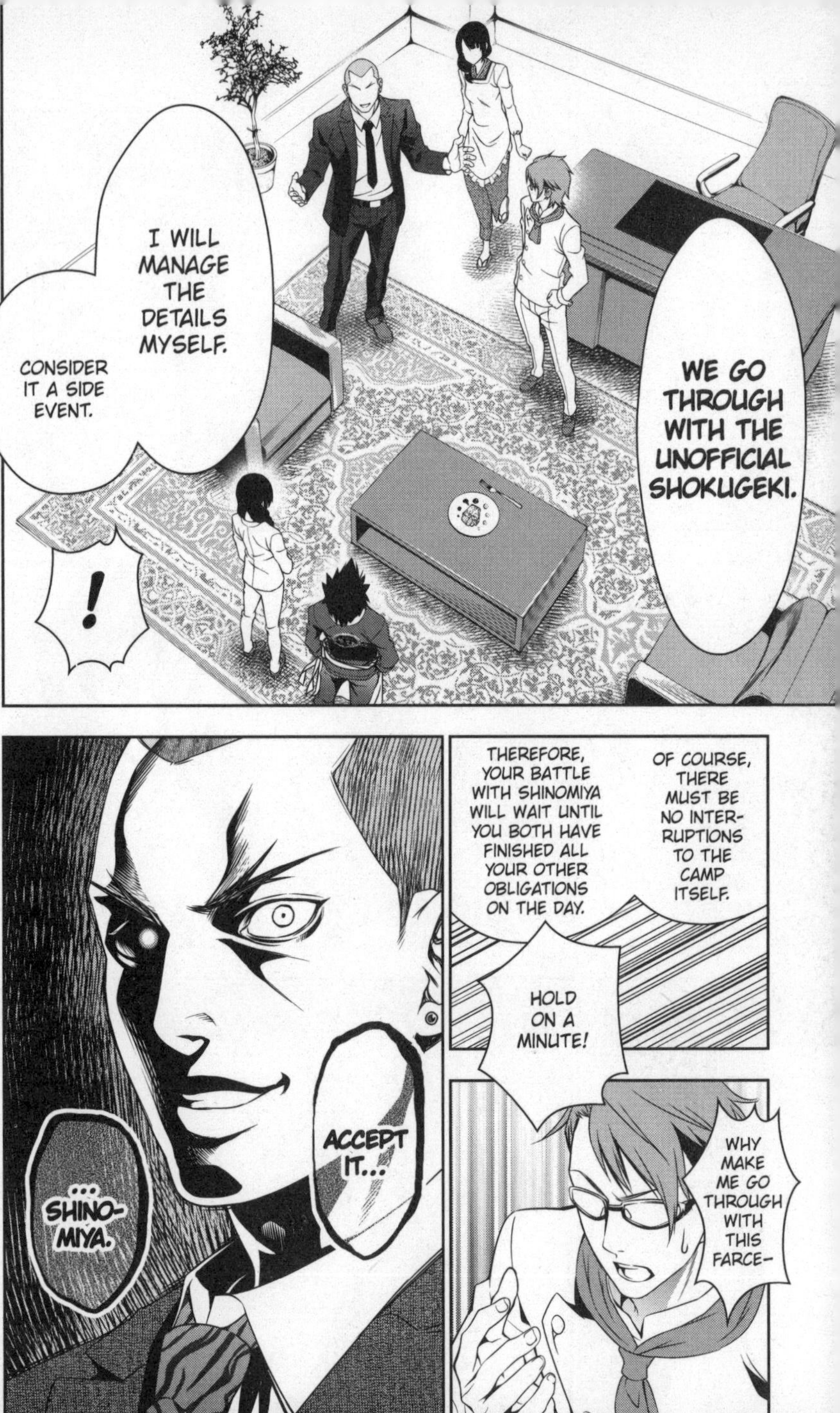
WE GO THROUGH WITH THE UNOFFICIAL SHOKUGEKI.
I WILL MANAGE THE DETAILS MYSELF.
CONSIDER IT A SIDE EVENT.
!
OF COURSE, THERE MUST BE NO INTER-RUPTIONS TO THE CAMP ITSELF.
THEREFORE, YOUR BATTLE WITH SHINOMIYA WILL WAIT UNTIL YOU BOTH HAVE FINISHED ALL YOUR OTHER OBLIGATIONS ON THE DAY.
HOLD ON A MINUTE!
WHY MAKE ME GO THROUGH WITH THIS FARCE-
ACCEPT IT...
...SHINOMIYA.

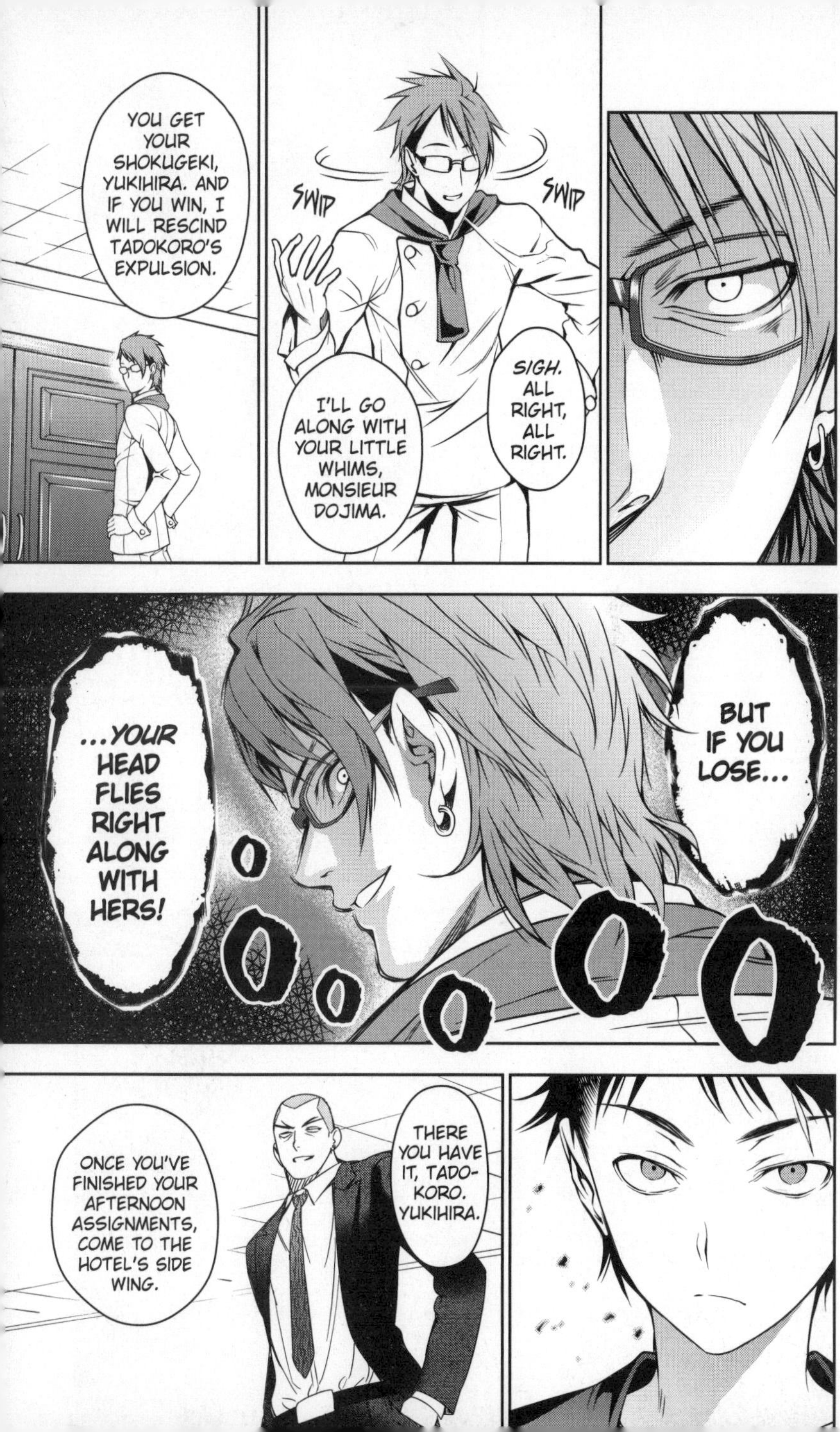
SWIP
SWIP
SIGH. ALL RIGHT, ALL RIGHT.
I'LL GO ALONG WITH YOUR LITTLE WHIMS, MONSIEUR DOJIMA.
YOU GET YOUR SHOKUGEKI, YUKIHIRA. AND IF YOU WIN, I WILL RESCIND TADOKORO'S EXPULSION.
BUT IF YOU LOSE...
...YOUR HEAD FLIES RIGHT ALONG WITH HERS!
THERE YOU HAVE IT, TADOKORO. YUKIHIRA.
ONCE YOU'VE FINISHED YOUR AFTERNOON ASSIGNMENTS, COME TO THE HOTEL'S SIDE WING.

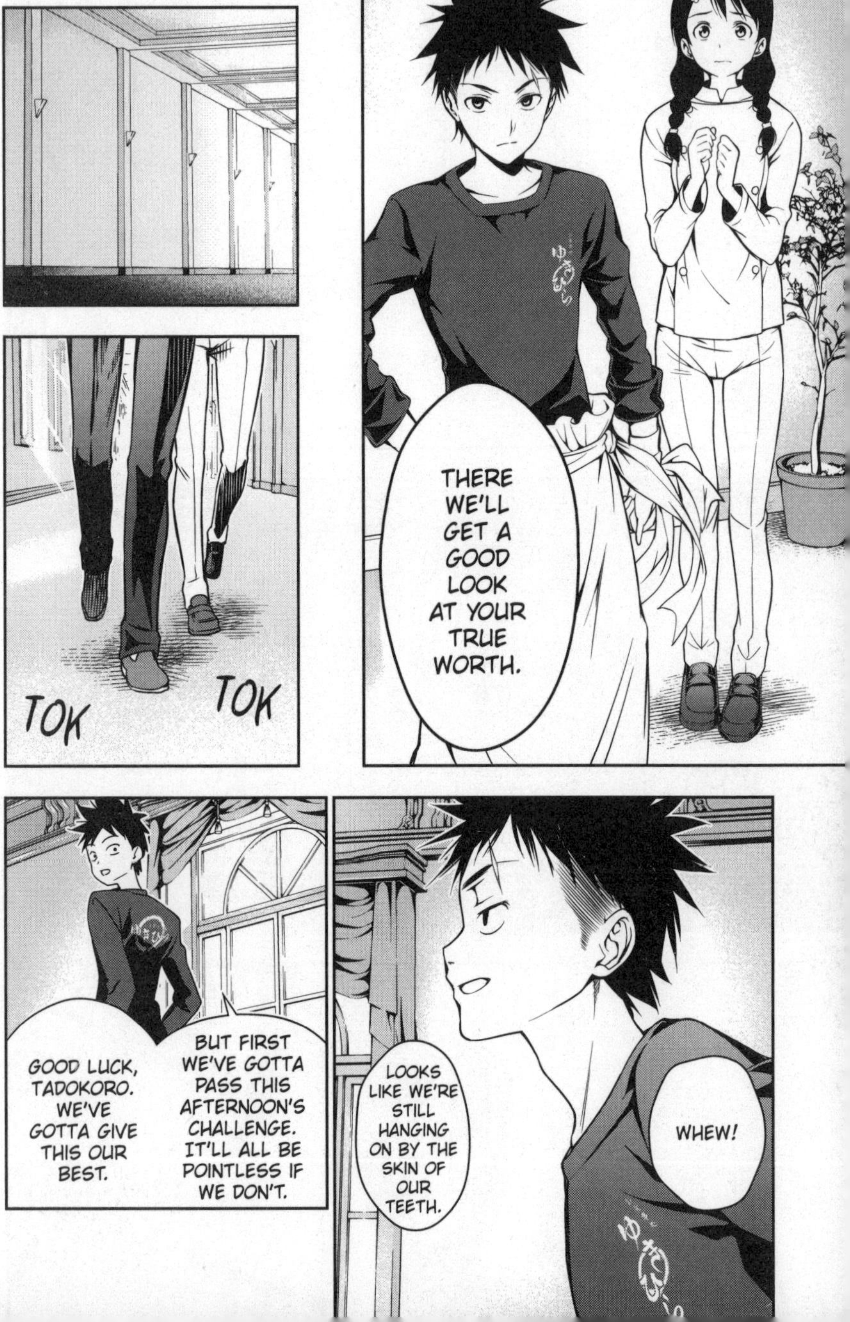
THERE WE'LL GET A GOOD LOOK AT YOUR TRUE WORTH.
TOK
TOK
WHEW!
LOOKS LIKE WE'RE STILL HANGING ON BY THE SKIN OF OUR TEETH.
BUT FIRST WE'VE GOTTA PASS THIS AFTERNOON'S CHALLENGE. IT'LL ALL BE POINTLESS IF WE DON'T.
GOOD LUCK, TADOKORO. WE'VE GOTTA GIVE THIS OUR BEST.

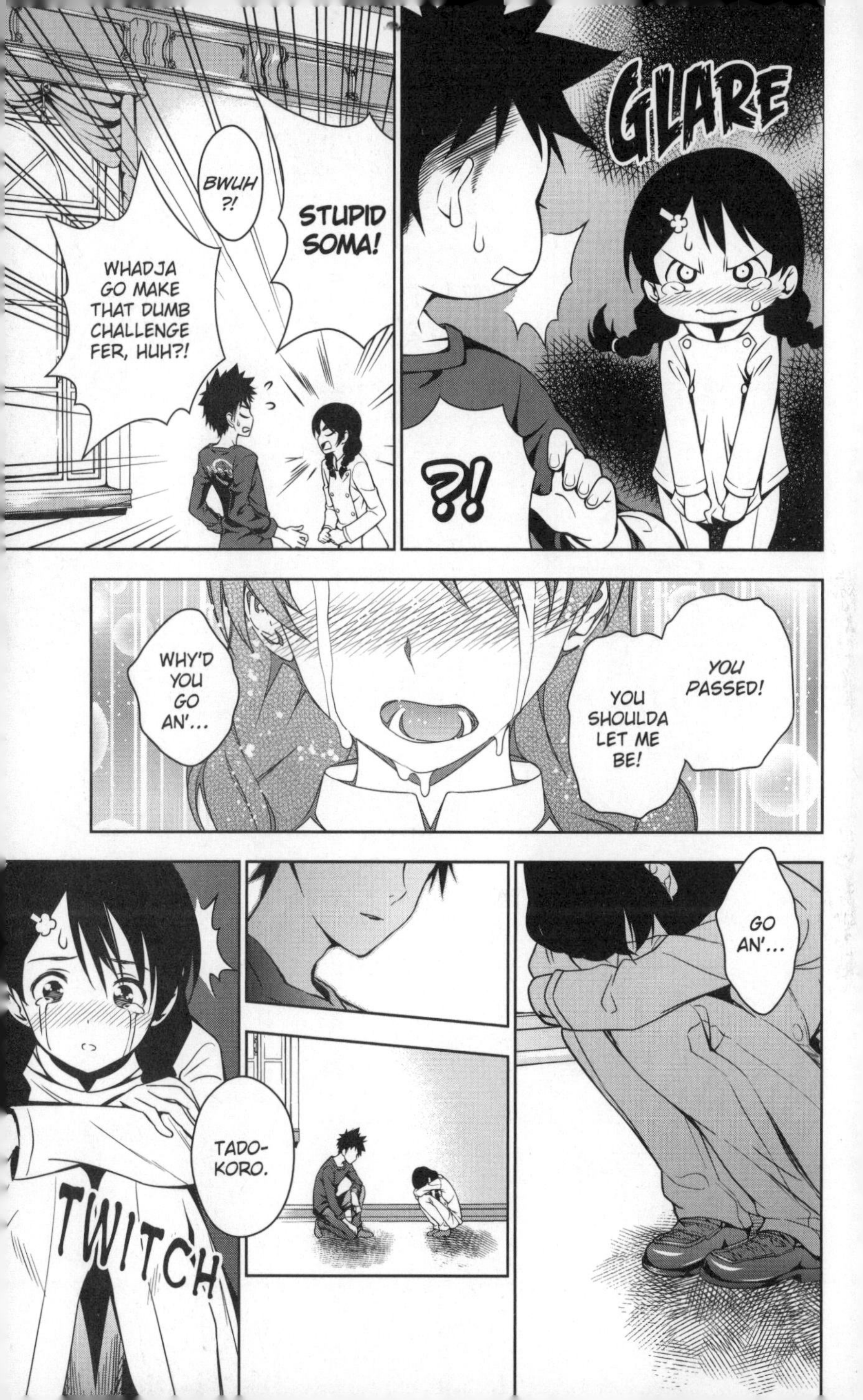
GLARE
?!
STUPID SOMA!
BWUH ?!
WHADJA GO MAKE THAT DUMB CHALLENGE FER, HUH?!
YOU PASSED!
YOU SHOULDA LET ME BE!
WHY'D YOU GO AN'...
GO AN'...
TADO-KORO.
TWITCH

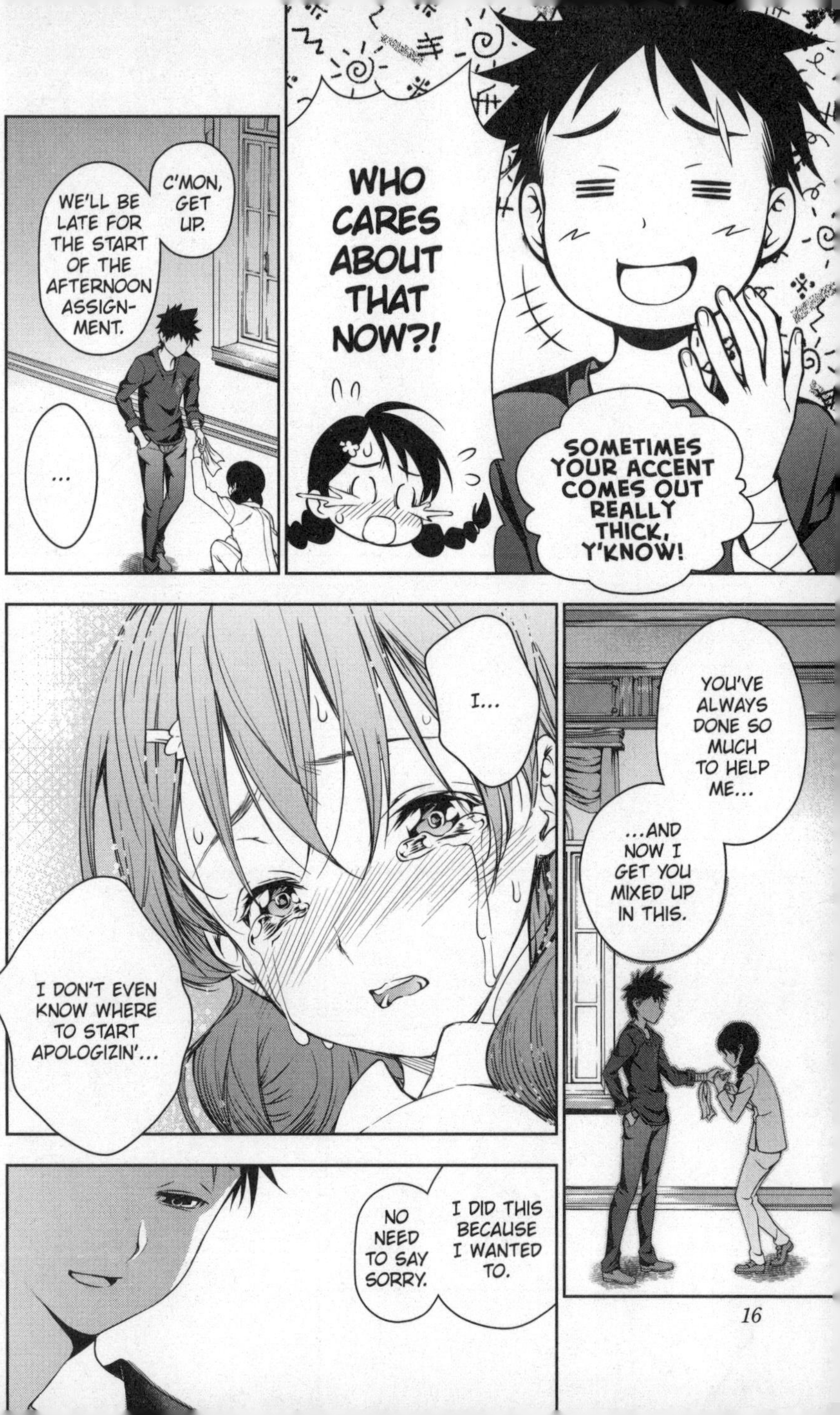
WHO CARES ABOUT THAT NOW?!
SOMETIMES YOUR ACCENT COMES OUT REALLY THICK, Y'KNOW!
C'MON, GET UP.
WE'LL BE LATE FOR THE START OF THE AFTERNOON ASSIGN-MENT.
...
YOU'VE ALWAYS DONE SO MUCH TO HELP ME...
...AND NOW I GET YOU MIXED UP IN THIS.
I...
I DON'T EVEN KNOW WHERE TO START APOLOGIZIN'...
I DID THIS BECAUSE I WANTED TO.
NO NEED TO SAY SORRY.

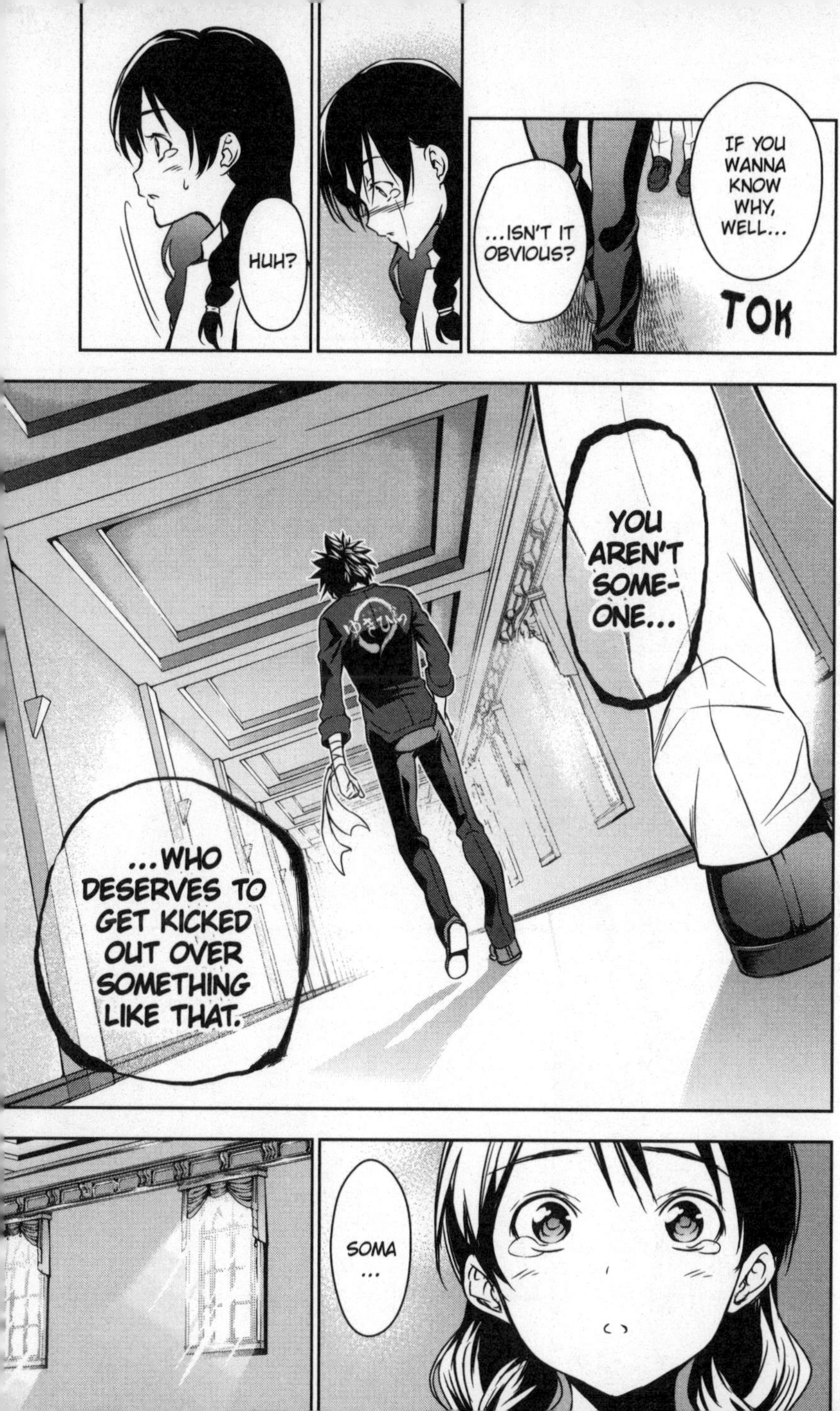
IF YOU WANNA KNOW WHY, WELL...
...ISN'T IT OBVIOUS?
TOK
HUH?
YOU AREN'T SOME-ONE...
...WHO DESERVES TO GET KICKED OUT OVER SOMETHING LIKE THAT.
SOMA ...

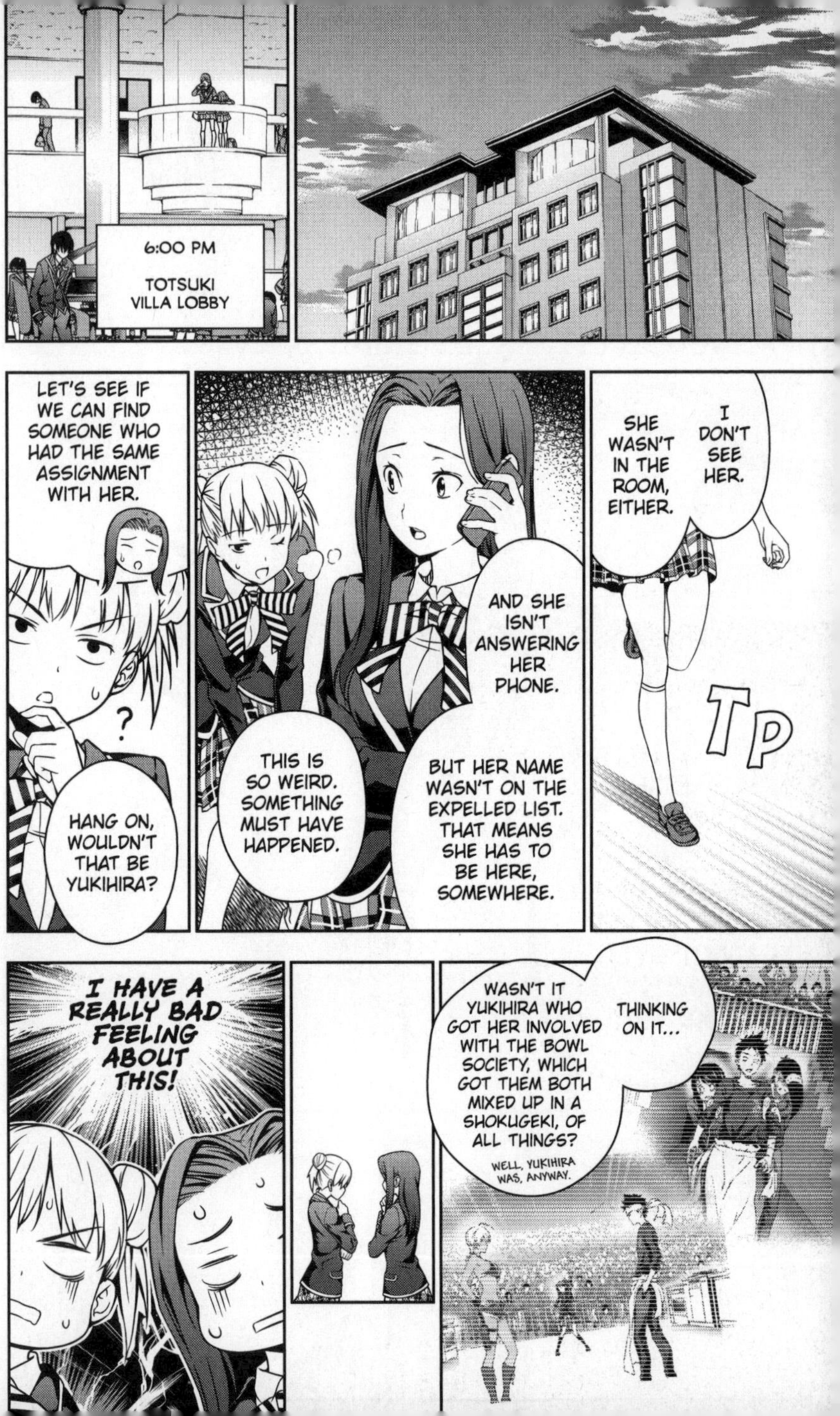
6:00 PM
TOTSUKI VILLA LOBBY
I DON'T SEE HER.
SHE WASN'T IN THE ROOM, EITHER.
TP
AND SHE ISN'T ANSWERING HER PHONE.
BUT HER NAME WASN'T ON THE EXPELLED LIST. THAT MEANS SHE HAS TO BE HERE, SOMEWHERE.
THIS IS SO WEIRD. SOMETHING MUST HAVE HAPPENED.
LET'S SEE IF WE CAN FIND SOMEONE WHO HAD THE SAME ASSIGNMENT WITH HER.
HANG ON, WOULDN'T THAT BE YUKIHIRA?
THINKING ON IT...
WASN'T IT YUKIHIRA WHO GOT HER INVOLVED WITH THE BOWL SOCIETY, WHICH GOT THEM BOTH MIXED UP IN A SHOKUGEKI, OF ALL THINGS?
WELL, YUKIHIRA WAS, ANYWAY.
I HAVE A REALLY BAD FEELING ABOUT THIS!

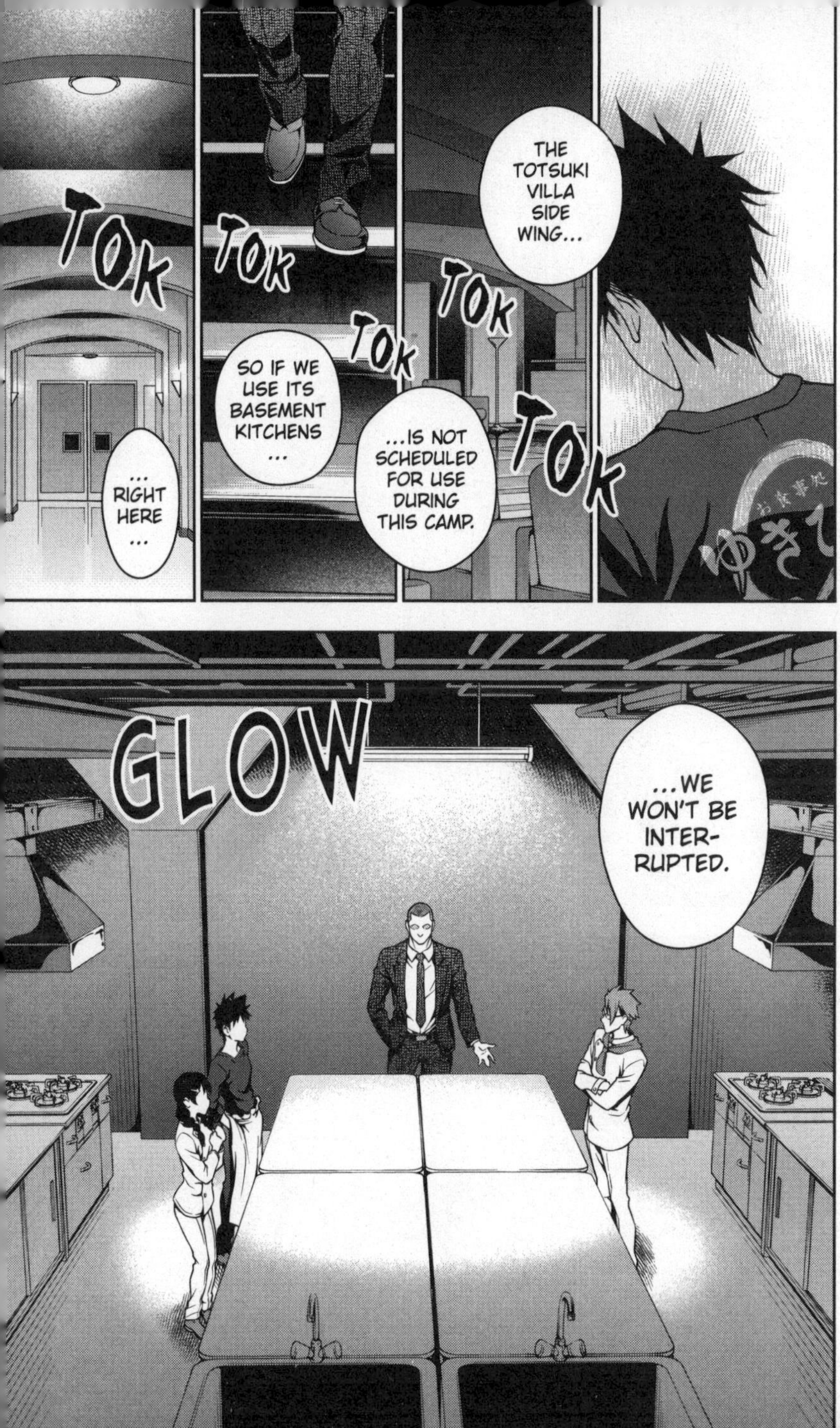
THE TOTSUKI VILLA SIDE WING...
TOK
TOK
...IS NOT SCHEDULED FOR USE DURING THIS CAMP.
TOK
SO IF WE USE ITS BASEMENT KITCHENS ...
TOK
TOK
... RIGHT HERE ...
GLOW
...WE WON'T BE INTER-RUPTED.

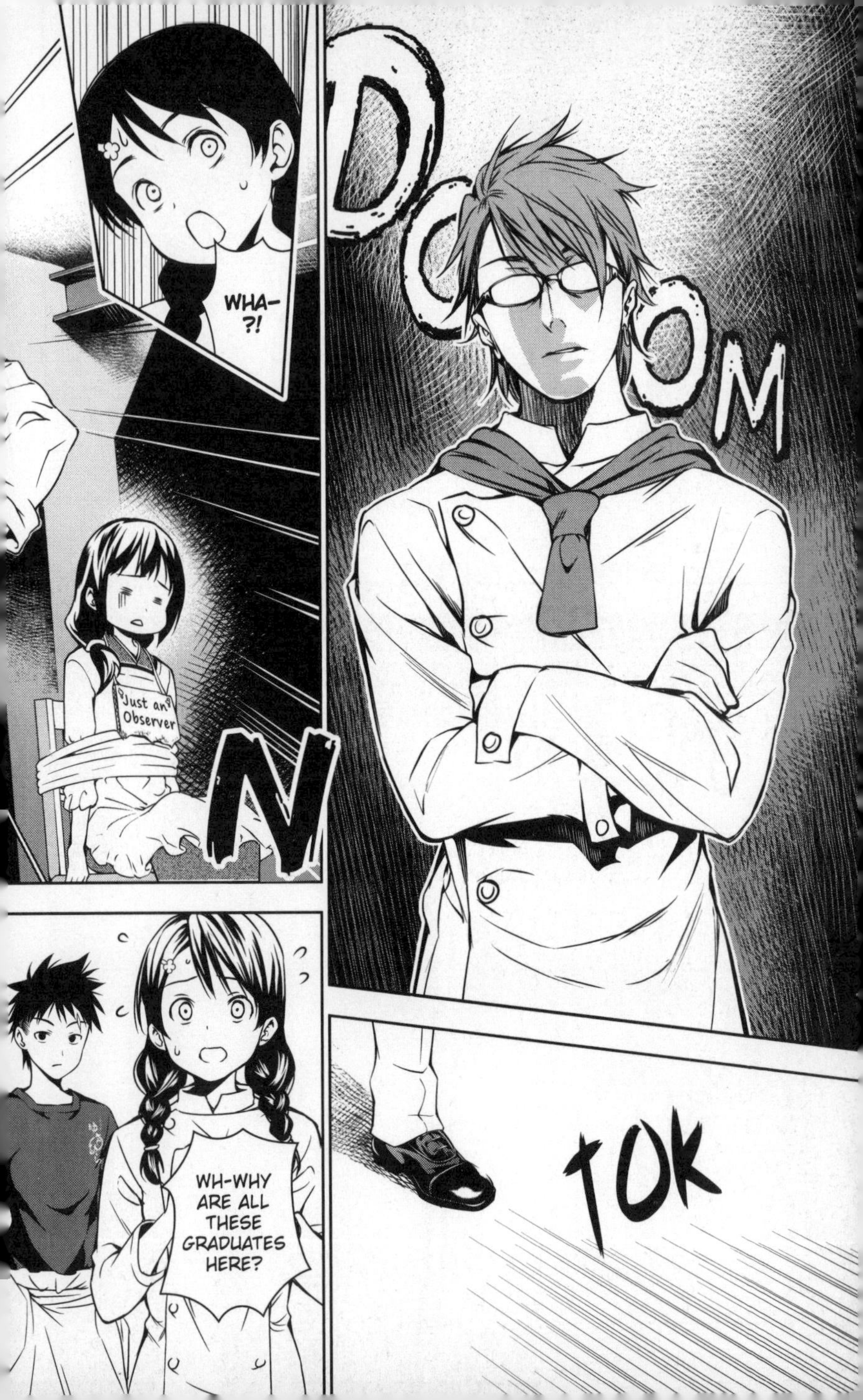
DOOOM
WHA-?!
Just an Observer
N
TOK
WH-WHY ARE ALL THESE GRADUATES HERE?

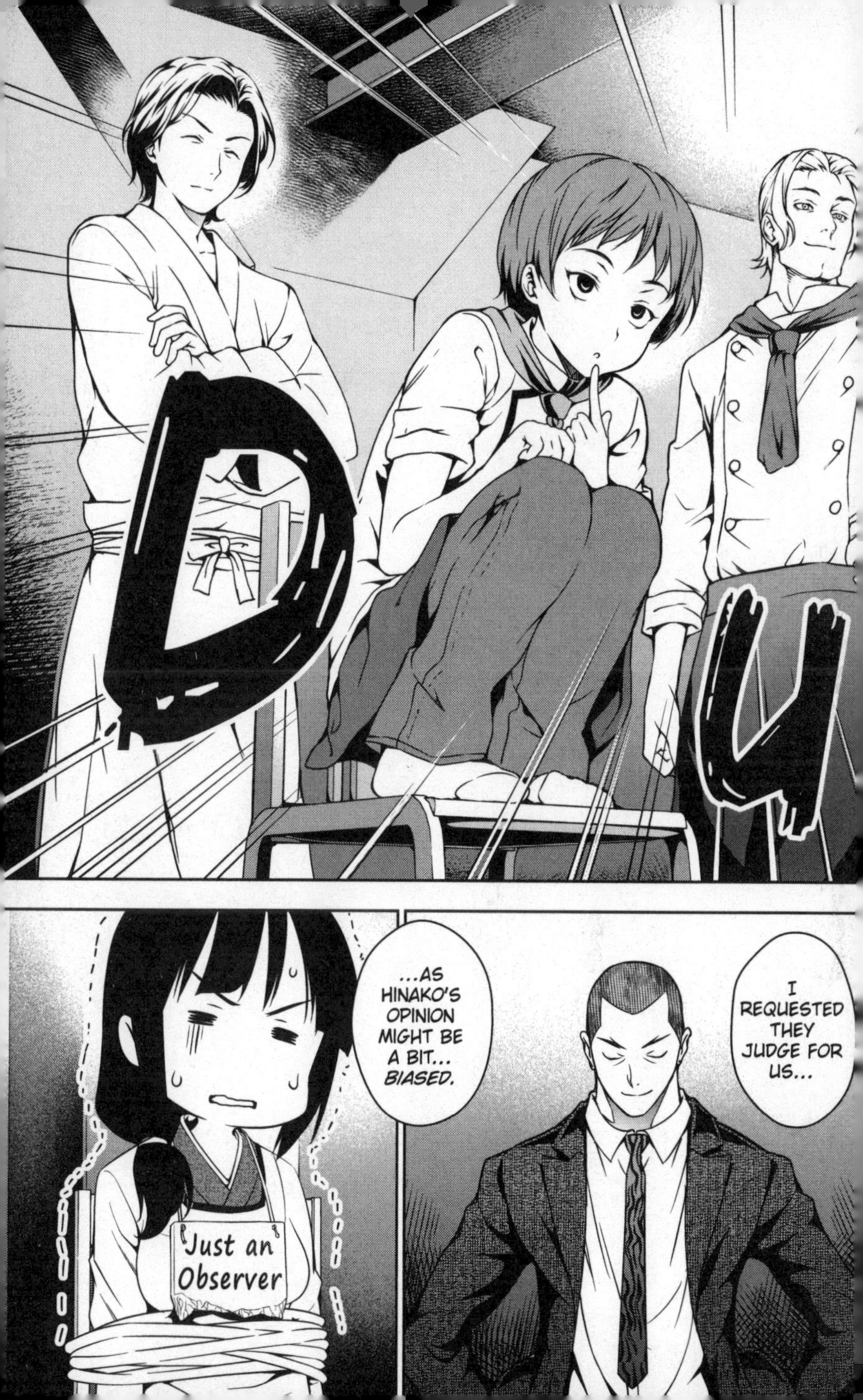
DU
I REQUESTED THEY JUDGE FOR US...
...AS HINAKO'S OPINION MIGHT BE A BIT... *BIASED.*
Just an Observer

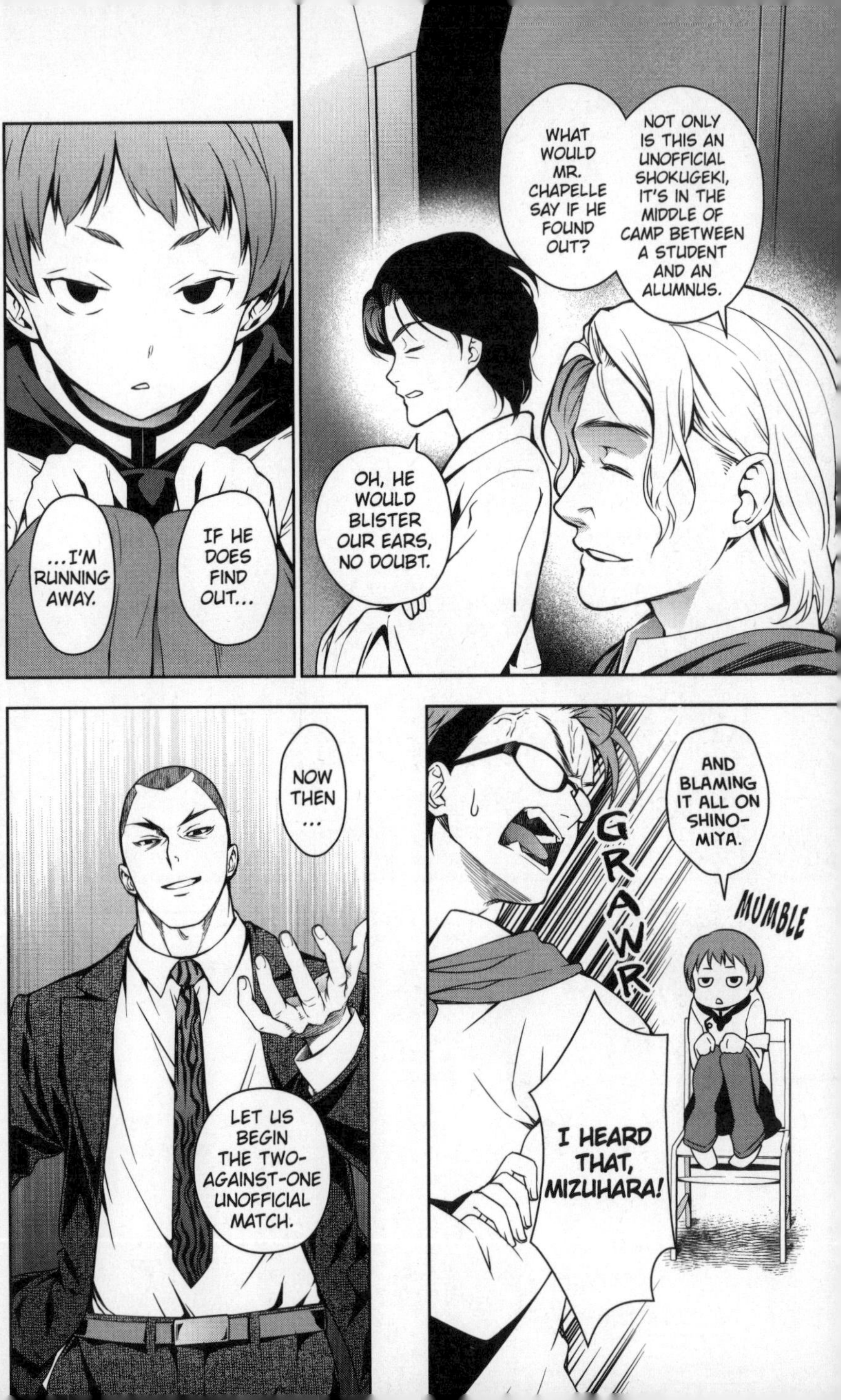
NOT ONLY IS THIS AN UNOFFICIAL SHOKUGEKI, IT'S IN THE MIDDLE OF CAMP BETWEEN A STUDENT AND AN ALUMNUS.
WHAT WOULD MR. CHAPELLE SAY IF HE FOUND OUT?
OH, HE WOULD BLISTER OUR EARS, NO DOUBT.
IF HE DOES FIND OUT...
...I'M RUNNING AWAY.
AND BLAMING IT ALL ON SHINO-MIYA.
MUMBLE
GRAWR
I HEARD THAT, MIZUHARA!
NOW THEN...
LET US BEGIN THE TWO-AGAINST-ONE UNOFFICIAL MATCH.

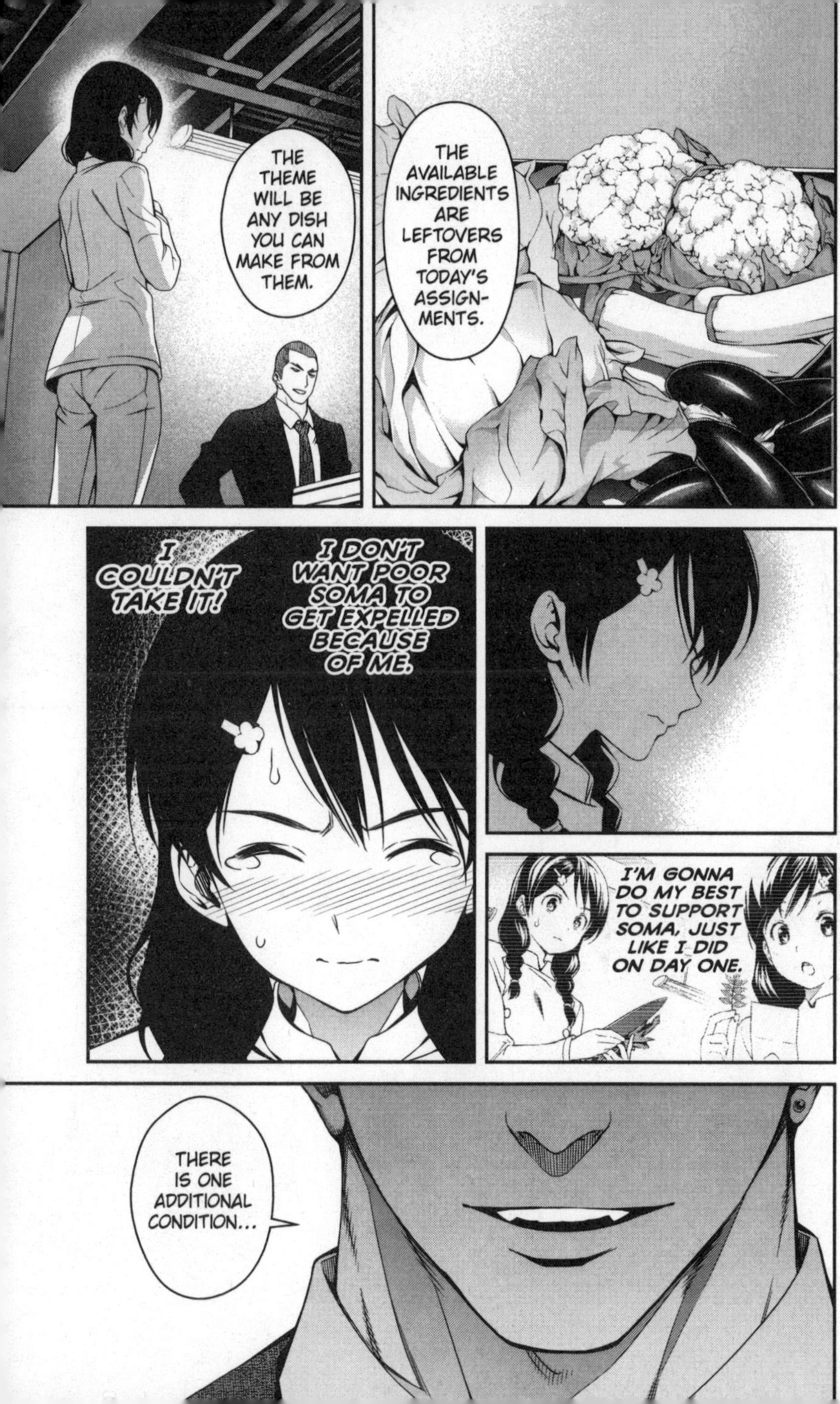
THE AVAILABLE INGREDIENTS ARE LEFTOVERS FROM TODAY'S ASSIGN-MENTS.
THE THEME WILL BE ANY DISH YOU CAN MAKE FROM THEM.
I'M GONNA DO MY BEST TO SUPPORT SOMA, JUST LIKE I DID ON DAY ONE.
I DON'T WANT POOR SOMA TO GET EXPELLED BECAUSE OF ME.
I COULDN'T TAKE IT!
THERE IS ONE ADDITIONAL CONDITION...

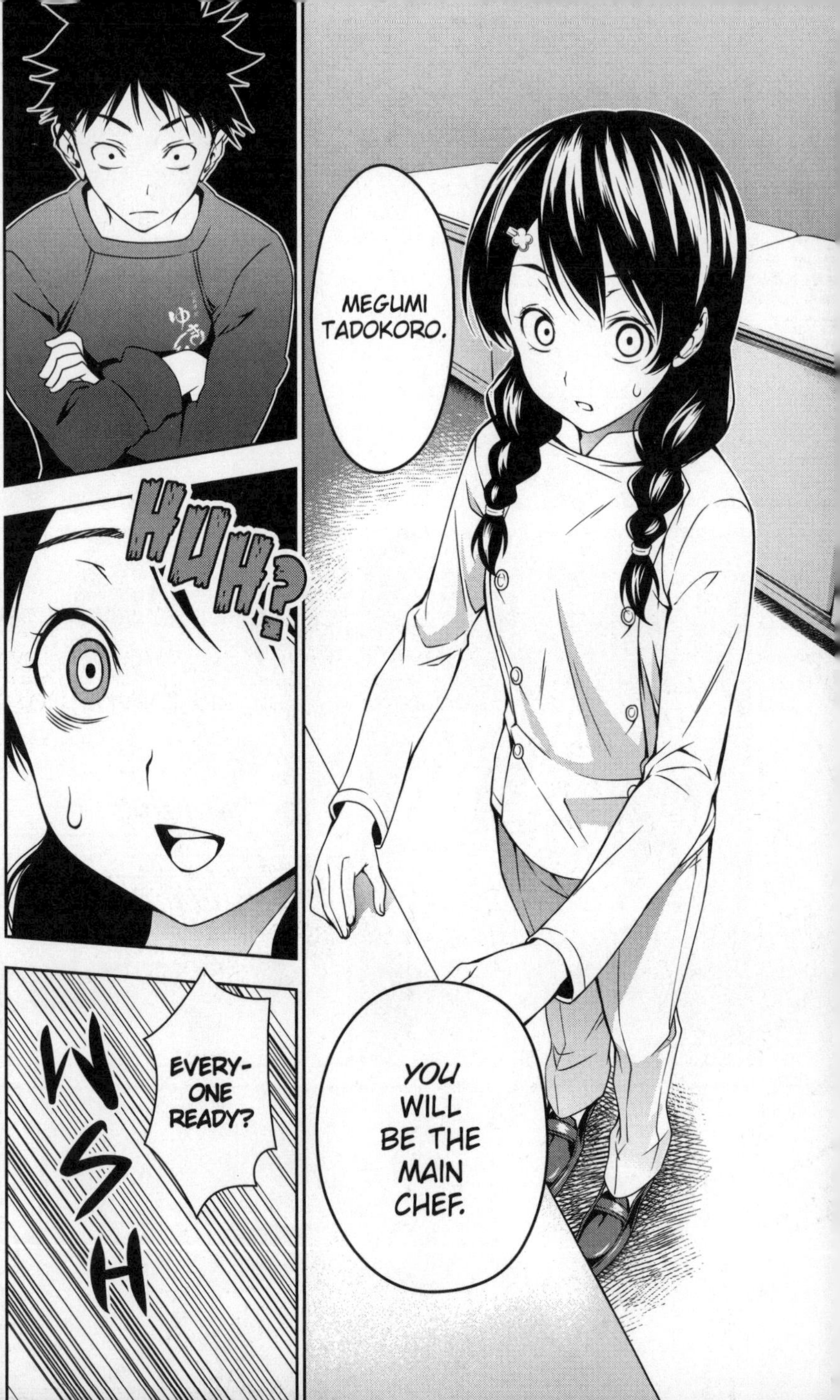
MEGUMI TADOKORO.
YOU WILL BE THE MAIN CHEF.
HUH?
EVERY-ONE READY?
WSH

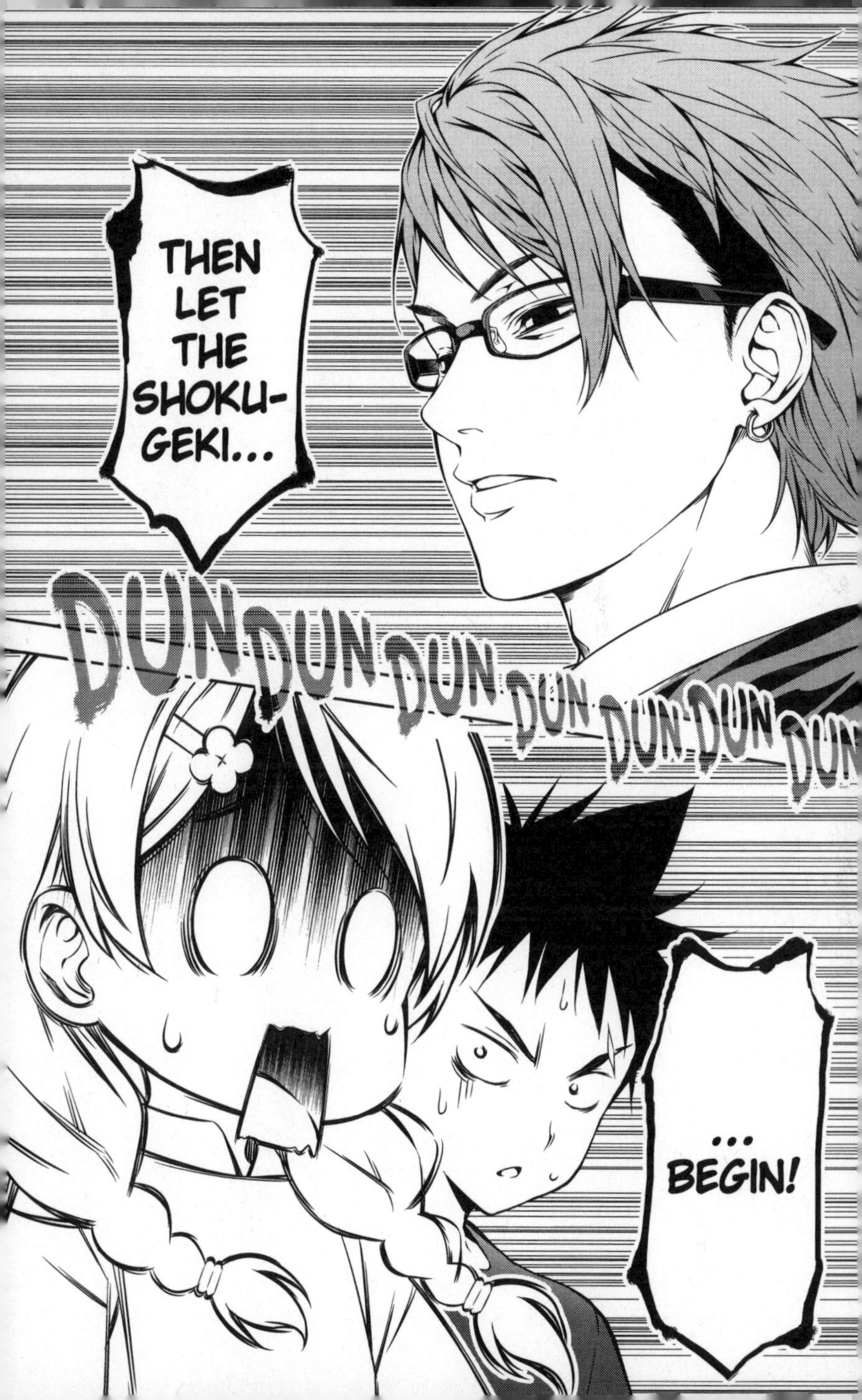
THEN LET THE SHOKU-GEKI...
DUN DUN DUN DUN DUN DUN DUN
... BEGIN!

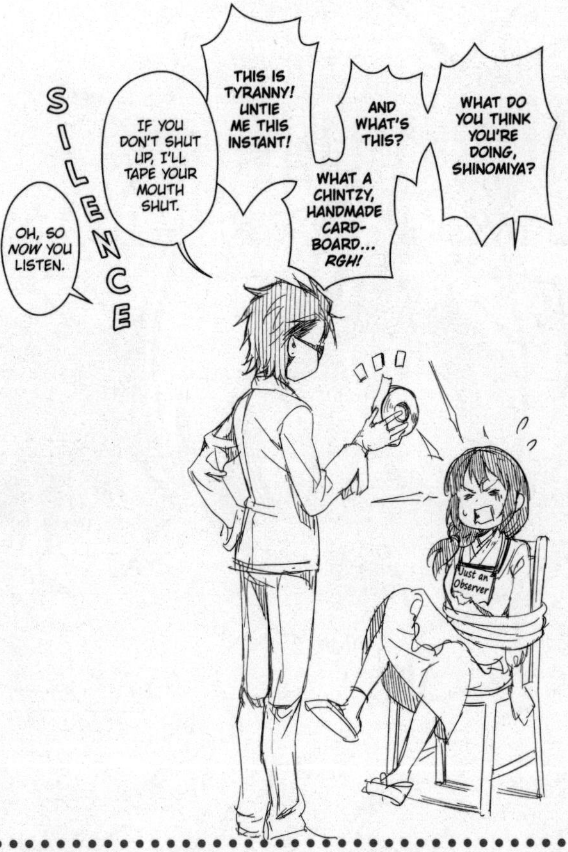
WHAT DO YOU THINK YOU'RE DOING, SHINOMIYA?
AND WHAT'S THIS?
WHAT A CHINTZY, HANDMADE CARD-BOARD... *RGH!*
Just an Observer
THIS IS TYRANNY! UNTIE ME THIS INSTANT!
IF YOU DON'T SHUT UP, I'LL TAPE YOUR MOUTH SHUT.
SILENCE
OH, SO *NOW* YOU LISTEN.

23 PROOF OF EXISTENCE

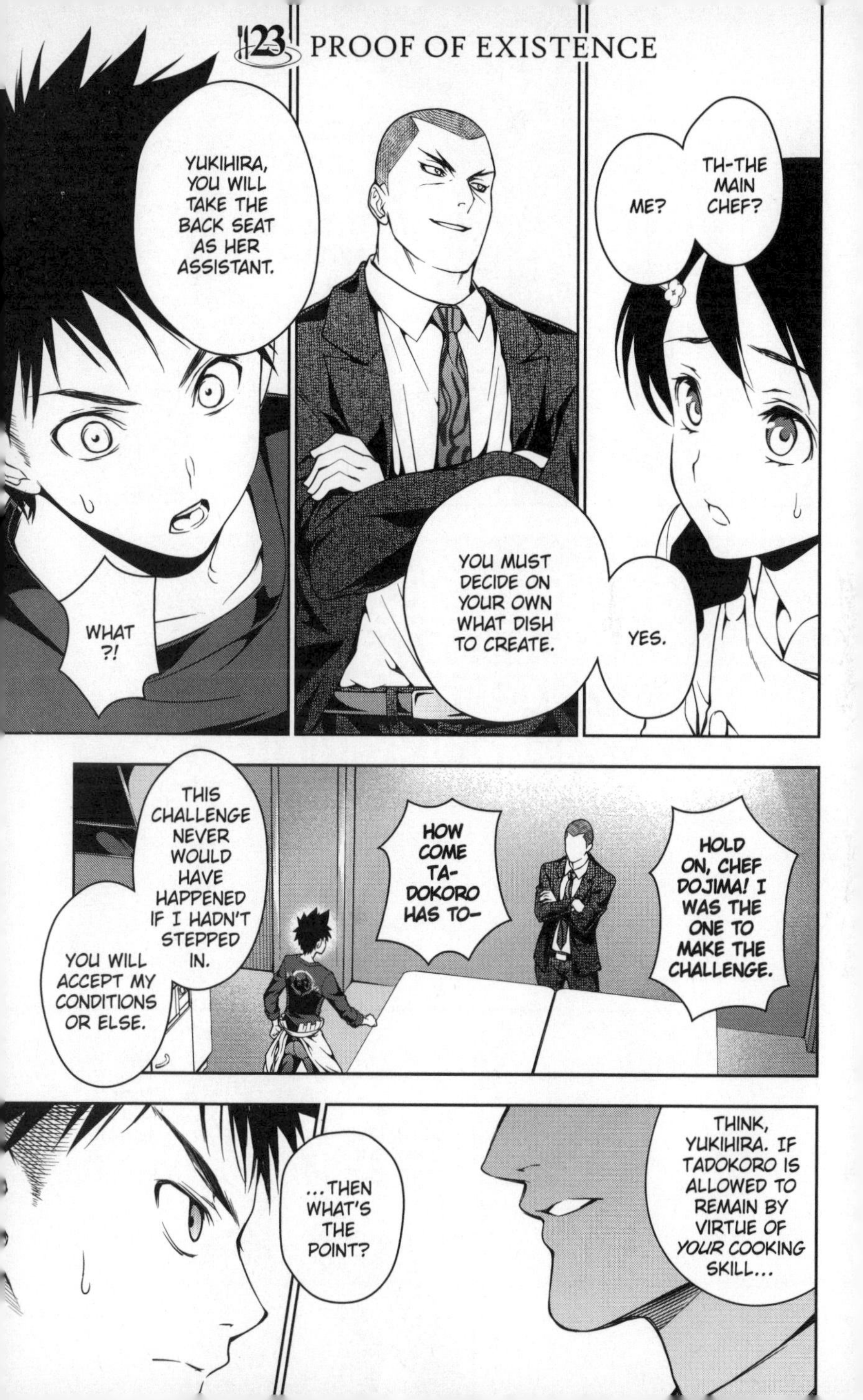
TH-THE MAIN CHEF?
ME?
YOU MUST DECIDE ON YOUR OWN WHAT DISH TO CREATE.
YES.
YUKIHIRA, YOU WILL TAKE THE BACK SEAT AS HER ASSISTANT.
WHAT?!
HOLD ON, CHEF DOJIMA! I WAS THE ONE TO MAKE THE CHALLENGE.
HOW COME TADOKORO HAS TO-
THIS CHALLENGE NEVER WOULD HAVE HAPPENED IF I HADN'T STEPPED IN.
YOU WILL ACCEPT MY CONDITIONS OR ELSE.
THINK, YUKIHIRA. IF TADOKORO IS ALLOWED TO REMAIN BY VIRTUE OF *YOUR* COOKING SKILL...
...THEN WHAT'S THE POINT?

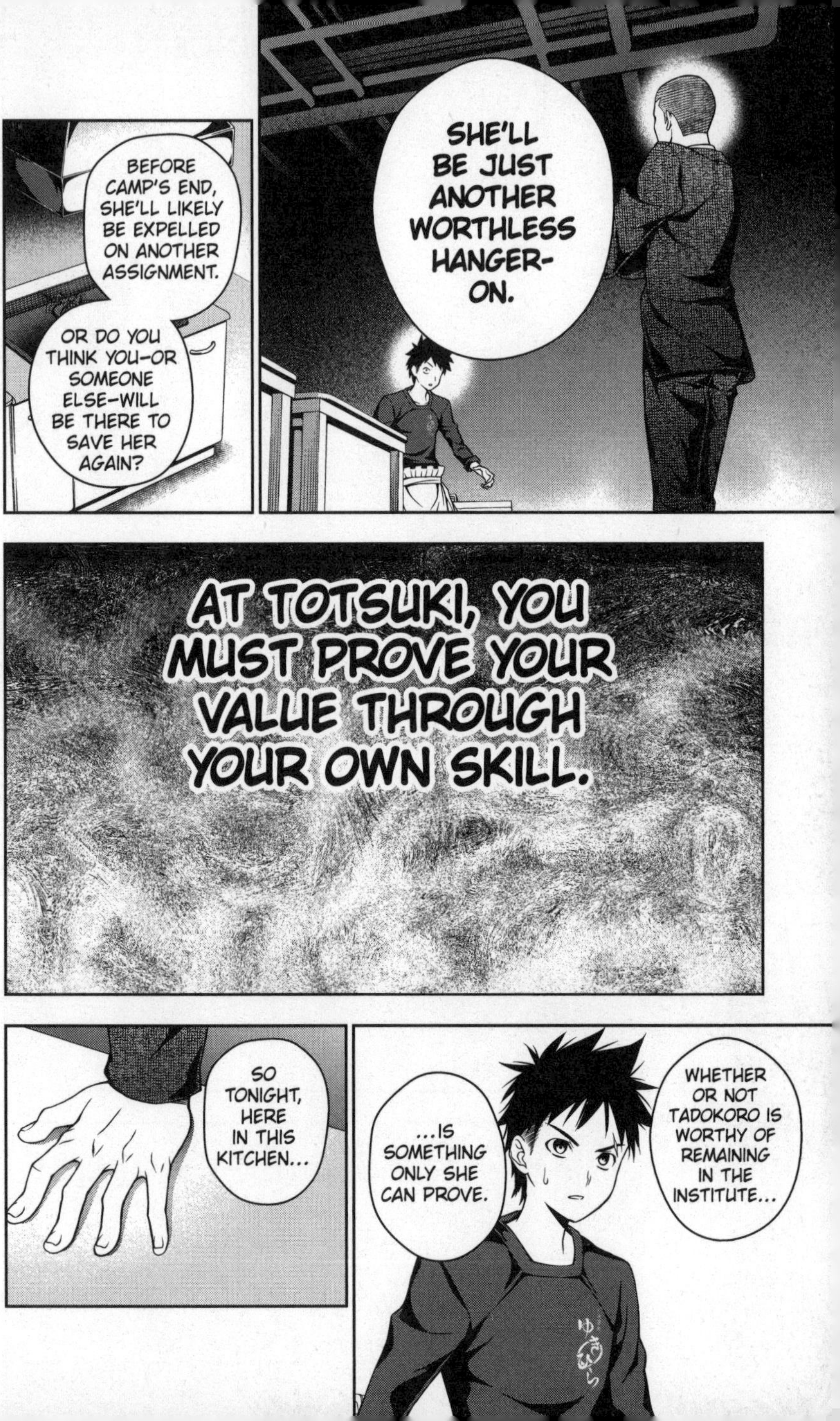
SHE'LL BE JUST ANOTHER WORTHLESS HANGER-ON.
BEFORE CAMP'S END, SHE'LL LIKELY BE EXPELLED ON ANOTHER ASSIGNMENT.
OR DO YOU THINK YOU—OR SOMEONE ELSE—WILL BE THERE TO SAVE HER AGAIN?
AT TOTSUKI, YOU MUST PROVE YOUR VALUE THROUGH YOUR OWN SKILL.
WHETHER OR NOT TADOKORO IS WORTHY OF REMAINING IN THE INSTITUTE...
...IS SOMETHING ONLY SHE CAN PROVE.
SO TONIGHT, HERE IN THIS KITCHEN...

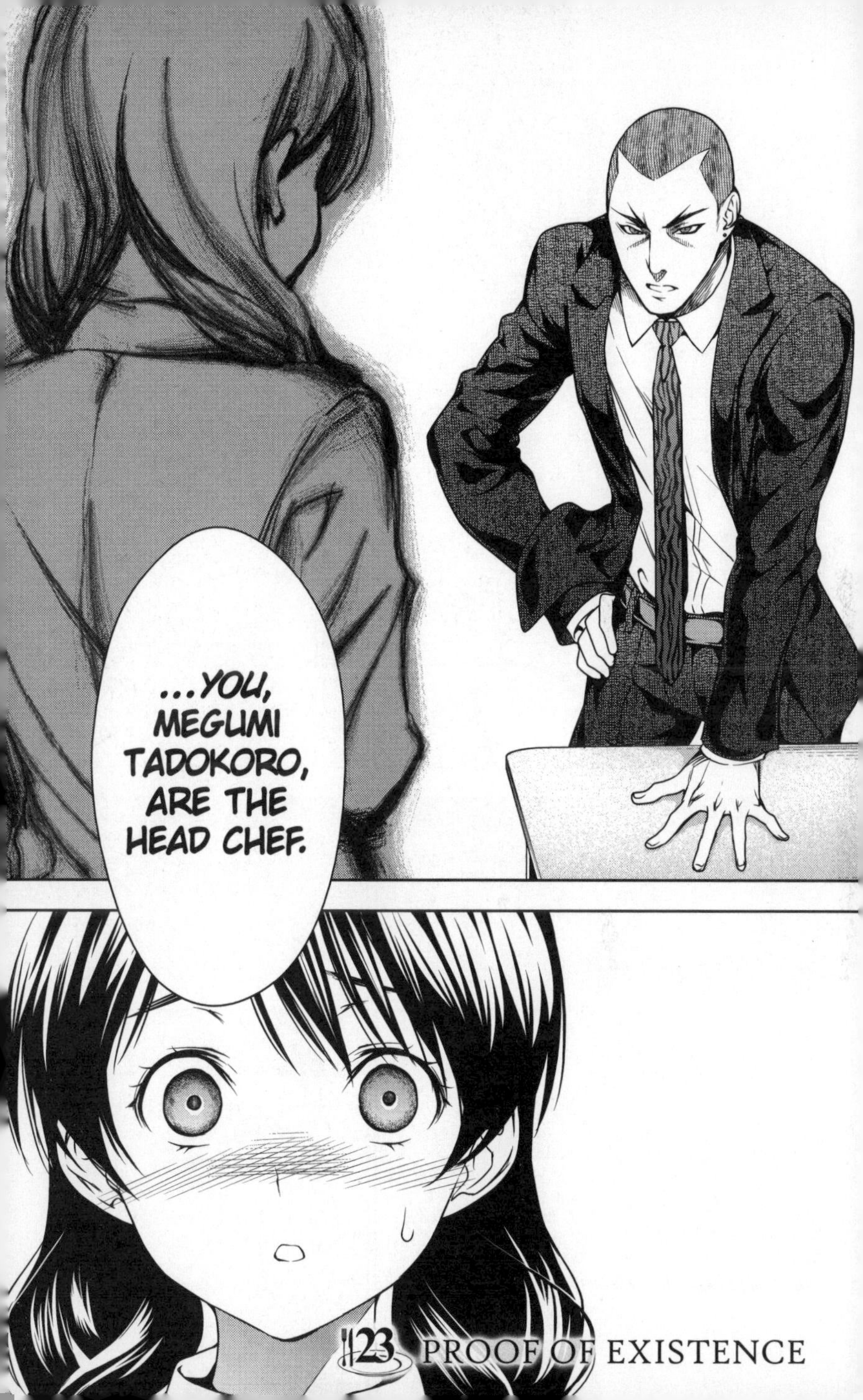
...YOU, MEGUMI TADOKORO, ARE THE HEAD CHEF.
23 PROOF OF EXISTENCE

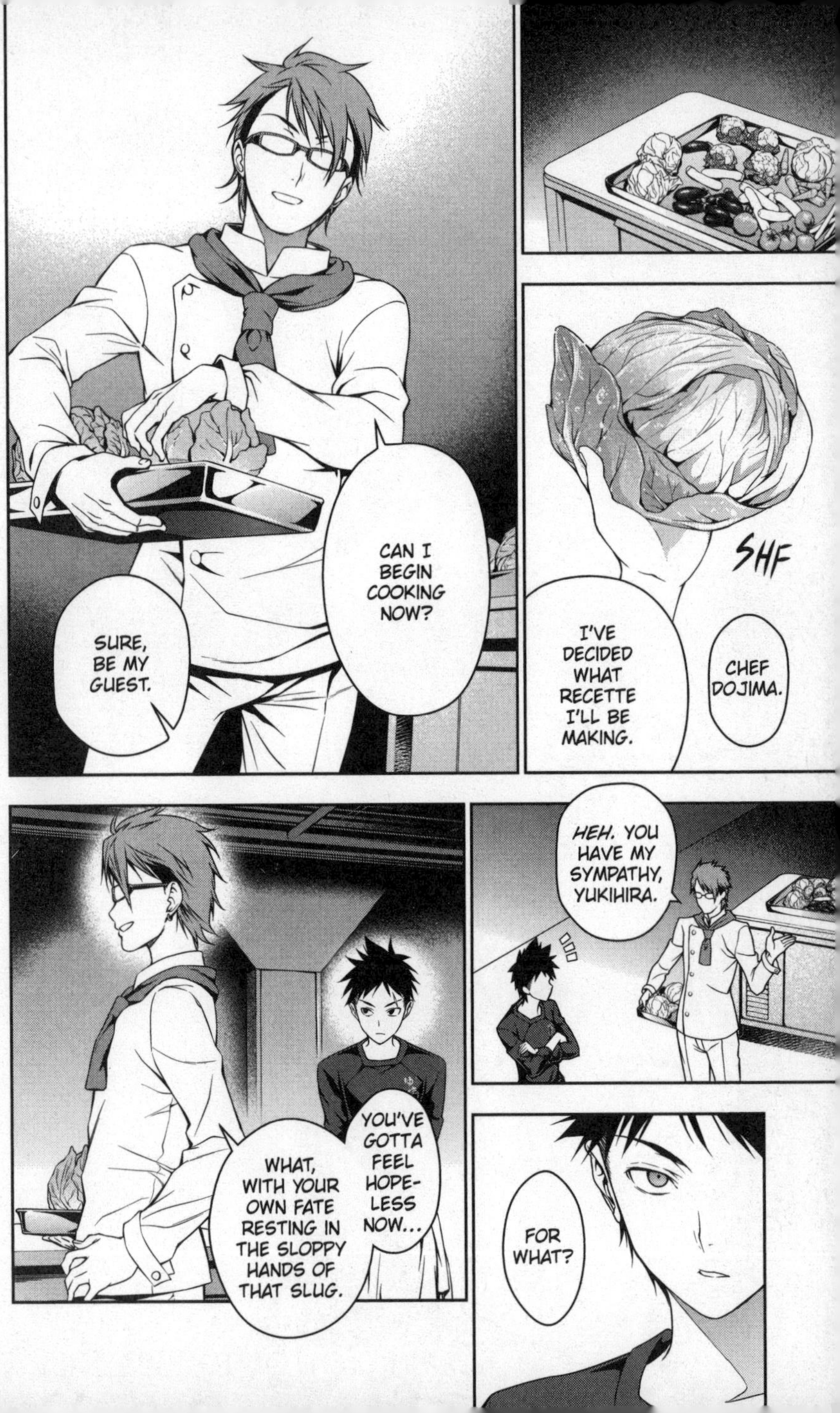
SHF
CHEF DOJIMA.
I'VE DECIDED WHAT RECETTE I'LL BE MAKING.
CAN I BEGIN COOKING NOW?
SURE, BE MY GUEST.
HEH. YOU HAVE MY SYMPATHY, YUKIHIRA.
FOR WHAT?
YOU'VE GOTTA FEEL HOPE-LESS NOW...
WHAT, WITH YOUR OWN FATE RESTING IN THE SLOPPY HANDS OF THAT SLUG.

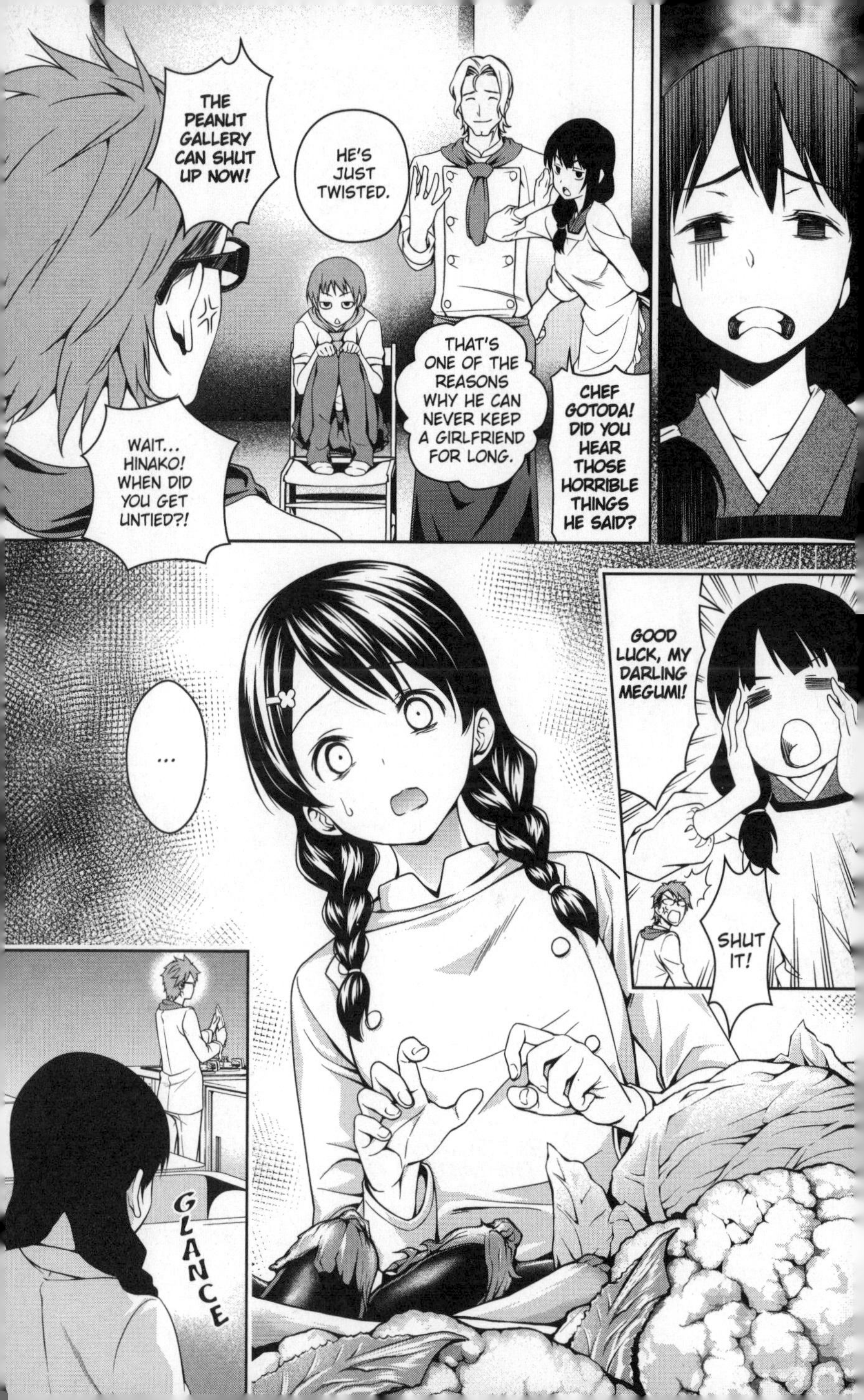
CHEF GOTODA! DID YOU HEAR THOSE HORRIBLE THINGS HE SAID?
HE'S JUST TWISTED.
THAT'S ONE OF THE REASONS WHY HE CAN NEVER KEEP A GIRLFRIEND FOR LONG.
THE PEANUT GALLERY CAN SHUT UP NOW!
WAIT... HINAKO! WHEN DID YOU GET UNTIED?!
GOOD LUCK, MY DARLING MEGUMI!
SHUT IT!
...
GLANCE

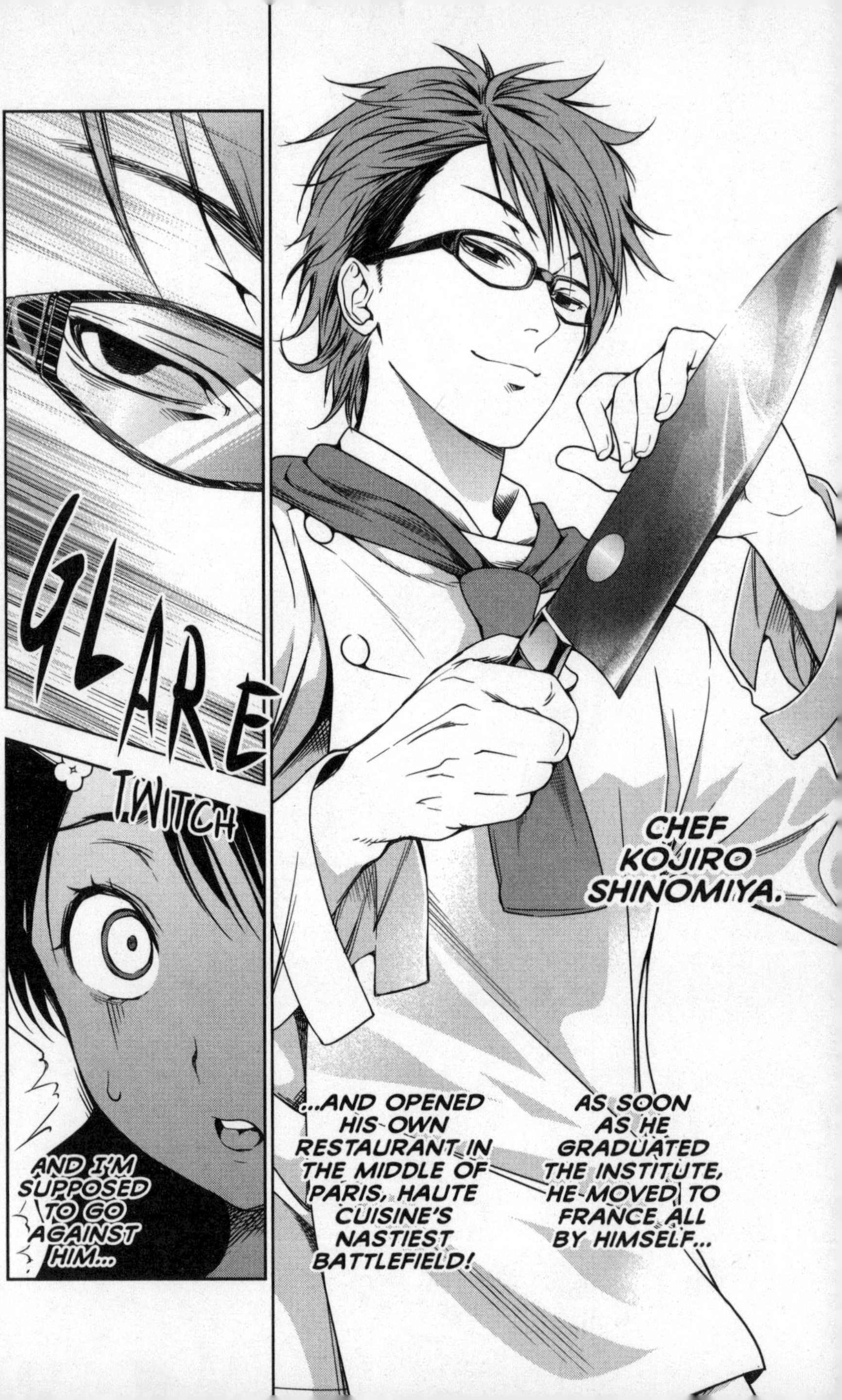
CHEF KOJIRO SHINOMIYA.
AS SOON AS HE GRADUATED THE INSTITUTE, HE MOVED TO FRANCE ALL BY HIMSELF...
...AND OPENED HIS OWN RESTAURANT IN THE MIDDLE OF PARIS, HAUTE CUISINE'S NASTIEST BATTLEFIELD!
GLARE
TWITCH
AND I'M SUPPOSED TO GO AGAINST HIM...

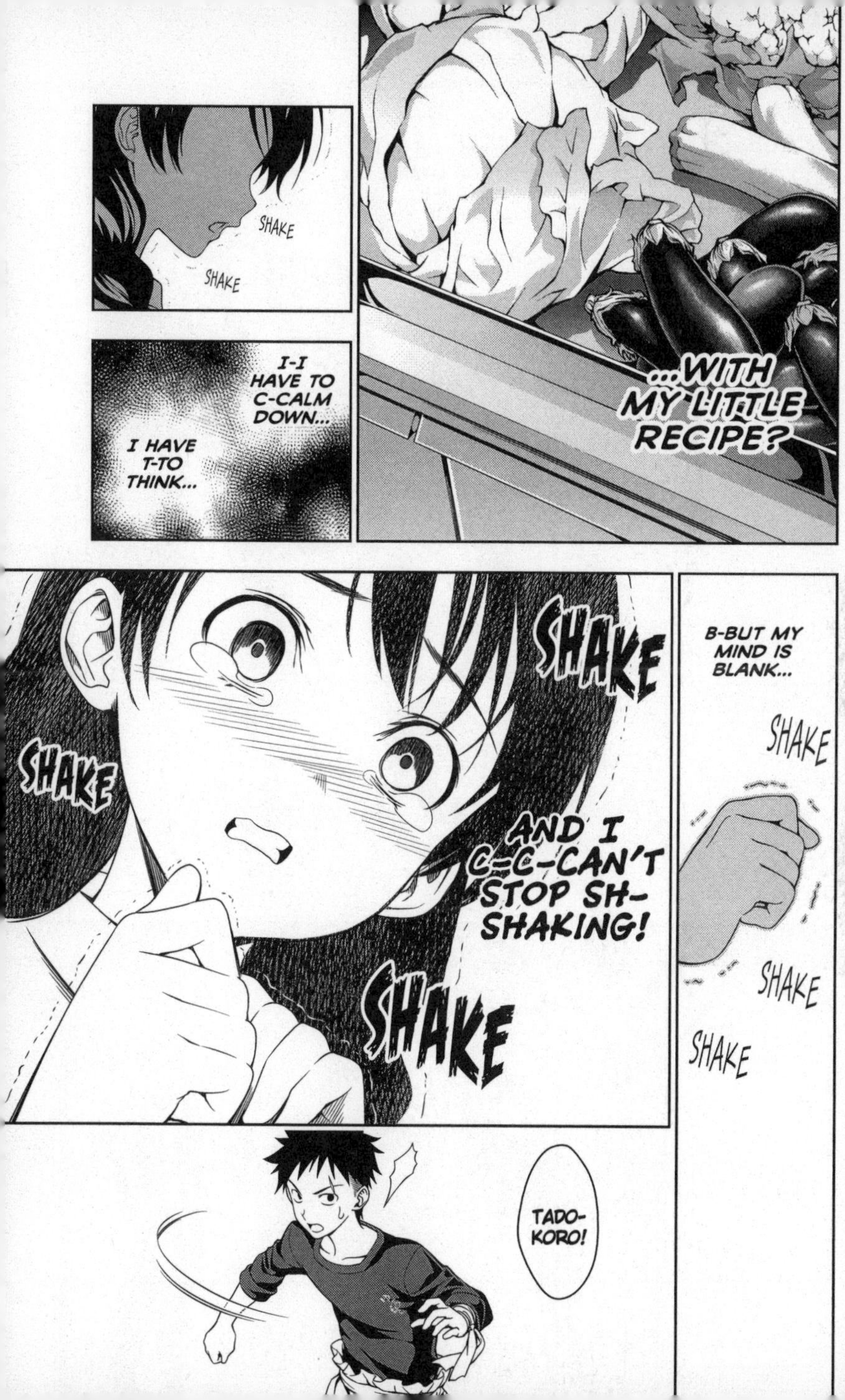
...WITH MY LITTLE RECIPE?
SHAKE
SHAKE
I-I HAVE TO C-CALM DOWN...
I HAVE T-TO THINK...
B-BUT MY MIND IS BLANK...
SHAKE
SHAKE
SHAKE
SHAKE
AND I C-C-CAN'T STOP SH-SHAKING!
SHAKE
SHAKE
TADO-KORO!

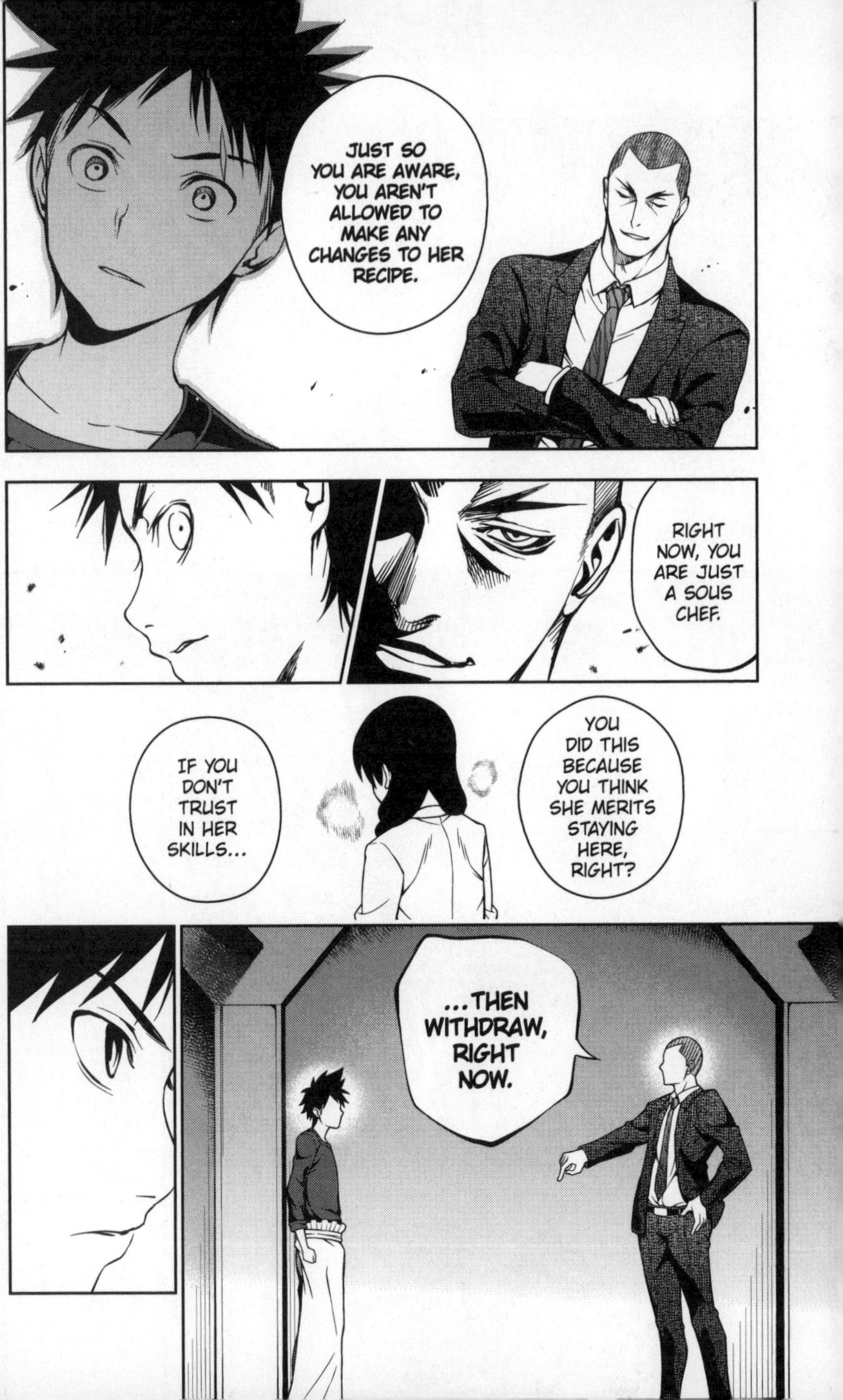
JUST SO YOU ARE AWARE, YOU AREN'T ALLOWED TO MAKE ANY CHANGES TO HER RECIPE.
RIGHT NOW, YOU ARE JUST A SOUS CHEF.
YOU DID THIS BECAUSE YOU THINK SHE MERITS STAYING HERE, RIGHT?
IF YOU DON'T TRUST IN HER SKILLS...
...THEN WITHDRAW, RIGHT NOW.

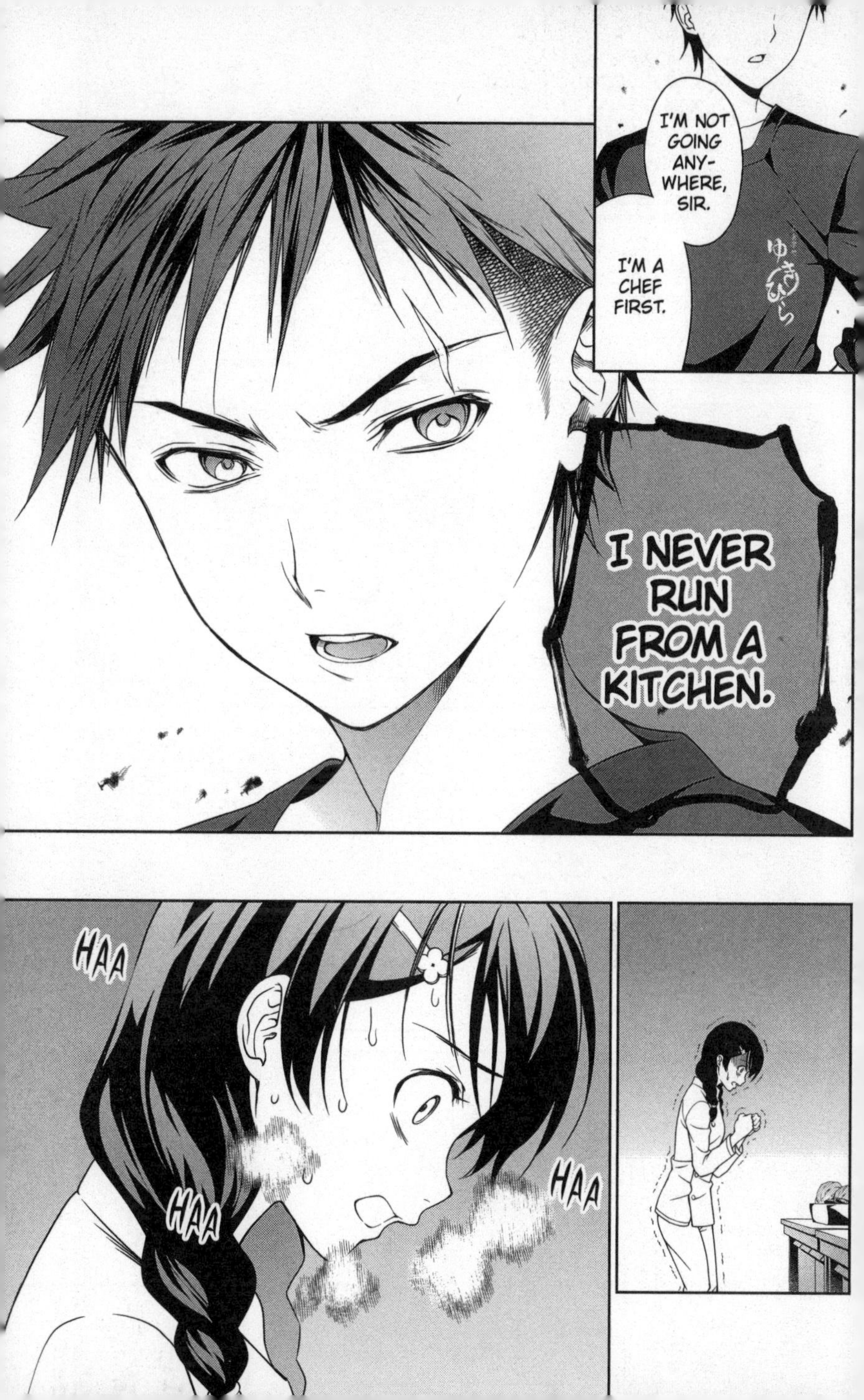
I'M NOT GOING ANY-WHERE, SIR.
I'M A CHEF FIRST.
I NEVER RUN FROM A KITCHEN.
HAA
HAA
HAA

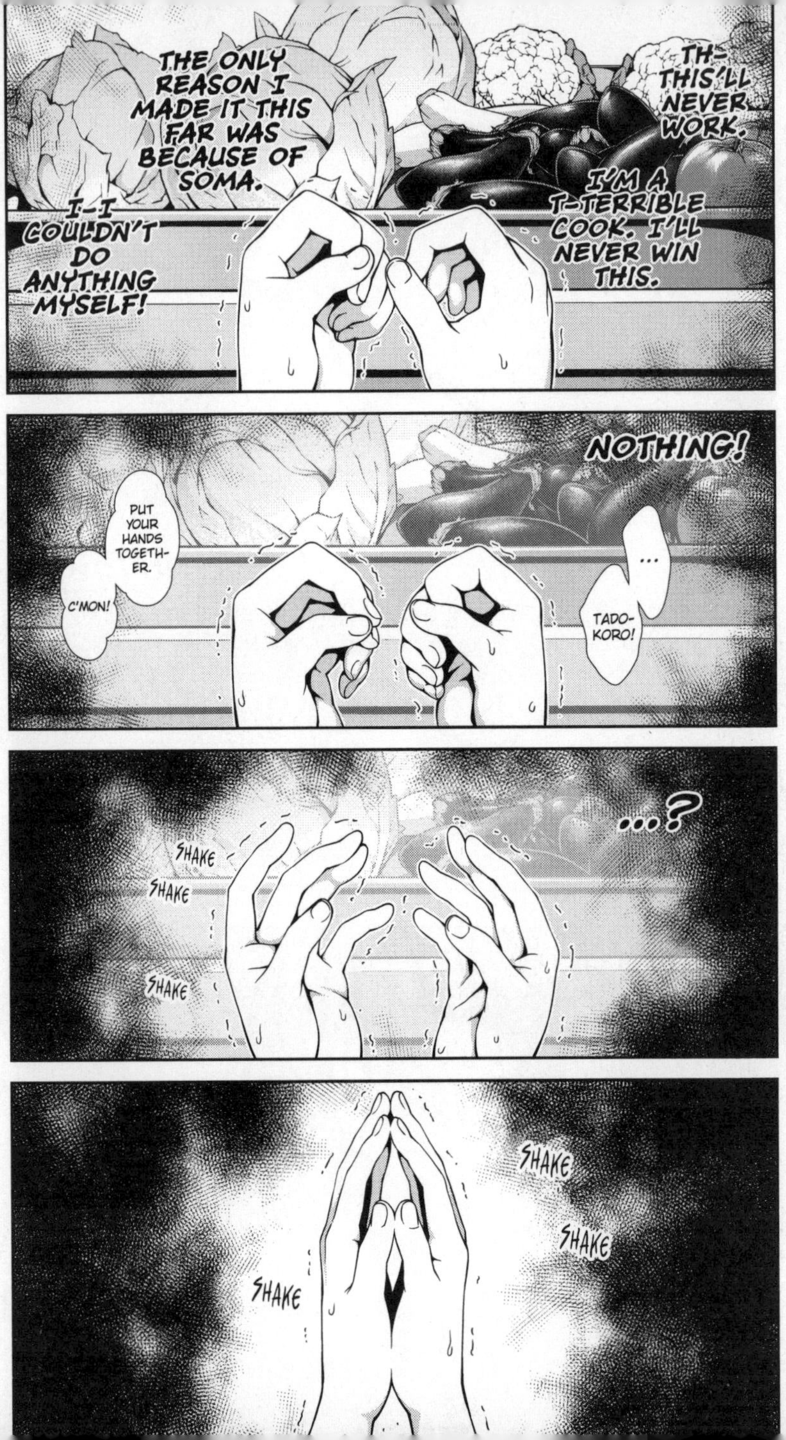
TH- THIS'LL NEVER WORK.
I'M A T-TERRIBLE COOK. I'LL NEVER WIN THIS.
THE ONLY REASON I MADE IT THIS FAR WAS BECAUSE OF SOMA.
I-I COULDN'T DO ANYTHING MYSELF!
NOTHING!
...
TADOKORO!
PUT YOUR HANDS TOGETHER.
C'MON!
...?
SHAKE
SHAKE
SHAKE
SHAKE
SHAKE
SHAKE

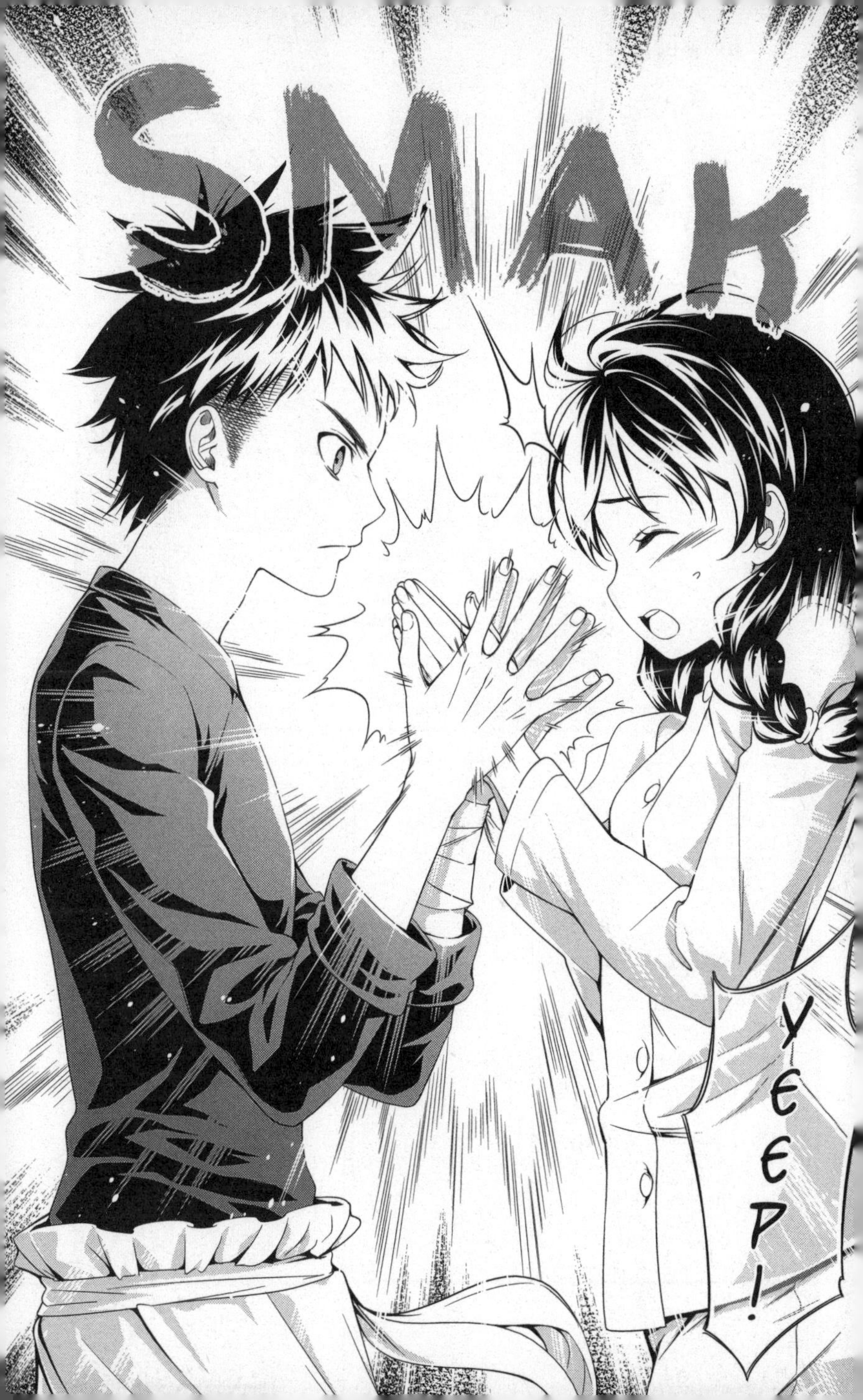
SMAK
YEEP!

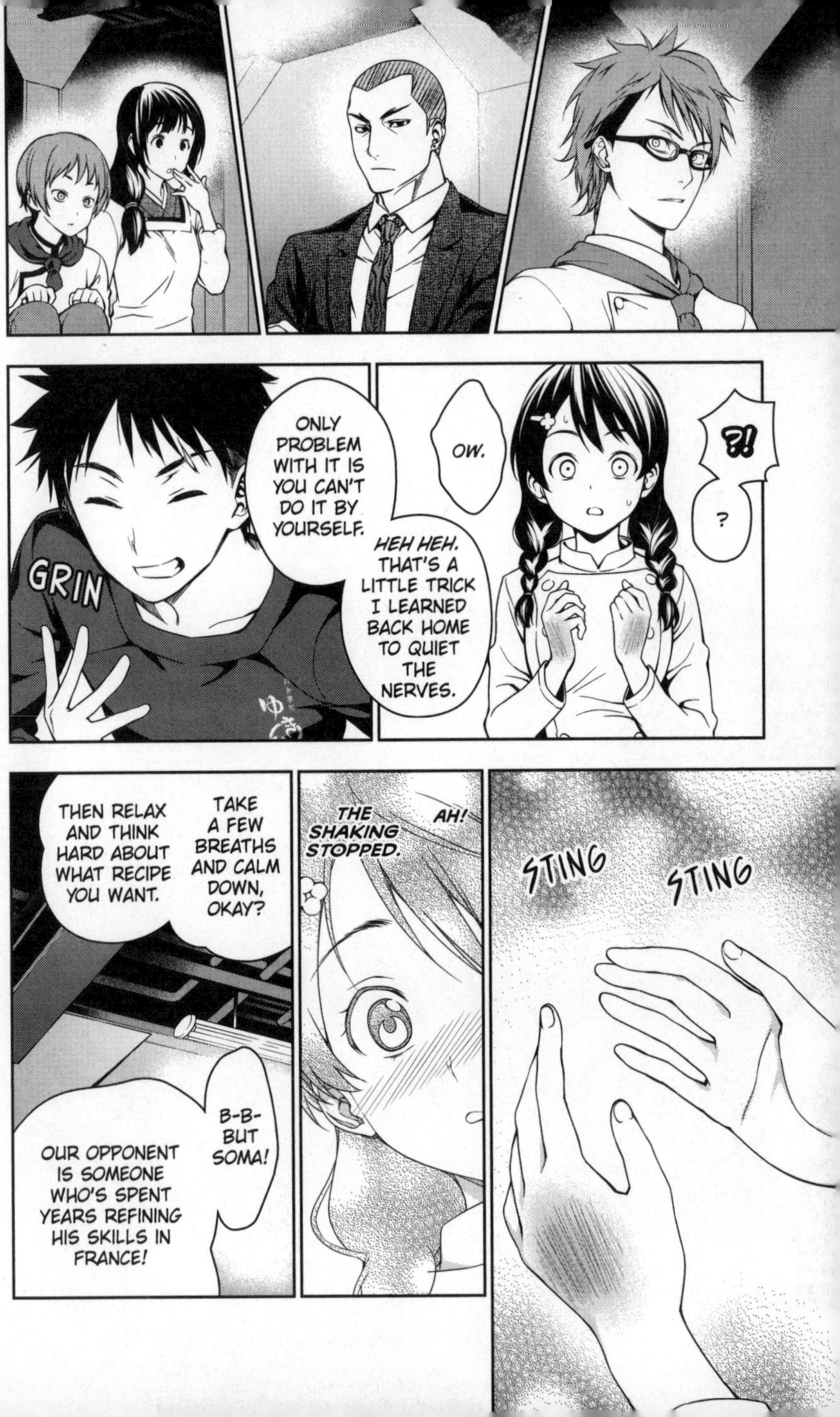
?!
?
OW.
HEH HEH. THAT'S A LITTLE TRICK I LEARNED BACK HOME TO QUIET THE NERVES.
ONLY PROBLEM WITH IT IS YOU CAN'T DO IT BY YOURSELF.
GRIN
STING
STING
AH!
THE SHAKING STOPPED.
TAKE A FEW BREATHS AND CALM DOWN, OKAY?
THEN RELAX AND THINK HARD ABOUT WHAT RECIPE YOU WANT.
B-B-BUT SOMA!
OUR OPPONENT IS SOMEONE WHO'S SPENT YEARS REFINING HIS SKILLS IN FRANCE!

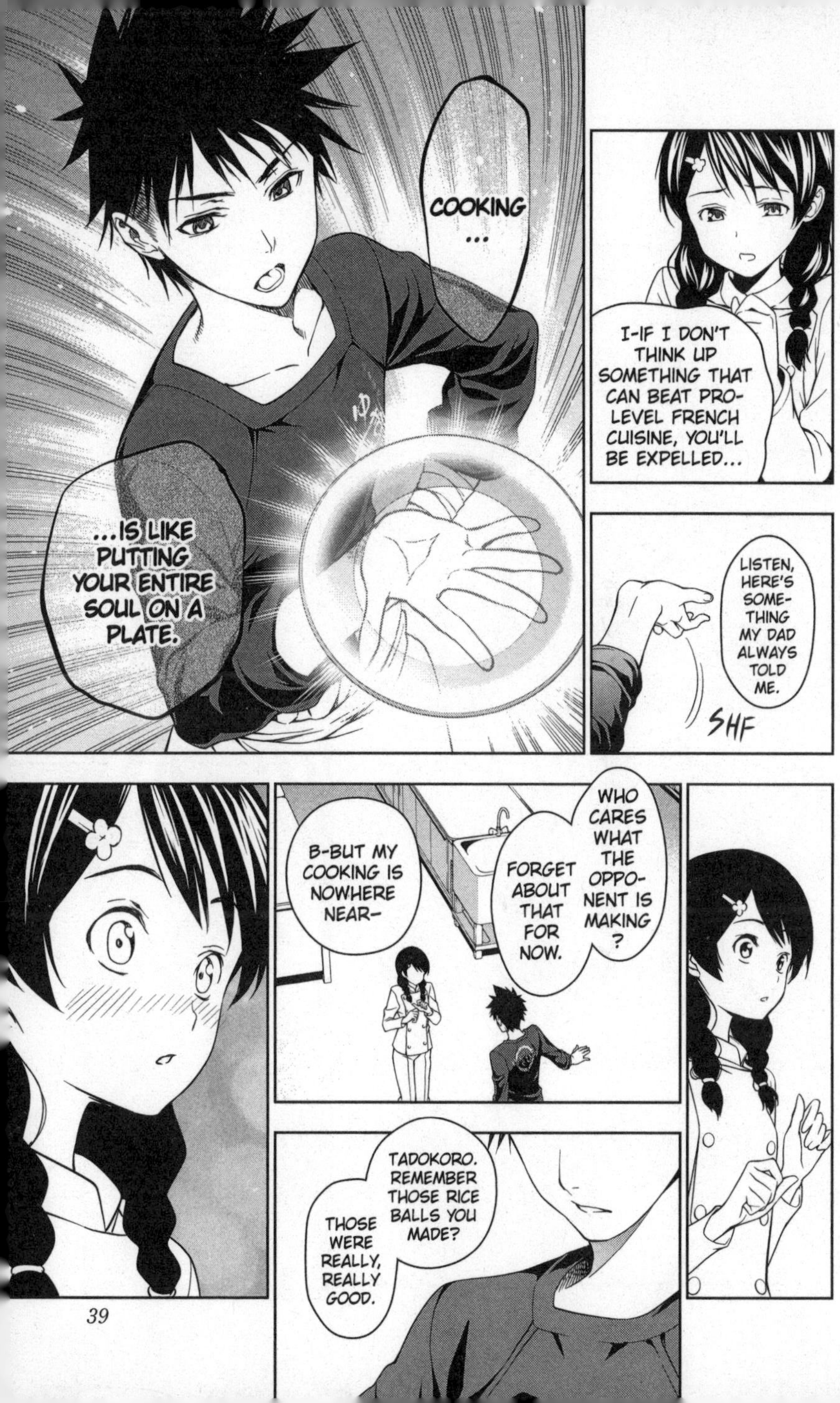
I-IF I DON'T THINK UP SOMETHING THAT CAN BEAT PRO-LEVEL FRENCH CUISINE, YOU'LL BE EXPELLED...
LISTEN, HERE'S SOME-THING MY DAD ALWAYS TOLD ME.
SHF
COOKING...
...IS LIKE PUTTING YOUR ENTIRE SOUL ON A PLATE.
WHO CARES WHAT THE OPPO-NENT IS MAKING?
FORGET ABOUT THAT FOR NOW.
B-BUT MY COOKING IS NOWHERE NEAR-
TADOKORO. REMEMBER THOSE RICE BALLS YOU MADE?
THOSE WERE REALLY, REALLY GOOD.

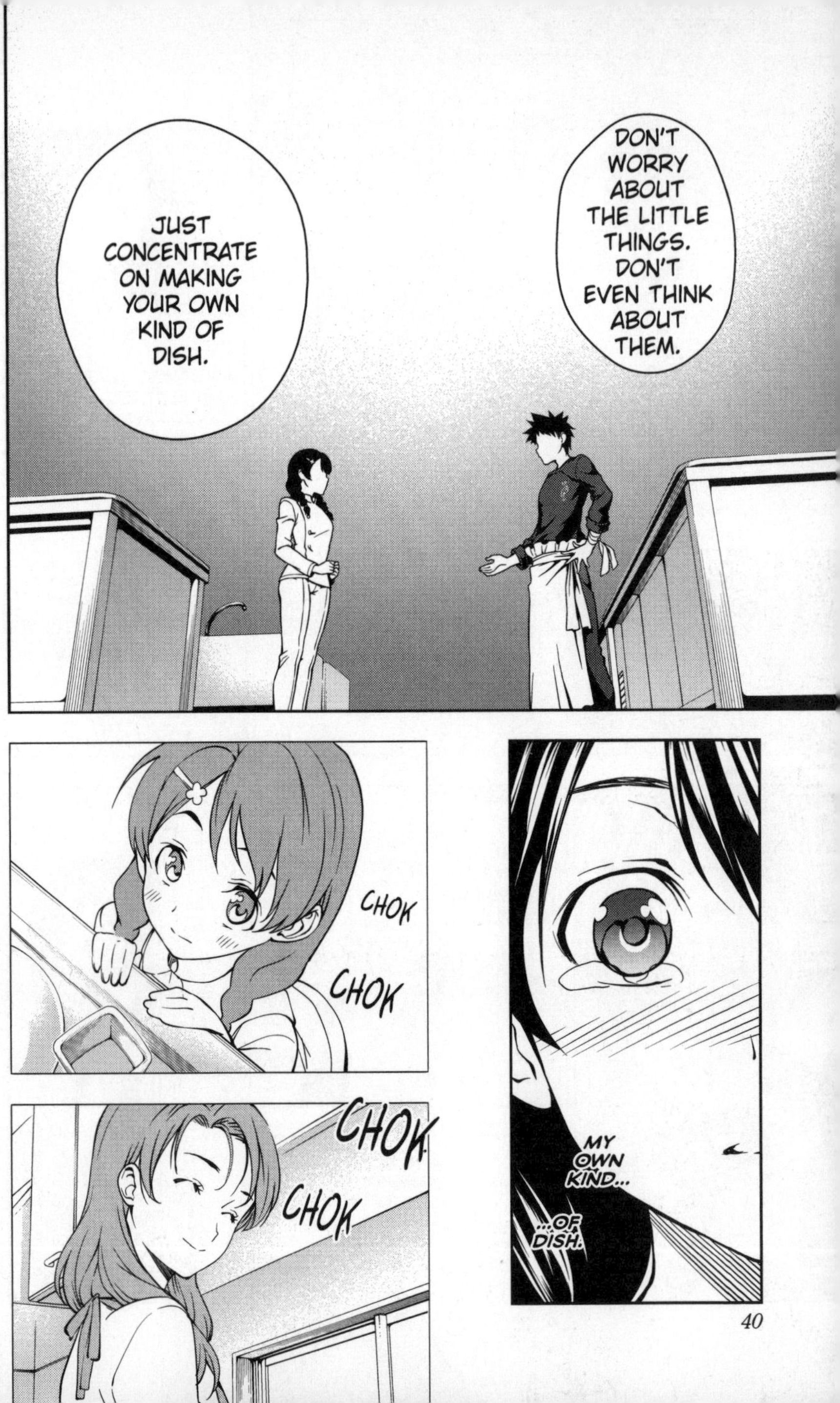
DON'T WORRY ABOUT THE LITTLE THINGS. DON'T EVEN THINK ABOUT THEM.
JUST CONCENTRATE ON MAKING YOUR OWN KIND OF DISH.
MY OWN KIND...
...OF DISH.
CHOK
CHOK
CHOK
CHOK

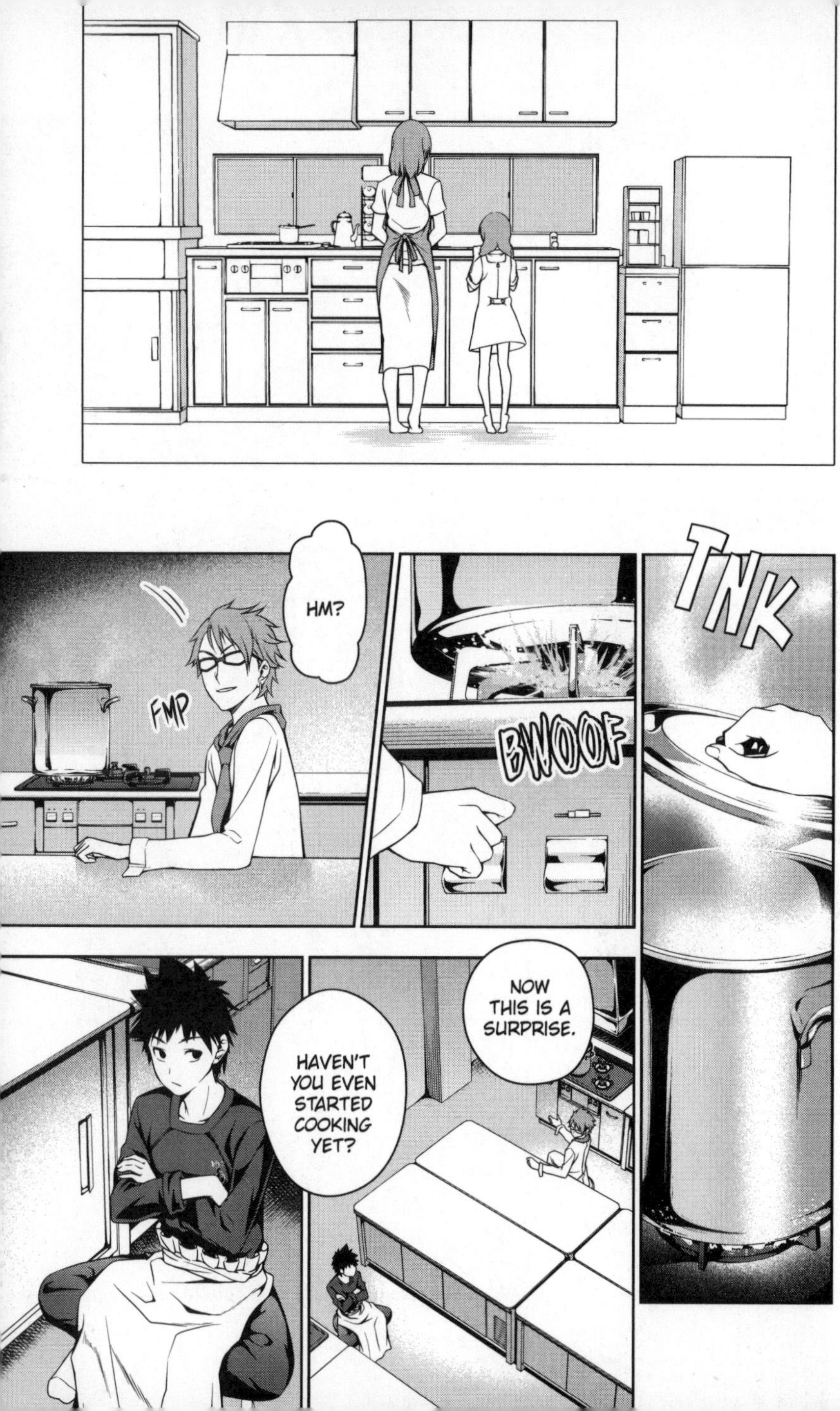
TNK
BWOOF
FMP
HM?
NOW THIS IS A SURPRISE.
HAVEN'T YOU EVEN STARTED COOKING YET?

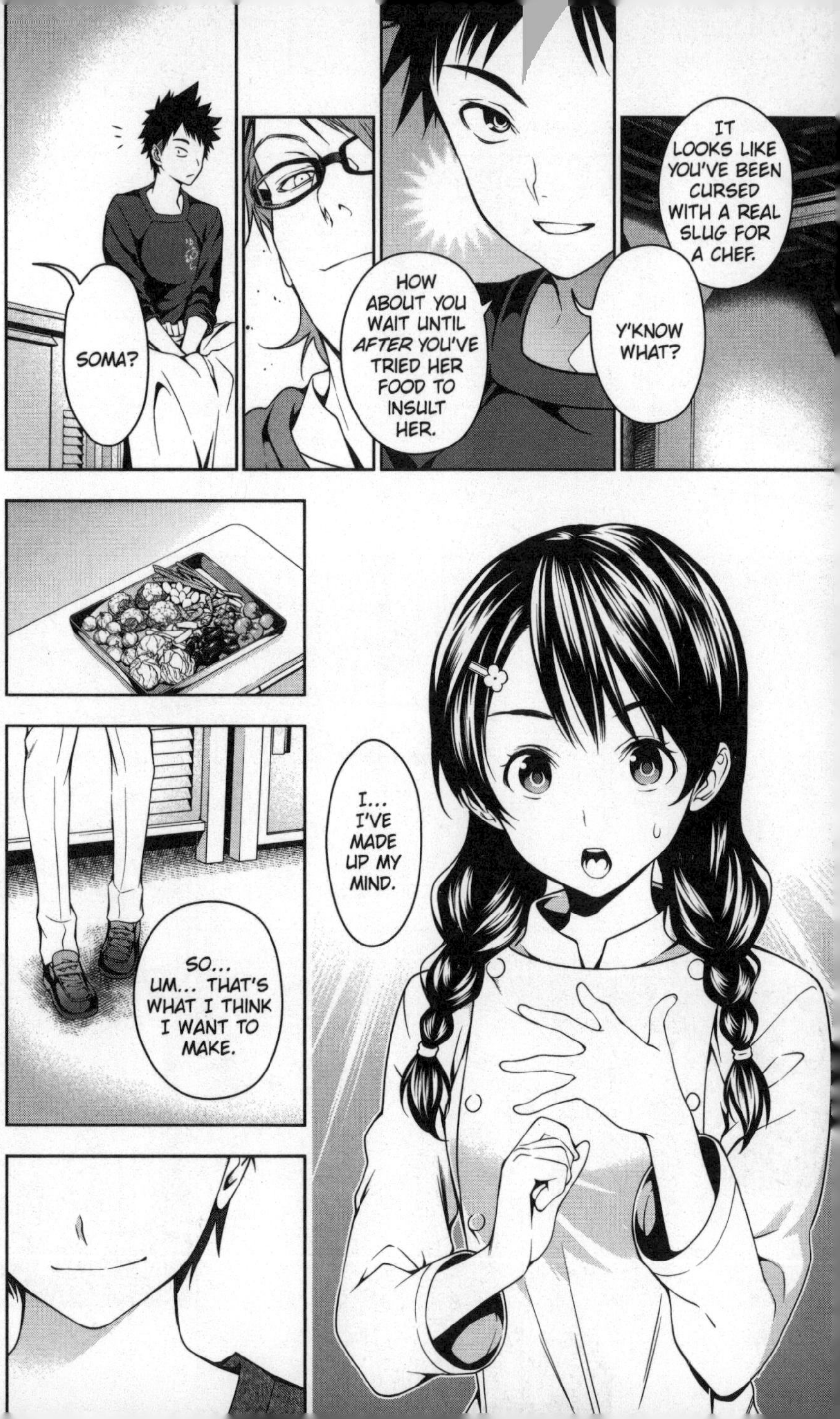
IT LOOKS LIKE YOU'VE BEEN CURSED WITH A REAL SLUG FOR A CHEF.
Y'KNOW WHAT?
HOW ABOUT YOU WAIT UNTIL *AFTER* YOU'VE TRIED HER FOOD TO INSULT HER.
SOMA?
I... I'VE MADE UP MY MIND.
SO... UM... THAT'S WHAT I THINK I WANT TO MAKE.

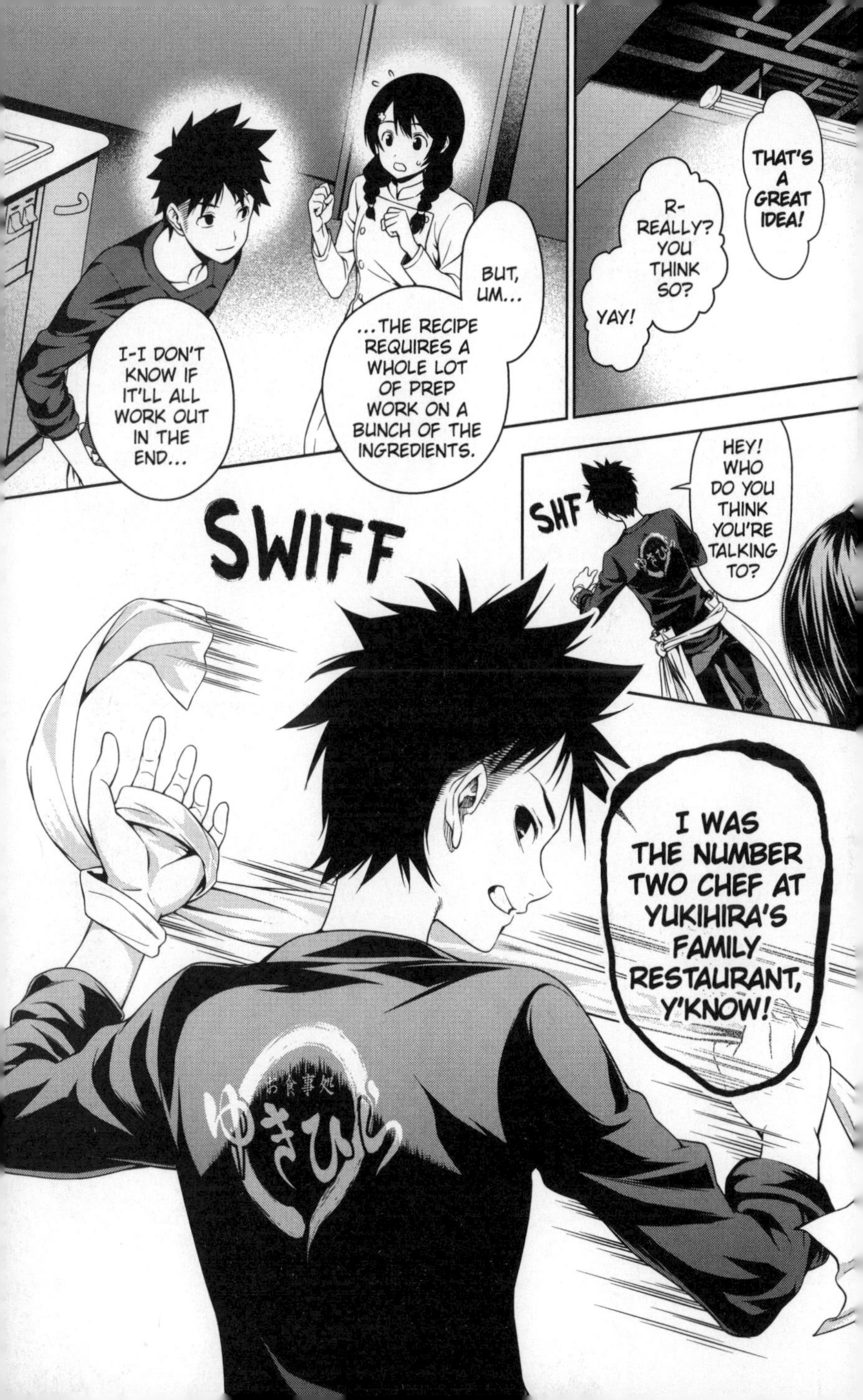
THAT'S A GREAT IDEA!
R-REALLY? YOU THINK SO?
YAY!
BUT, UM...
...THE RECIPE REQUIRES A WHOLE LOT OF PREP WORK ON A BUNCH OF THE INGREDIENTS.
I-I DON'T KNOW IF IT'LL ALL WORK OUT IN THE END...
SHF
HEY! WHO DO YOU THINK YOU'RE TALKING TO?
SWIFF
I WAS THE NUMBER TWO CHEF AT YUKIHIRA'S FAMILY RESTAURANT, Y'KNOW!
ゆきひら

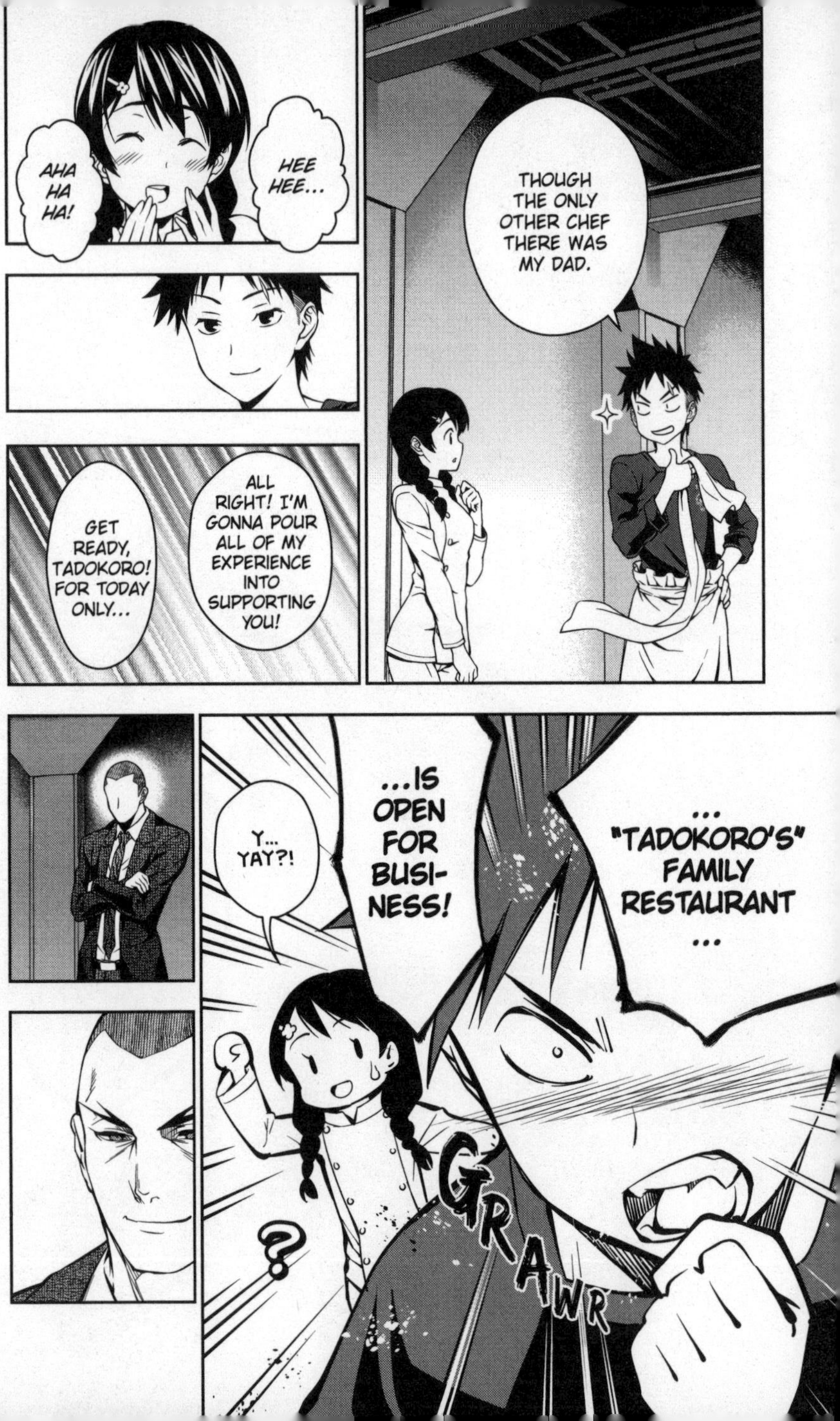
THOUGH THE ONLY OTHER CHEF THERE WAS MY DAD.
HEE HEE...
AHA HA HA!
ALL RIGHT! I'M GONNA POUR ALL OF MY EXPERIENCE INTO SUPPORTING YOU!
GET READY, TADOKORO! FOR TODAY ONLY...
... "TADOKORO'S" FAMILY RESTAURANT ...
...IS OPEN FOR BUSI-NESS!
Y... YAY?!
GRAWR
?!

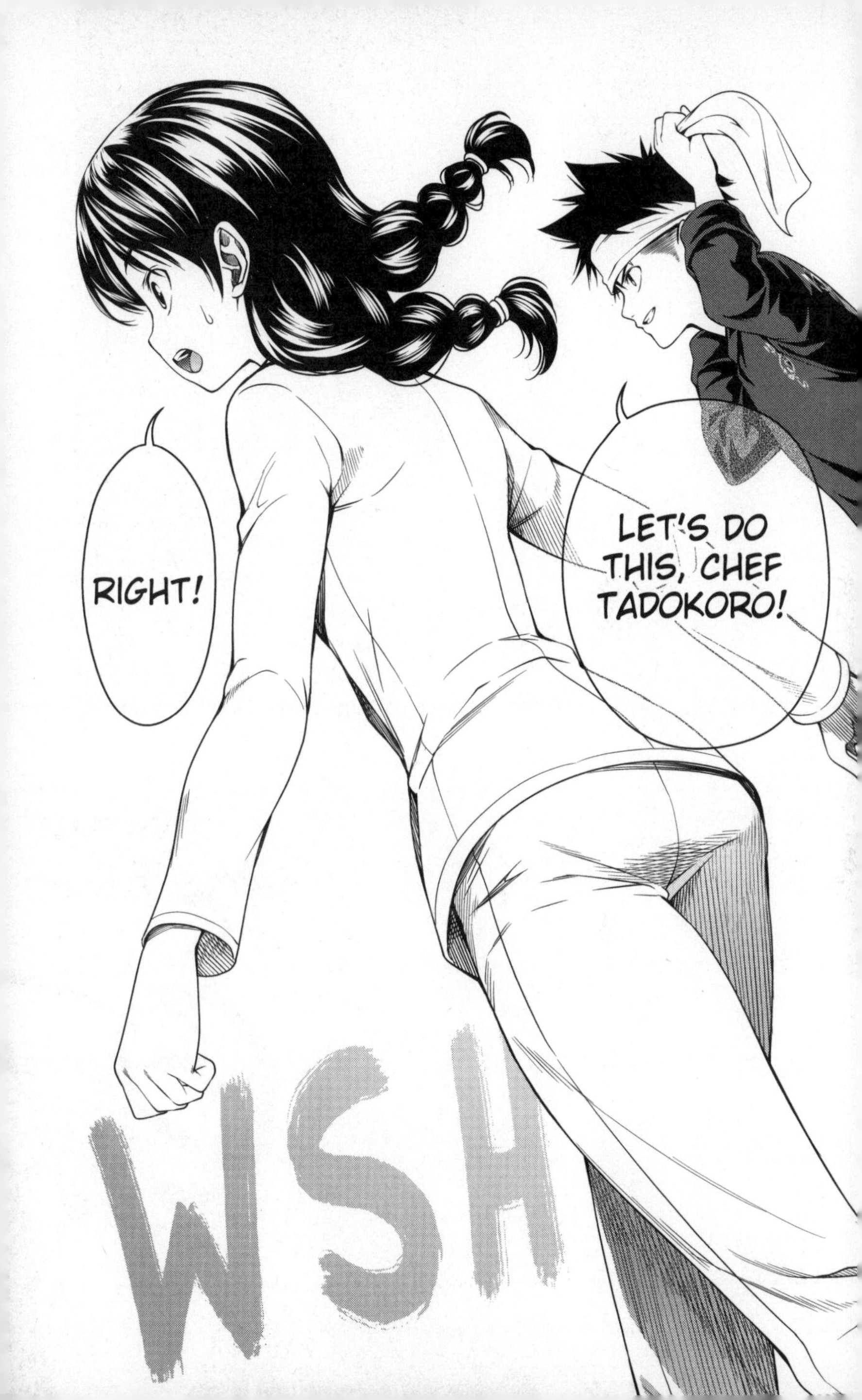
LET'S DO THIS, CHEF TADOKORO!
RIGHT!
WSH

お食事処

たどころ

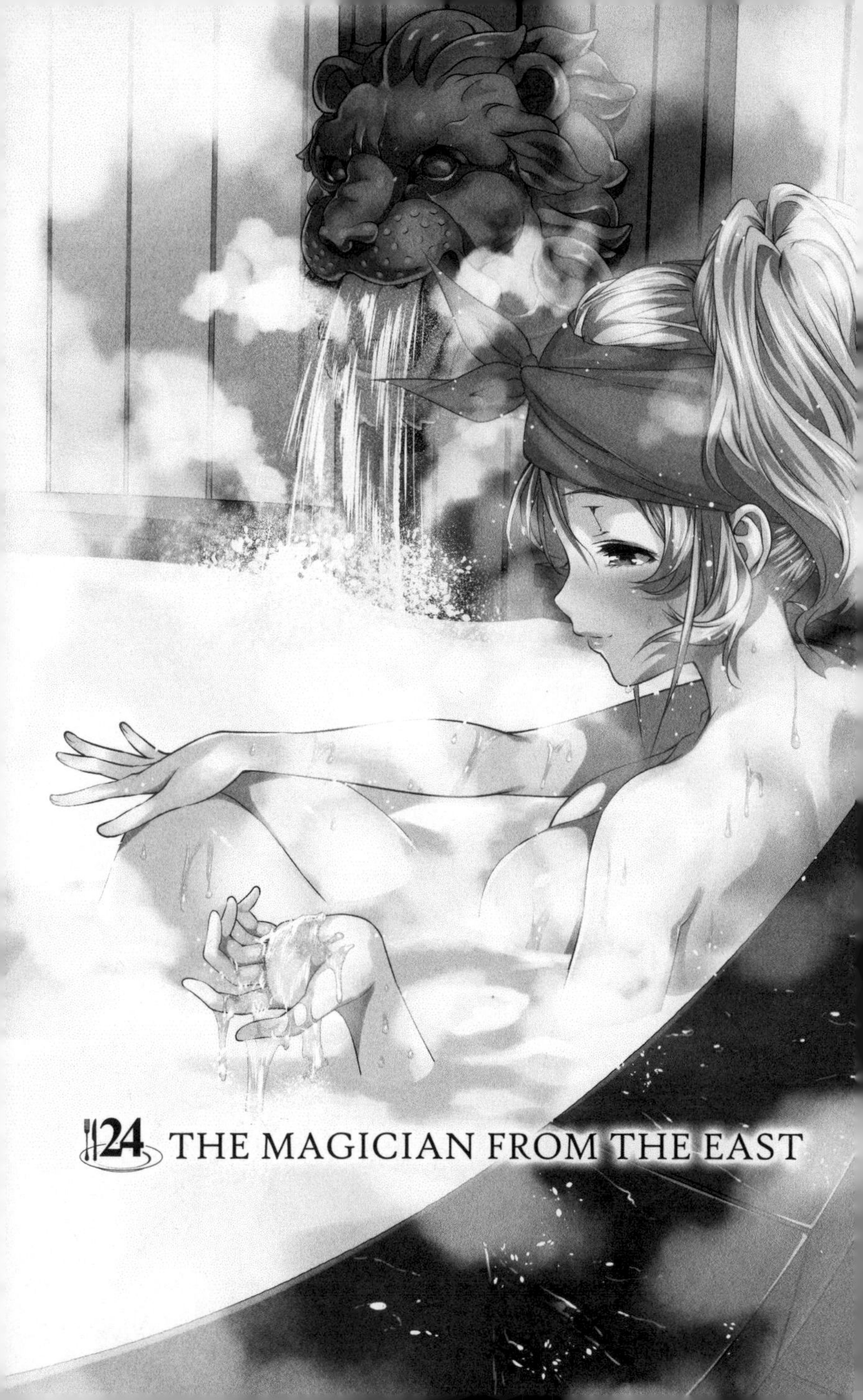

24 THE MAGICIAN FROM THE EAST

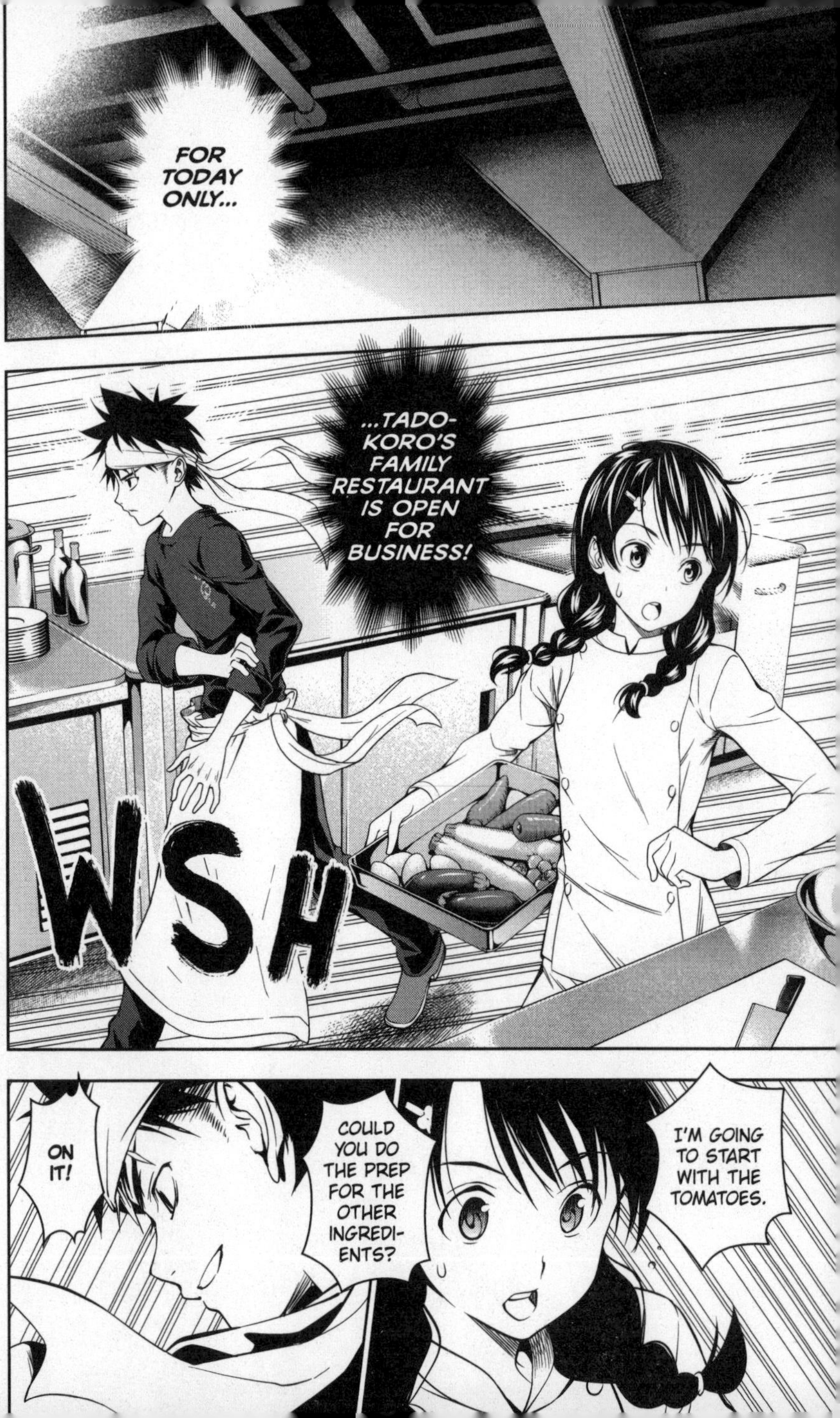
FOR TODAY ONLY...
...TADO-KORO'S FAMILY RESTAURANT IS OPEN FOR BUSINESS!
WSH
I'M GOING TO START WITH THE TOMATOES.
COULD YOU DO THE PREP FOR THE OTHER INGREDI-ENTS?
ON IT!

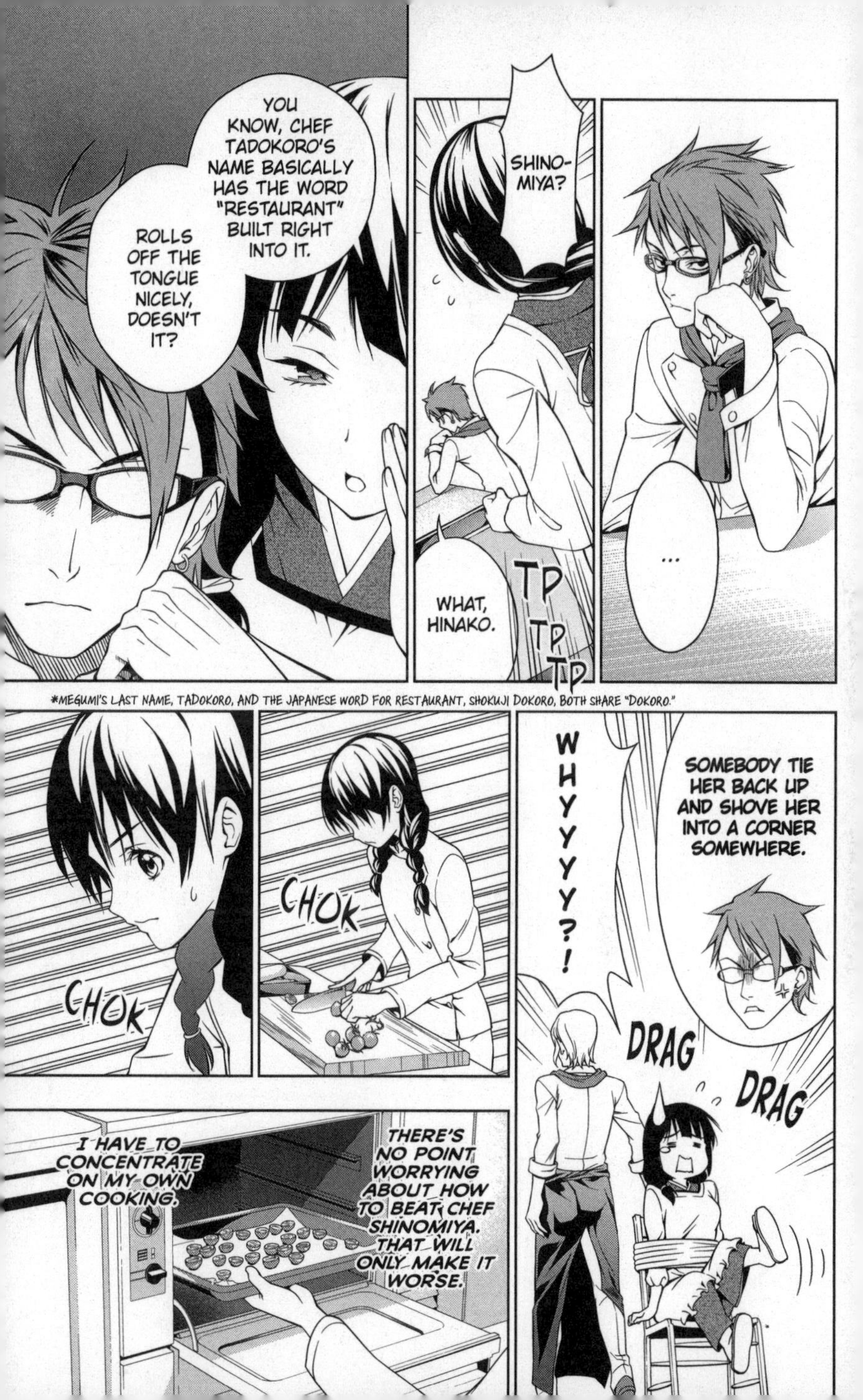
...
SHINO-MIYA?
WHAT, HINAKO.
TP TP TP
YOU KNOW, CHEF TADOKORO'S NAME BASICALLY HAS THE WORD "RESTAURANT" BUILT RIGHT INTO IT.
ROLLS OFF THE TONGUE NICELY, DOESN'T IT?
SOMEBODY TIE HER BACK UP AND SHOVE HER INTO A CORNER SOMEWHERE.
WHYYYYY?!
DRAG
DRAG
CHOK
CHOK
THERE'S NO POINT WORRYING ABOUT HOW TO BEAT CHEF SHINOMIYA. THAT WILL ONLY MAKE IT WORSE.
I HAVE TO CONCENTRATE ON MY OWN COOKING.

*MEGUMI'S LAST NAME, TADOKORO, AND THE JAPANESE WORD FOR RESTAURANT, SHOKUJI DOKORO, BOTH SHARE "DOKORO."

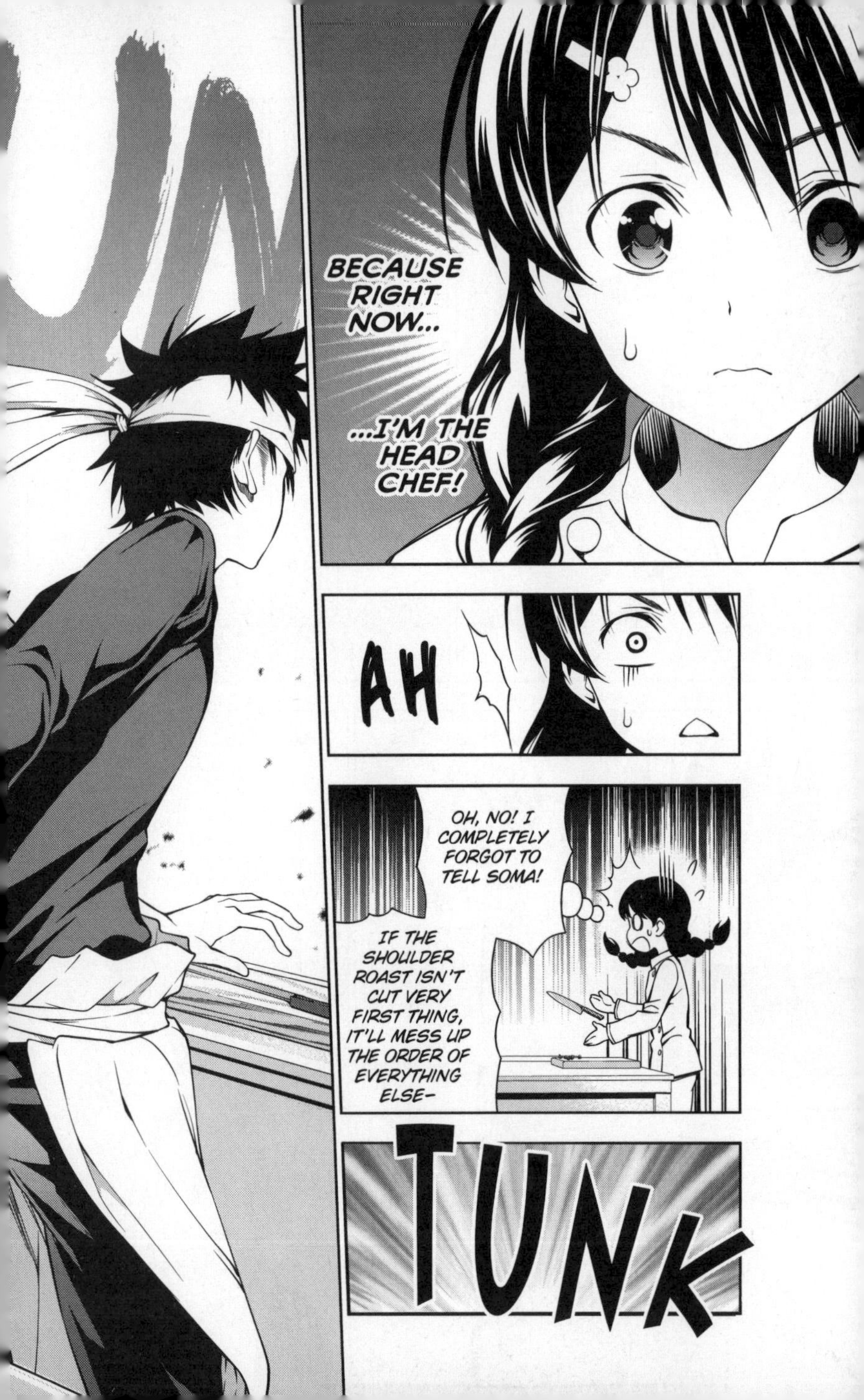
BECAUSE RIGHT NOW...
...I'M THE HEAD CHEF!
AH
OH, NO! I COMPLETELY FORGOT TO TELL SOMA!
IF THE SHOULDER ROAST ISN'T CUT VERY FIRST THING, IT'LL MESS UP THE ORDER OF EVERYTHING ELSE-
TUNK

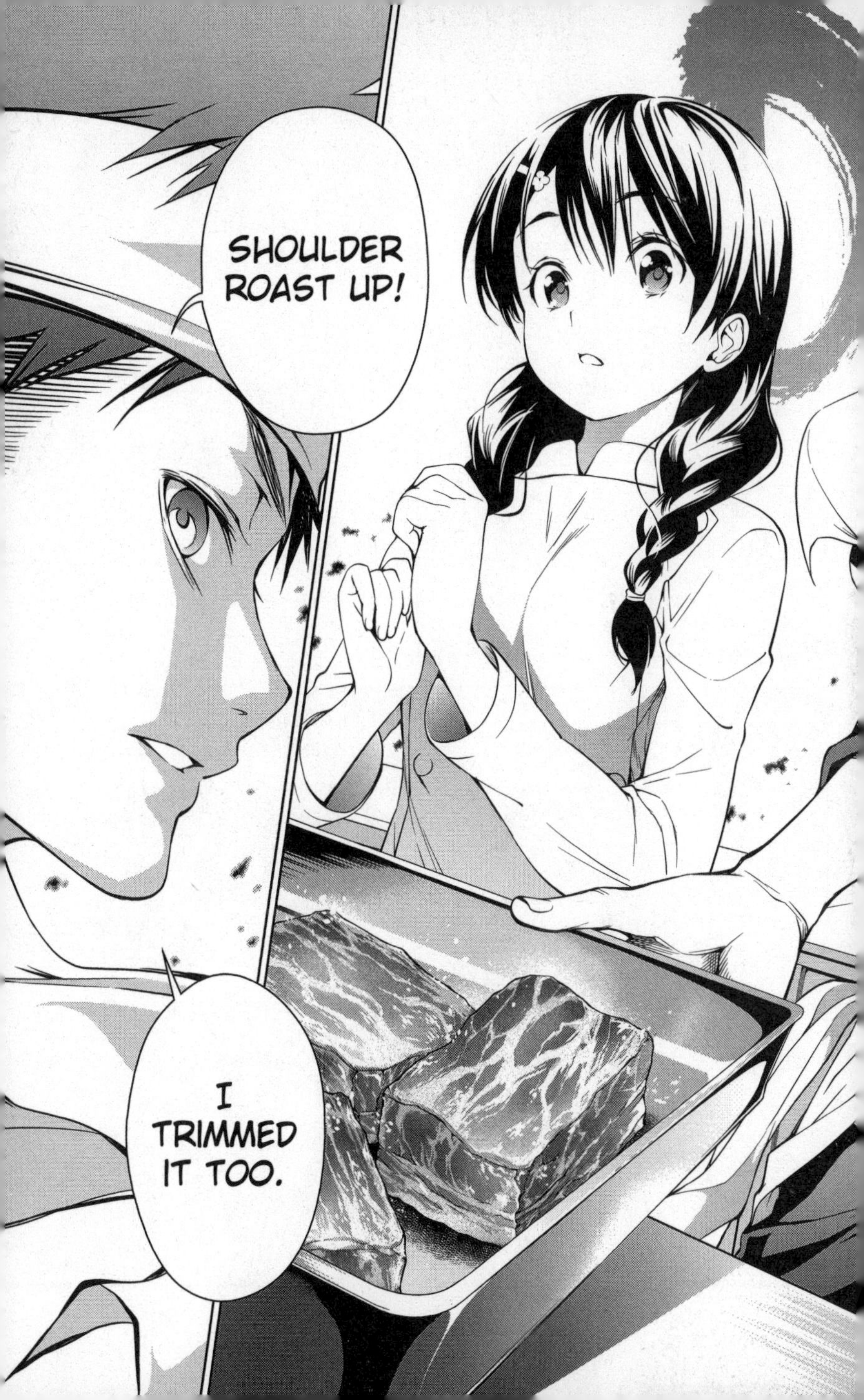
SHOULDER ROAST UP!
I TRIMMED IT TOO.

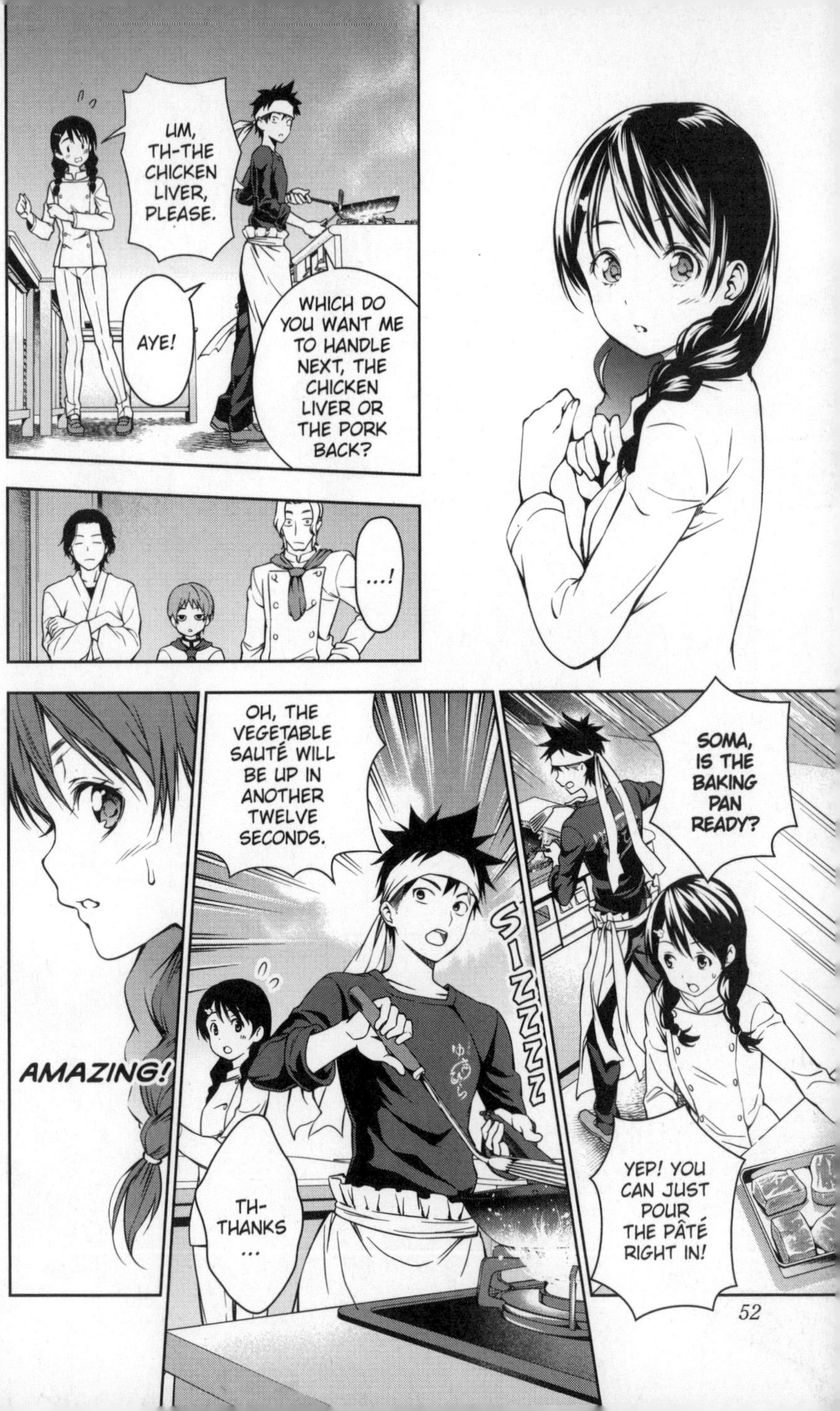
WHICH DO YOU WANT ME TO HANDLE NEXT, THE CHICKEN LIVER OR THE PORK BACK?
UM, TH-THE CHICKEN LIVER, PLEASE.
AYE!
...!
SOMA, IS THE BAKING PAN READY?
YEP! YOU CAN JUST POUR THE PÂTÉ RIGHT IN!
OH, THE VEGETABLE SAUTÉ WILL BE UP IN ANOTHER TWELVE SECONDS.
SIZZZZZ
TH-THANKS...
AMAZING!

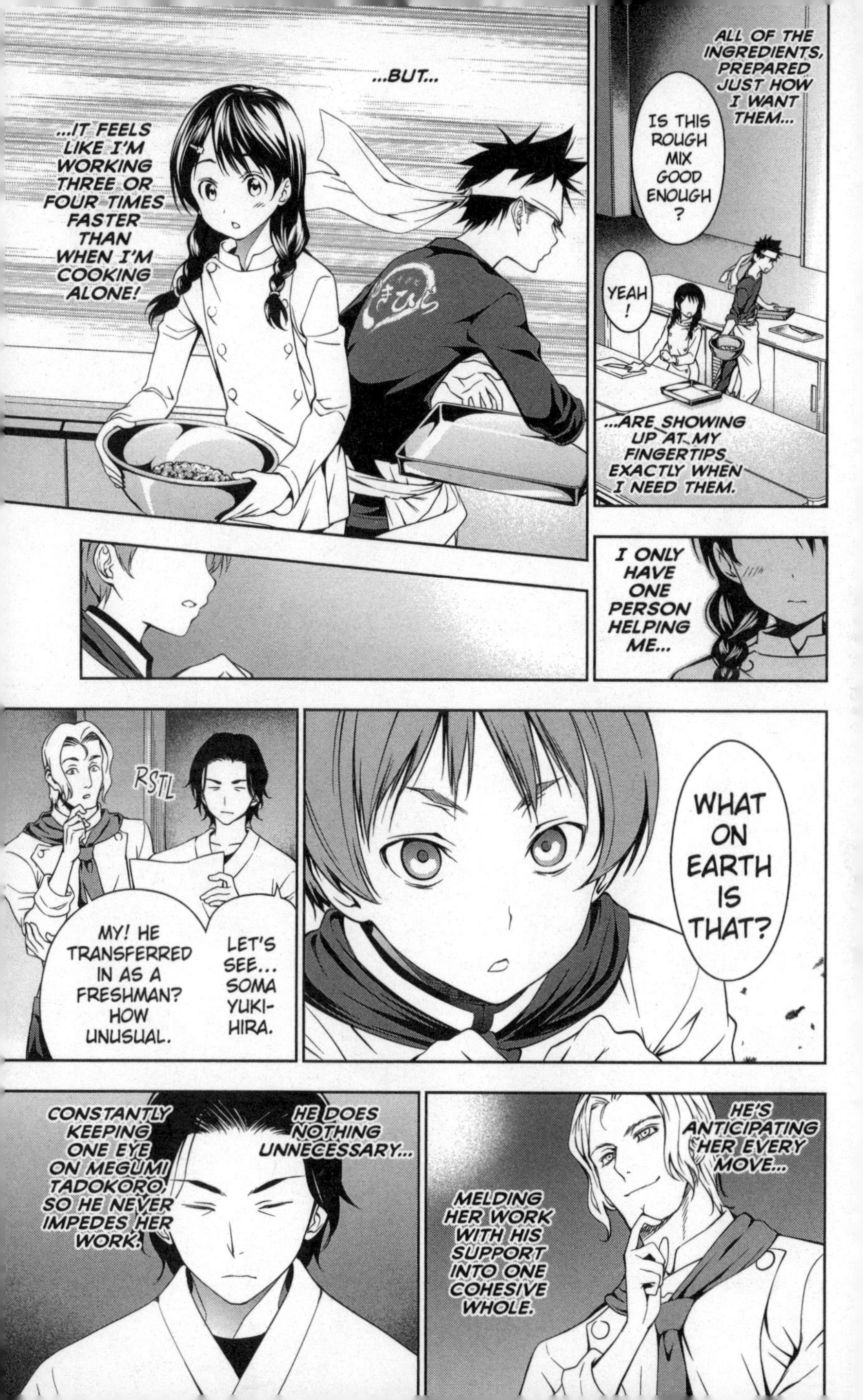
ALL OF THE INGREDIENTS, PREPARED JUST HOW I WANT THEM...
IS THIS ROUGH MIX GOOD ENOUGH?
YEAH!
...ARE SHOWING UP AT MY FINGERTIPS EXACTLY WHEN I NEED THEM.
I ONLY HAVE ONE PERSON HELPING ME...
...BUT...
...IT FEELS LIKE I'M WORKING THREE OR FOUR TIMES FASTER THAN WHEN I'M COOKING ALONE!
WHAT ON EARTH IS THAT?
RSTL
LET'S SEE... SOMA YUKIHIRA.
MY! HE TRANSFERRED IN AS A FRESHMAN? HOW UNUSUAL.
HE'S ANTICIPATING HER EVERY MOVE...
MELDING HER WORK WITH HIS SUPPORT INTO ONE COHESIVE WHOLE.
HE DOES NOTHING UNNECESSARY...
CONSTANTLY KEEPING ONE EYE ON MEGUMI TADOKORO, SO HE NEVER IMPEDES HER WORK.

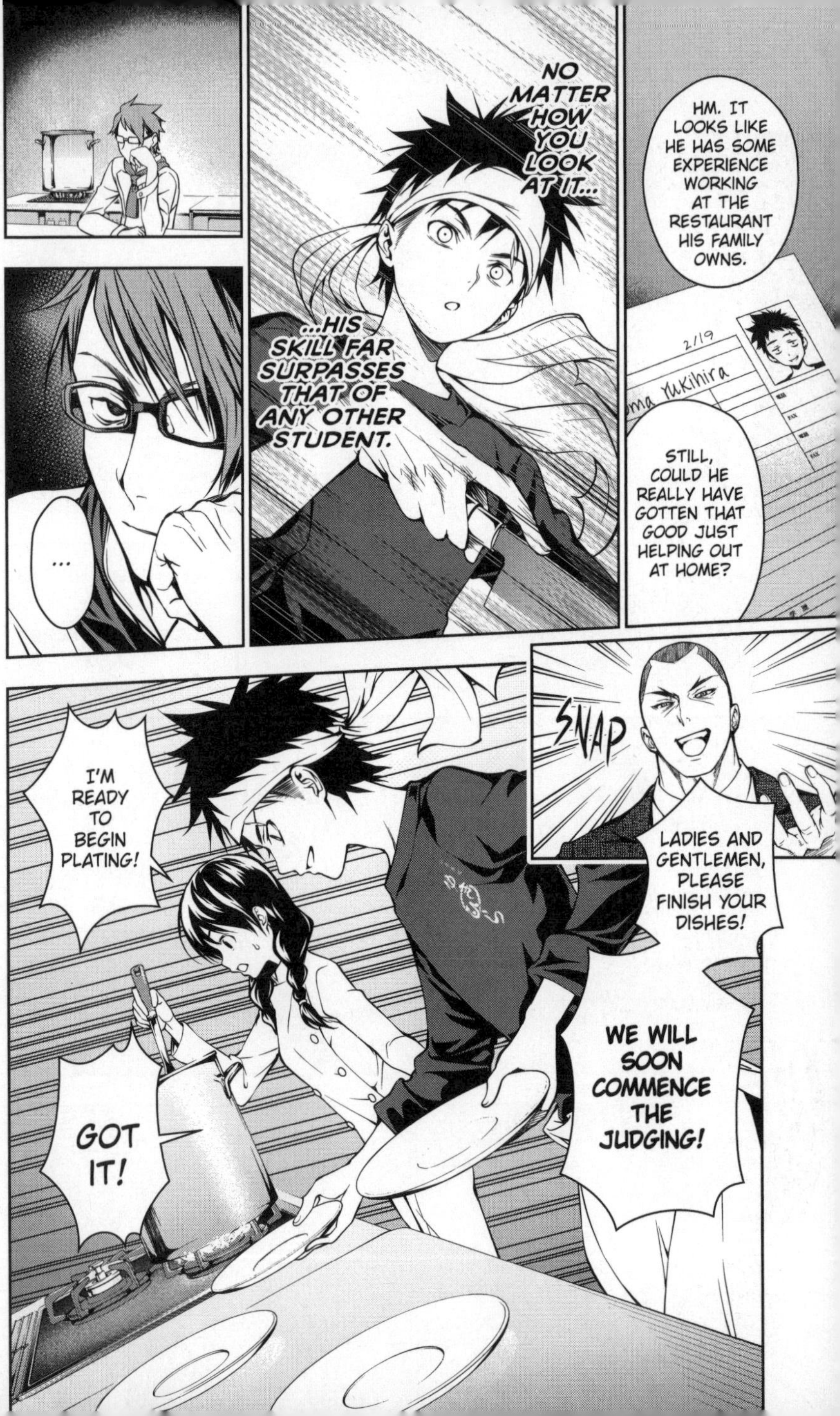
HM. IT LOOKS LIKE HE HAS SOME EXPERIENCE WORKING AT THE RESTAURANT HIS FAMILY OWNS.
2/19
ma Yukihira
STILL, COULD HE REALLY HAVE GOTTEN THAT GOOD JUST HELPING OUT AT HOME?
NO MATTER HOW YOU LOOK AT IT...
...HIS SKILL FAR SURPASSES THAT OF ANY OTHER STUDENT.
...
SNAP
LADIES AND GENTLEMEN, PLEASE FINISH YOUR DISHES!
WE WILL SOON COMMENCE THE JUDGING!
I'M READY TO BEGIN PLATING!
GOT IT!

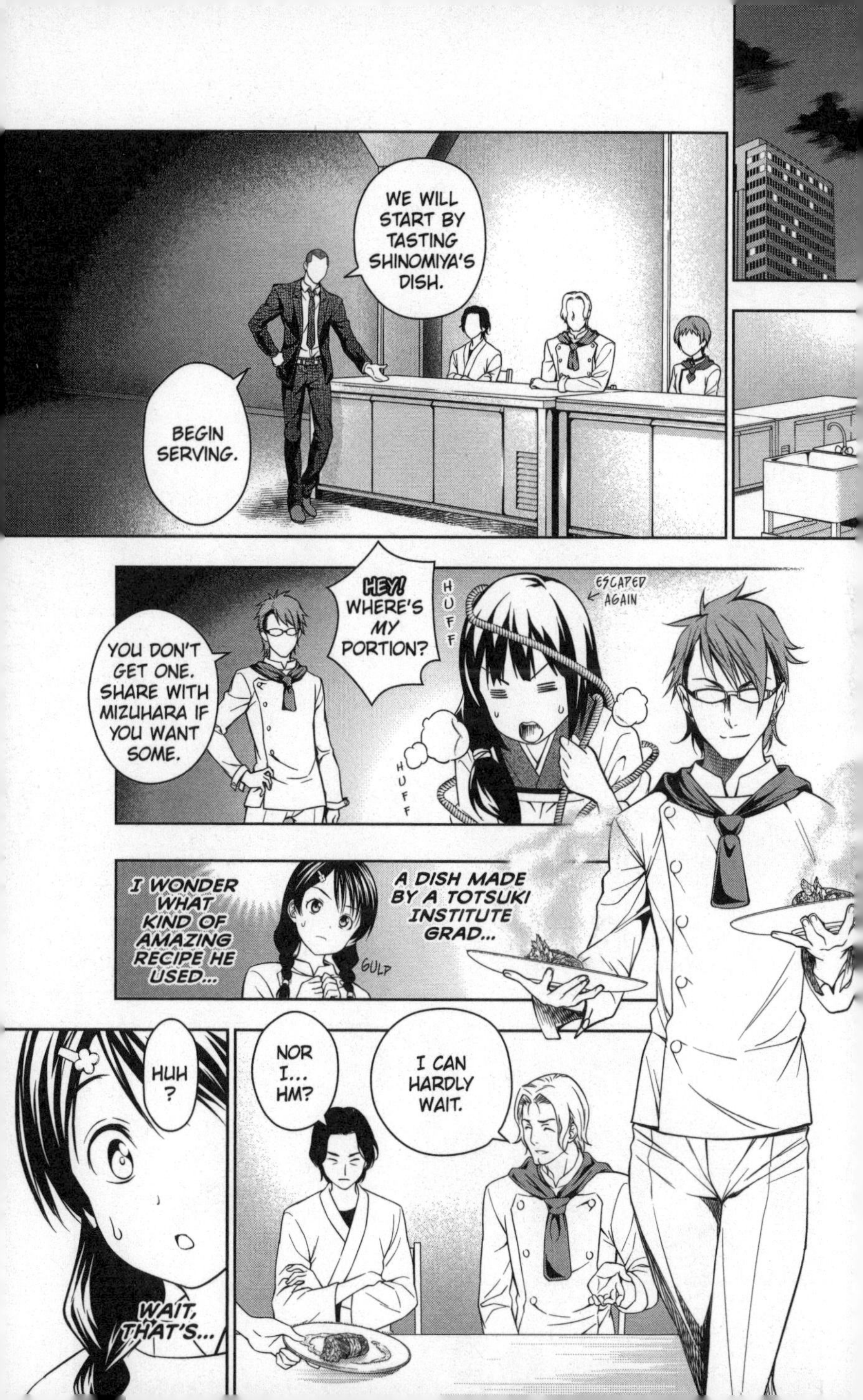
WE WILL START BY TASTING SHINOMIYA'S DISH.
BEGIN SERVING.
ESCAPED AGAIN
HUFF
HEY! WHERE'S MY PORTION?
HUFF
YOU DON'T GET ONE. SHARE WITH MIZUHARA IF YOU WANT SOME.
A DISH MADE BY A TOTSUKI INSTITUTE GRAD...
I WONDER WHAT KIND OF AMAZING RECIPE HE USED...
GULP
I CAN HARDLY WAIT.
NOR I... HM?
HUH?
WAIT, THAT'S...

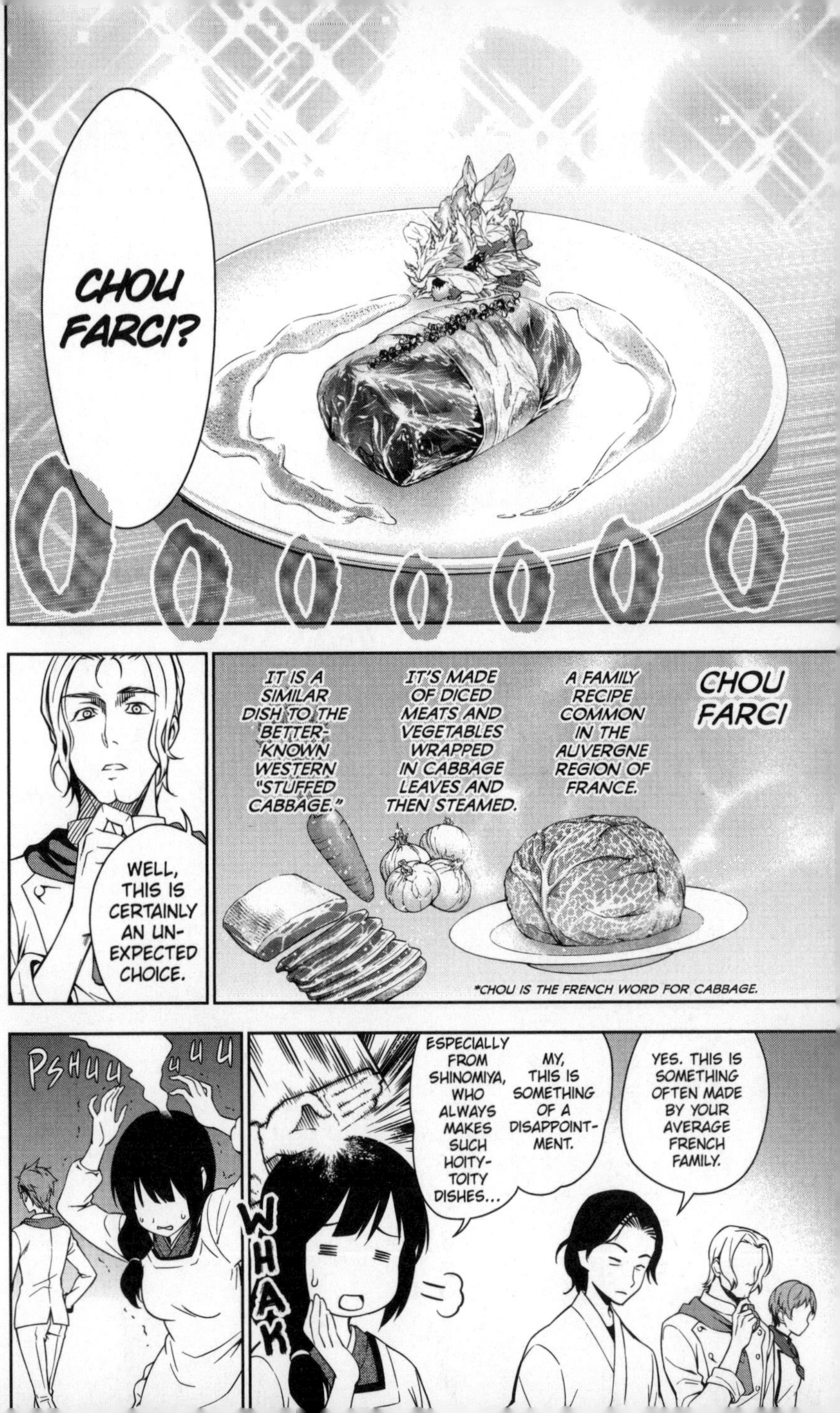
CHOU FARCI?
CHOU FARCI
A FAMILY RECIPE COMMON IN THE AUVERGNE REGION OF FRANCE.
IT'S MADE OF DICED MEATS AND VEGETABLES WRAPPED IN CABBAGE LEAVES AND THEN STEAMED.
IT IS A SIMILAR DISH TO THE BETTER-KNOWN WESTERN "STUFFED CABBAGE."
*CHOU IS THE FRENCH WORD FOR CABBAGE.
WELL, THIS IS CERTAINLY AN UN-EXPECTED CHOICE.
YES. THIS IS SOMETHING OFTEN MADE BY YOUR AVERAGE FRENCH FAMILY.
MY, THIS IS SOMETHING OF A DISAPPOINT-MENT.
ESPECIALLY FROM SHINOMIYA, WHO ALWAYS MAKES SUCH HOITY-TOITY DISHES...
WHAK
PSHUUUUU

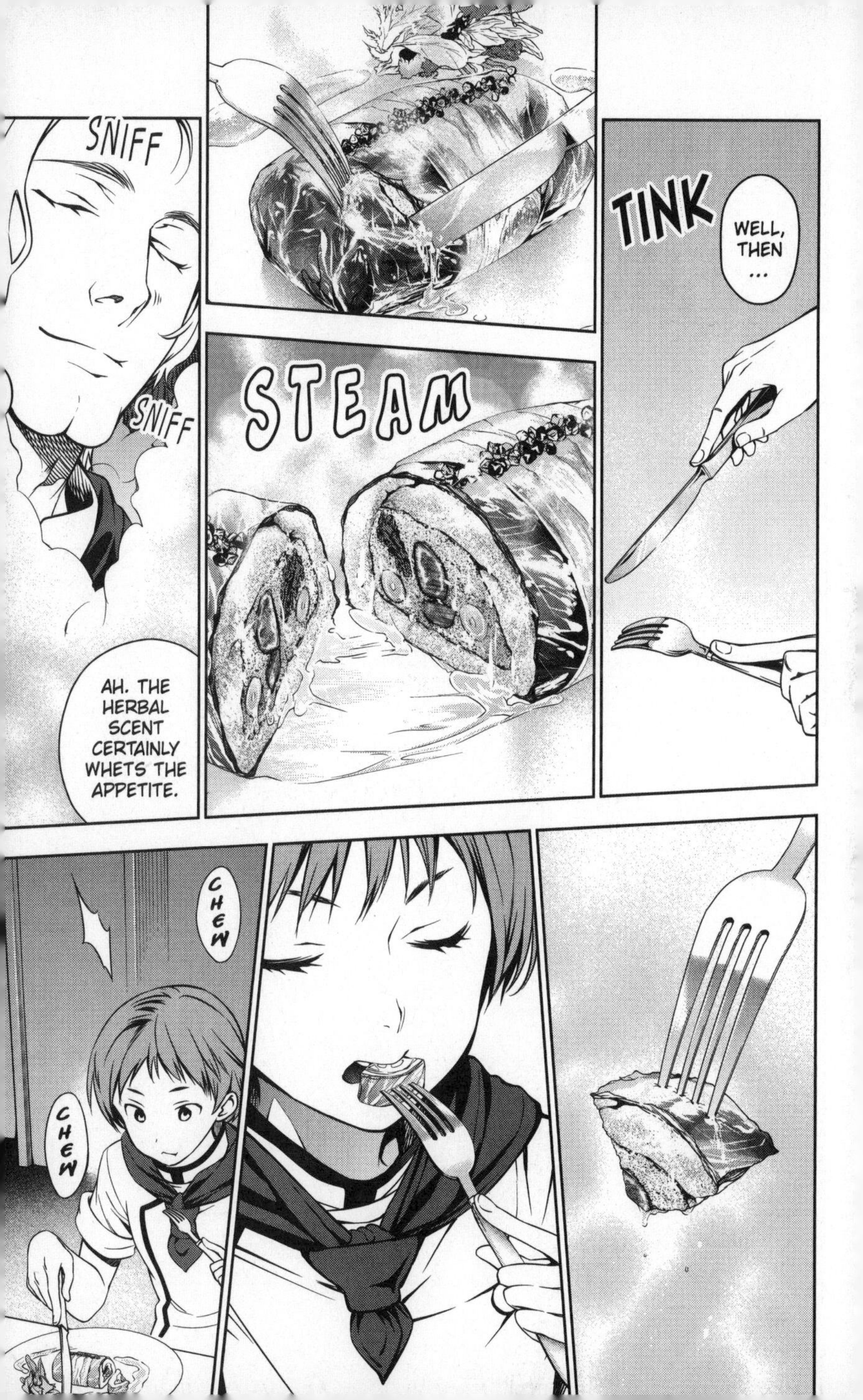
TINK
WELL, THEN ...
STEAM
SNIFF
SNIFF
AH. THE HERBAL SCENT CERTAINLY WHETS THE APPETITE.
CHEW
CHEW

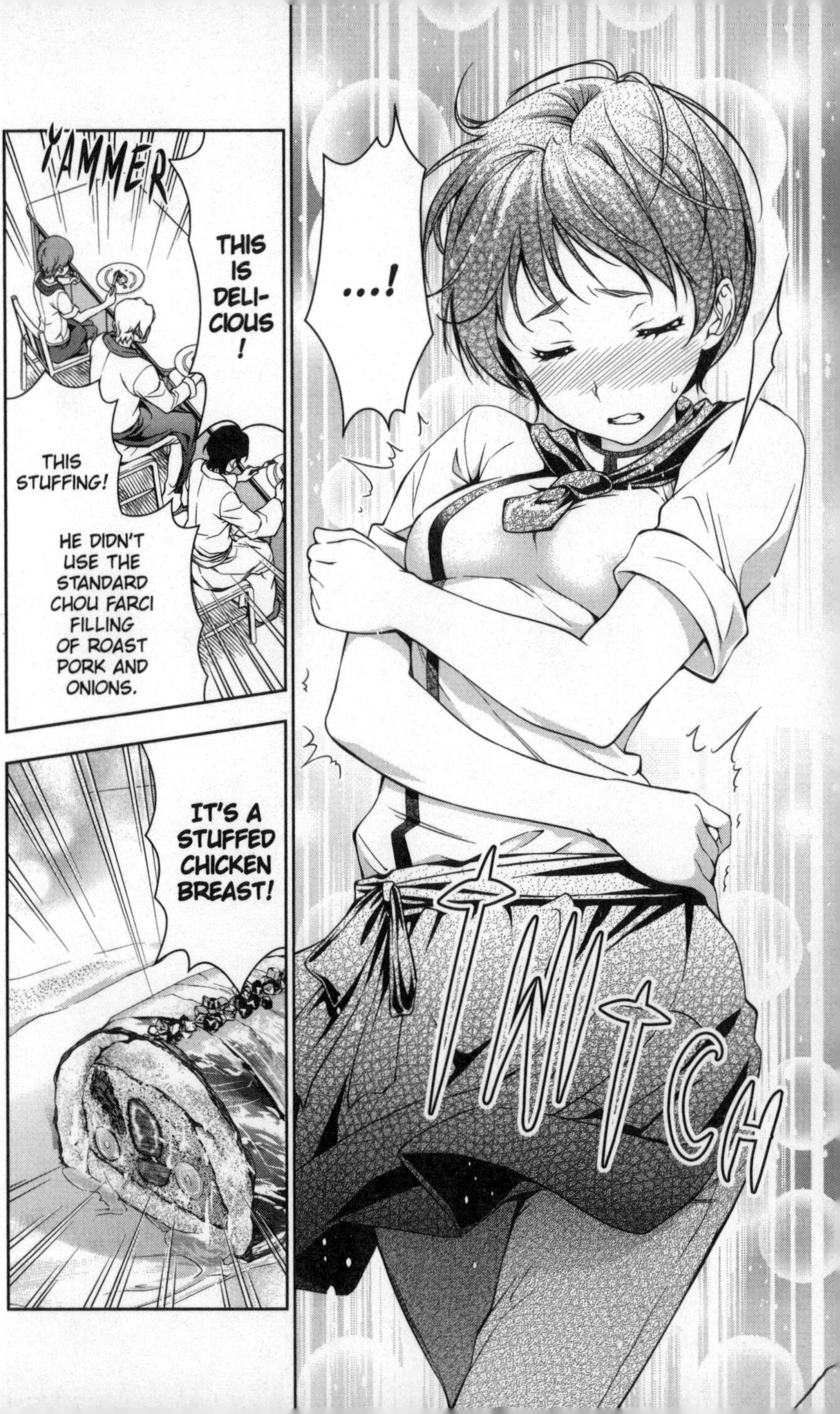
...!
TWITCH
YAMMER
THIS IS DELI-CIOUS!
THIS STUFFING!
HE DIDN'T USE THE STANDARD CHOU FARCI FILLING OF ROAST PORK AND ONIONS.
IT'S A STUFFED CHICKEN BREAST!

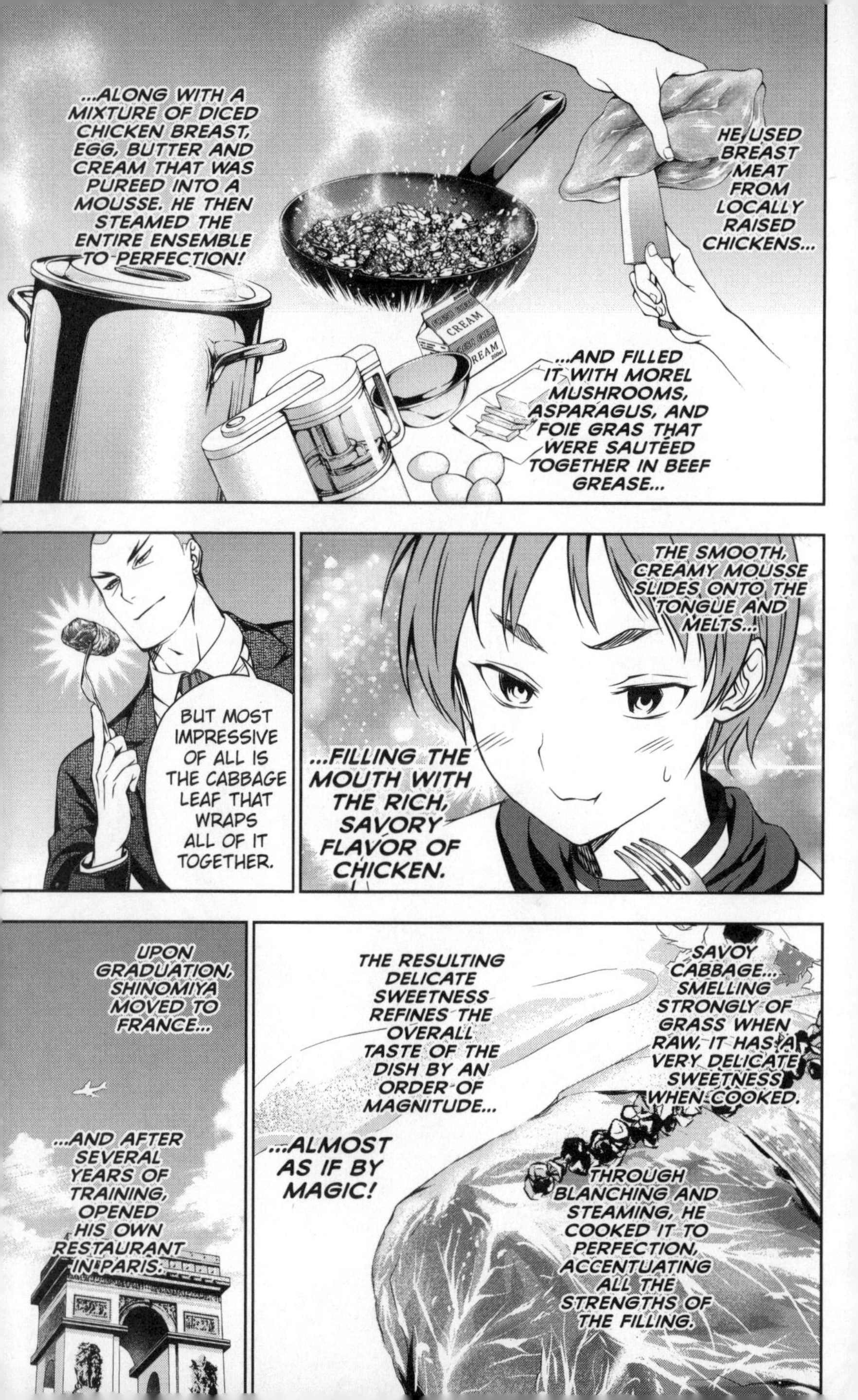
HE USED BREAST MEAT FROM LOCALLY RAISED CHICKENS...
...AND FILLED IT WITH MOREL MUSHROOMS, ASPARAGUS, AND FOIE GRAS THAT WERE SAUTÉED TOGETHER IN BEEF GREASE...
...ALONG WITH A MIXTURE OF DICED CHICKEN BREAST, EGG, BUTTER AND CREAM THAT WAS PUREED INTO A MOUSSE. HE THEN STEAMED THE ENTIRE ENSEMBLE TO PERFECTION!
CREAM
THE SMOOTH, CREAMY MOUSSE SLIDES ONTO THE TONGUE AND MELTS...
...FILLING THE MOUTH WITH THE RICH, SAVORY FLAVOR OF CHICKEN.
BUT MOST IMPRESSIVE OF ALL IS THE CABBAGE LEAF THAT WRAPS ALL OF IT TOGETHER.
SAVOY CABBAGE... SMELLING STRONGLY OF GRASS WHEN RAW, IT HAS A VERY DELICATE SWEETNESS WHEN COOKED.
THROUGH BLANCHING AND STEAMING, HE COOKED IT TO PERFECTION, ACCENTUATING ALL THE STRENGTHS OF THE FILLING.
THE RESULTING DELICATE SWEETNESS REFINES THE OVERALL TASTE OF THE DISH BY AN ORDER OF MAGNITUDE...
...ALMOST AS IF BY MAGIC!
UPON GRADUATION, SHINOMIYA MOVED TO FRANCE...
...AND AFTER SEVERAL YEARS OF TRAINING, OPENED HIS OWN RESTAURANT IN PARIS.

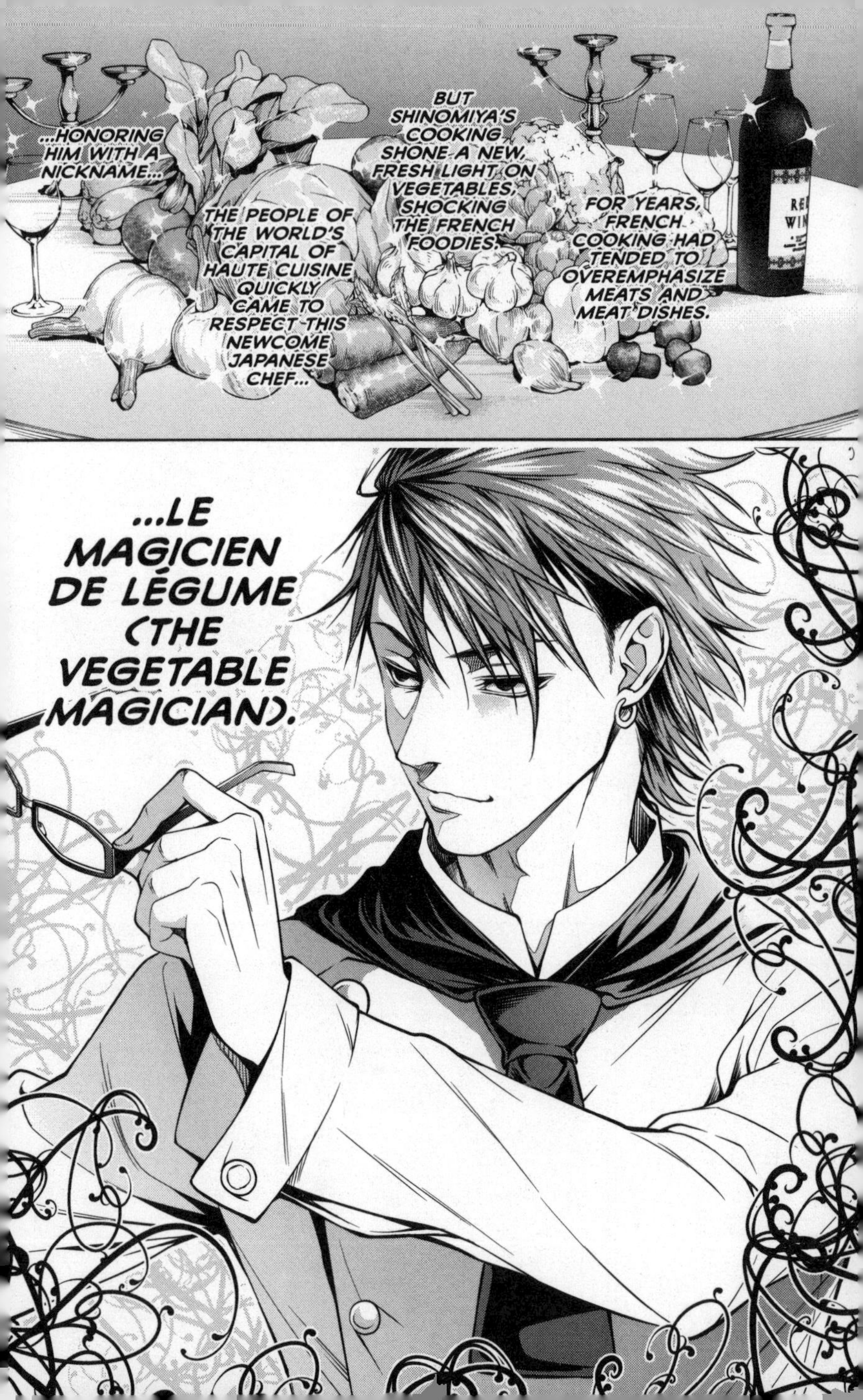
FOR YEARS, FRENCH COOKING HAD TENDED TO OVEREMPHASIZE MEATS AND MEAT DISHES.
BUT SHINOMIYA'S COOKING SHONE A NEW, FRESH LIGHT ON VEGETABLES, SHOCKING THE FRENCH FOODIES.
THE PEOPLE OF THE WORLD'S CAPITAL OF HAUTE CUISINE QUICKLY CAME TO RESPECT THIS NEWCOME JAPANESE CHEF...
...HONORING HIM WITH A NICKNAME...
...LE MAGICIEN DE LÉGUME (THE VEGETABLE MAGICIAN).

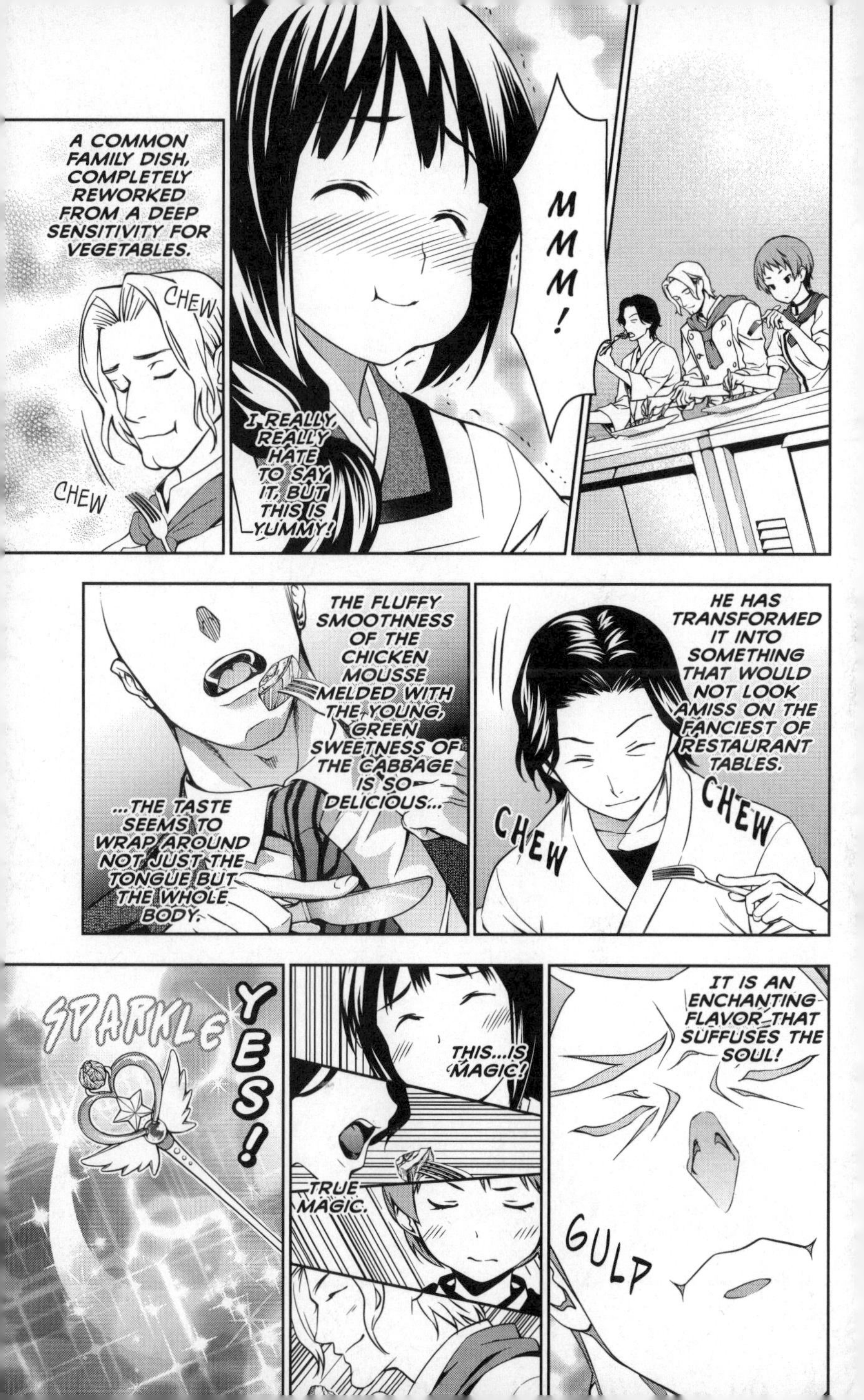
MMM!
I REALLY, REALLY HATE TO SAY IT, BUT THIS IS YUMMY!
A COMMON FAMILY DISH, COMPLETELY REWORKED FROM A DEEP SENSITIVITY FOR VEGETABLES.
CHEW
CHEW
HE HAS TRANSFORMED IT INTO SOMETHING THAT WOULD NOT LOOK AMISS ON THE FANCIEST OF RESTAURANT TABLES.
CHEW
CHEW
THE FLUFFY SMOOTHNESS OF THE CHICKEN MOUSSE MELDED WITH THE YOUNG, GREEN SWEETNESS OF THE CABBAGE IS SO DELICIOUS...
...THE TASTE SEEMS TO WRAP AROUND NOT JUST THE TONGUE BUT THE WHOLE BODY.
IT IS AN ENCHANTING FLAVOR THAT SUFFUSES THE SOUL!
GULP
THIS...IS MAGIC!
TRUE MAGIC.
YES!
SPARKLE

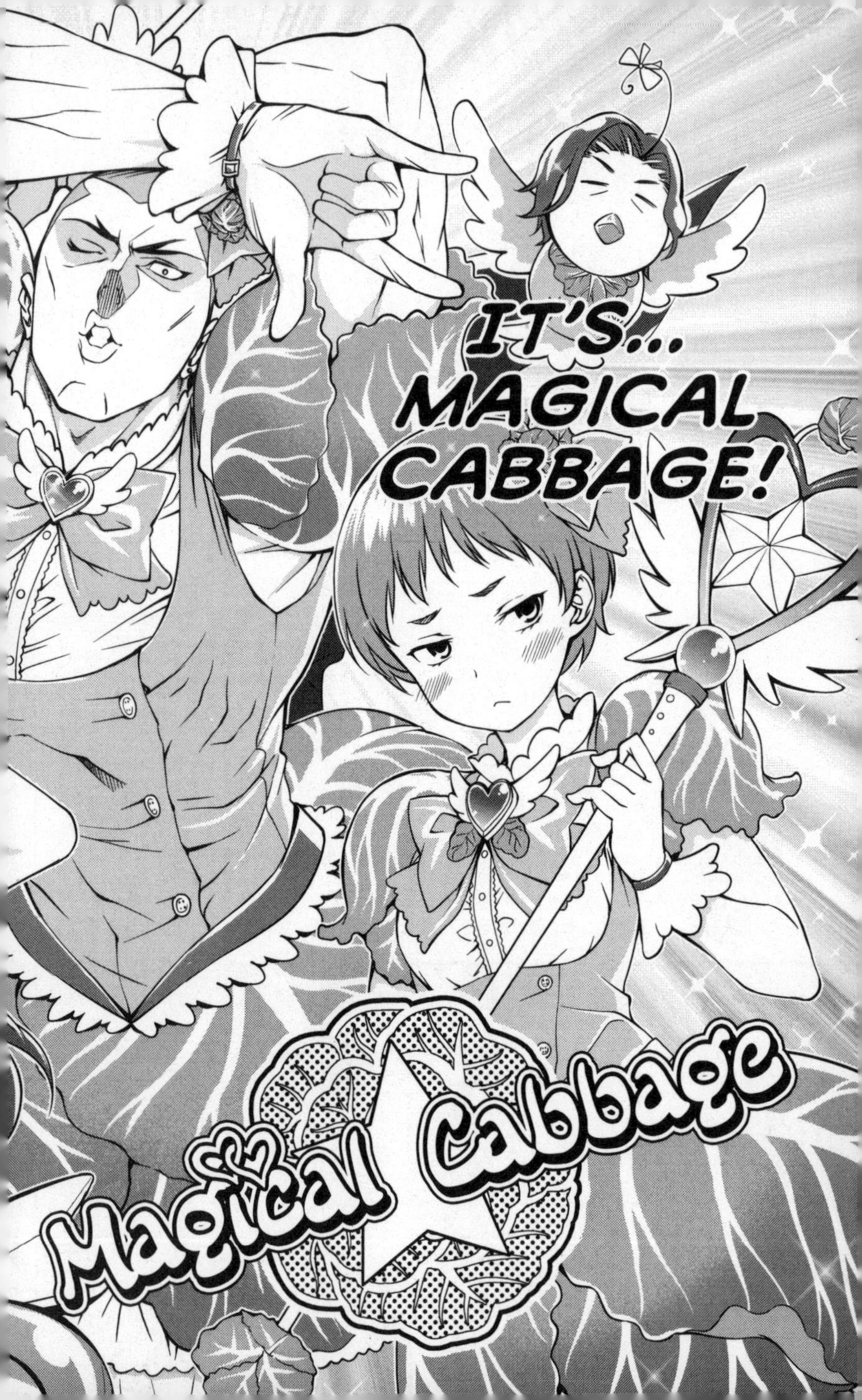
IT'S... MAGICAL CABBAGE!
Magical Cabbage

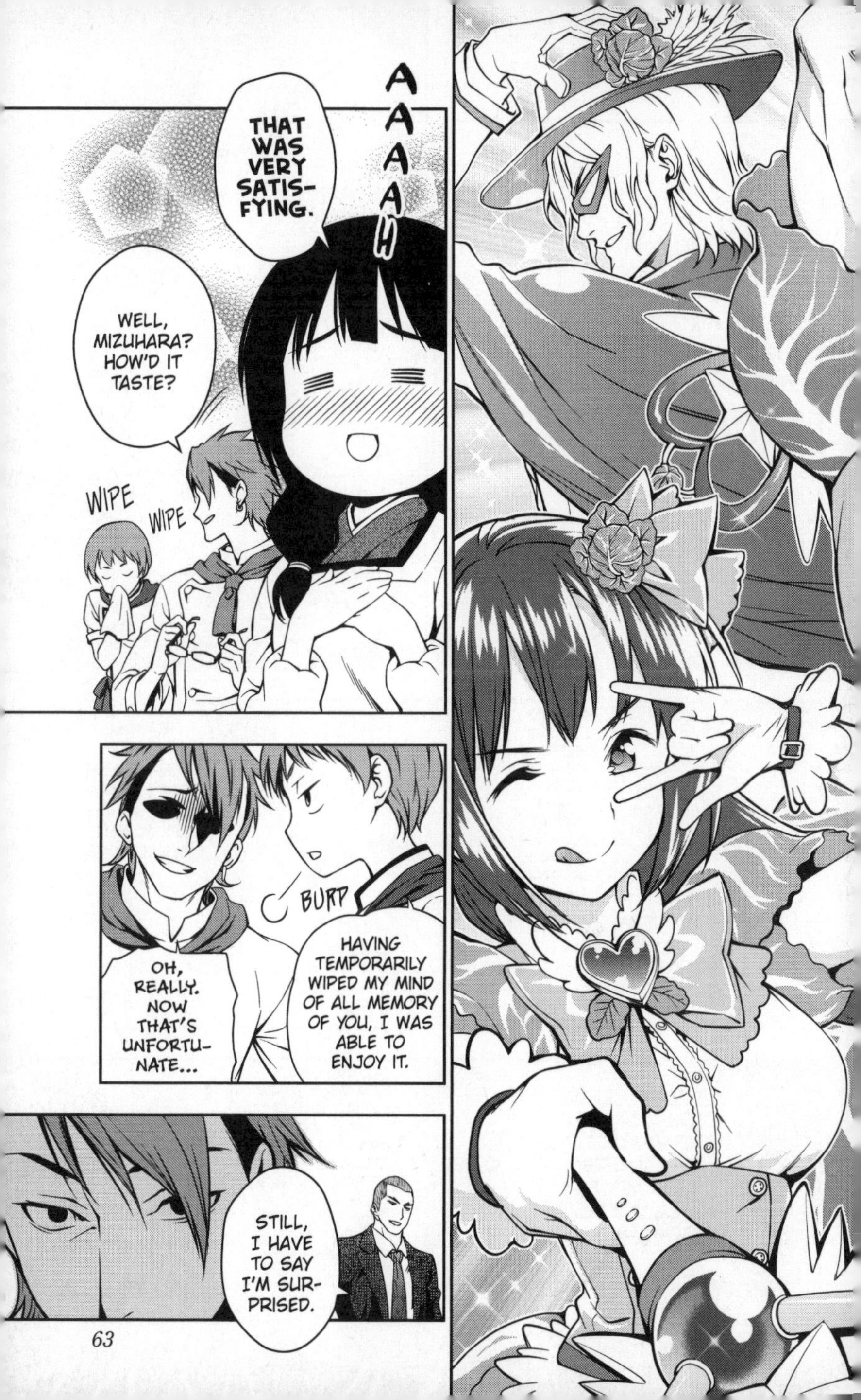
AAAAH
THAT WAS VERY SATIS-FYING.
WELL, MIZUHARA? HOW'D IT TASTE?
WIPE
WIPE
BURP
HAVING TEMPORARILY WIPED MY MIND OF ALL MEMORY OF YOU, I WAS ABLE TO ENJOY IT.
OH, REALLY. NOW THAT'S UNFORTU-NATE...
STILL, I HAVE TO SAY I'M SUR-PRISED.

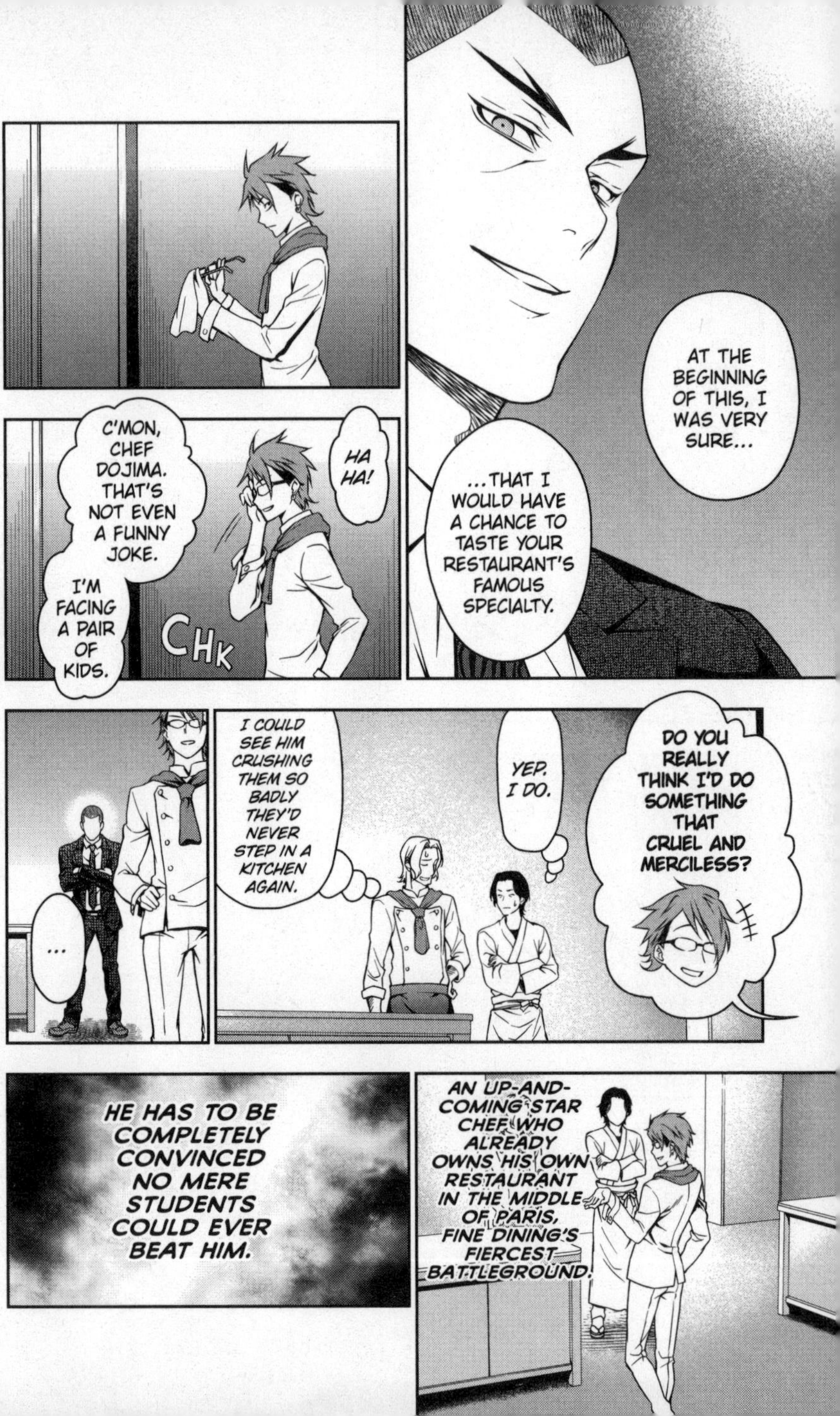
AT THE BEGINNING OF THIS, I WAS VERY SURE...
...THAT I WOULD HAVE A CHANCE TO TASTE YOUR RESTAURANT'S FAMOUS SPECIALTY.
HA HA!
C'MON, CHEF DOJIMA. THAT'S NOT EVEN A FUNNY JOKE.
I'M FACING A PAIR OF KIDS.
CHK
DO YOU REALLY THINK I'D DO SOMETHING THAT CRUEL AND MERCILESS?
YEP. I DO.
I COULD SEE HIM CRUSHING THEM SO BADLY THEY'D NEVER STEP IN A KITCHEN AGAIN.
...
AN UP-AND-COMING STAR CHEF WHO ALREADY OWNS HIS OWN RESTAURANT IN THE MIDDLE OF PARIS, FINE DINING'S FIERCEST BATTLEGROUND.
HE HAS TO BE COMPLETELY CONVINCED NO MERE STUDENTS COULD EVER BEAT HIM.

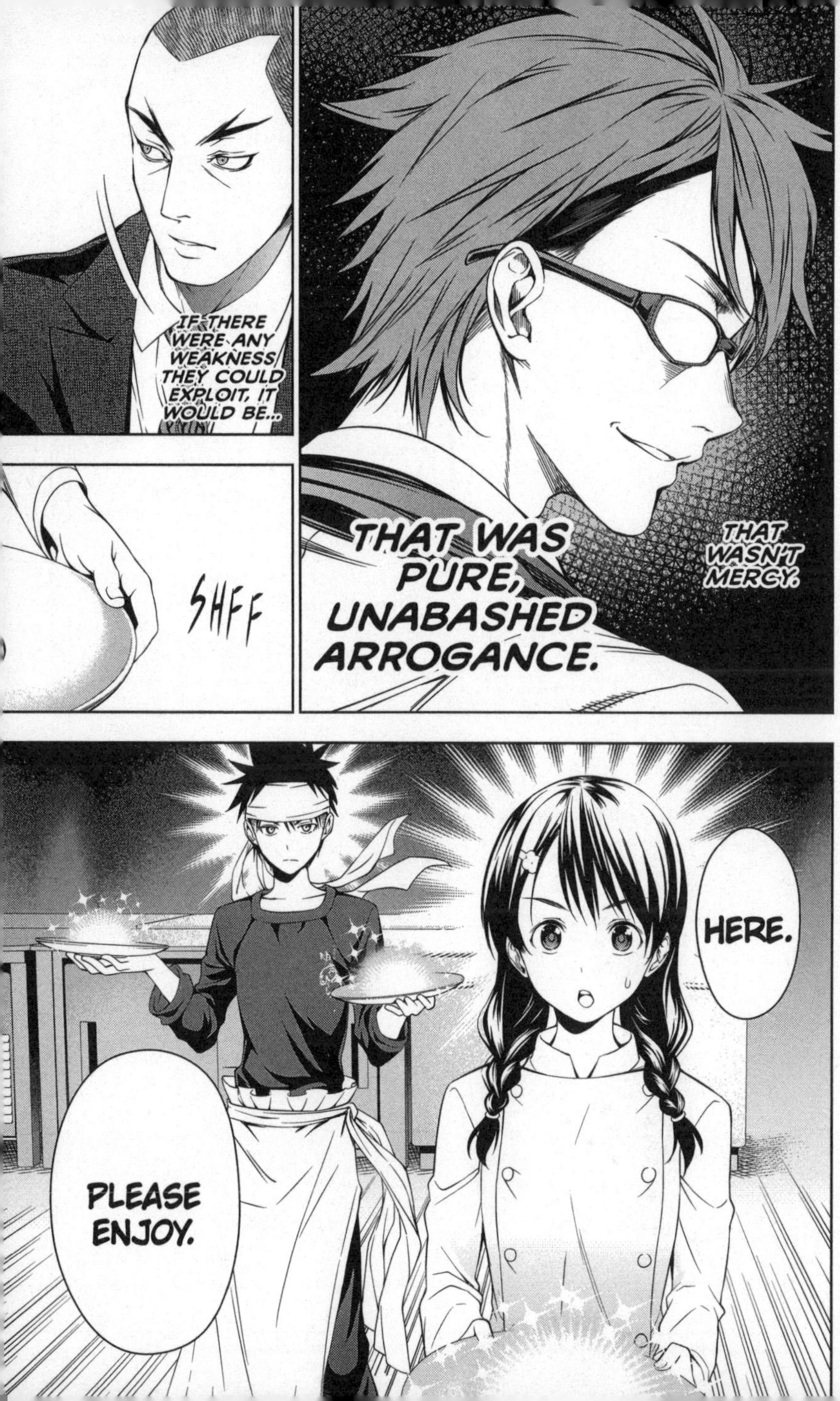
THAT WASN'T MERCY.
THAT WAS PURE, UNABASHED ARROGANCE.
IF THERE WERE ANY WEAKNESS THEY COULD EXPLOIT, IT WOULD BE...
SHFF
HERE.
PLEASE ENJOY.

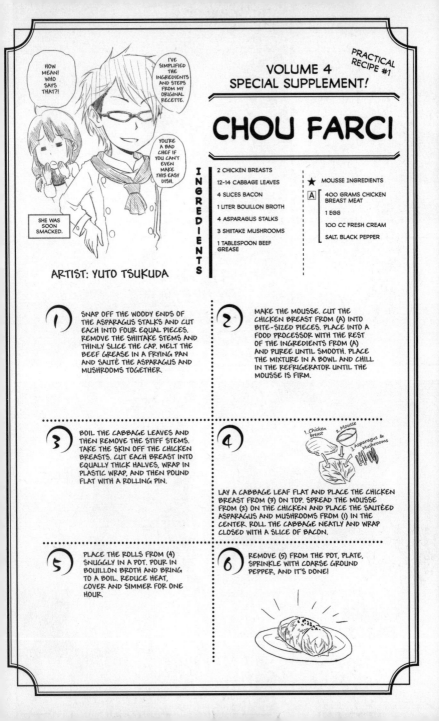

I'VE SIMPLIFIED THE INGREDIENTS AND STEPS FROM MY ORIGINAL RECETTE.
YOU'RE A BAD CHEF IF YOU CAN'T EVEN MAKE THIS EASY DISH.
HOW MEAN! WHO SAYS THAT?!
SHE WAS SOON SMACKED.

ARTIST: YUTO TSUKUDA

PRACTICAL RECIPE #1

VOLUME 4 SPECIAL SUPPLEMENT!

CHOU FARCI

INGREDIENTS

- 2 CHICKEN BREASTS
- 12-14 CABBAGE LEAVES
- 4 SLICES BACON
- 1 LITER BOUILLON BROTH
- 4 ASPARAGUS STALKS
- 3 SHIITAKE MUSHROOMS
- 1 TABLESPOON BEEF GREASE

★ MOUSSE INGREDIENTS

A
- 400 GRAMS CHICKEN BREAST MEAT
- 1 EGG
- 100 CC FRESH CREAM
- SALT, BLACK PEPPER

1. SNAP OFF THE WOODY ENDS OF THE ASPARAGUS STALKS AND CUT EACH INTO FOUR EQUAL PIECES. REMOVE THE SHIITAKE STEMS AND THINLY SLICE THE CAP. MELT THE BEEF GREASE IN A FRYING PAN AND SAUTÉ THE ASPARAGUS AND MUSHROOMS TOGETHER.

2. MAKE THE MOUSSE. CUT THE CHICKEN BREAST FROM (A) INTO BITE-SIZED PIECES. PLACE INTO A FOOD PROCESSOR WITH THE REST OF THE INGREDIENTS FROM (A) AND PUREE UNTIL SMOOTH. PLACE THE MIXTURE IN A BOWL AND CHILL IN THE REFRIGERATOR UNTIL THE MOUSSE IS FIRM.

3. BOIL THE CABBAGE LEAVES AND THEN REMOVE THE STIFF STEMS. TAKE THE SKIN OFF THE CHICKEN BREASTS. CUT EACH BREAST INTO EQUALLY THICK HALVES, WRAP IN PLASTIC WRAP, AND THEN POUND FLAT WITH A ROLLING PIN.

4.
1. Chicken breast
2. Mousse
3. Asparagus & Mushrooms

LAY A CABBAGE LEAF FLAT AND PLACE THE CHICKEN BREAST FROM (3) ON TOP. SPREAD THE MOUSSE FROM (2) ON THE CHICKEN AND PLACE THE SAUTÉED ASPARAGUS AND MUSHROOMS FROM (1) IN THE CENTER. ROLL THE CABBAGE NEATLY AND WRAP CLOSED WITH A SLICE OF BACON.

5. PLACE THE ROLLS FROM (4) SNUGGLY IN A POT. POUR IN BOUILLON BROTH AND BRING TO A BOIL. REDUCE HEAT, COVER AND SIMMER FOR ONE HOUR.

6. REMOVE (5) FROM THE POT, PLATE, SPRINKLE WITH COARSE GROUND PEPPER, AND IT'S DONE!

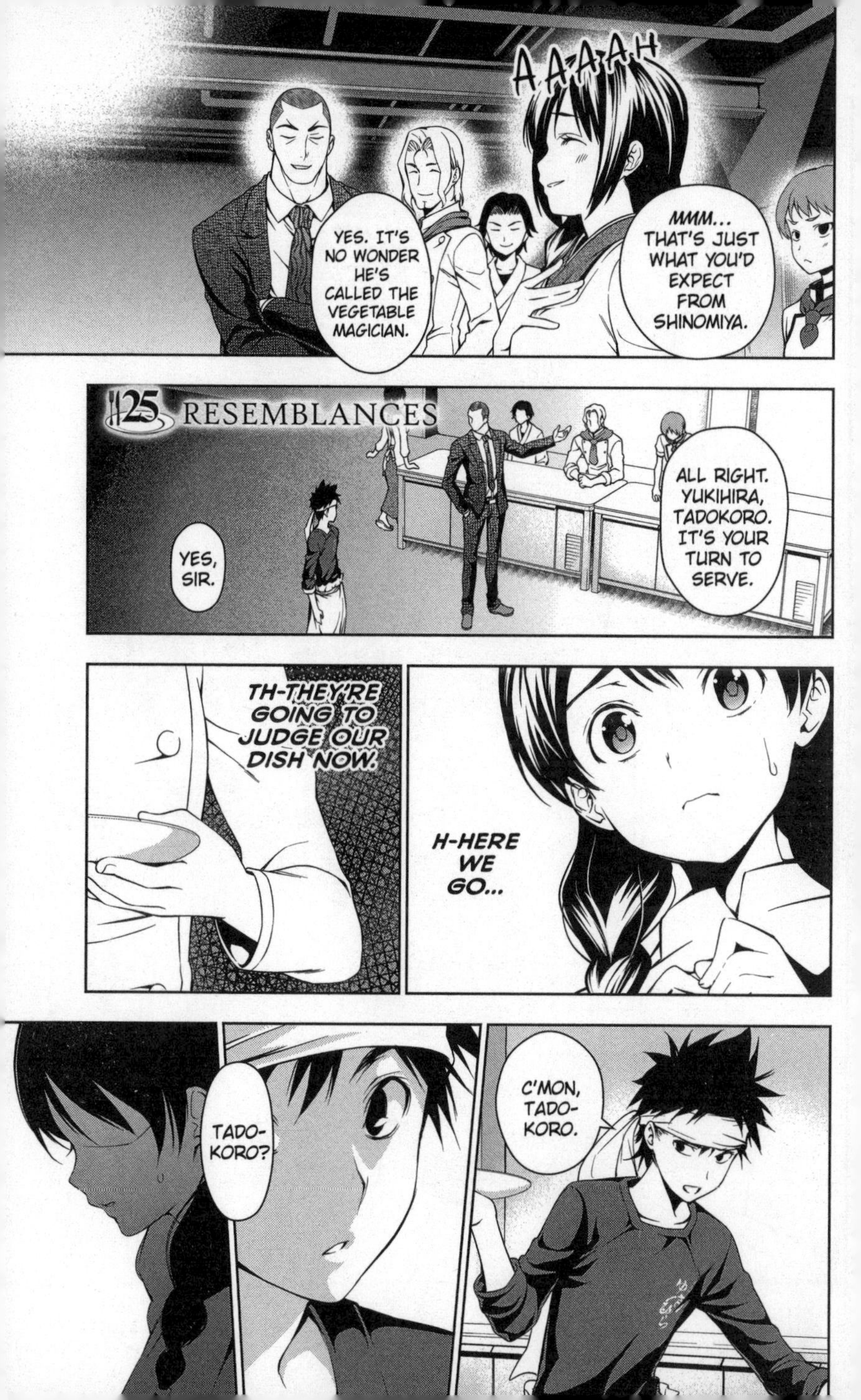
AAAAH
MMM... THAT'S JUST WHAT YOU'D EXPECT FROM SHINOMIYA.
YES. IT'S NO WONDER HE'S CALLED THE VEGETABLE MAGICIAN.
25 RESEMBLANCES
ALL RIGHT. YUKIHIRA, TADOKORO. IT'S YOUR TURN TO SERVE.
YES, SIR.
H-HERE WE GO...
TH-THEY'RE GOING TO JUDGE OUR DISH NOW.
C'MON, TADO-KORO.
TADO-KORO?

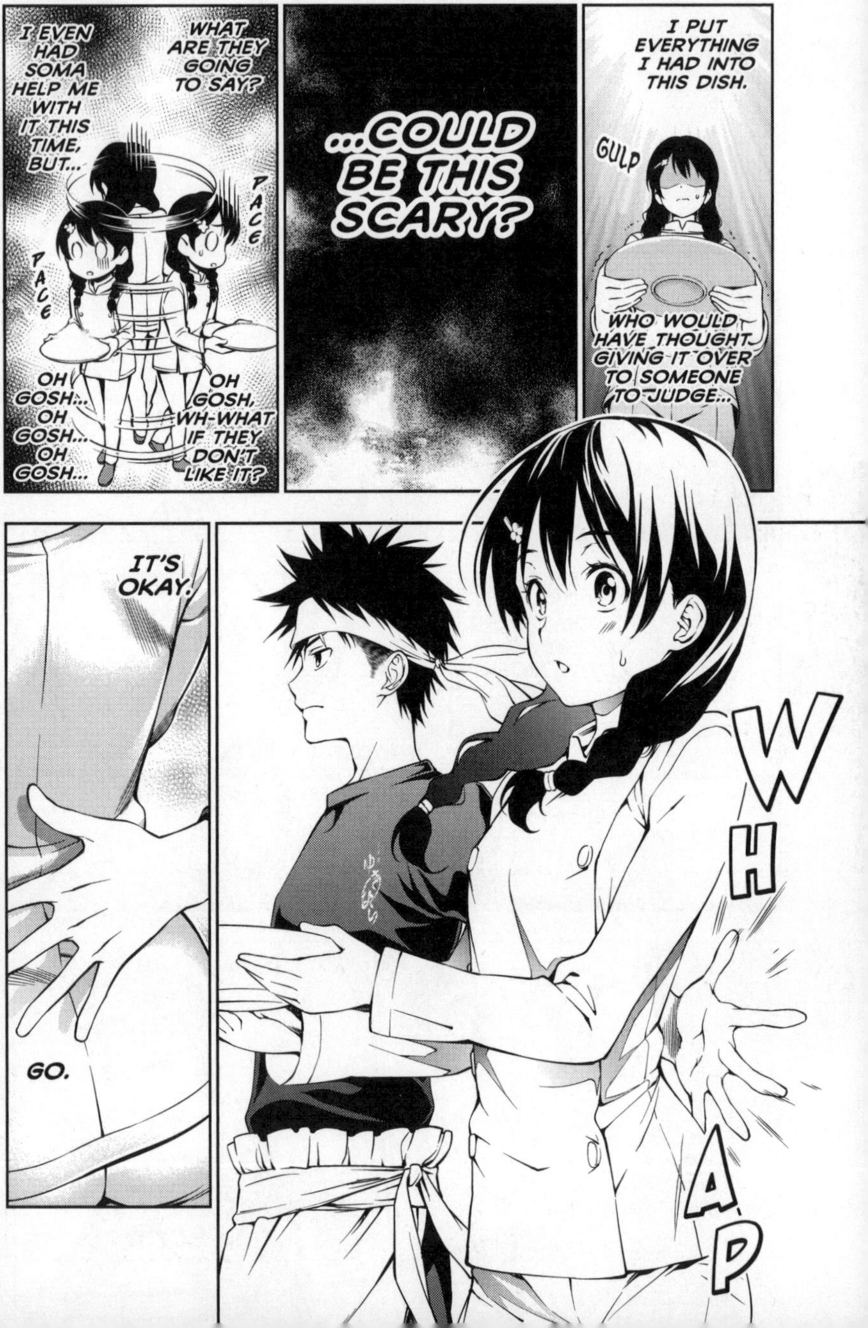
I PUT EVERYTHING I HAD INTO THIS DISH.
GULP
WHO WOULD HAVE THOUGHT GIVING IT OVER TO SOMEONE TO JUDGE...
...COULD BE THIS SCARY?
WHAT ARE THEY GOING TO SAY?
I EVEN HAD SOMA HELP ME WITH IT THIS TIME, BUT...
PACE
PACE
OH GOSH, WH-WHAT IF THEY DON'T LIKE IT?
OH GOSH... OH GOSH... OH GOSH...
WHAP
IT'S OKAY.
GO.

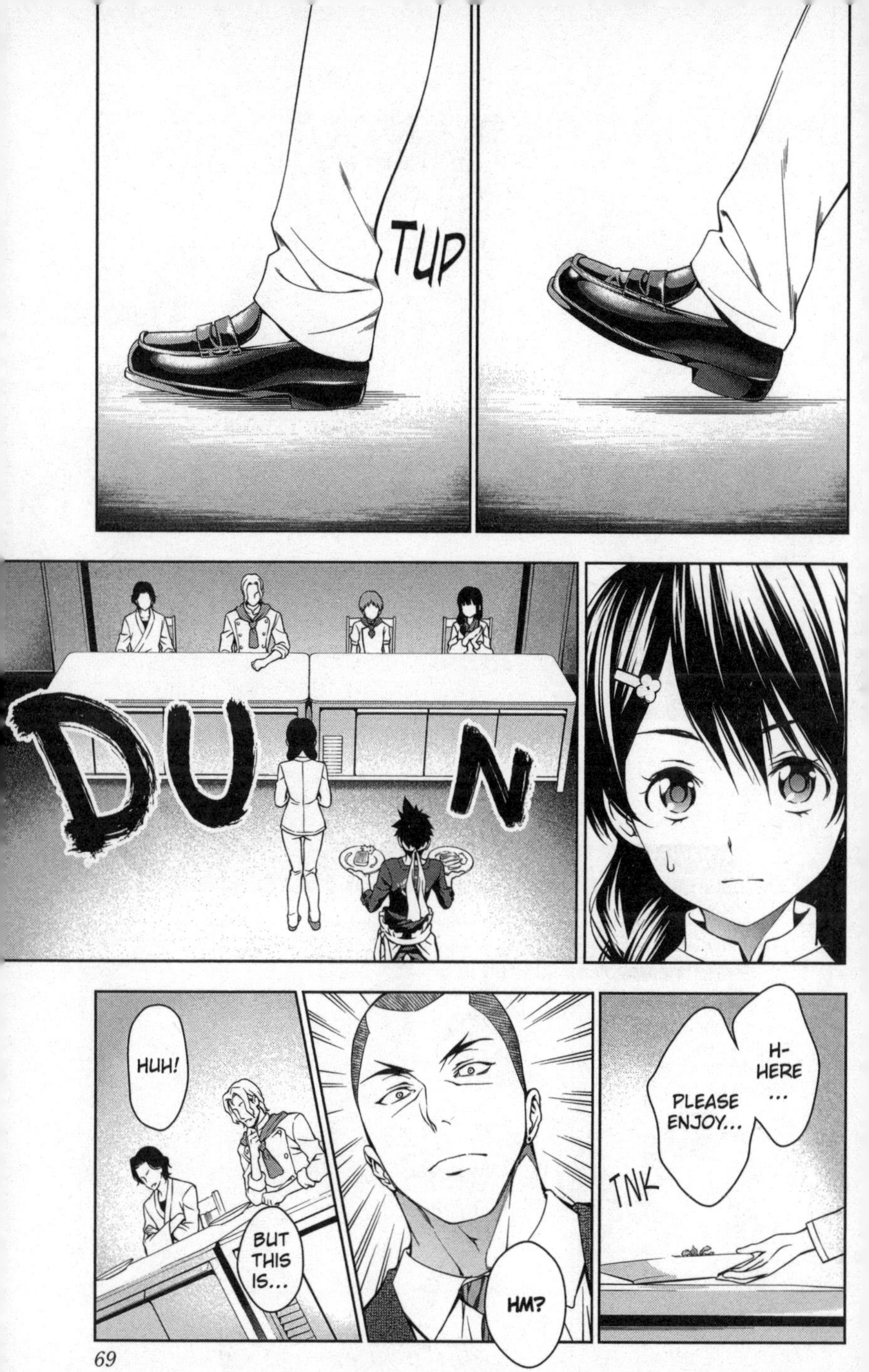
TUP
DUN
H-HERE...
PLEASE ENJOY...
TNK
HM?
HUH!
BUT THIS IS...

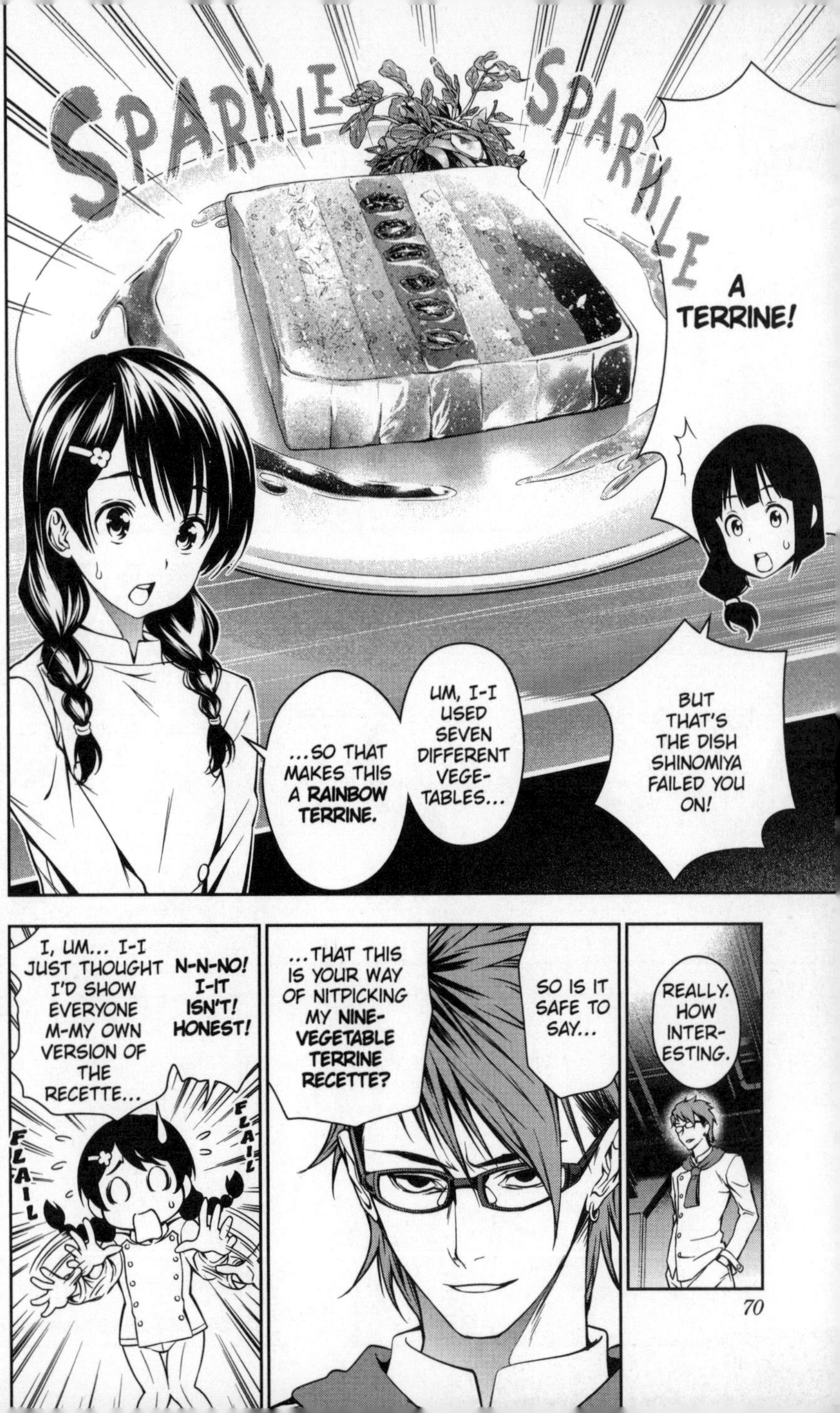
SPARKLE
SPARKLE
A TERRINE!
BUT THAT'S THE DISH SHINOMIYA FAILED YOU ON!
UM, I-I USED SEVEN DIFFERENT VEGE-TABLES...
...SO THAT MAKES THIS A **RAINBOW TERRINE.**
REALLY. HOW INTER-ESTING.
SO IS IT SAFE TO SAY...
...THAT THIS IS YOUR WAY OF NITPICKING MY **NINE-VEGETABLE TERRINE RECETTE?**
N-N-NO! I-IT ISN'T! HONEST!
I, UM... I-I JUST THOUGHT I'D SHOW EVERYONE M-MY OWN VERSION OF THE RECETTE...
FLAIL
FLAIL

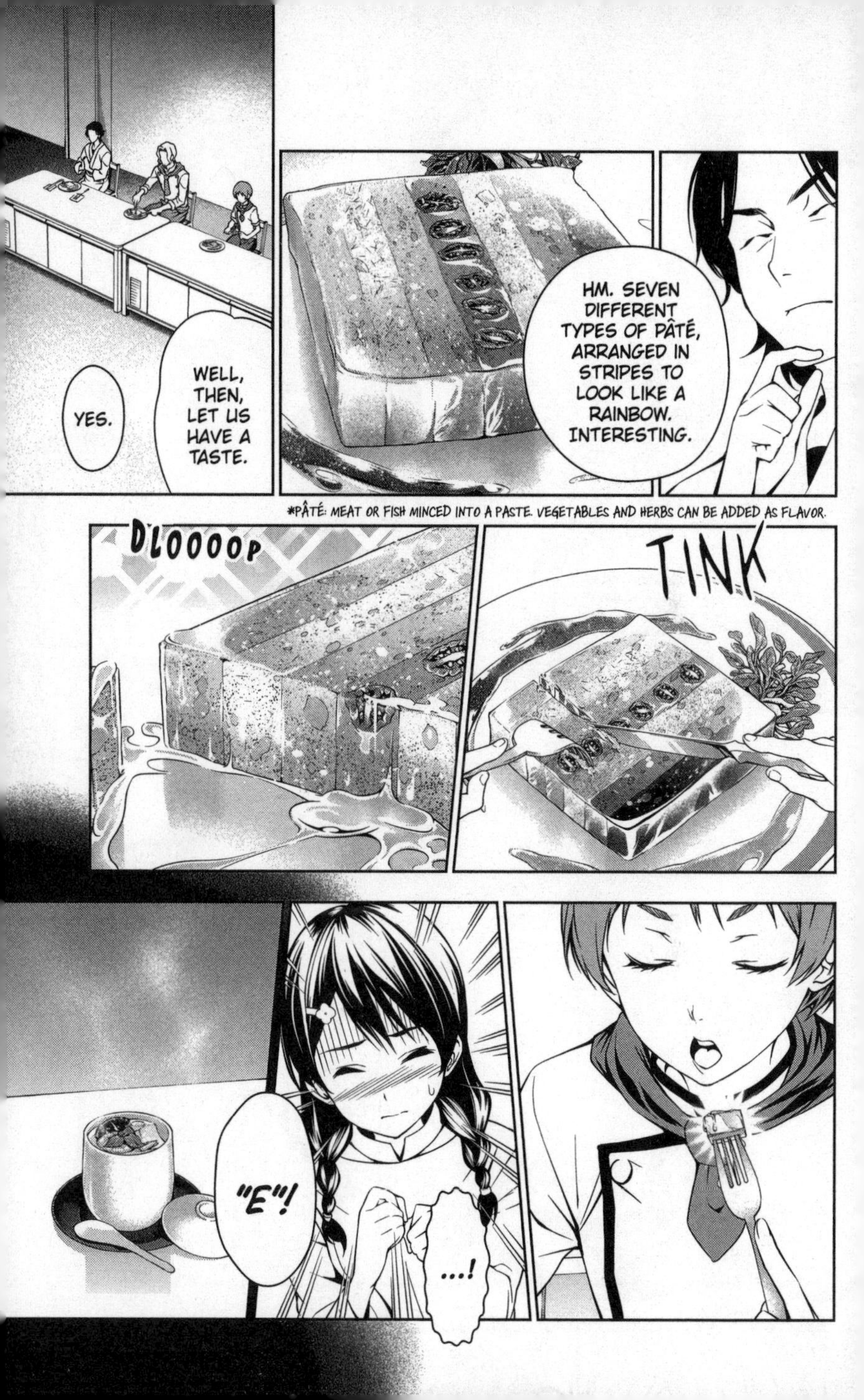
WELL, THEN, LET US HAVE A TASTE.
YES.
HM. SEVEN DIFFERENT TYPES OF PÂTÉ, ARRANGED IN STRIPES TO LOOK LIKE A RAINBOW. INTERESTING.
*PÂTÉ: MEAT OR FISH MINCED INTO A PASTE. VEGETABLES AND HERBS CAN BE ADDED AS FLAVOR.
TINK
DLOOOOP
"E"!
...!

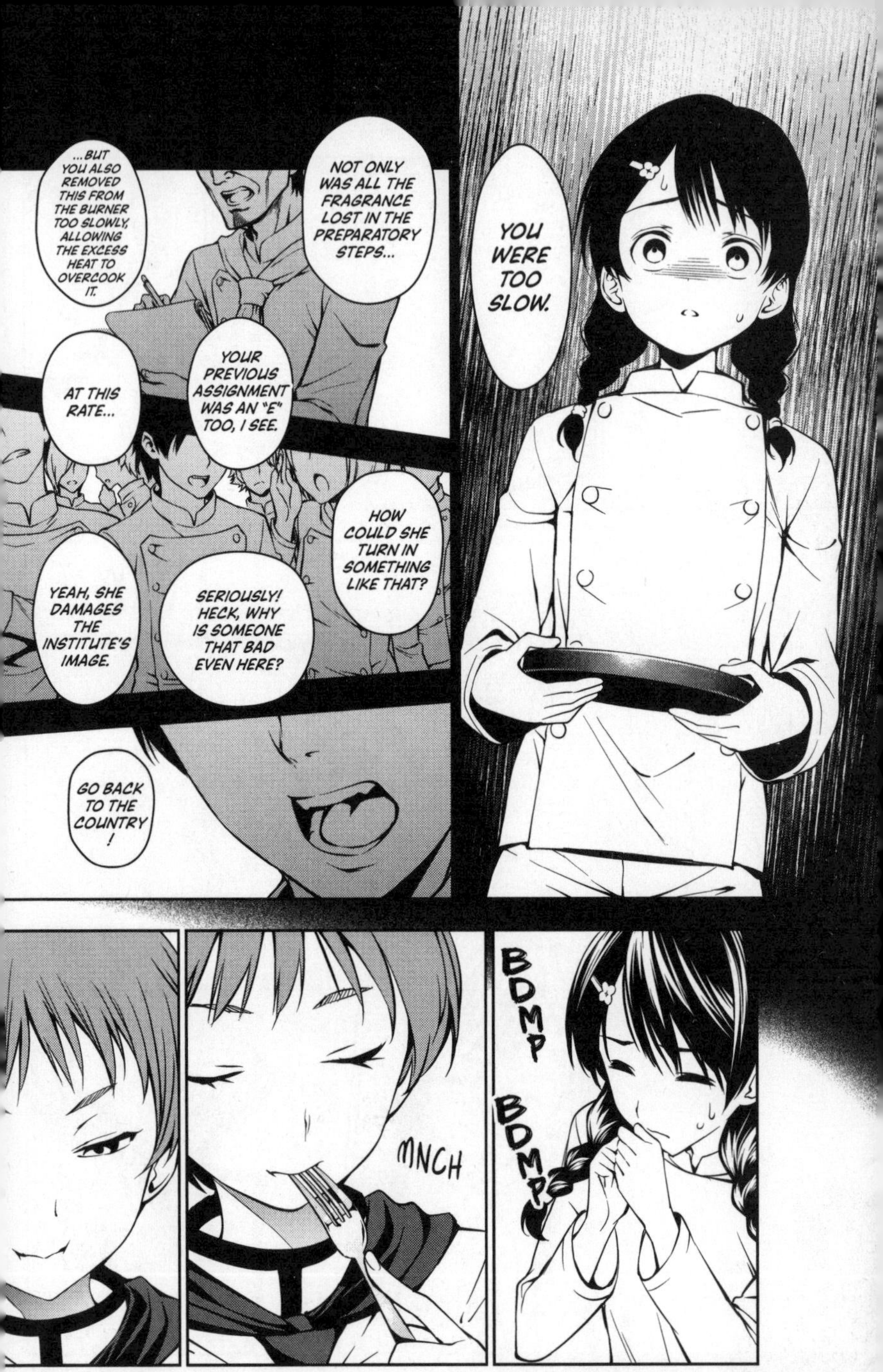
YOU WERE TOO SLOW.
NOT ONLY WAS ALL THE FRAGRANCE LOST IN THE PREPARATORY STEPS...
...BUT YOU ALSO REMOVED THIS FROM THE BURNER TOO SLOWLY, ALLOWING THE EXCESS HEAT TO OVERCOOK IT.
YOUR PREVIOUS ASSIGNMENT WAS AN "E" TOO, I SEE.
AT THIS RATE...
HOW COULD SHE TURN IN SOMETHING LIKE THAT?
SERIOUSLY! HECK, WHY IS SOMEONE THAT BAD EVEN HERE?
YEAH, SHE DAMAGES THE INSTITUTE'S IMAGE.
GO BACK TO THE COUNTRY!
BDMP
BDMP
MNCH

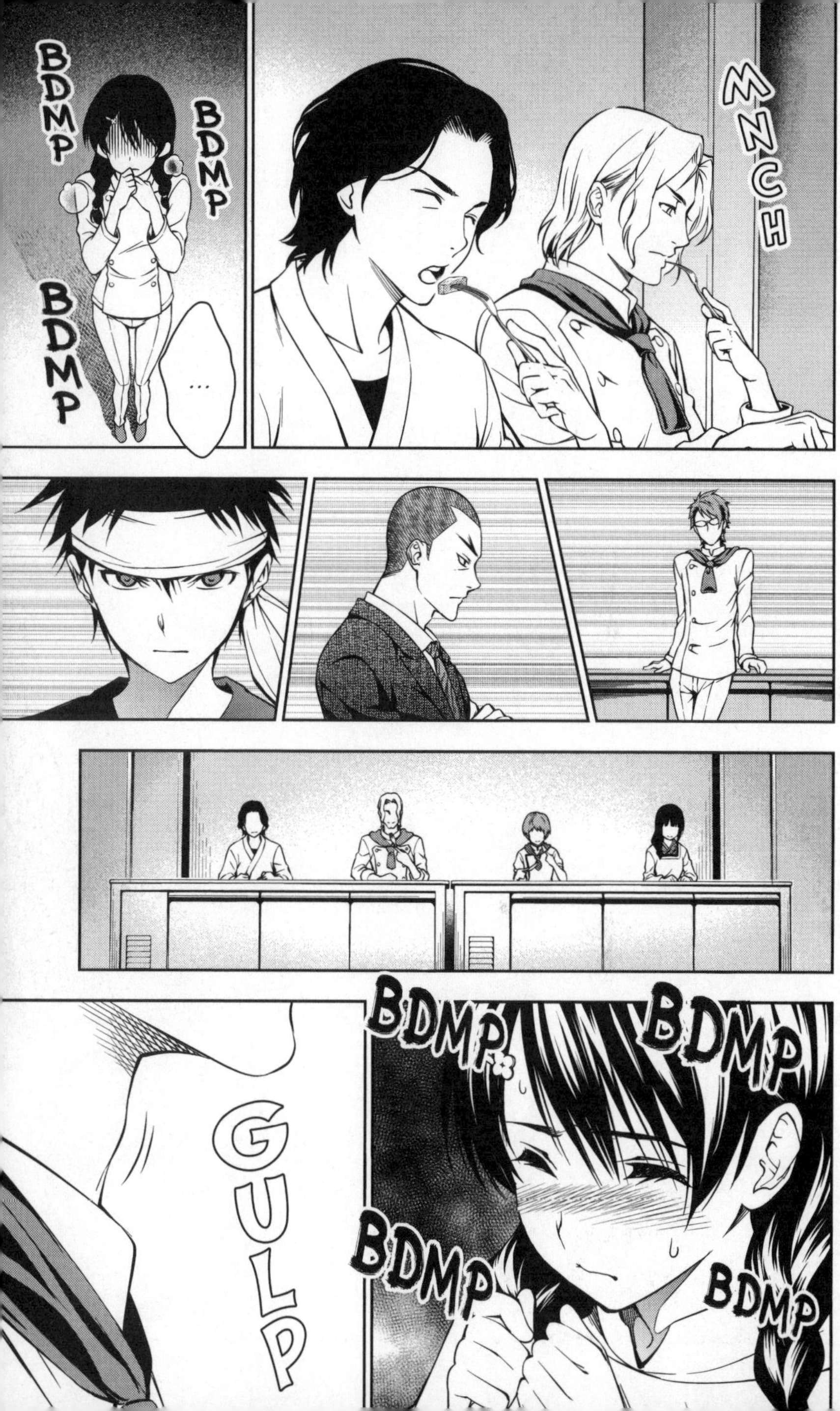
MNCH
BDMP
BDMP
...
BDMP
BDMP
BDMP
BDMP
BDMP
GULP

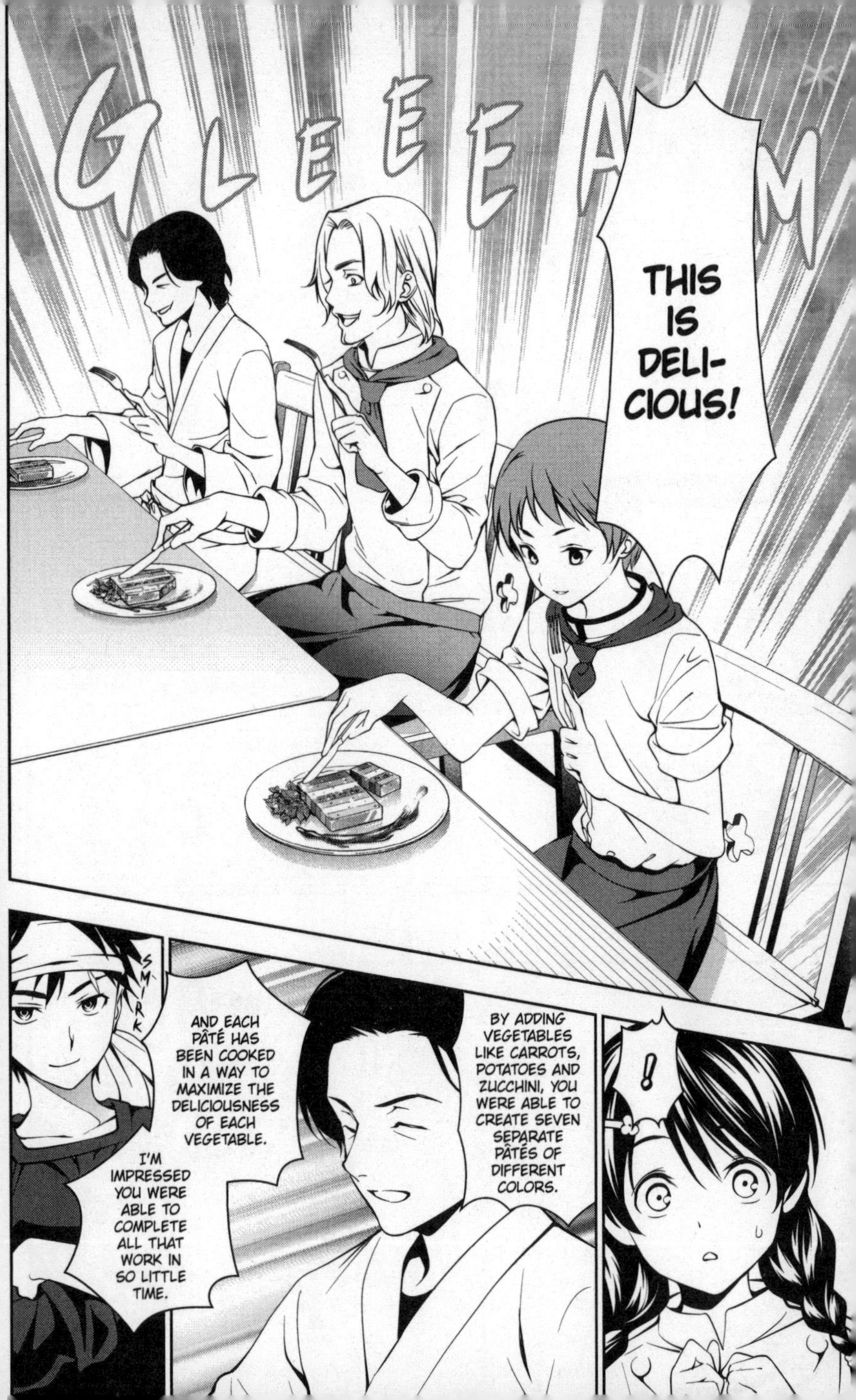
GLEEEAM
THIS IS DELI-CIOUS!
!
BY ADDING VEGETABLES LIKE CARROTS, POTATOES AND ZUCCHINI, YOU WERE ABLE TO CREATE SEVEN SEPARATE PÂTÉS OF DIFFERENT COLORS.
SMIRK
AND EACH PÂTÉ HAS BEEN COOKED IN A WAY TO MAXIMIZE THE DELICIOUSNESS OF EACH VEGETABLE.
I'M IMPRESSED YOU WERE ABLE TO COMPLETE ALL THAT WORK IN SO LITTLE TIME.

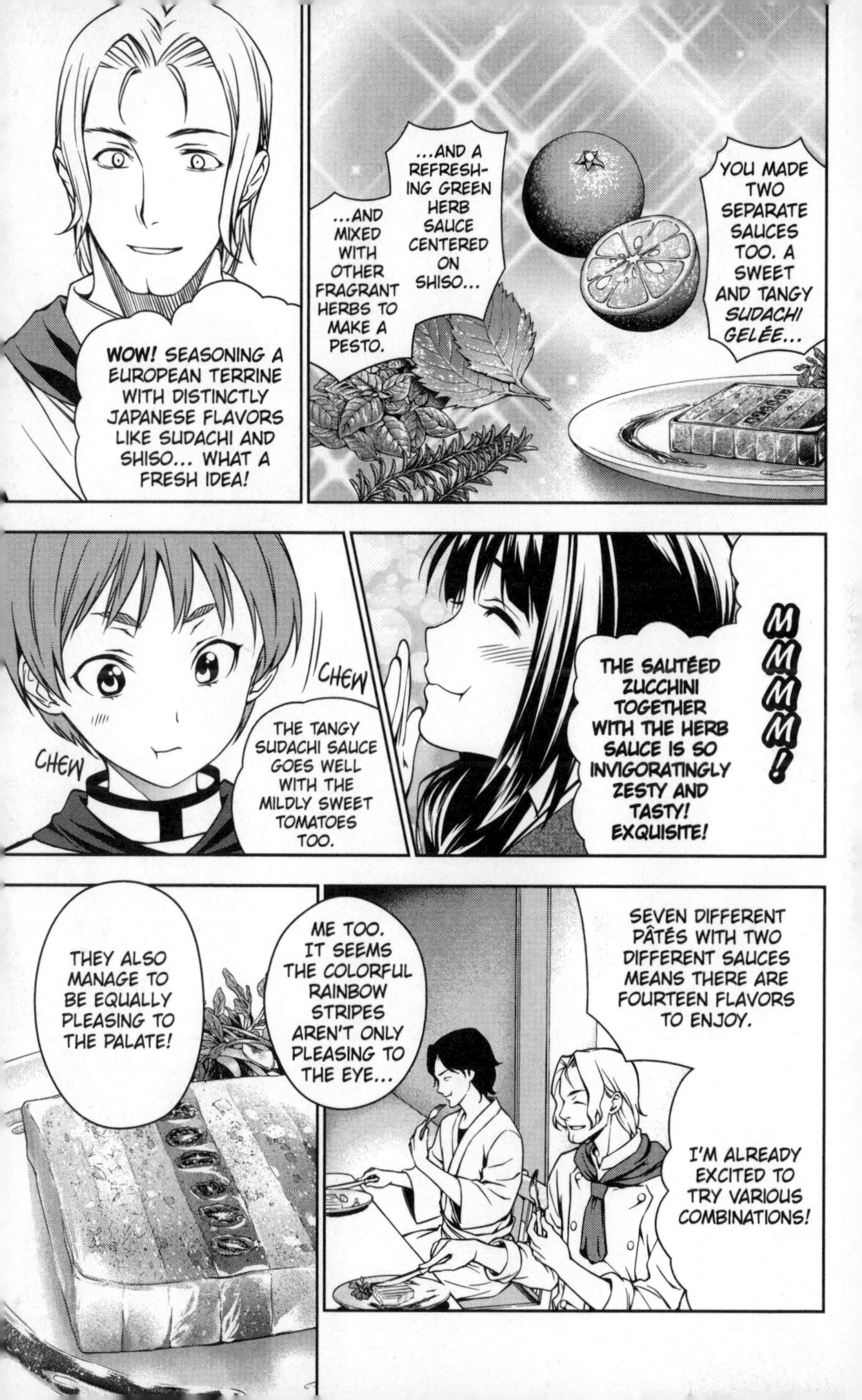
YOU MADE TWO SEPARATE SAUCES TOO. A SWEET AND TANGY SUDACHI GELÉE...
...AND A REFRESHING GREEN HERB SAUCE CENTERED ON SHISO...
...AND MIXED WITH OTHER FRAGRANT HERBS TO MAKE A PESTO.
WOW! SEASONING A EUROPEAN TERRINE WITH DISTINCTLY JAPANESE FLAVORS LIKE SUDACHI AND SHISO... WHAT A FRESH IDEA!
MMMMM!
THE SAUTÉED ZUCCHINI TOGETHER WITH THE HERB SAUCE IS SO INVIGORATINGLY ZESTY AND TASTY! EXQUISITE!
CHEW
CHEW
THE TANGY SUDACHI SAUCE GOES WELL WITH THE MILDLY SWEET TOMATOES TOO.
SEVEN DIFFERENT PÂTÉS WITH TWO DIFFERENT SAUCES MEANS THERE ARE FOURTEEN FLAVORS TO ENJOY.
I'M ALREADY EXCITED TO TRY VARIOUS COMBINATIONS!
ME TOO. IT SEEMS THE COLORFUL RAINBOW STRIPES AREN'T ONLY PLEASING TO THE EYE...
THEY ALSO MANAGE TO BE EQUALLY PLEASING TO THE PALATE!

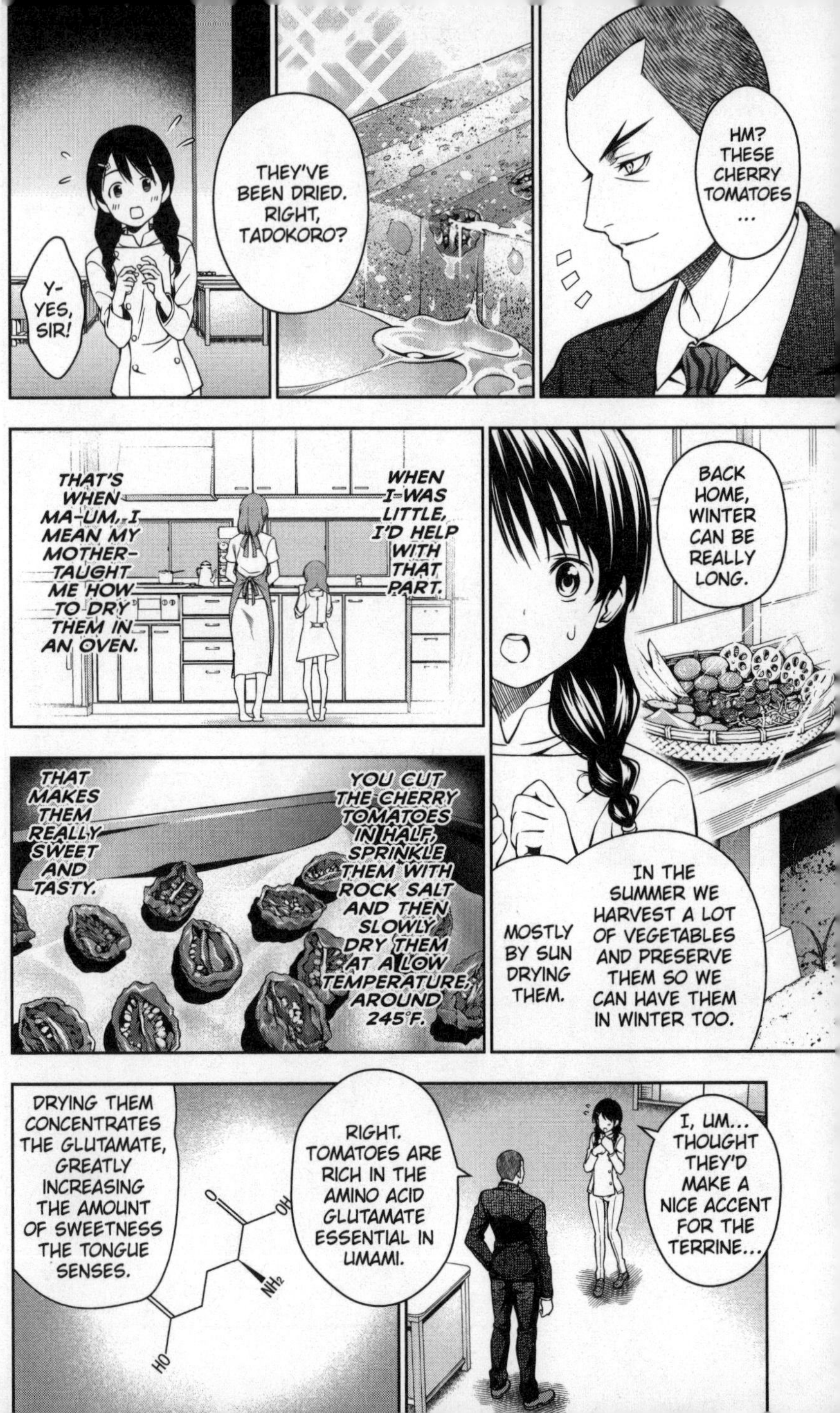
HM? THESE CHERRY TOMATOES ...
THEY'VE BEEN DRIED. RIGHT, TADOKORO?
Y-YES, SIR!
BACK HOME, WINTER CAN BE REALLY LONG.
IN THE SUMMER WE HARVEST A LOT OF VEGETABLES AND PRESERVE THEM SO WE CAN HAVE THEM IN WINTER TOO.
MOSTLY BY SUN DRYING THEM.
WHEN I WAS LITTLE, I'D HELP WITH THAT PART.
THAT'S WHEN MA—UM, I MEAN MY MOTHER—TAUGHT ME HOW TO DRY THEM IN AN OVEN.
YOU CUT THE CHERRY TOMATOES IN HALF, SPRINKLE THEM WITH ROCK SALT AND THEN SLOWLY DRY THEM AT A LOW TEMPERATURE, AROUND 245°F.
THAT MAKES THEM REALLY SWEET AND TASTY.
I, UM... THOUGHT THEY'D MAKE A NICE ACCENT FOR THE TERRINE...
RIGHT. TOMATOES ARE RICH IN THE AMINO ACID GLUTAMATE ESSENTIAL IN UMAMI.
DRYING THEM CONCENTRATES THE GLUTAMATE, GREATLY INCREASING THE AMOUNT OF SWEETNESS THE TONGUE SENSES.
OH
NH2
HO

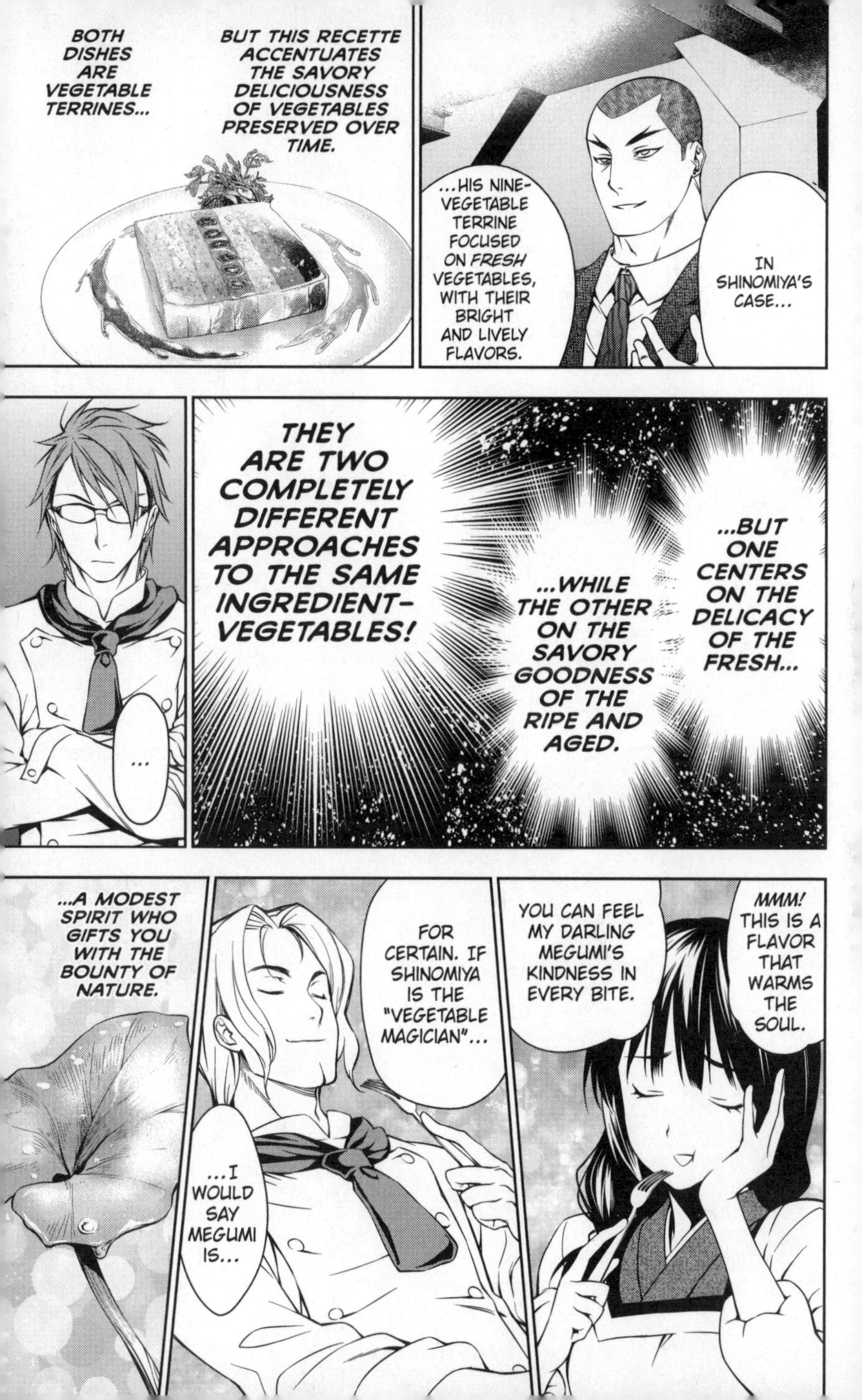
IN SHINOMIYA'S CASE...
...HIS NINE-VEGETABLE TERRINE FOCUSED ON FRESH VEGETABLES, WITH THEIR BRIGHT AND LIVELY FLAVORS.
BOTH DISHES ARE VEGETABLE TERRINES...
BUT THIS RECETTE ACCENTUATES THE SAVORY DELICIOUSNESS OF VEGETABLES PRESERVED OVER TIME.
THEY ARE TWO COMPLETELY DIFFERENT APPROACHES TO THE SAME INGREDIENT—VEGETABLES!
...BUT ONE CENTERS ON THE DELICACY OF THE FRESH...
...WHILE THE OTHER ON THE SAVORY GOODNESS OF THE RIPE AND AGED.
...
MMM! THIS IS A FLAVOR THAT WARMS THE SOUL.
YOU CAN FEEL MY DARLING MEGUMI'S KINDNESS IN EVERY BITE.
FOR CERTAIN. IF SHINOMIYA IS THE "VEGETABLE MAGICIAN"...
...I WOULD SAY MEGUMI IS...
...A MODEST SPIRIT WHO GIFTS YOU WITH THE BOUNTY OF NATURE.

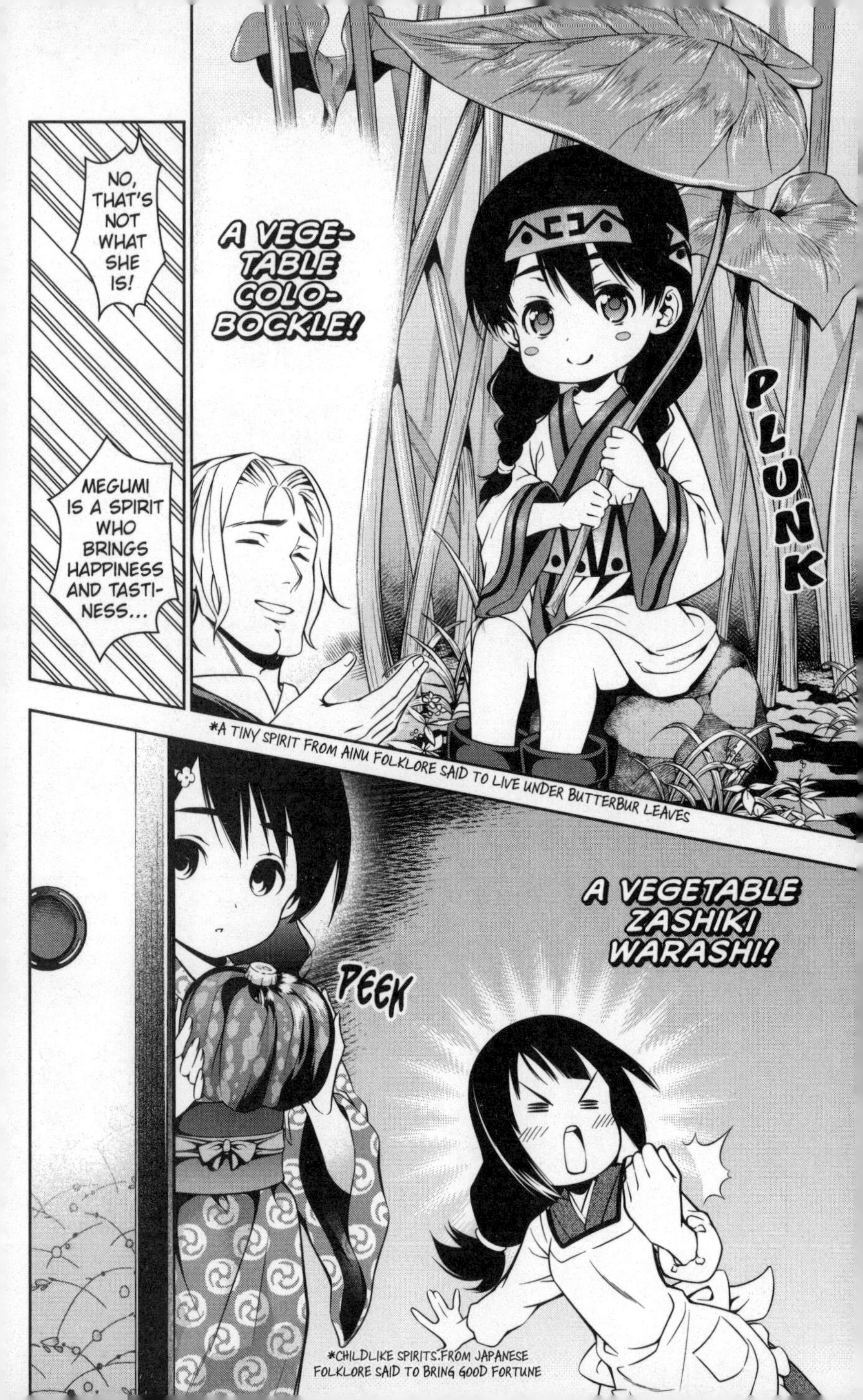
A VEGE-TABLE COLO-BOCKLE!
PLUNK
*A TINY SPIRIT FROM AINU FOLKLORE SAID TO LIVE UNDER BUTTERBUR LEAVES
NO, THAT'S NOT WHAT SHE IS!
MEGUMI IS A SPIRIT WHO BRINGS HAPPINESS AND TASTI-NESS...
A VEGETABLE ZASHIKI WARASHI!
PEEK
*CHILDLIKE SPIRITS FROM JAPANESE FOLKLORE SAID TO BRING GOOD FORTUNE

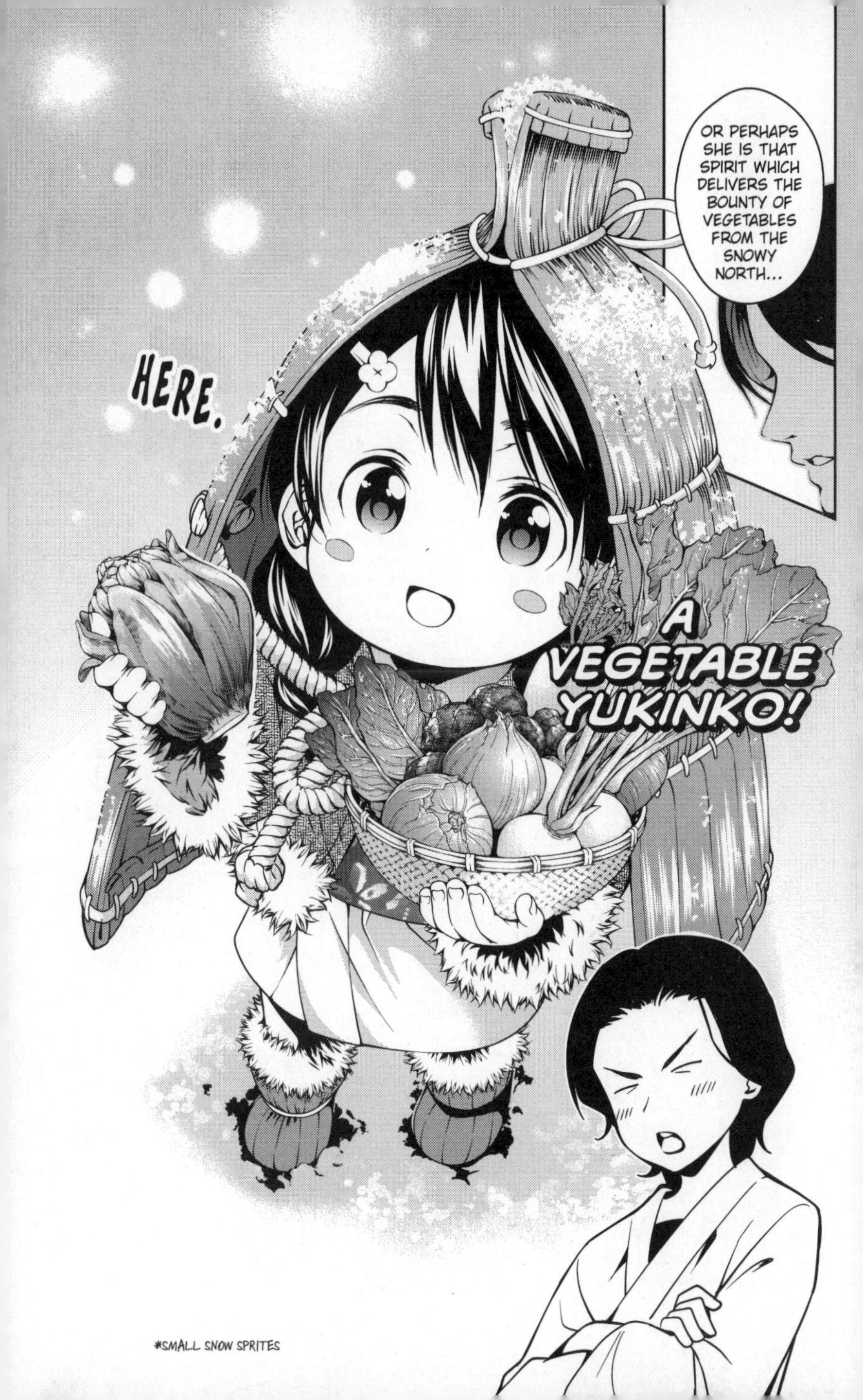
OR PERHAPS SHE IS THAT SPIRIT WHICH DELIVERS THE BOUNTY OF VEGETABLES FROM THE SNOWY NORTH...
A VEGETABLE YUKINKO!
HERE.

*SMALL SNOW SPRITES

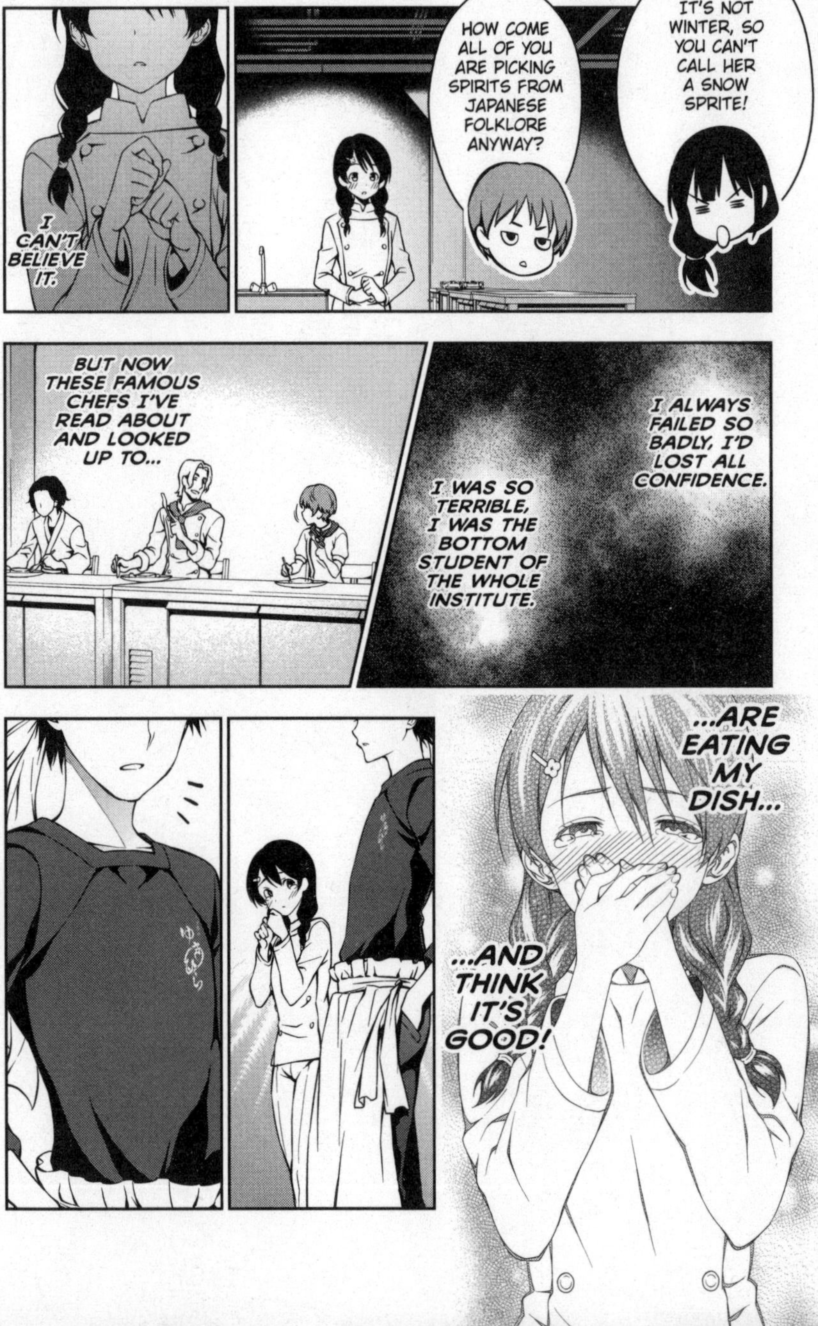
IT'S NOT WINTER, SO YOU CAN'T CALL HER A SNOW SPRITE!
HOW COME ALL OF YOU ARE PICKING SPIRITS FROM JAPANESE FOLKLORE ANYWAY?
I CAN'T BELIEVE IT.
I ALWAYS FAILED SO BADLY, I'D LOST ALL CONFIDENCE.
I WAS SO TERRIBLE, I WAS THE BOTTOM STUDENT OF THE WHOLE INSTITUTE.
BUT NOW THESE FAMOUS CHEFS I'VE READ ABOUT AND LOOKED UP TO...
...ARE EATING MY DISH...
...AND THINK IT'S GOOD!

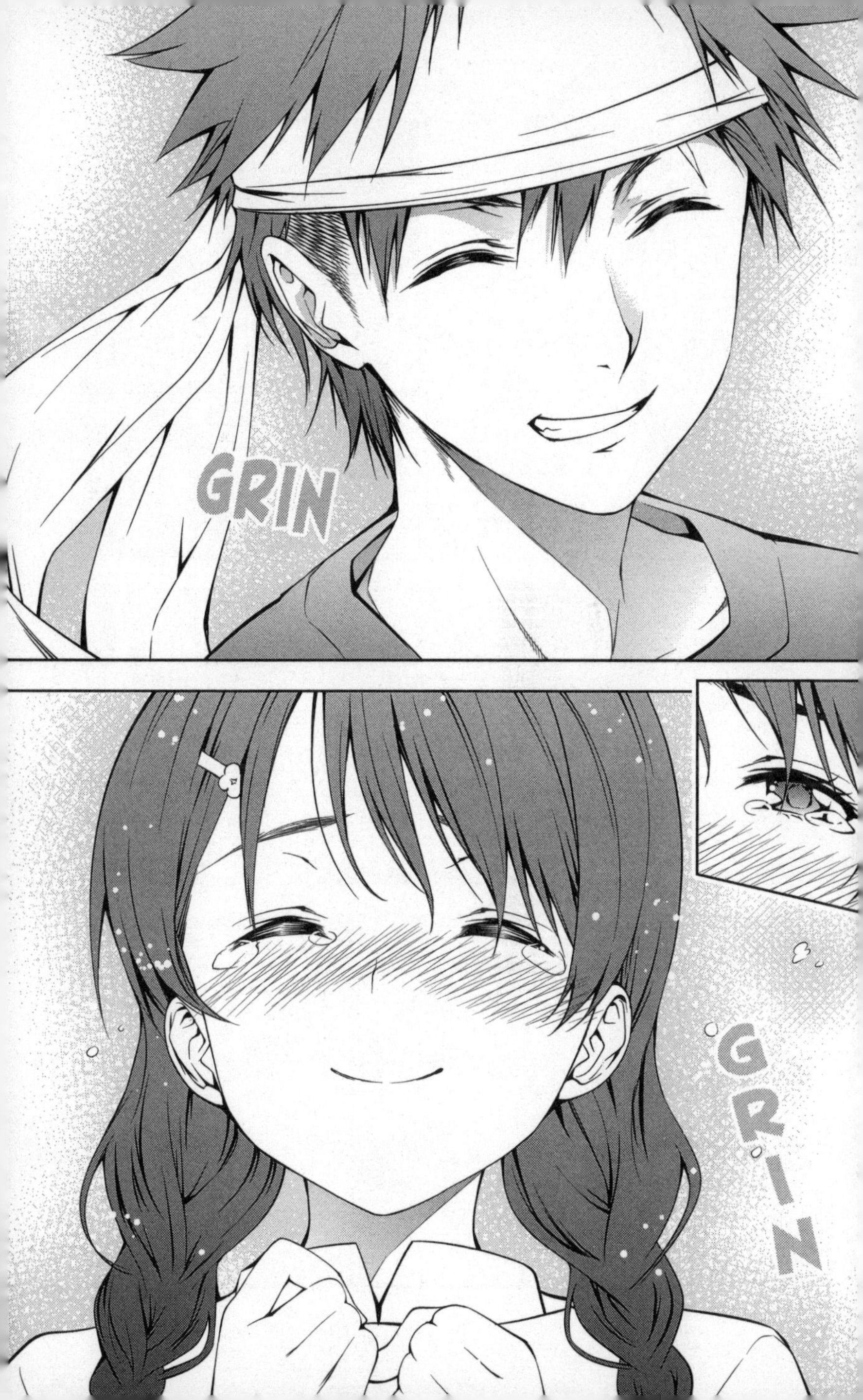
GRIN
GRIN

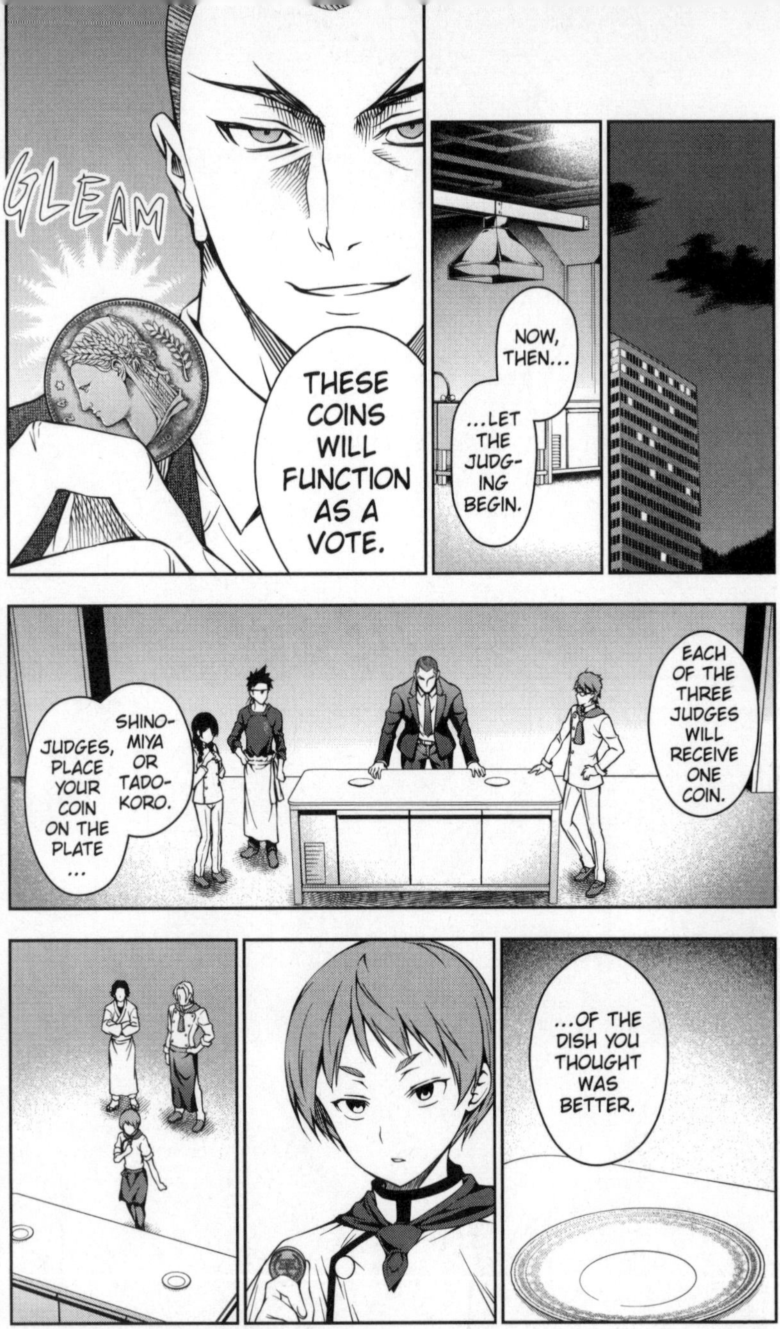
NOW, THEN...
...LET THE JUDG-ING BEGIN.
THESE COINS WILL FUNCTION AS A VOTE.
GLEAM
EACH OF THE THREE JUDGES WILL RECEIVE ONE COIN.
SHINO-MIYA OR TADO-KORO.
JUDGES, PLACE YOUR COIN ON THE PLATE ...
...OF THE DISH YOU THOUGHT WAS BETTER.

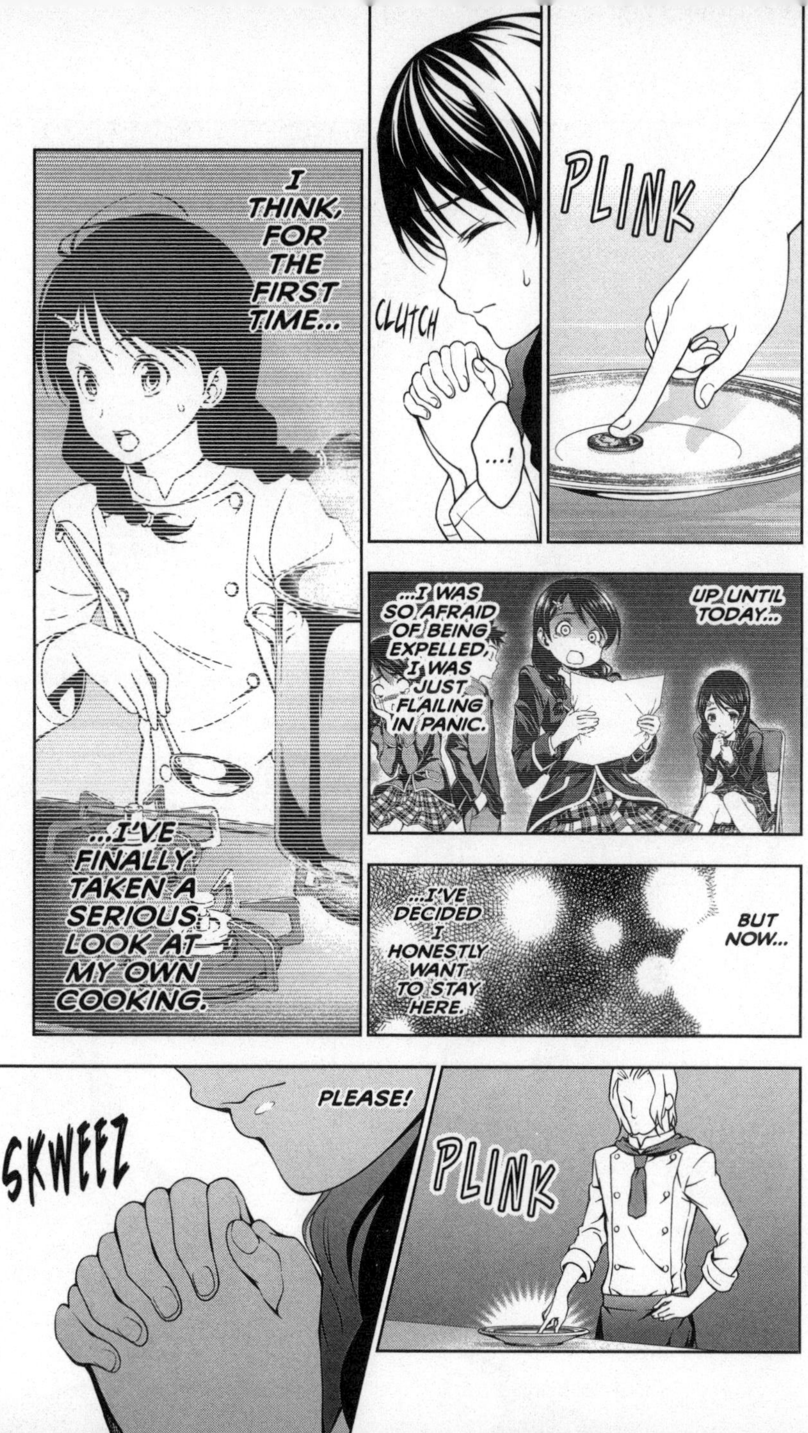
PLINK
CLUTCH
...!
UP UNTIL TODAY...
...I WAS SO AFRAID OF BEING EXPELLED, I WAS JUST FLAILING IN PANIC.
BUT NOW...
...I'VE DECIDED I HONESTLY WANT TO STAY HERE.
I THINK, FOR THE FIRST TIME...
...I'VE FINALLY TAKEN A SERIOUS LOOK AT MY OWN COOKING.
PLINK
PLEASE!
SKWEEZ

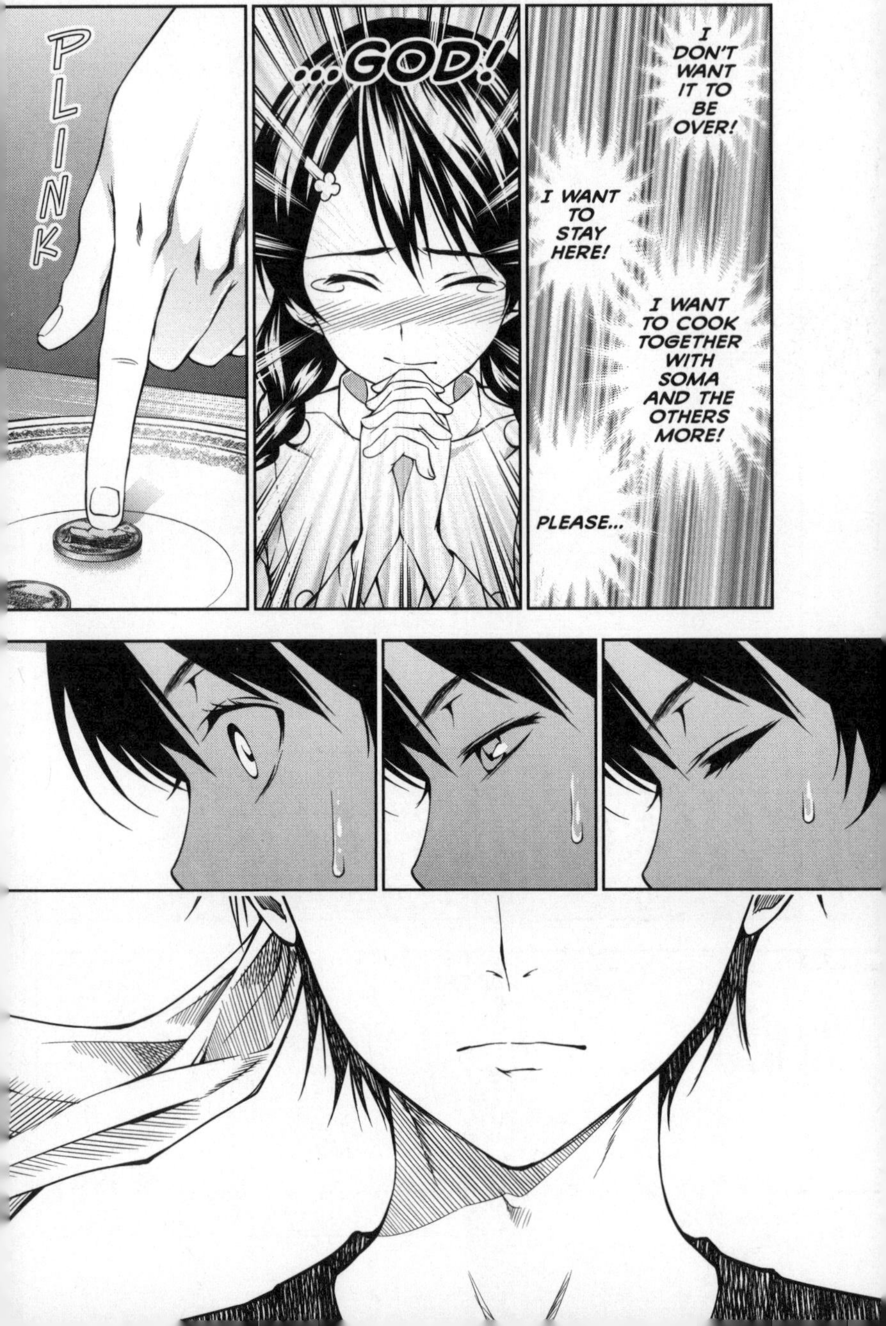
I DON'T WANT IT TO BE OVER!
I WANT TO STAY HERE!
I WANT TO COOK TOGETHER WITH SOMA AND THE OTHERS MORE!
PLEASE...
...GOD!
PLINK

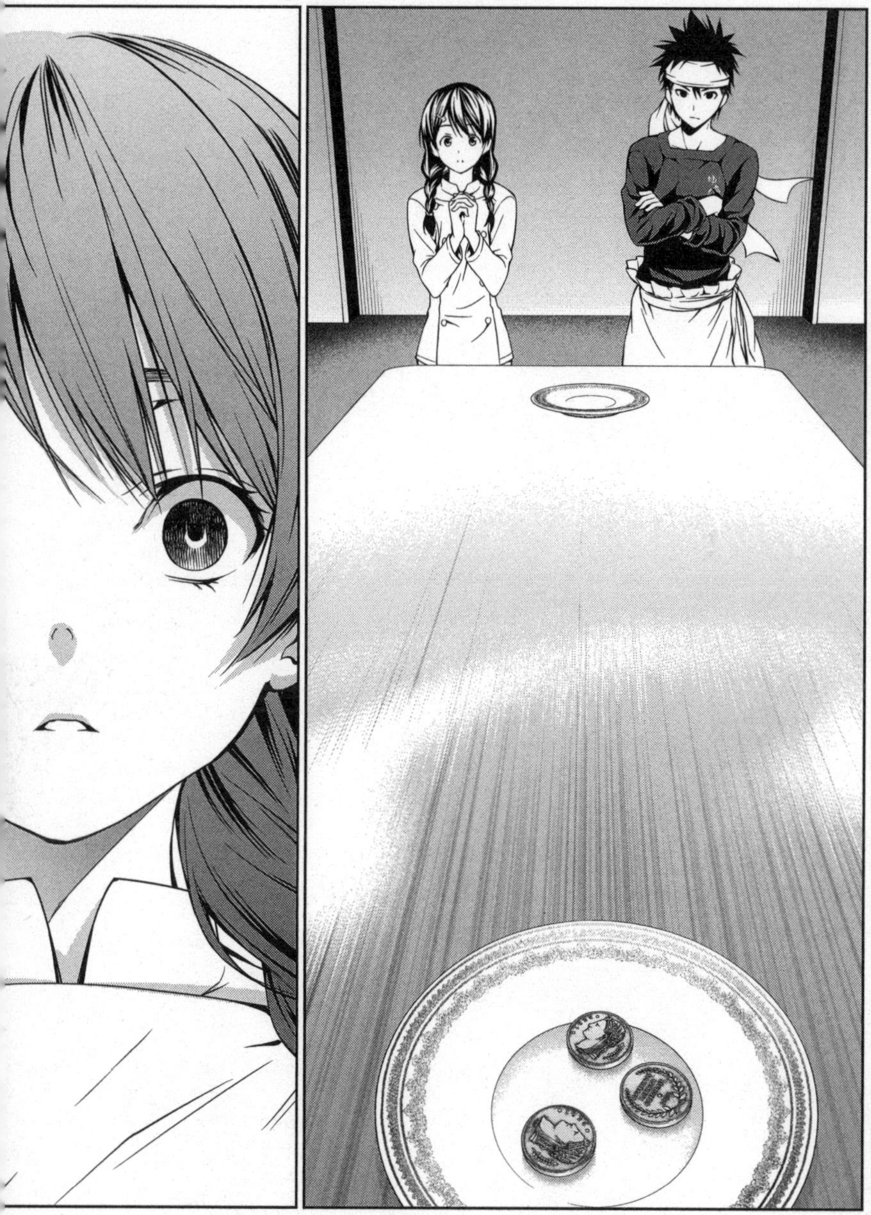

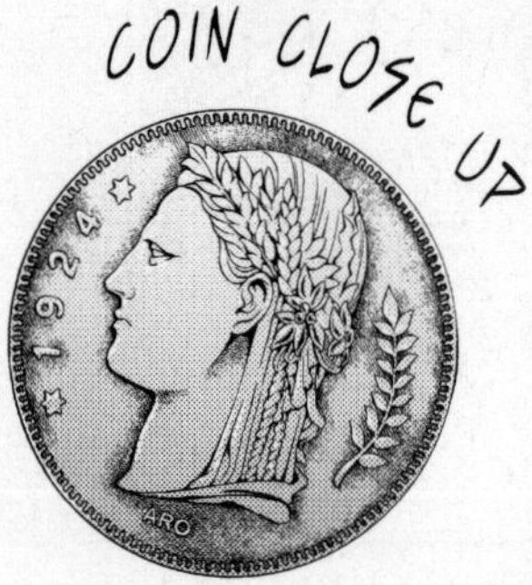
COIN CLOSE UP
1924
ARO

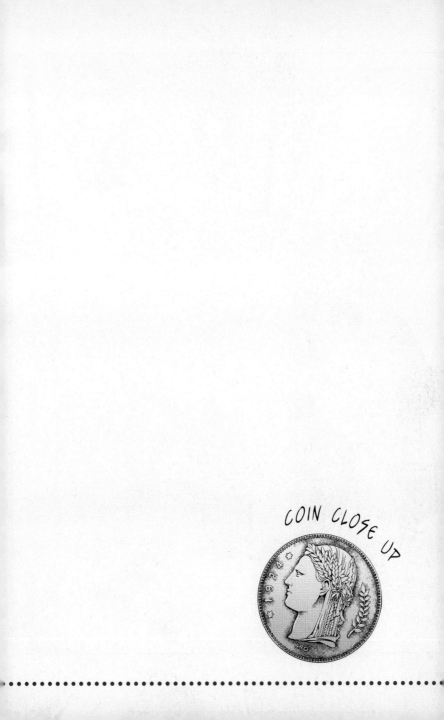

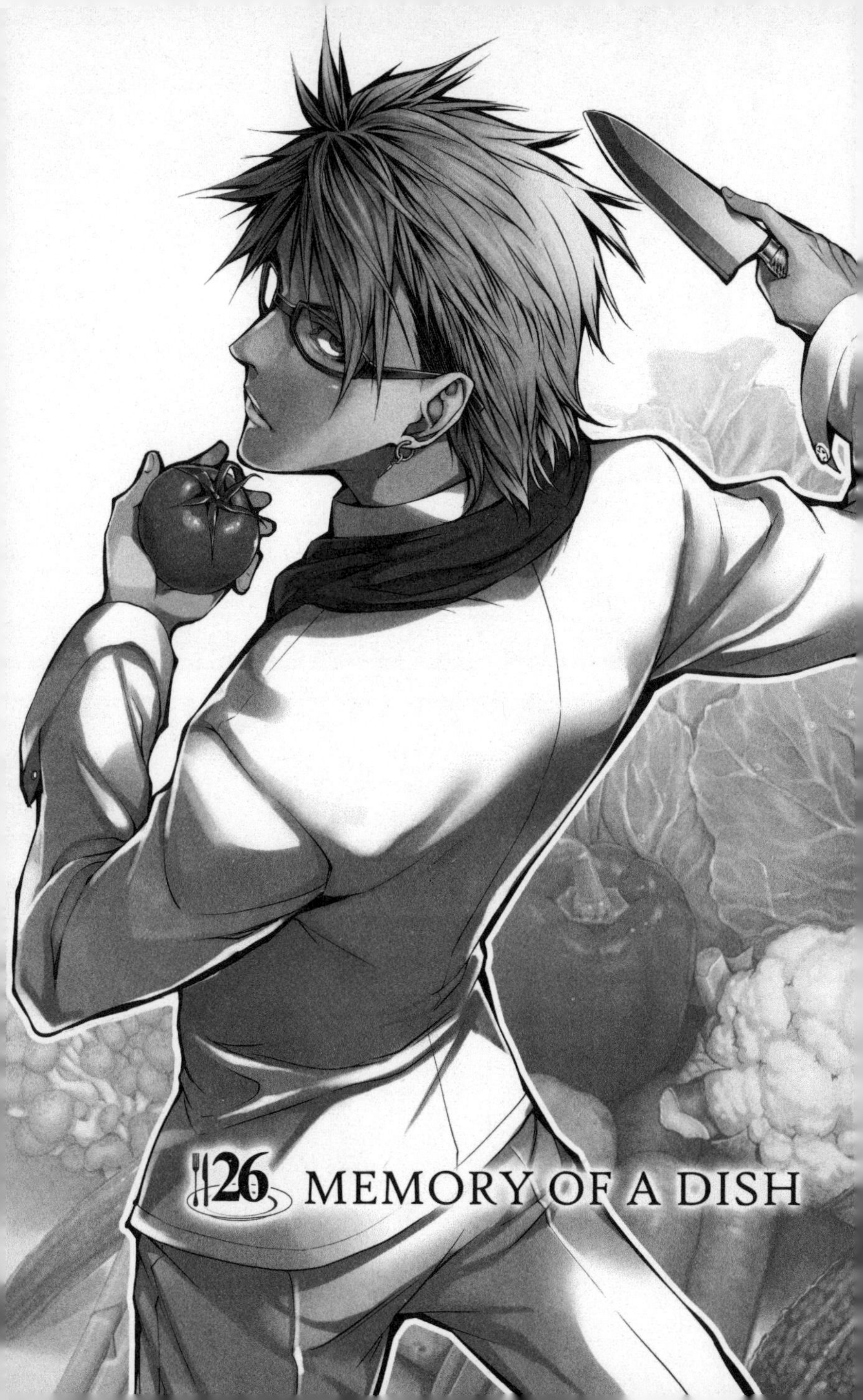
26
MEMORY OF A DISH

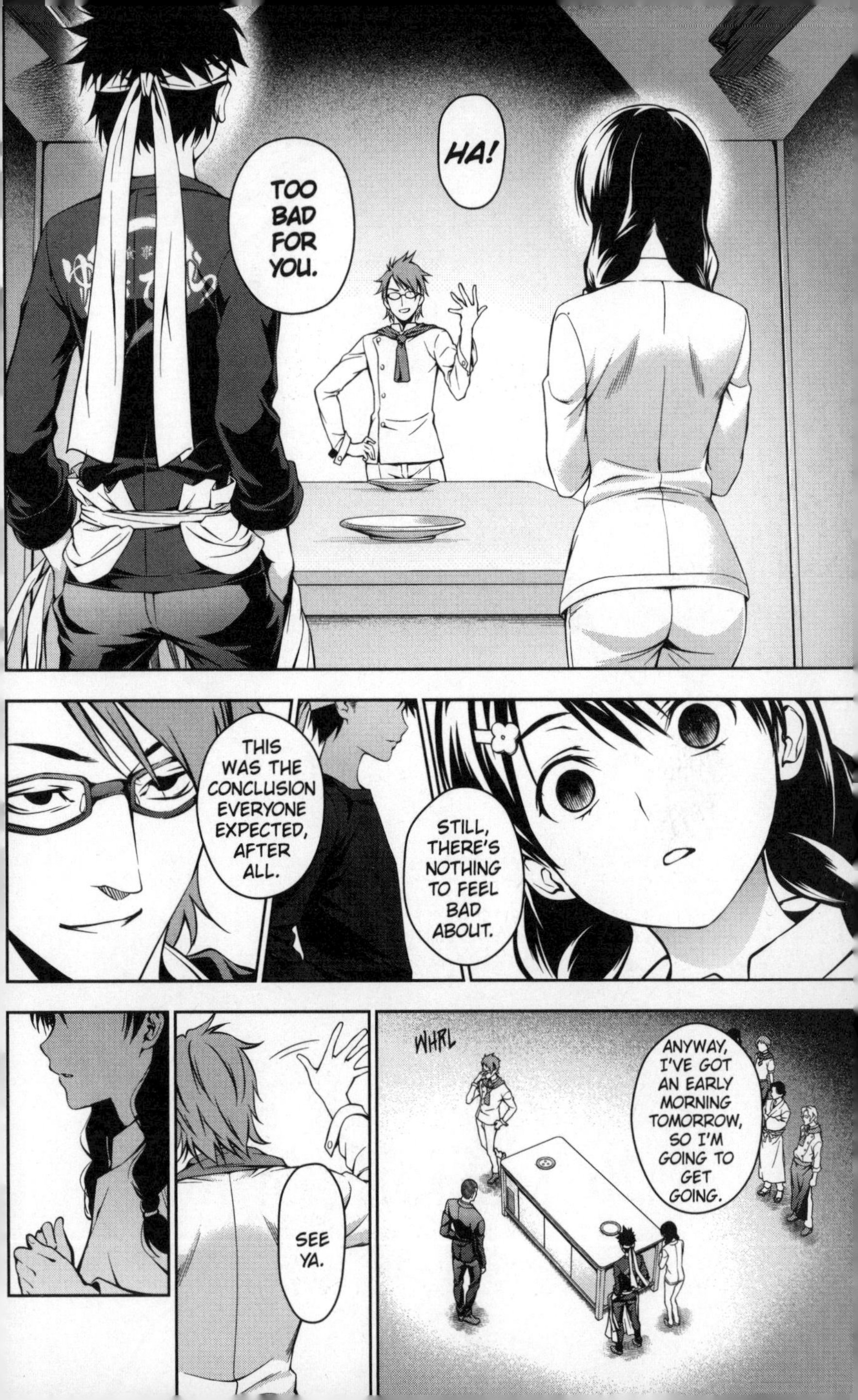
HA!
TOO BAD FOR YOU.
STILL, THERE'S NOTHING TO FEEL BAD ABOUT.
THIS WAS THE CONCLUSION EVERYONE EXPECTED, AFTER ALL.
ANYWAY, I'VE GOT AN EARLY MORNING TOMORROW, SO I'M GOING TO GET GOING.
WHRL
SEE YA.

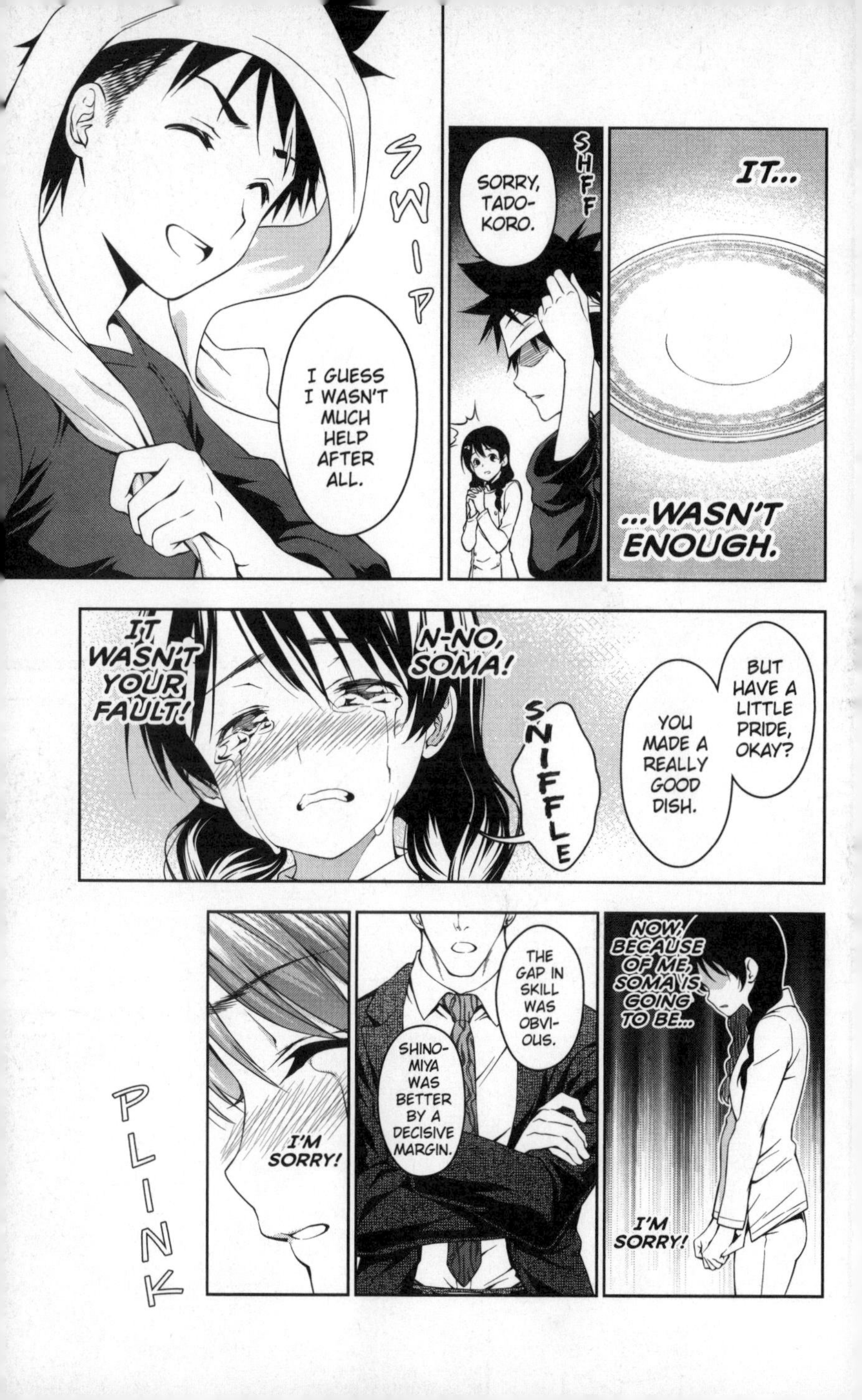
IT...
...WASN'T ENOUGH.
SHFF
SORRY, TADO-KORO.
SWIP
I GUESS I WASN'T MUCH HELP AFTER ALL.
BUT HAVE A LITTLE PRIDE, OKAY?
YOU MADE A REALLY GOOD DISH.
SNIFFLE
N-NO, SOMA!
IT WASN'T YOUR FAULT!
NOW, BECAUSE OF ME, SOMA IS GOING TO BE...
I'M SORRY!
THE GAP IN SKILL WAS OBVI-OUS.
SHINO-MIYA WAS BETTER BY A DECISIVE MARGIN.
I'M SORRY!
PLINK

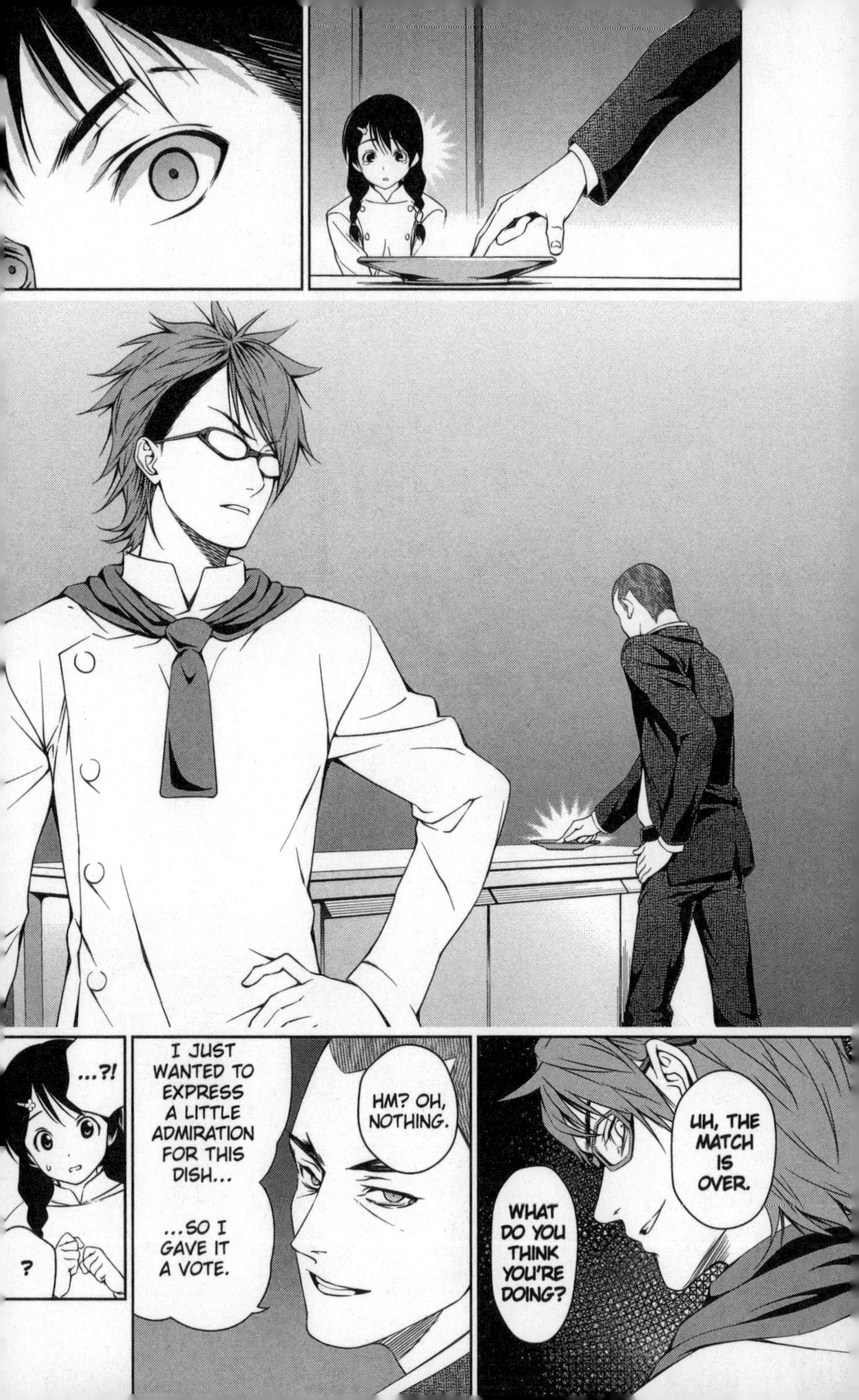
UH, THE MATCH IS OVER.
WHAT DO YOU THINK YOU'RE DOING?
HM? OH, NOTHING.
I JUST WANTED TO EXPRESS A LITTLE ADMIRATION FOR THIS DISH...
...SO I GAVE IT A VOTE.
...?!
?

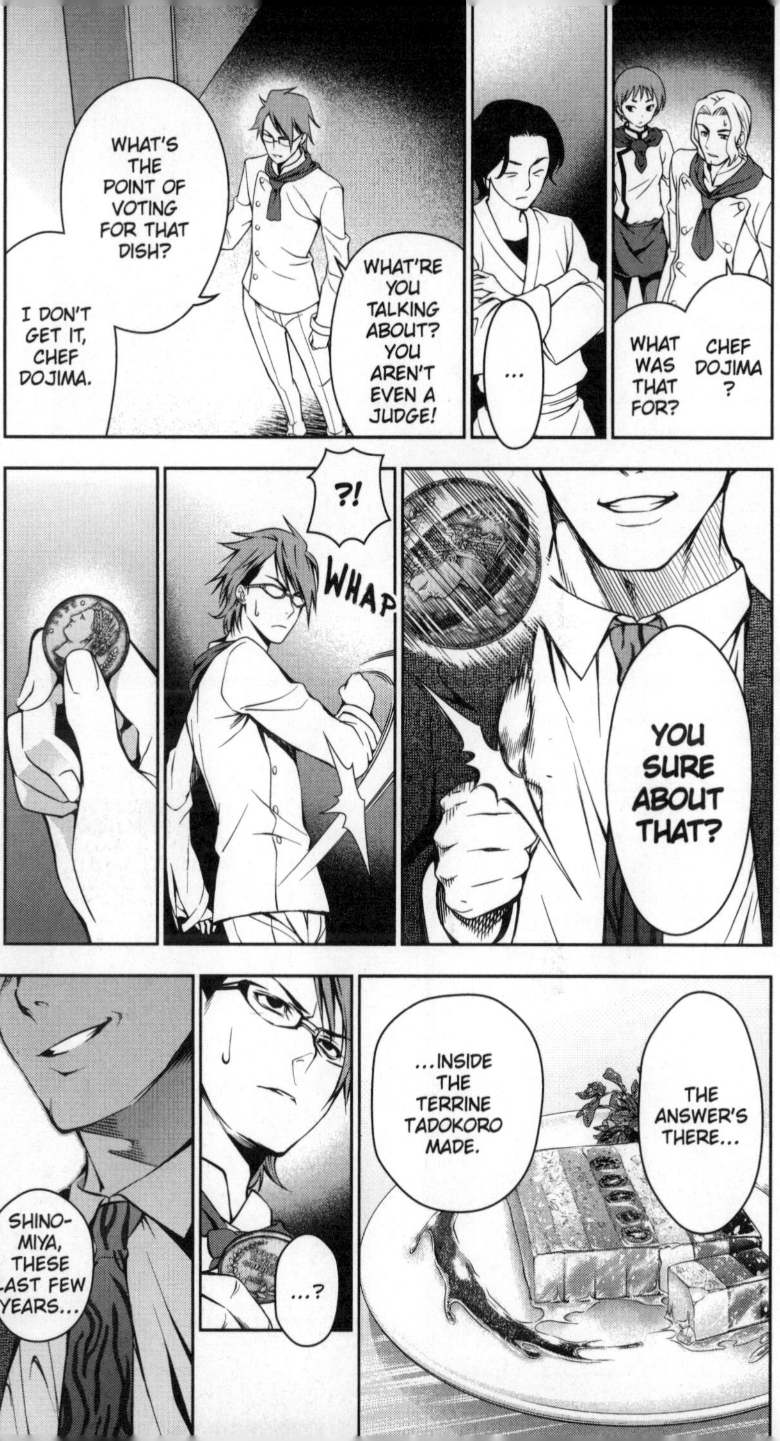
CHEF DOJIMA?
WHAT WAS THAT FOR?
...
WHAT'S THE POINT OF VOTING FOR THAT DISH?
WHAT'RE YOU TALKING ABOUT? YOU AREN'T EVEN A JUDGE!
I DON'T GET IT, CHEF DOJIMA.
YOU SURE ABOUT THAT?
?!
WHAP
THE ANSWER'S THERE...
...INSIDE THE TERRINE TADOKORO MADE.
...?
SHINO-MIYA, THESE LAST FEW YEARS...

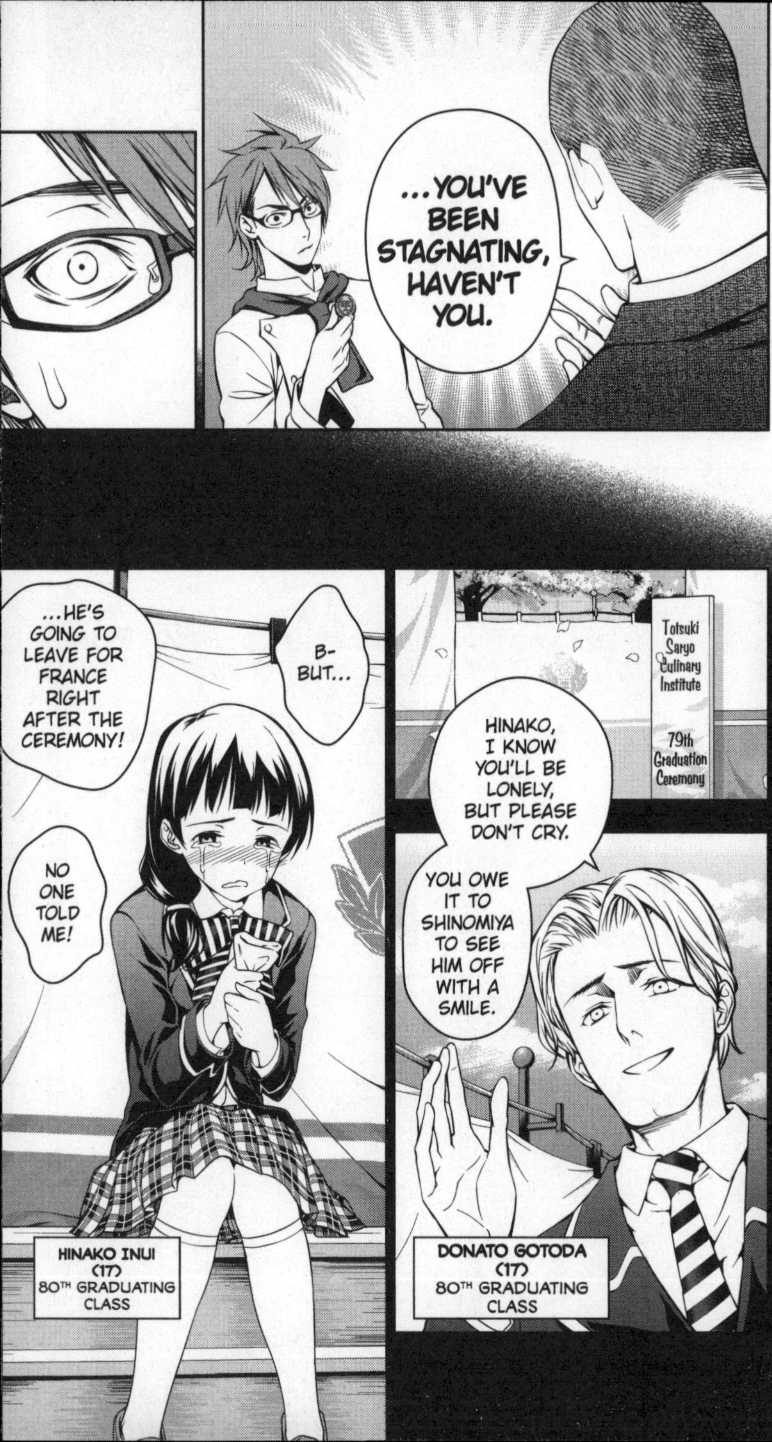
...YOU'VE BEEN STAGNATING, HAVEN'T YOU.
Totsuki Saryo Culinary Institute
79th Graduation Ceremony
HINAKO, I KNOW YOU'LL BE LONELY, BUT PLEASE DON'T CRY.
YOU OWE IT TO SHINOMIYA TO SEE HIM OFF WITH A SMILE.
DONATO GOTODA (17) 80TH GRADUATING CLASS
B-BUT...
...HE'S GOING TO LEAVE FOR FRANCE RIGHT AFTER THE CEREMONY!
NO ONE TOLD ME!
HINAKO INUI (17) 80TH GRADUATING CLASS

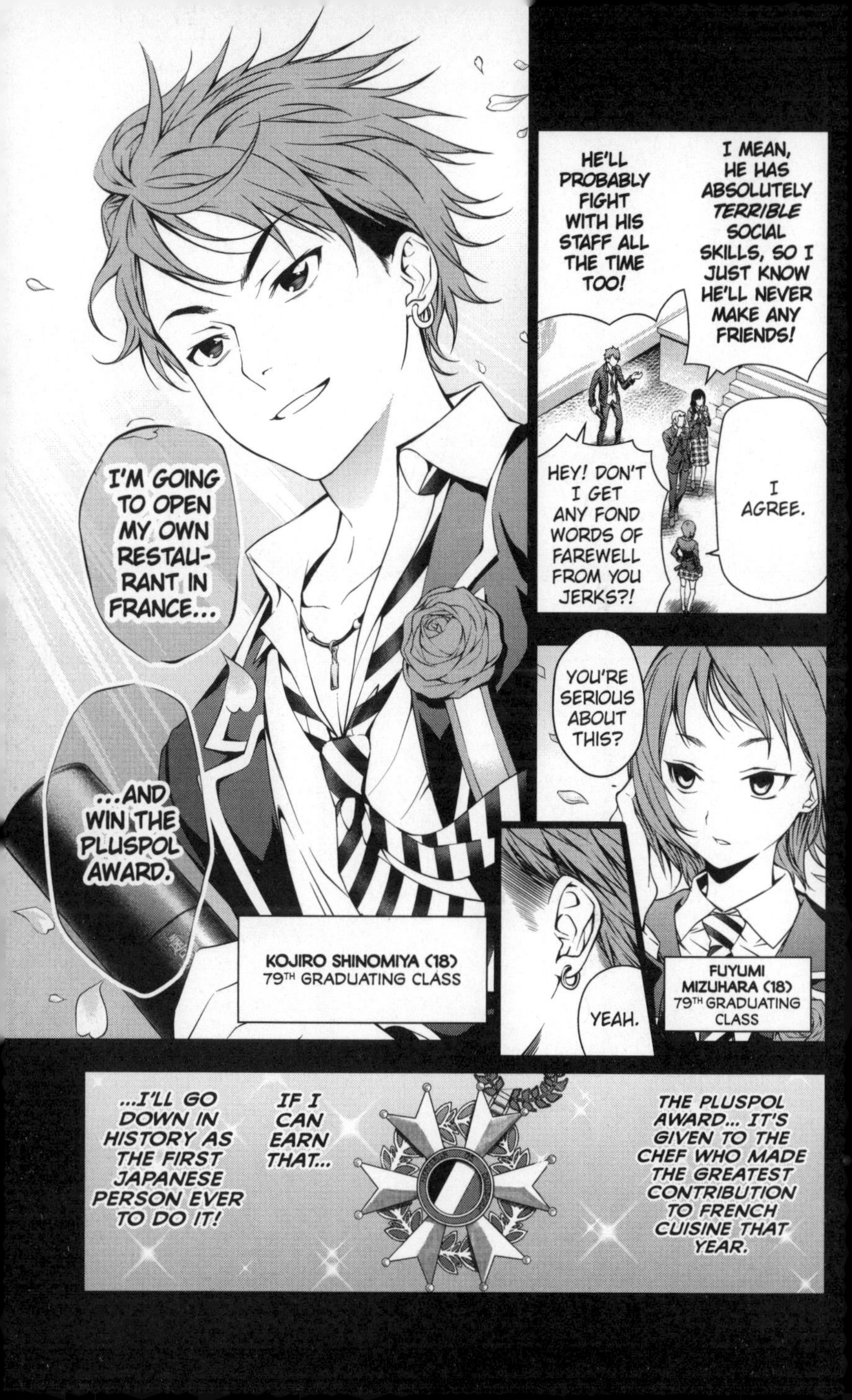
I MEAN, HE HAS ABSOLUTELY TERRIBLE SOCIAL SKILLS, SO I JUST KNOW HE'LL NEVER MAKE ANY FRIENDS!
HE'LL PROBABLY FIGHT WITH HIS STAFF ALL THE TIME TOO!
I AGREE.
HEY! DON'T I GET ANY FOND WORDS OF FAREWELL FROM YOU JERKS?!
YOU'RE SERIOUS ABOUT THIS?
FUYUMI MIZUHARA (18) 79TH GRADUATING CLASS
YEAH.
I'M GOING TO OPEN MY OWN RESTAURANT IN FRANCE...
...AND WIN THE PLUSPOL AWARD.
KOJIRO SHINOMIYA (18) 79TH GRADUATING CLASS
THE PLUSPOL AWARD... IT'S GIVEN TO THE CHEF WHO MADE THE GREATEST CONTRIBUTION TO FRENCH CUISINE THAT YEAR.
IF I CAN EARN THAT...
...I'LL GO DOWN IN HISTORY AS THE FIRST JAPANESE PERSON EVER TO DO IT!

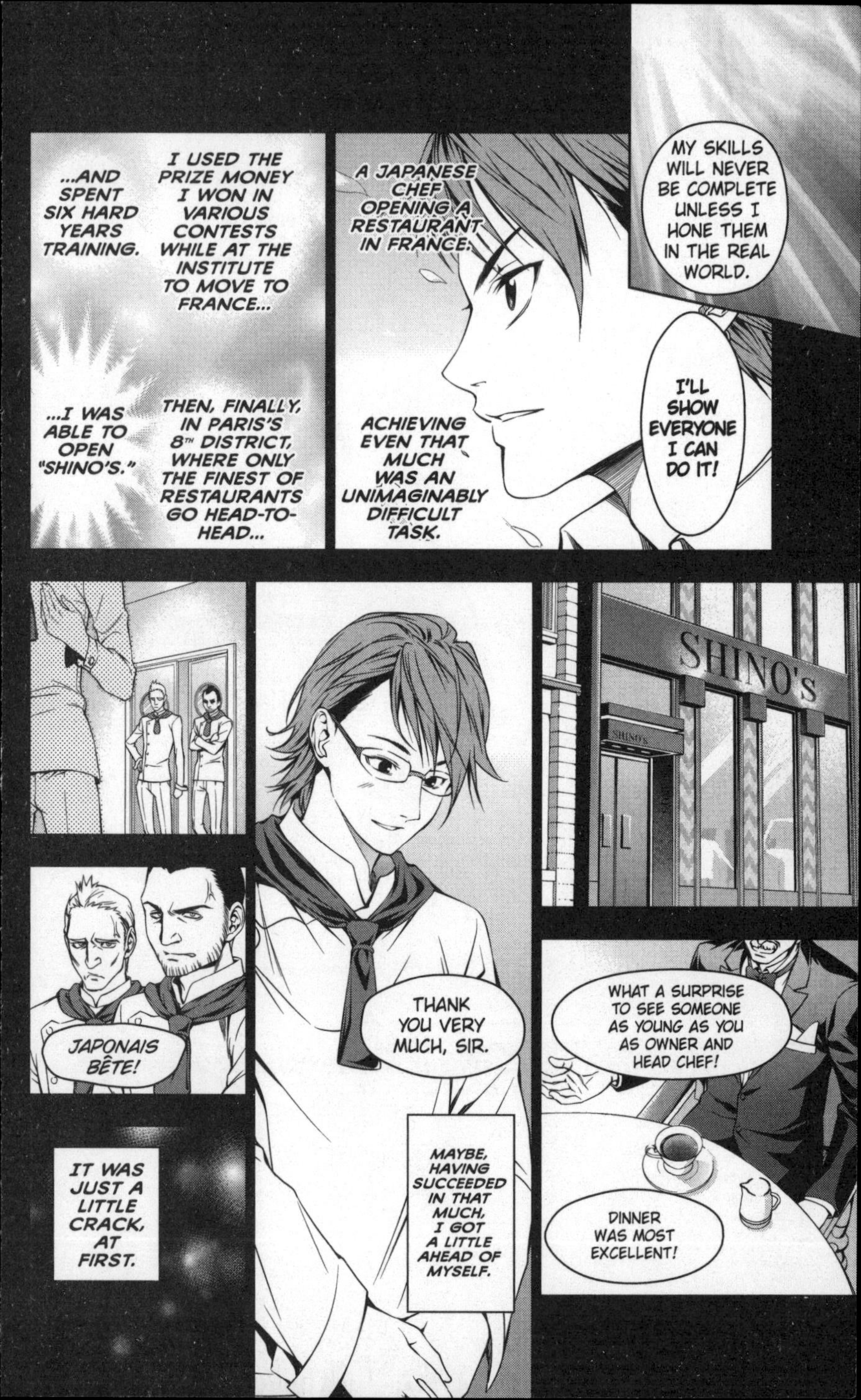
MY SKILLS WILL NEVER BE COMPLETE UNLESS I HONE THEM IN THE REAL WORLD.
I'LL SHOW EVERYONE I CAN DO IT!
A JAPANESE CHEF OPENING A RESTAURANT IN FRANCE.
ACHIEVING EVEN THAT MUCH WAS AN UNIMAGINABLY DIFFICULT TASK.
I USED THE PRIZE MONEY I WON IN VARIOUS CONTESTS WHILE AT THE INSTITUTE TO MOVE TO FRANCE...
...AND SPENT SIX HARD YEARS TRAINING.
THEN, FINALLY, IN PARIS'S 8TH DISTRICT, WHERE ONLY THE FINEST OF RESTAURANTS GO HEAD-TO-HEAD...
...I WAS ABLE TO OPEN "SHINO'S."
SHINO's
WHAT A SURPRISE TO SEE SOMEONE AS YOUNG AS YOU AS OWNER AND HEAD CHEF!
DINNER WAS MOST EXCELLENT!
THANK YOU VERY MUCH, SIR.
MAYBE, HAVING SUCCEEDED IN THAT MUCH, I GOT A LITTLE AHEAD OF MYSELF.
JAPONAIS BÊTE!
IT WAS JUST A LITTLE CRACK, AT FIRST.

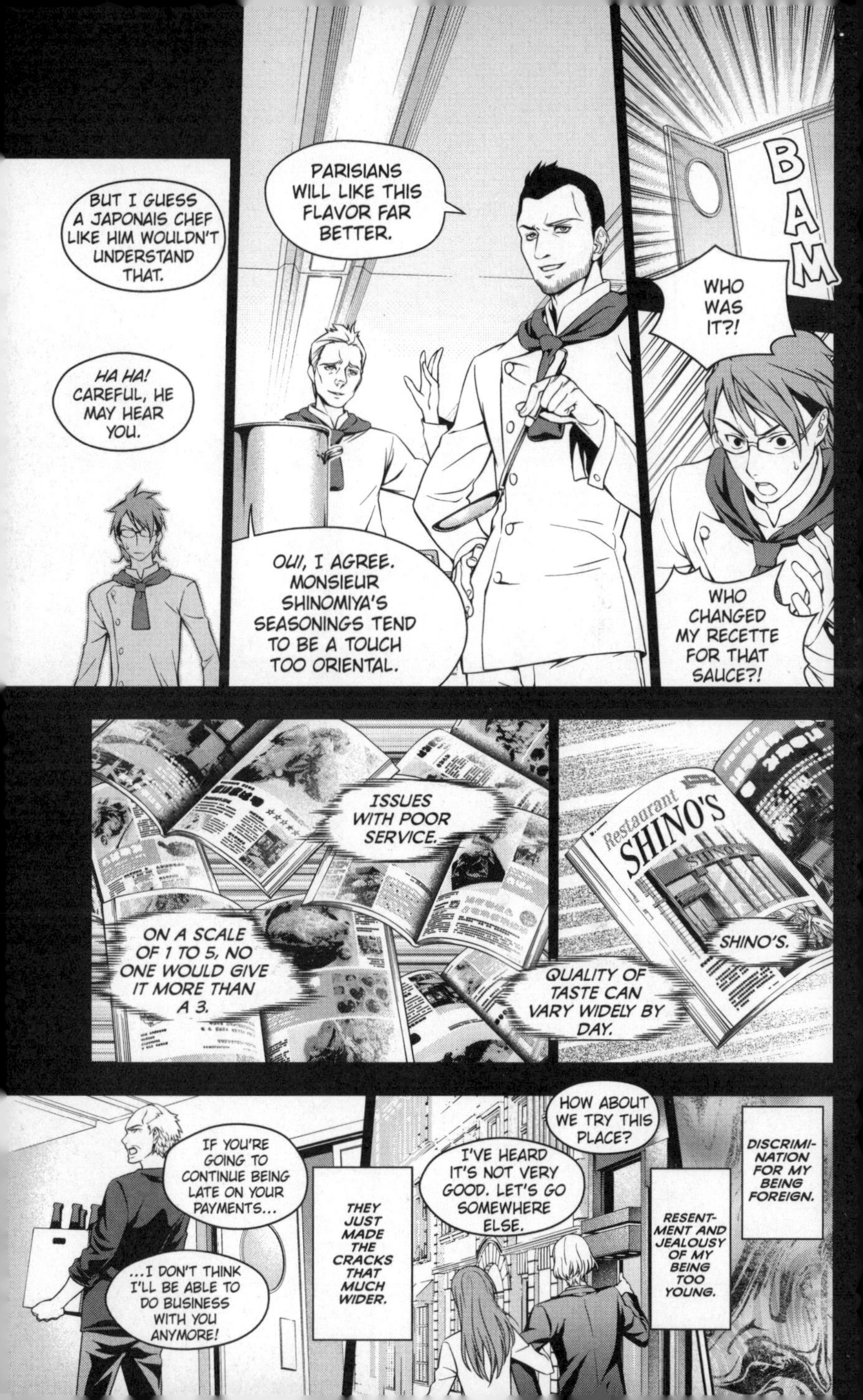
BAM
WHO WAS IT?!
WHO CHANGED MY RECETTE FOR THAT SAUCE?!
PARISIANS WILL LIKE THIS FLAVOR FAR BETTER.
OUI, I AGREE. MONSIEUR SHINOMIYA'S SEASONINGS TEND TO BE A TOUCH TOO ORIENTAL.
BUT I GUESS A JAPONAIS CHEF LIKE HIM WOULDN'T UNDERSTAND THAT.
HA HA! CAREFUL, HE MAY HEAR YOU.
Restaurant SHINO'S
SHINO'S.
QUALITY OF TASTE CAN VARY WIDELY BY DAY.
ISSUES WITH POOR SERVICE.
ON A SCALE OF 1 TO 5, NO ONE WOULD GIVE IT MORE THAN A 3.
DISCRIMINATION FOR MY BEING FOREIGN.
RESENTMENT AND JEALOUSY OF MY BEING TOO YOUNG.
HOW ABOUT WE TRY THIS PLACE?
I'VE HEARD IT'S NOT VERY GOOD. LET'S GO SOMEWHERE ELSE.
THEY JUST MADE THE CRACKS THAT MUCH WIDER.
IF YOU'RE GOING TO CONTINUE BEING LATE ON YOUR PAYMENTS...
...I DON'T THINK I'LL BE ABLE TO DO BUSINESS WITH YOU ANYMORE!

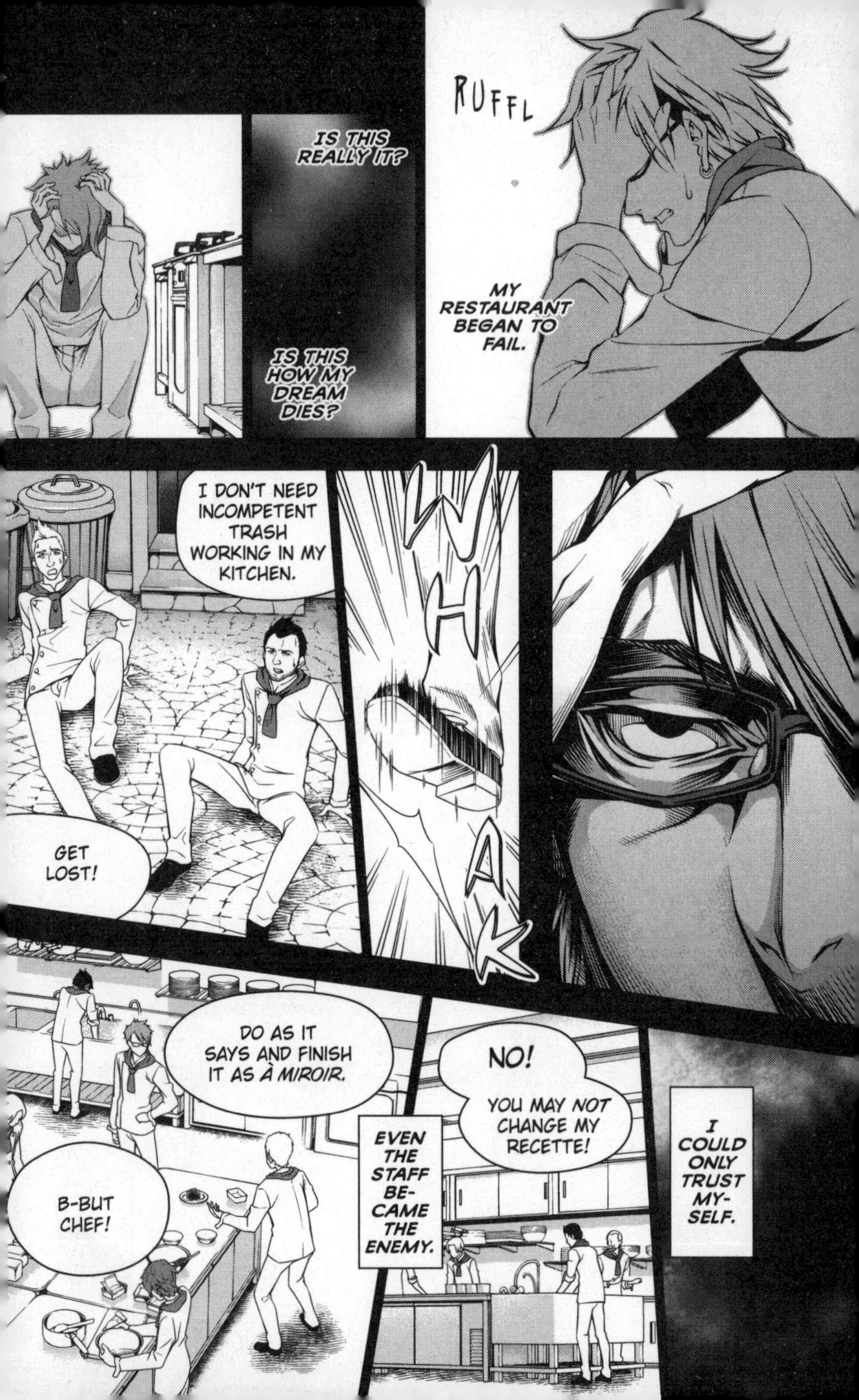
RUFFL
MY RESTAURANT BEGAN TO FAIL.
IS THIS REALLY IT?
IS THIS HOW MY DREAM DIES?
WHAK
I DON'T NEED INCOMPETENT TRASH WORKING IN MY KITCHEN.
GET LOST!
I COULD ONLY TRUST MY-SELF.
NO!
YOU MAY *NOT* CHANGE MY RECETTE!
EVEN THE STAFF BE-CAME THE ENEMY.
DO AS IT SAYS AND FINISH IT AS *À MIROIR*.
B-BUT CHEF!

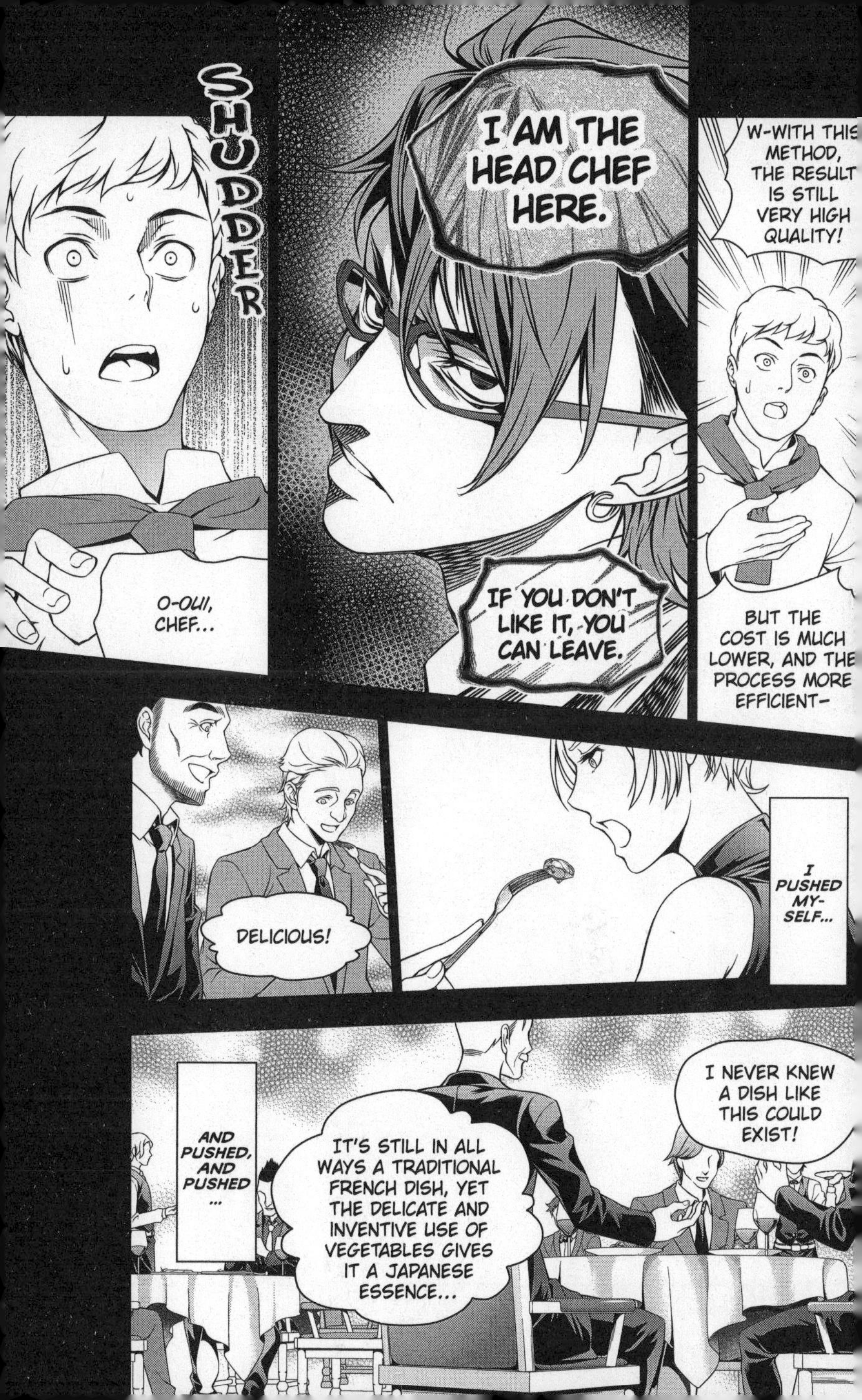
W-WITH THIS METHOD, THE RESULT IS STILL VERY HIGH QUALITY!
BUT THE COST IS MUCH LOWER, AND THE PROCESS MORE EFFICIENT-
I AM THE HEAD CHEF HERE.
IF YOU DON'T LIKE IT, YOU CAN LEAVE.
SHUDDER
O-OUI, CHEF...
I PUSHED MY-SELF...
DELICIOUS!
I NEVER KNEW A DISH LIKE THIS COULD EXIST!
AND PUSHED, AND PUSHED ...
IT'S STILL IN ALL WAYS A TRADITIONAL FRENCH DISH, YET THE DELICATE AND INVENTIVE USE OF VEGETABLES GIVES IT A JAPANESE ESSENCE...

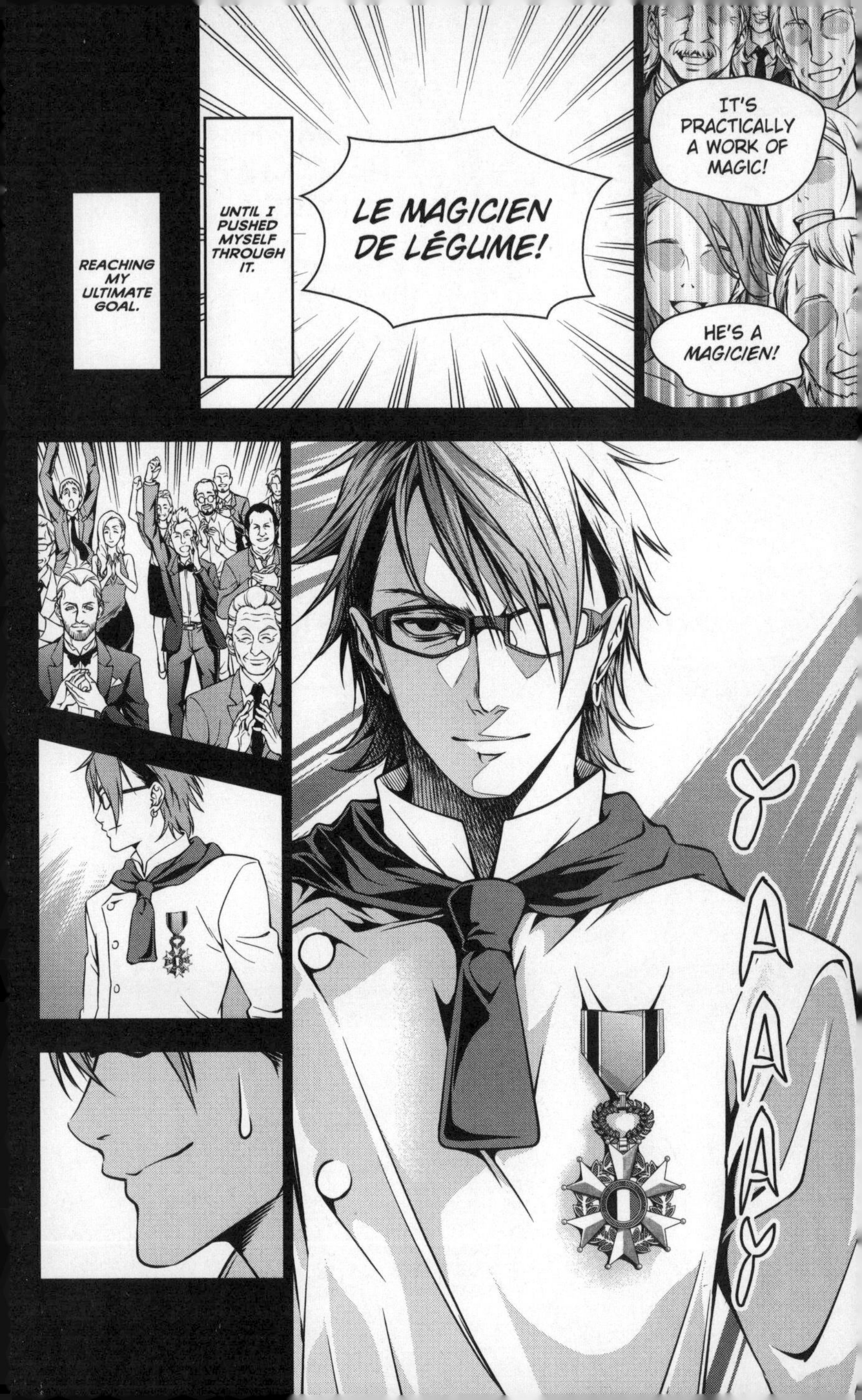
IT'S PRACTICALLY A WORK OF MAGIC!
HE'S A MAGICIEN!
LE MAGICIEN DE LÉGUME!
UNTIL I PUSHED MYSELF THROUGH IT.
REACHING MY ULTIMATE GOAL.
YAAAAY

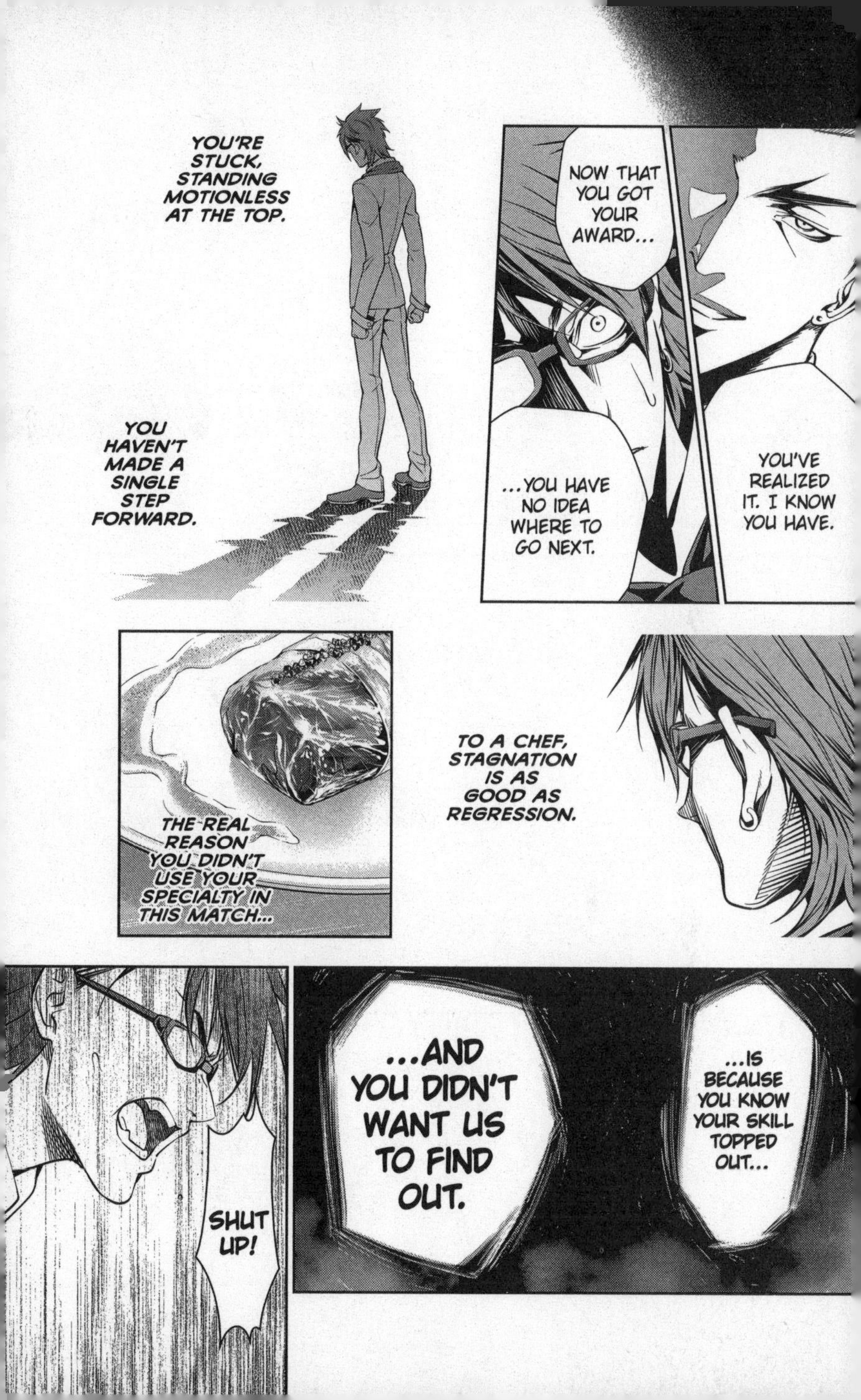
YOU'VE REALIZED IT. I KNOW YOU HAVE.
NOW THAT YOU GOT YOUR AWARD...
...YOU HAVE NO IDEA WHERE TO GO NEXT.
YOU'RE STUCK, STANDING MOTIONLESS AT THE TOP.
YOU HAVEN'T MADE A SINGLE STEP FORWARD.
TO A CHEF, STAGNATION IS AS GOOD AS REGRESSION.
THE REAL REASON YOU DIDN'T USE YOUR SPECIALTY IN THIS MATCH...
...IS BECAUSE YOU KNOW YOUR SKILL TOPPED OUT...
...AND YOU DIDN'T WANT US TO FIND OUT.
SHUT UP!

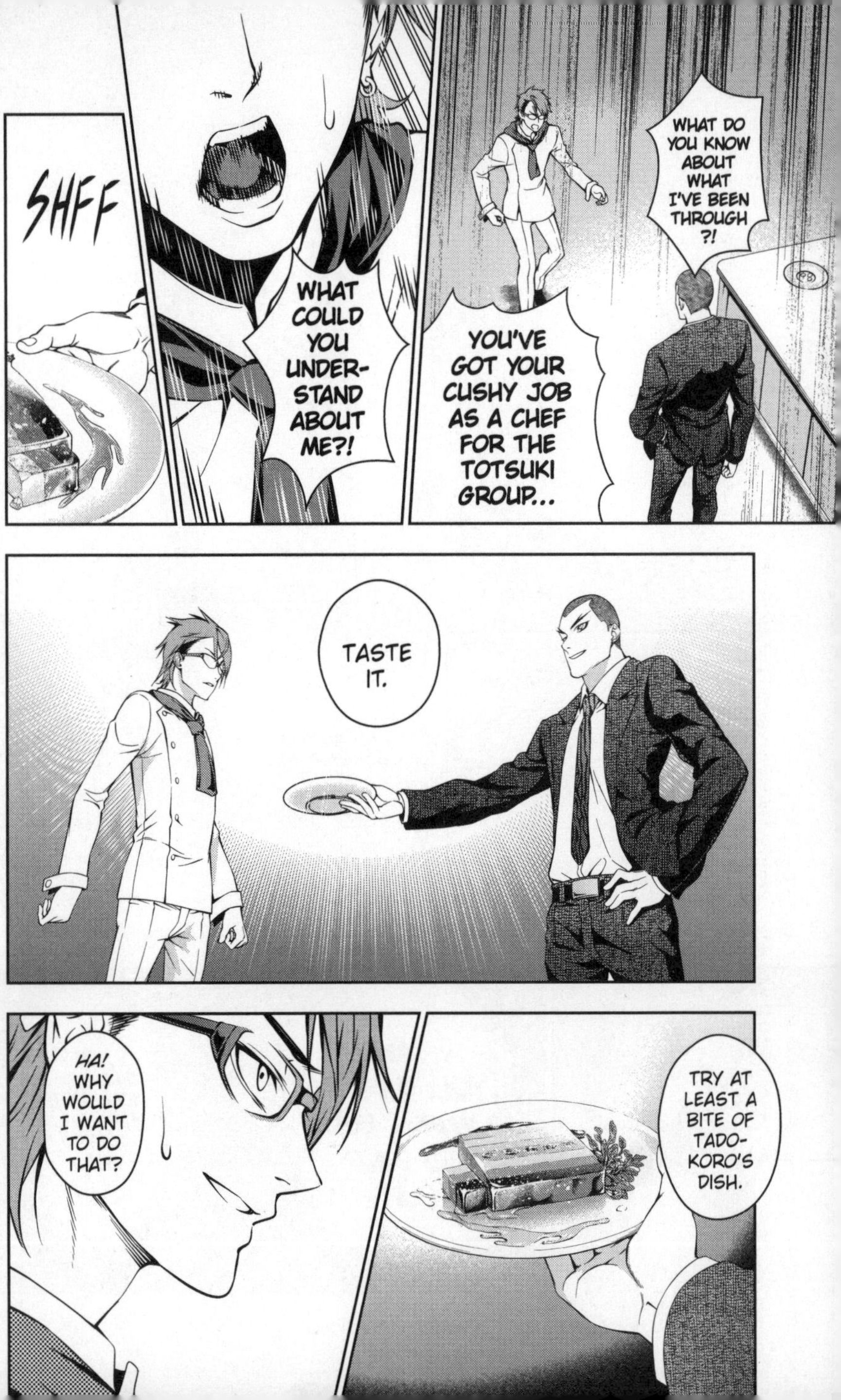
WHAT DO YOU KNOW ABOUT WHAT I'VE BEEN THROUGH?!
YOU'VE GOT YOUR CUSHY JOB AS A CHEF FOR THE TOTSUKI GROUP...
WHAT COULD YOU UNDER-STAND ABOUT ME?!
SHFF
TASTE IT.
TRY AT LEAST A BITE OF TADO-KORO'S DISH.
HA! WHY WOULD I WANT TO DO THAT?

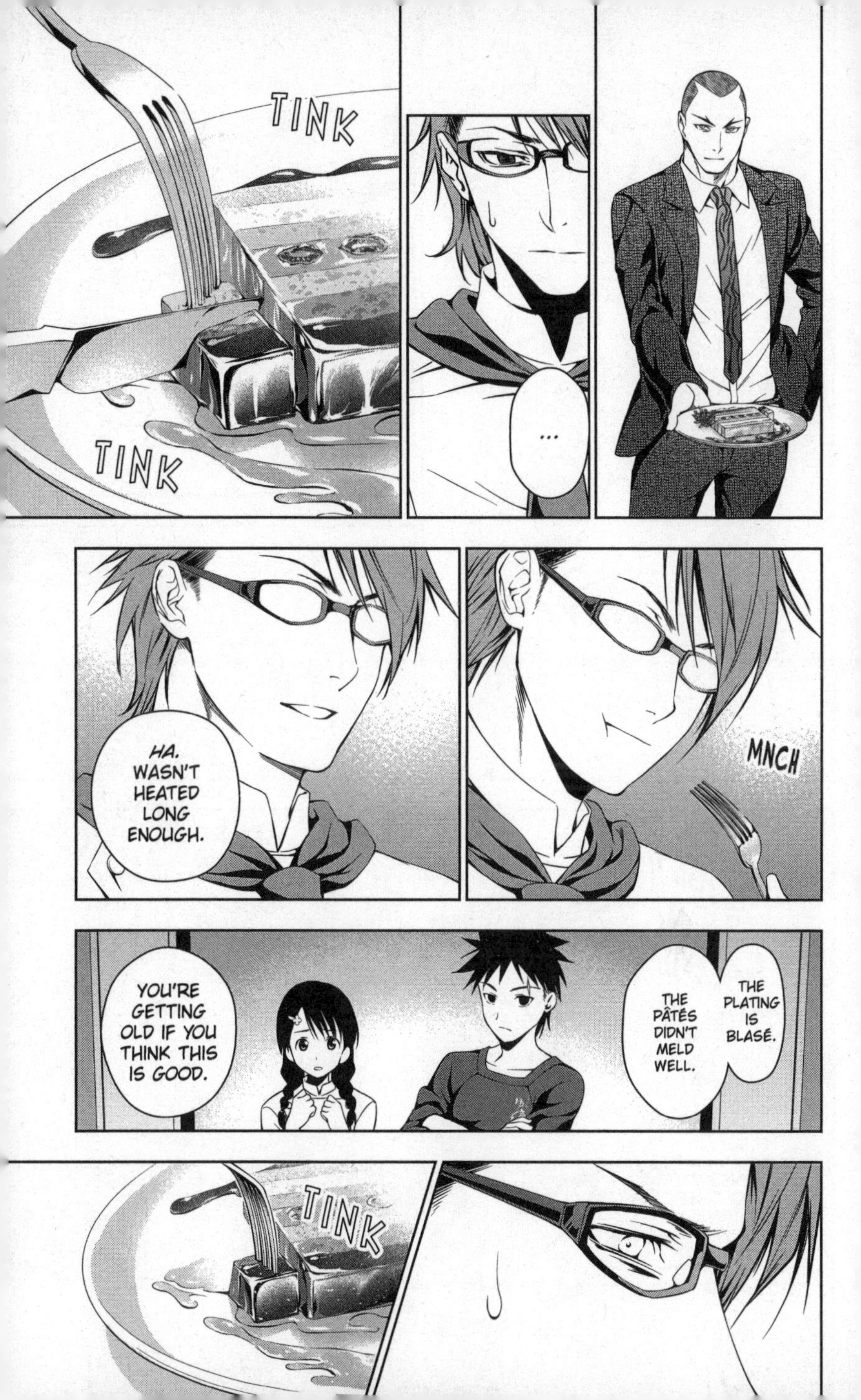
...
TINK
TINK
MNCH
HA. WASN'T HEATED LONG ENOUGH.
THE PLATING IS BLASÉ.
THE PÂTÉS DIDN'T MELD WELL.
YOU'RE GETTING OLD IF YOU THINK THIS IS GOOD.
TINK

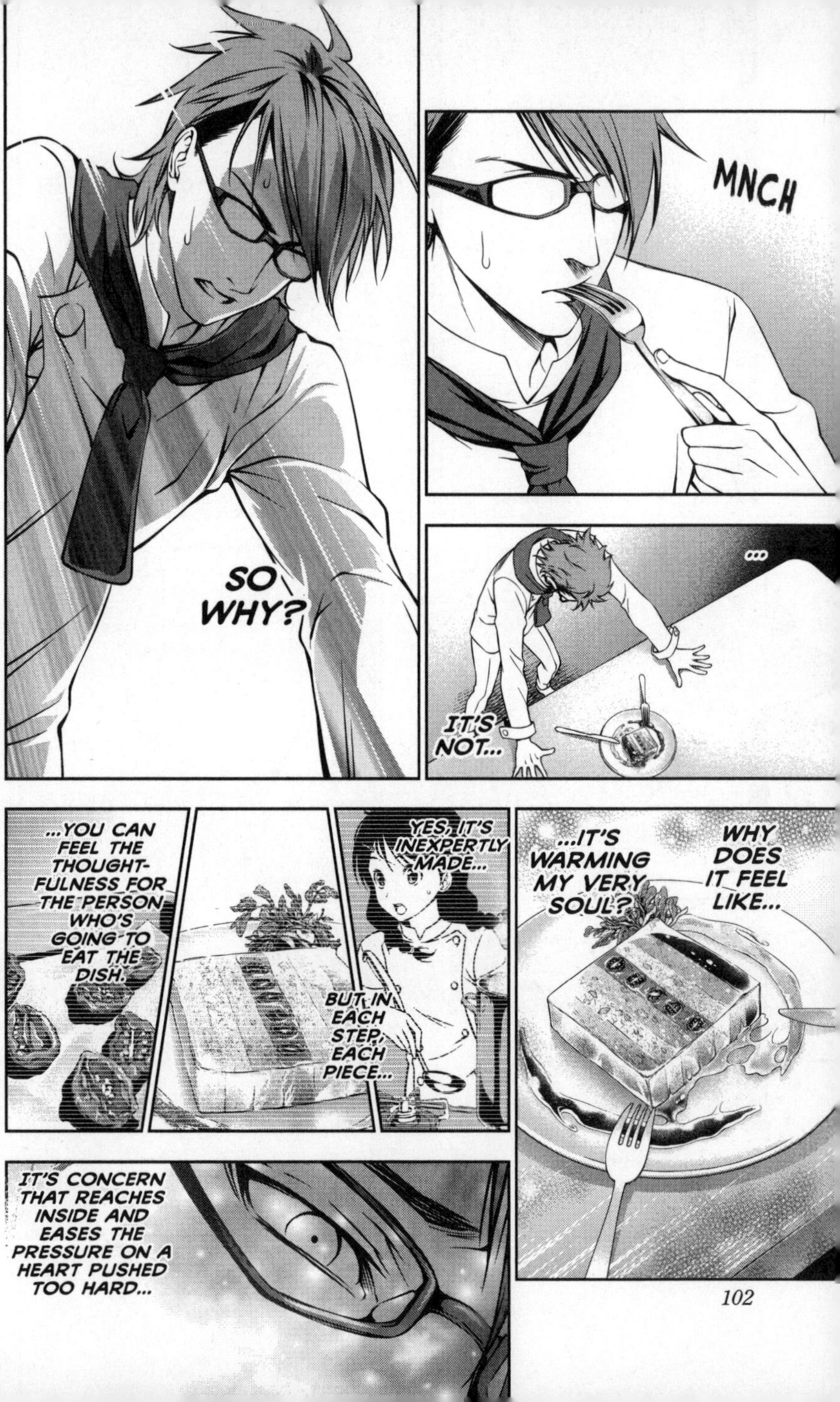
MNCH
...
IT'S NOT...
SO WHY?
WHY DOES IT FEEL LIKE...
...IT'S WARMING MY VERY SOUL?
YES, IT'S INEXPERTLY MADE...
BUT IN EACH STEP, EACH PIECE...
...YOU CAN FEEL THE THOUGHT-FULNESS FOR THE PERSON WHO'S GOING TO EAT THE DISH.
IT'S CONCERN THAT REACHES INSIDE AND EASES THE PRESSURE ON A HEART PUSHED TOO HARD...

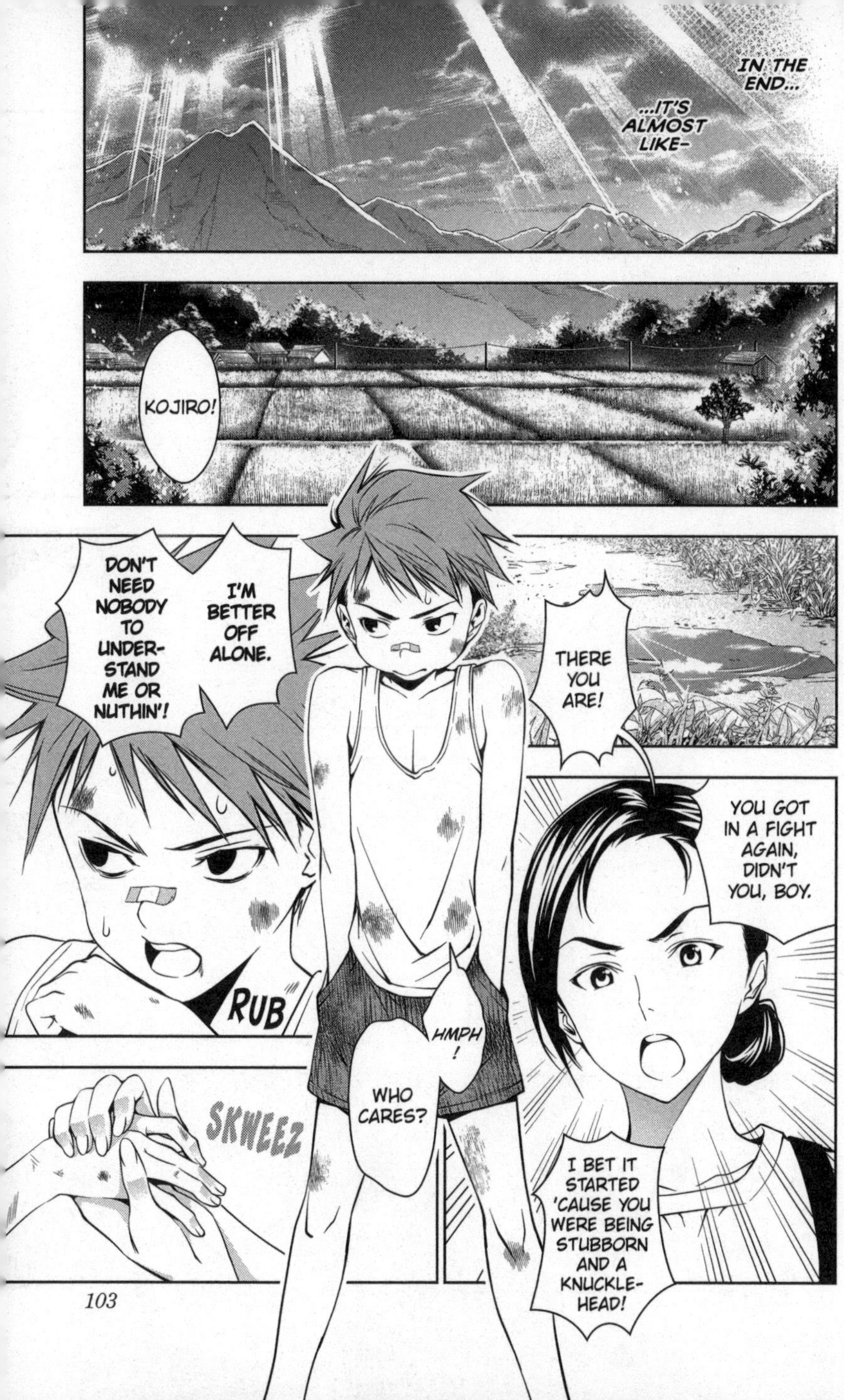
IN THE END...
...IT'S ALMOST LIKE–
KOJIRO!
THERE YOU ARE!
YOU GOT IN A FIGHT AGAIN, DIDN'T YOU, BOY.
I BET IT STARTED 'CAUSE YOU WERE BEING STUBBORN AND A KNUCKLE-HEAD!
HMPH!
WHO CARES?
I'M BETTER OFF ALONE.
DON'T NEED NOBODY TO UNDER-STAND ME OR NUTHIN'!
RUB
SKWEEZ

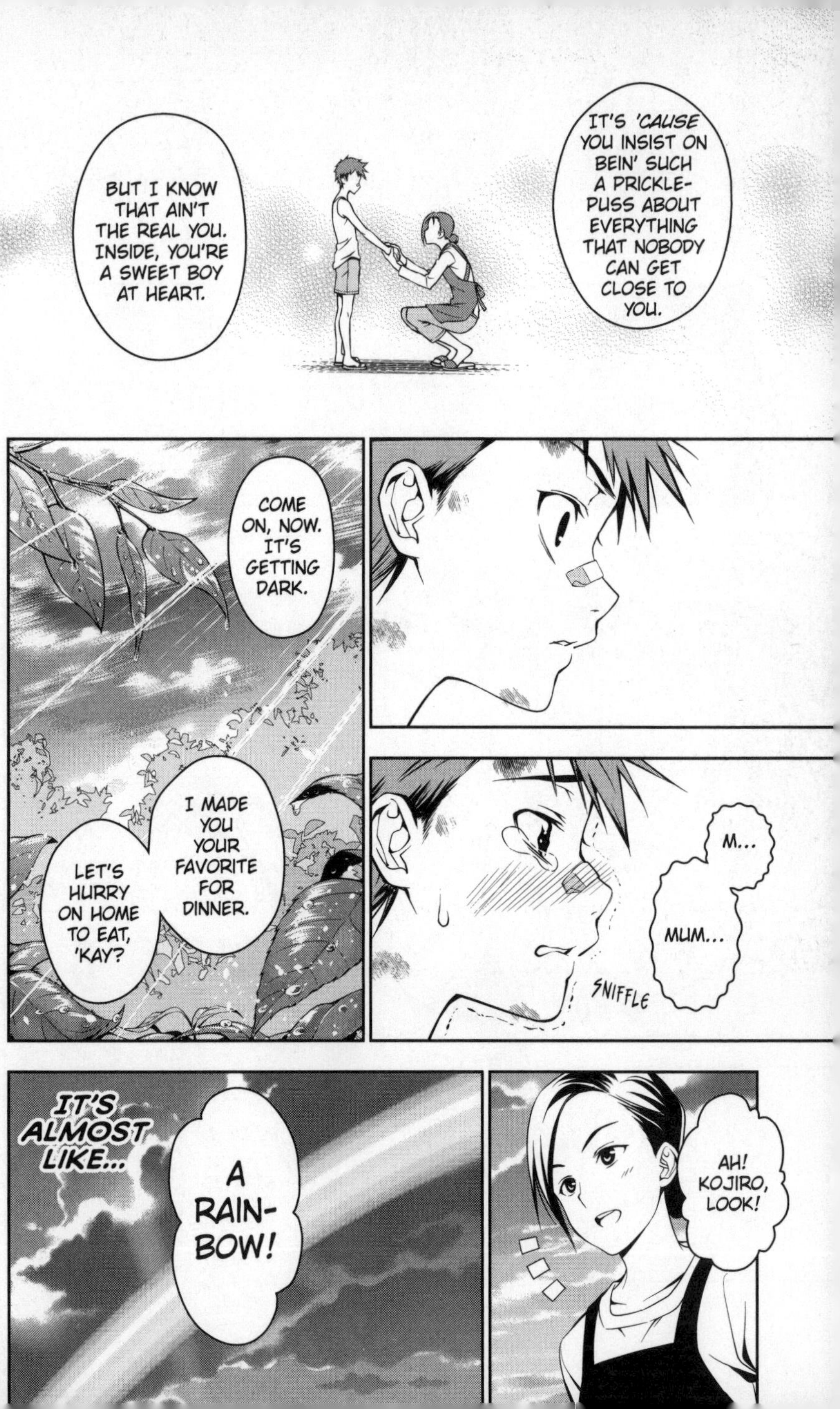

IT'S 'CAUSE YOU INSIST ON BEIN' SUCH A PRICKLE-PUSS ABOUT EVERYTHING THAT NOBODY CAN GET CLOSE TO YOU.
BUT I KNOW THAT AIN'T THE REAL YOU. INSIDE, YOU'RE A SWEET BOY AT HEART.
M...
MUM...
SNIFFLE
COME ON, NOW. IT'S GETTING DARK.
I MADE YOU YOUR FAVORITE FOR DINNER.
LET'S HURRY ON HOME TO EAT, 'KAY?
AH! KOJIRO, LOOK!
A RAIN-BOW!
IT'S ALMOST LIKE...

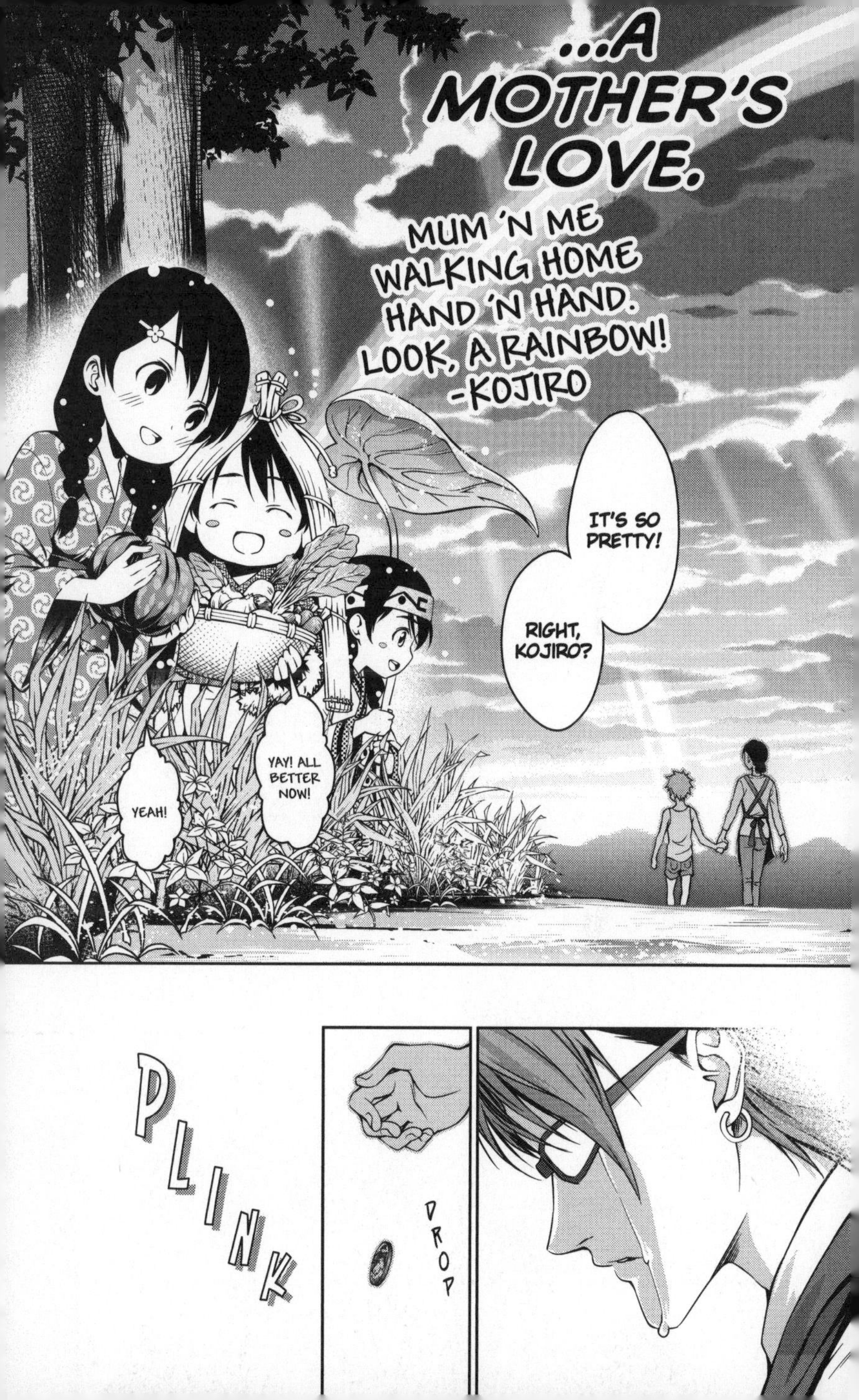
...A MOTHER'S LOVE.
MUM 'N ME WALKING HOME HAND 'N HAND. LOOK, A RAINBOW! -KOJIRO
IT'S SO PRETTY!
RIGHT, KOJIRO?
YAY! ALL BETTER NOW!
YEAH!
DROP
PLINK

**MEGUMI SPRITE
MINI PLUSHIES**

**THREE VARIETIES
600 YEN EACH, PLUS TAX
*THESE ARE MEANT AS TOYS**

ACTUAL SALE
ITEMS NOT
FINALIZED

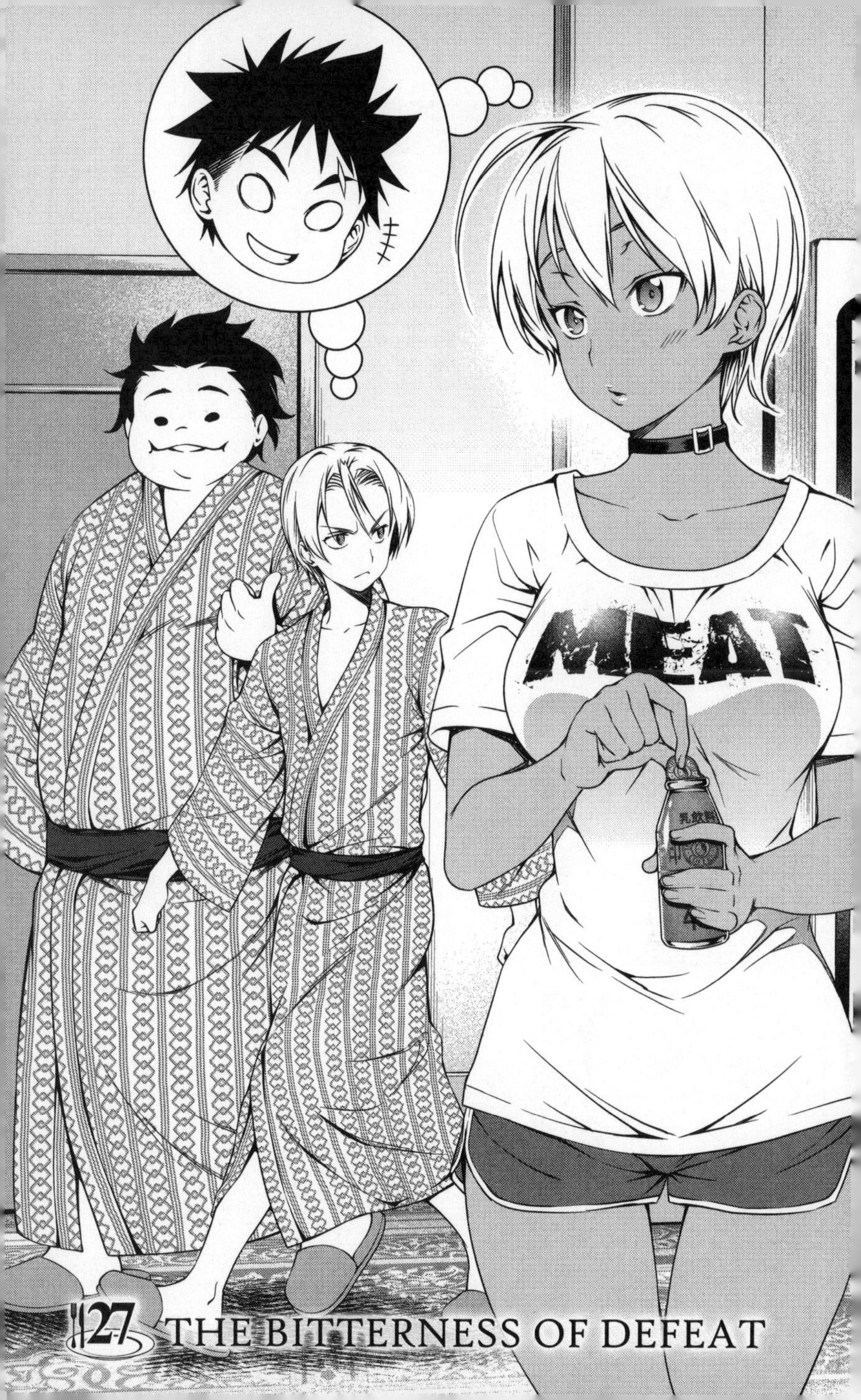
MEAT

27 THE BITTERNESS OF DEFEAT

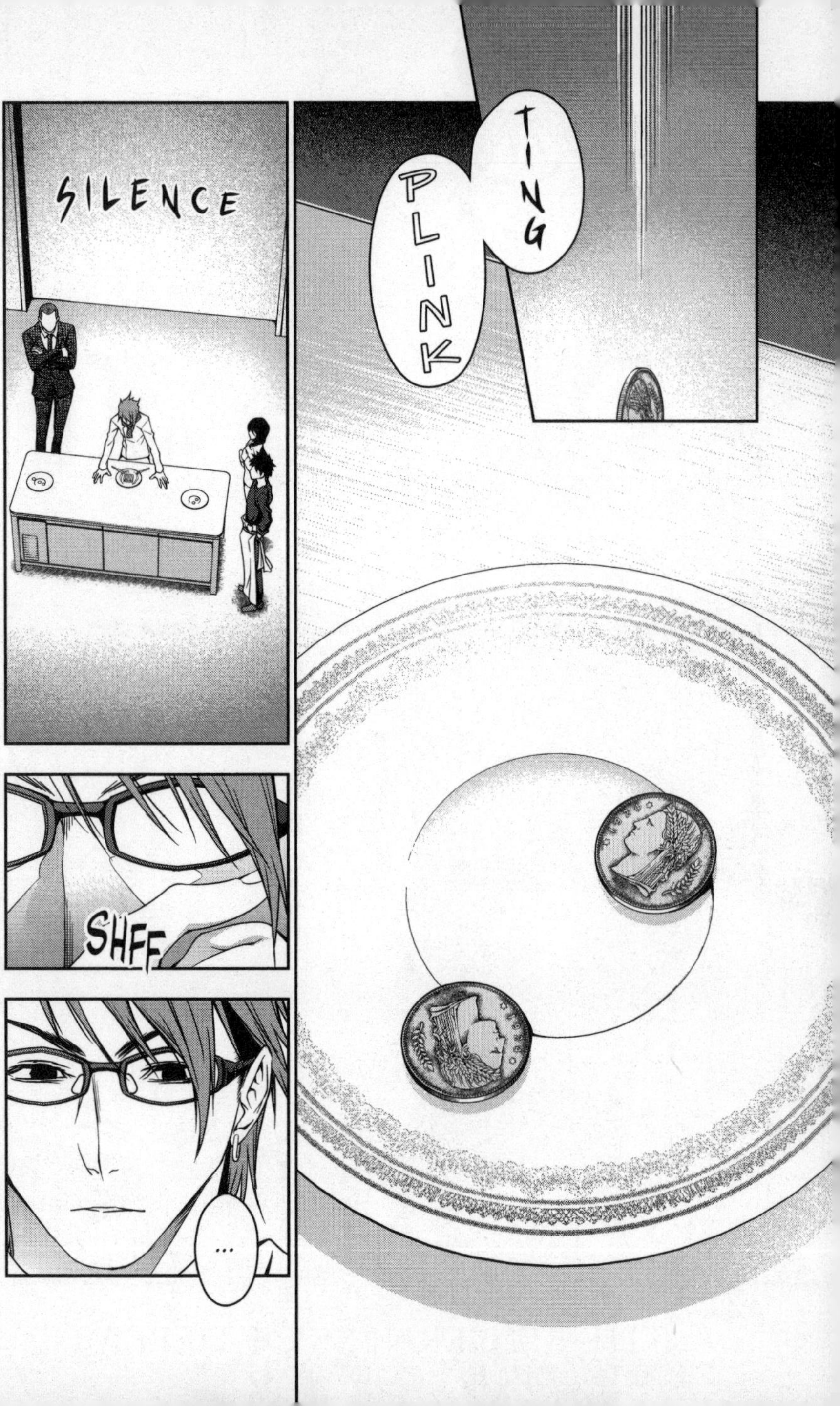

TING
PLINK
SILENCE
SHFF
...

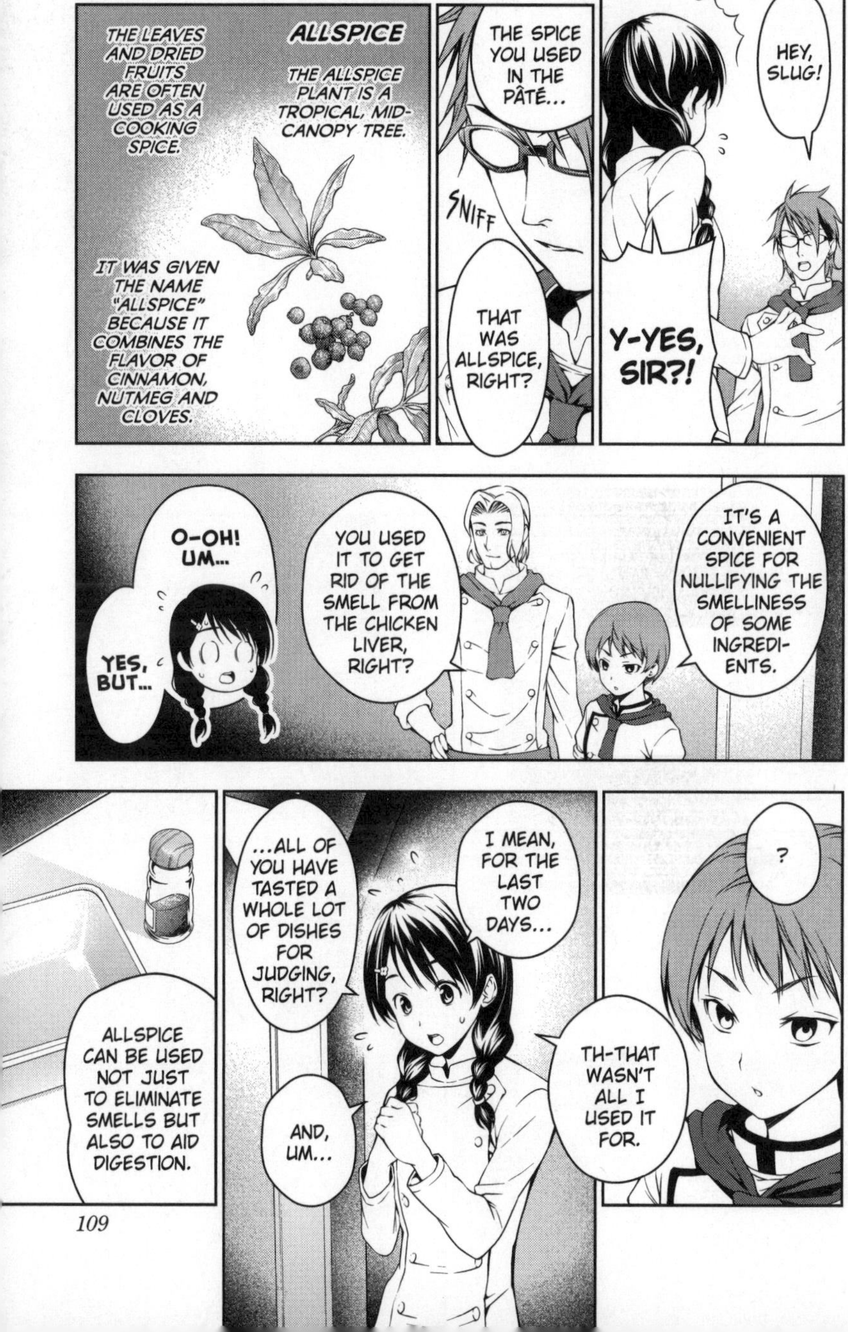
HEY, SLUG!
Y-YES, SIR?!
THE SPICE YOU USED IN THE PÂTÉ...
SNIFF
THAT WAS ALLSPICE, RIGHT?
ALLSPICE
THE ALLSPICE PLANT IS A TROPICAL, MID-CANOPY TREE.
THE LEAVES AND DRIED FRUITS ARE OFTEN USED AS A COOKING SPICE.
IT WAS GIVEN THE NAME "ALLSPICE" BECAUSE IT COMBINES THE FLAVOR OF CINNAMON, NUTMEG AND CLOVES.
IT'S A CONVENIENT SPICE FOR NULLIFYING THE SMELLINESS OF SOME INGREDI-ENTS.
YOU USED IT TO GET RID OF THE SMELL FROM THE CHICKEN LIVER, RIGHT?
O-OH! UM...
YES, BUT...
?
TH-THAT WASN'T ALL I USED IT FOR.
I MEAN, FOR THE LAST TWO DAYS...
...ALL OF YOU HAVE TASTED A WHOLE LOT OF DISHES FOR JUDGING, RIGHT?
AND, UM...
ALLSPICE CAN BE USED NOT JUST TO ELIMINATE SMELLS BUT ALSO TO AID DIGESTION.

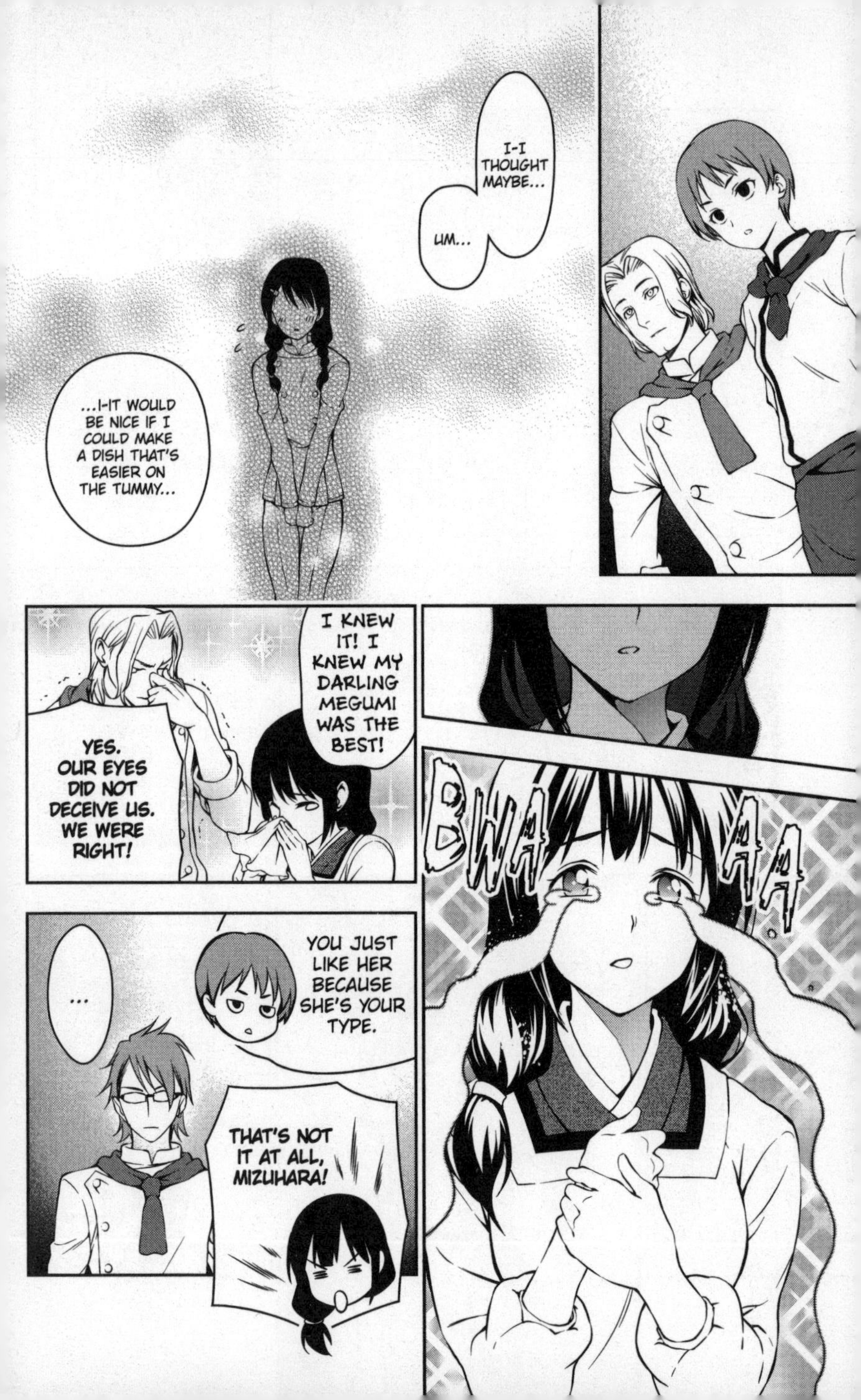
I-I THOUGHT MAYBE...
UM...
...I-IT WOULD BE NICE IF I COULD MAKE A DISH THAT'S EASIER ON THE TUMMY...
BWAAA
I KNEW IT! I KNEW MY DARLING MEGUMI WAS THE BEST!
YES. OUR EYES DID NOT DECEIVE US. WE WERE RIGHT!
YOU JUST LIKE HER BECAUSE SHE'S YOUR TYPE.
...
THAT'S NOT IT AT ALL, MIZUHARA!

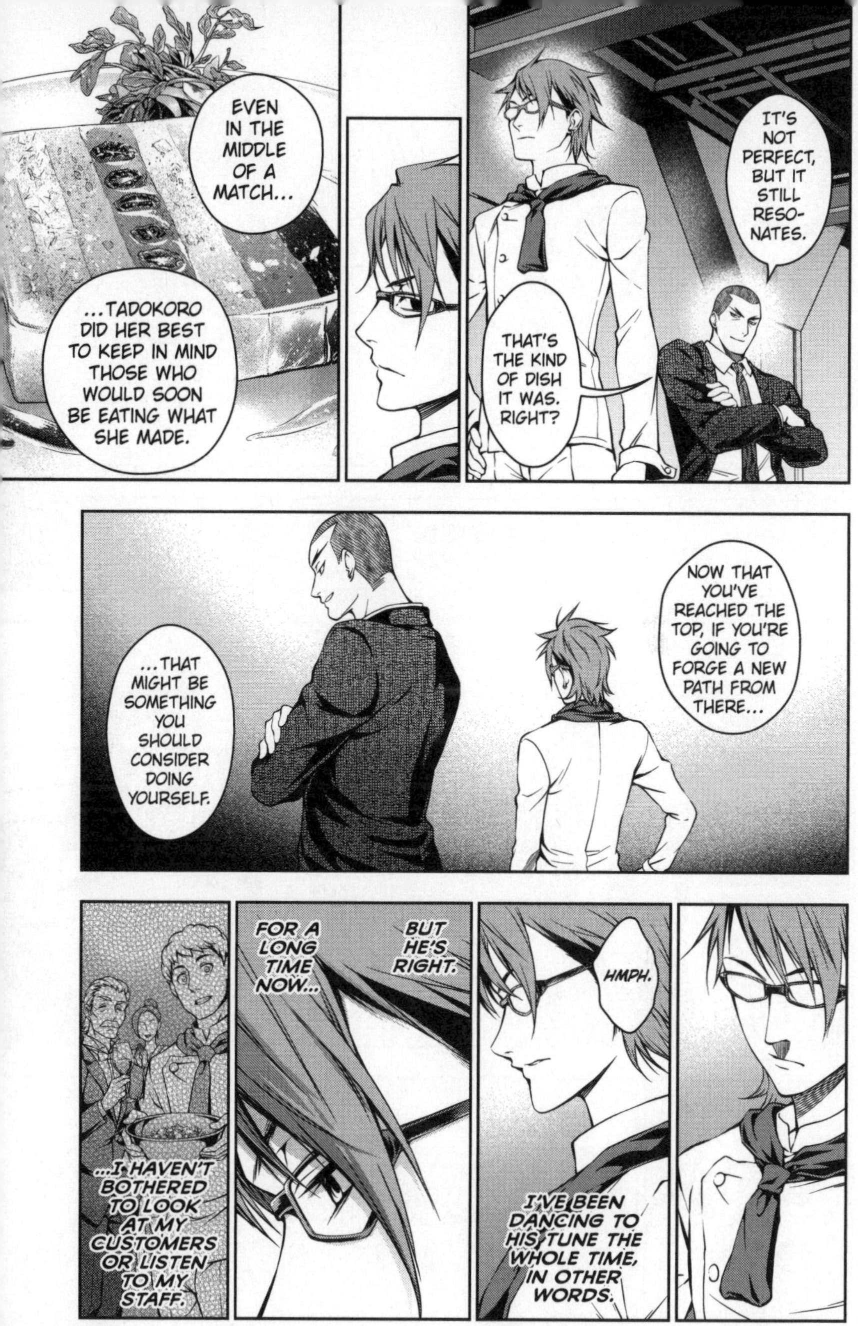
IT'S NOT PERFECT, BUT IT STILL RESONATES.
THAT'S THE KIND OF DISH IT WAS. RIGHT?
EVEN IN THE MIDDLE OF A MATCH...
...TADOKORO DID HER BEST TO KEEP IN MIND THOSE WHO WOULD SOON BE EATING WHAT SHE MADE.
NOW THAT YOU'VE REACHED THE TOP, IF YOU'RE GOING TO FORGE A NEW PATH FROM THERE...
...THAT MIGHT BE SOMETHING YOU SHOULD CONSIDER DOING YOURSELF.
HMPH.
I'VE BEEN DANCING TO HIS TUNE THE WHOLE TIME, IN OTHER WORDS.
BUT HE'S RIGHT.
FOR A LONG TIME NOW...
...I HAVEN'T BOTHERED TO LOOK AT MY CUSTOMERS OR LISTEN TO MY STAFF.

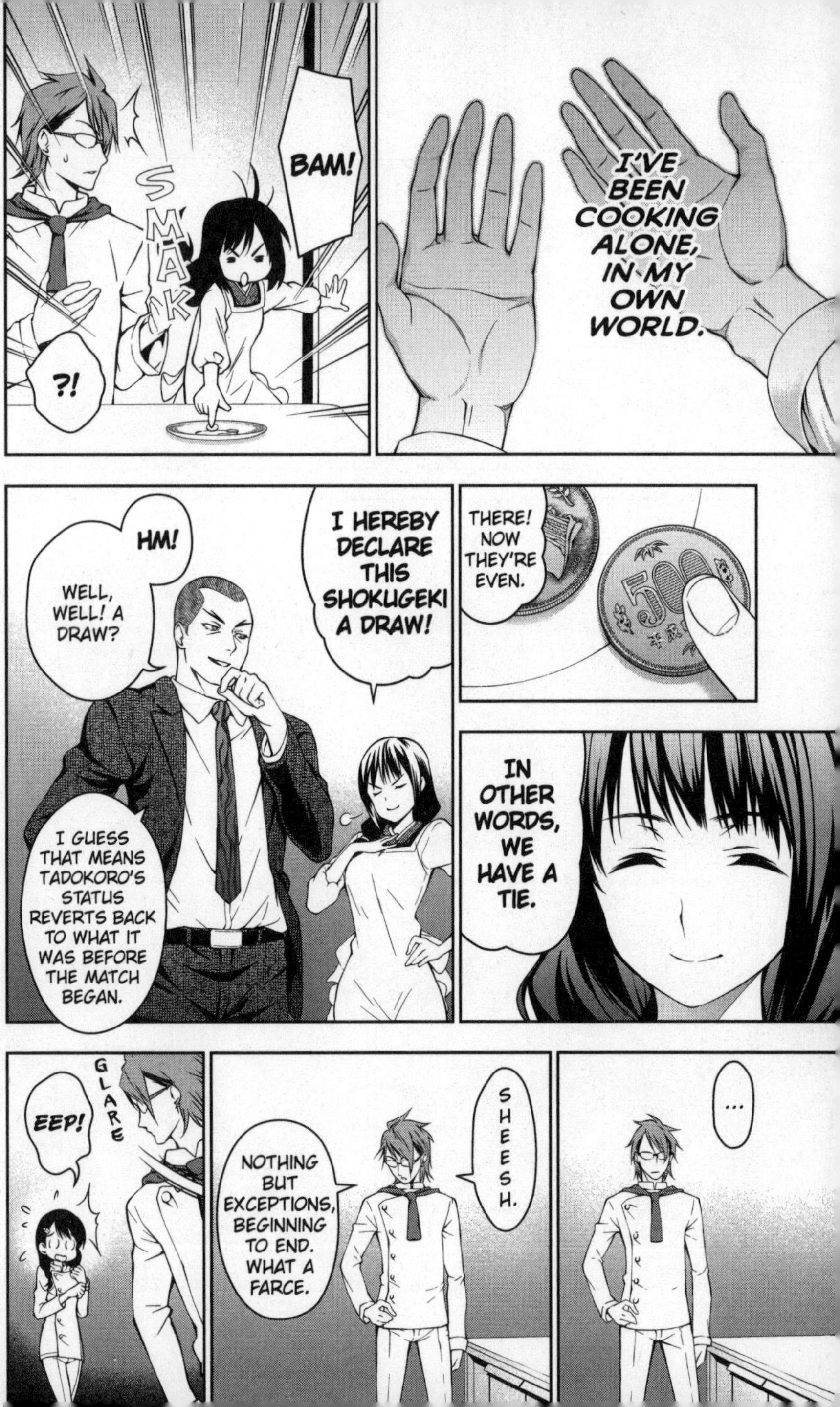
I'VE BEEN COOKING ALONE, IN MY OWN WORLD.
BAM!
SMAK
?!
THERE! NOW THEY'RE EVEN.
IN OTHER WORDS, WE HAVE A TIE.
I HEREBY DECLARE THIS SHOKUGEKI A DRAW!
HM!
WELL, WELL! A DRAW?
I GUESS THAT MEANS TADOKORO'S STATUS REVERTS BACK TO WHAT IT WAS BEFORE THE MATCH BEGAN.
...
SHEESH.
NOTHING BUT EXCEPTIONS, BEGINNING TO END. WHAT A FARCE.
GLARE
EEP!

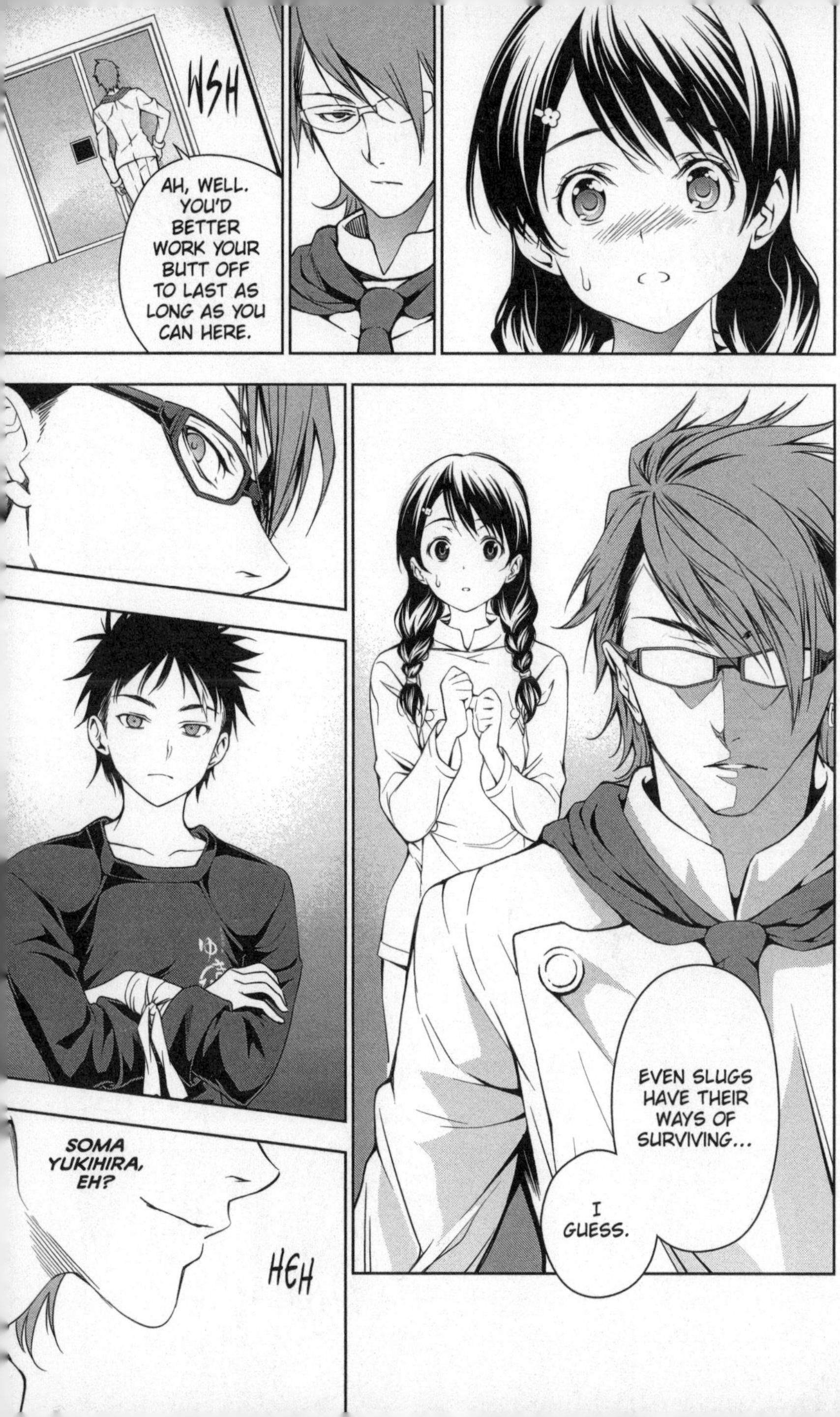
WSH
AH, WELL. YOU'D BETTER WORK YOUR BUTT OFF TO LAST AS LONG AS YOU CAN HERE.
EVEN SLUGS HAVE THEIR WAYS OF SURVIVING...
I GUESS.
SOMA YUKIHIRA, EH?
HEH

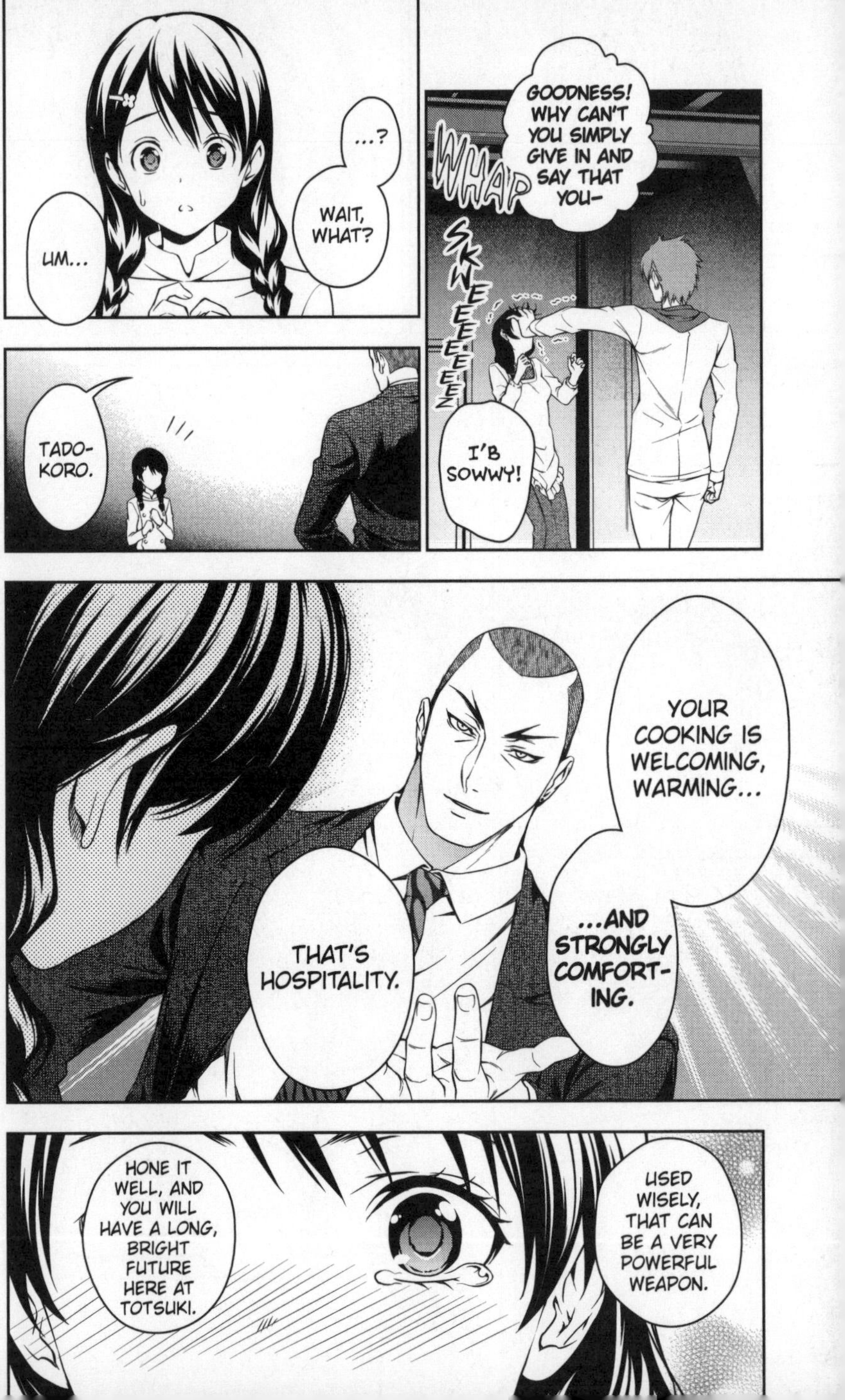
GOODNESS! WHY CAN'T YOU SIMPLY GIVE IN AND SAY THAT YOU-
WHAP
SKWEEEEEEEZ
I'B SOWWY!
...?
WAIT, WHAT?
UM...
TADO-KORO.
YOUR COOKING IS WELCOMING, WARMING...
...AND STRONGLY COMFORT-ING.
THAT'S HOSPITALITY.
USED WISELY, THAT CAN BE A VERY POWERFUL WEAPON.
HONE IT WELL, AND YOU WILL HAVE A LONG, BRIGHT FUTURE HERE AT TOTSUKI.

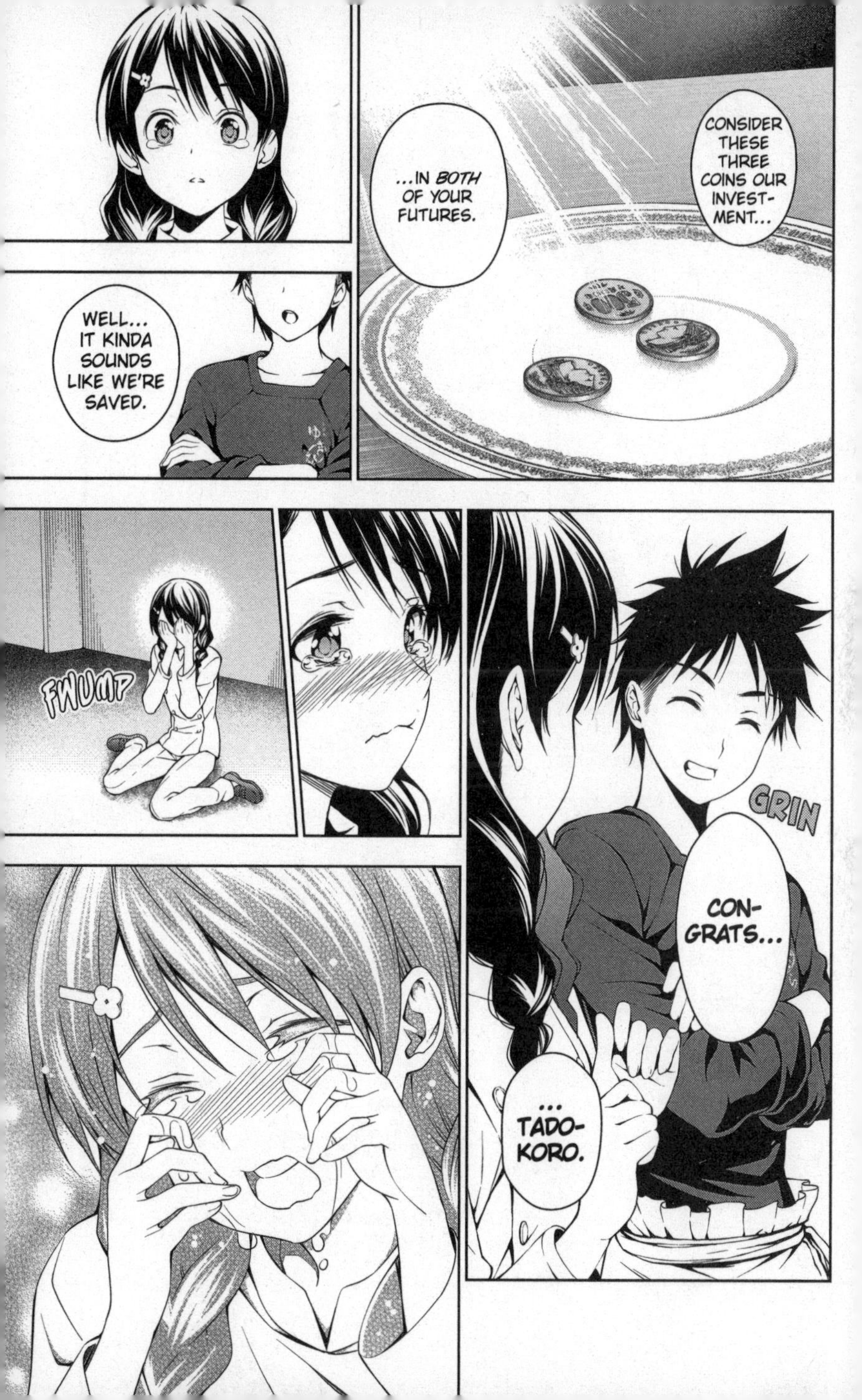
CONSIDER THESE THREE COINS OUR INVEST-MENT...
...IN *BOTH* OF YOUR FUTURES.
WELL... IT KINDA SOUNDS LIKE WE'RE SAVED.
GRIN
CON-GRATS...
... TADO-KORO.
FWUMP

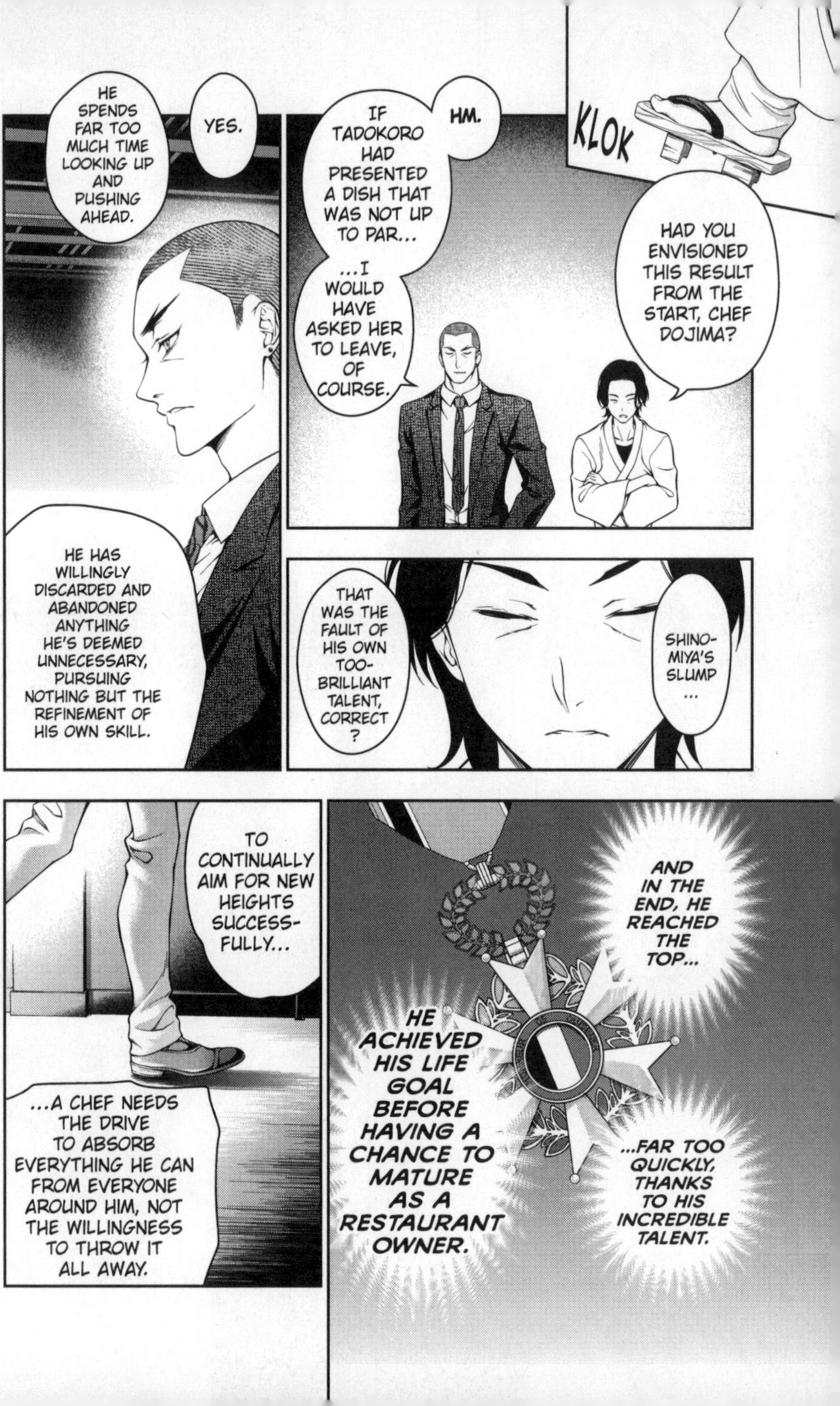
KLOK
HAD YOU ENVISIONED THIS RESULT FROM THE START, CHEF DOJIMA?
HM.
IF TADOKORO HAD PRESENTED A DISH THAT WAS NOT UP TO PAR...
...I WOULD HAVE ASKED HER TO LEAVE, OF COURSE.
SHINO-MIYA'S SLUMP...
THAT WAS THE FAULT OF HIS OWN TOO-BRILLIANT TALENT, CORRECT?
YES.
HE SPENDS FAR TOO MUCH TIME LOOKING UP AND PUSHING AHEAD.
HE HAS WILLINGLY DISCARDED AND ABANDONED ANYTHING HE'S DEEMED UNNECESSARY, PURSUING NOTHING BUT THE REFINEMENT OF HIS OWN SKILL.
AND IN THE END, HE REACHED THE TOP...
...FAR TOO QUICKLY, THANKS TO HIS INCREDIBLE TALENT.
HE ACHIEVED HIS LIFE GOAL BEFORE HAVING A CHANCE TO MATURE AS A RESTAURANT OWNER.
TO CONTINUALLY AIM FOR NEW HEIGHTS SUCCESS-FULLY...
...A CHEF NEEDS THE DRIVE TO ABSORB EVERYTHING HE CAN FROM EVERYONE AROUND HIM, NOT THE WILLINGNESS TO THROW IT ALL AWAY.

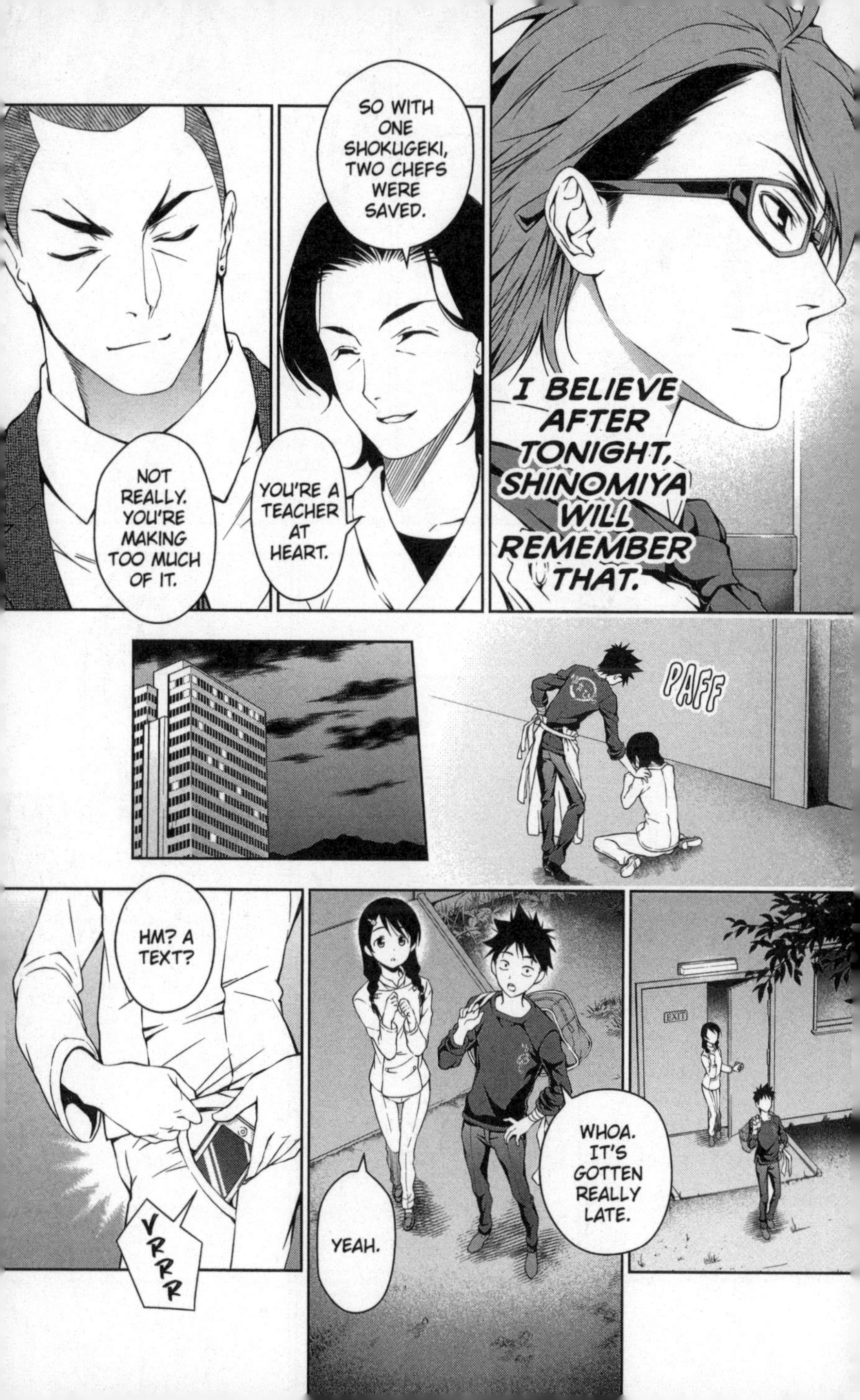

I BELIEVE AFTER TONIGHT, SHINOMIYA WILL REMEMBER THAT.
SO WITH ONE SHOKUGEKI, TWO CHEFS WERE SAVED.
YOU'RE A TEACHER AT HEART.
NOT REALLY. YOU'RE MAKING TOO MUCH OF IT.
PAFF
WHOA. IT'S GOTTEN REALLY LATE.
YEAH.
HM? A TEXT?
VRRR

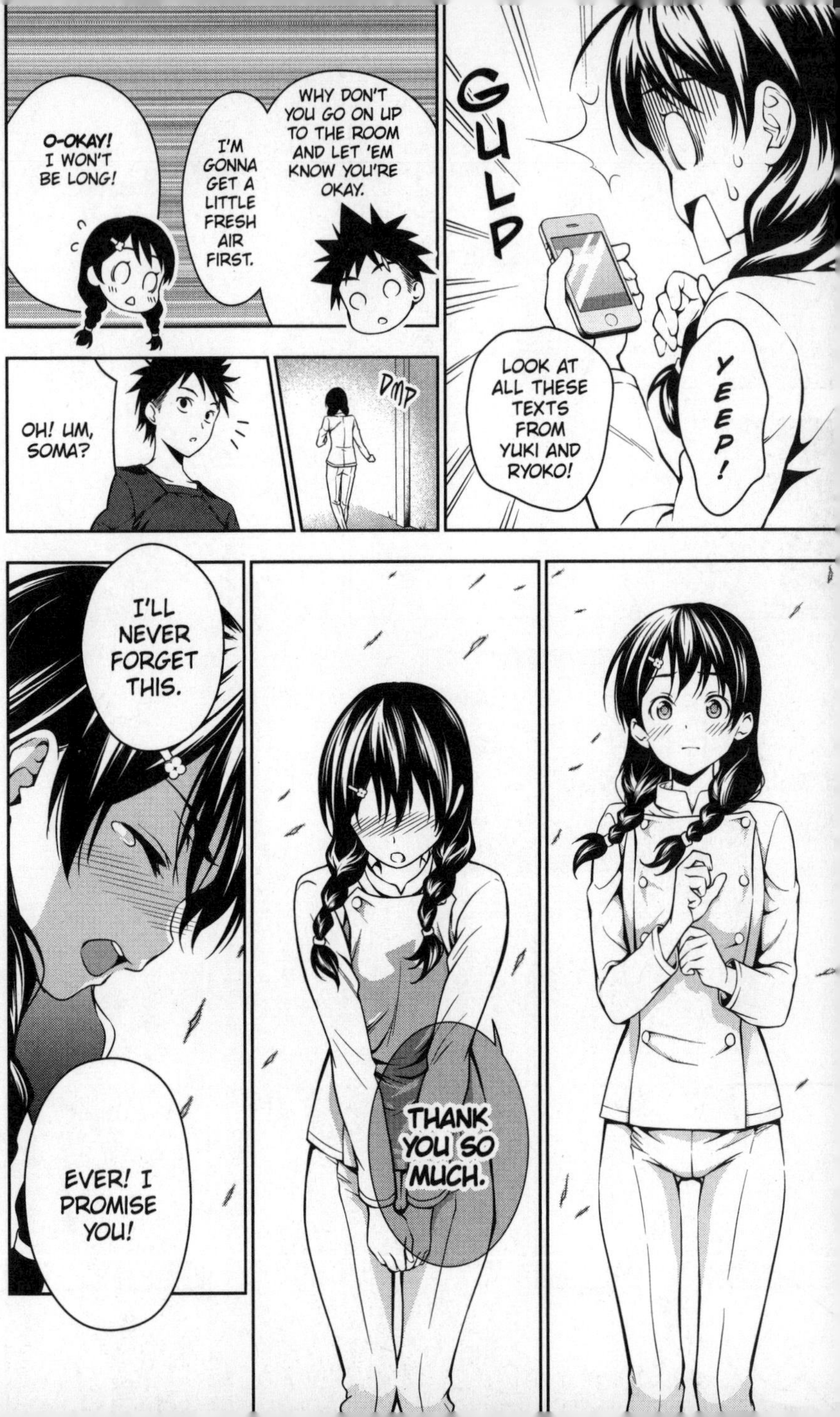
GULP
YEEP!
LOOK AT ALL THESE TEXTS FROM YUKI AND RYOKO!
WHY DON'T YOU GO ON UP TO THE ROOM AND LET 'EM KNOW YOU'RE OKAY.
I'M GONNA GET A LITTLE FRESH AIR FIRST.
O-OKAY! I WON'T BE LONG!
DMP
OH! UM, SOMA?
THANK YOU SO MUCH.
I'LL NEVER FORGET THIS.
EVER! I PROMISE YOU!

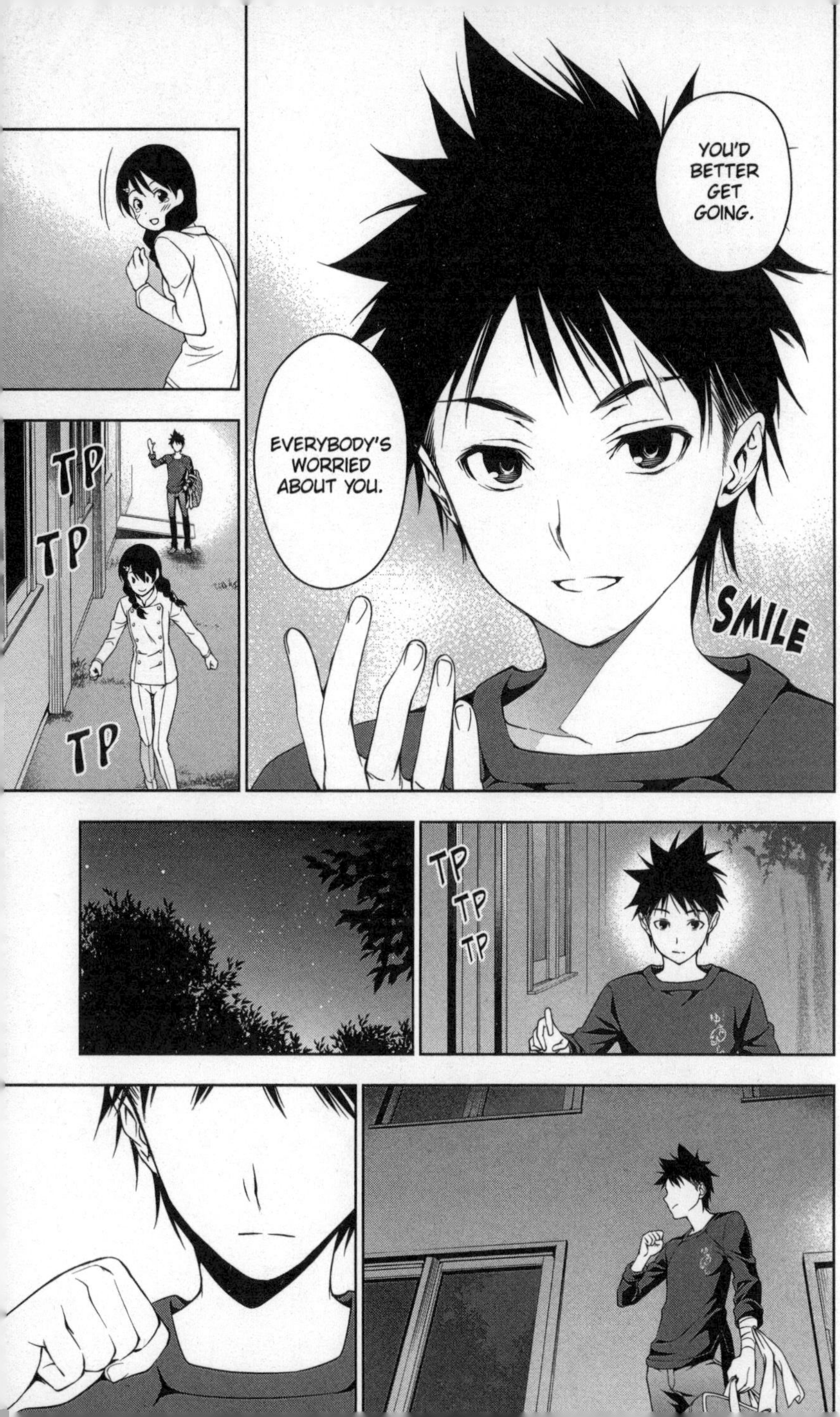
YOU'D BETTER GET GOING.
EVERYBODY'S WORRIED ABOUT YOU.
SMILE
TP
TP
TP
TP
TP
TP

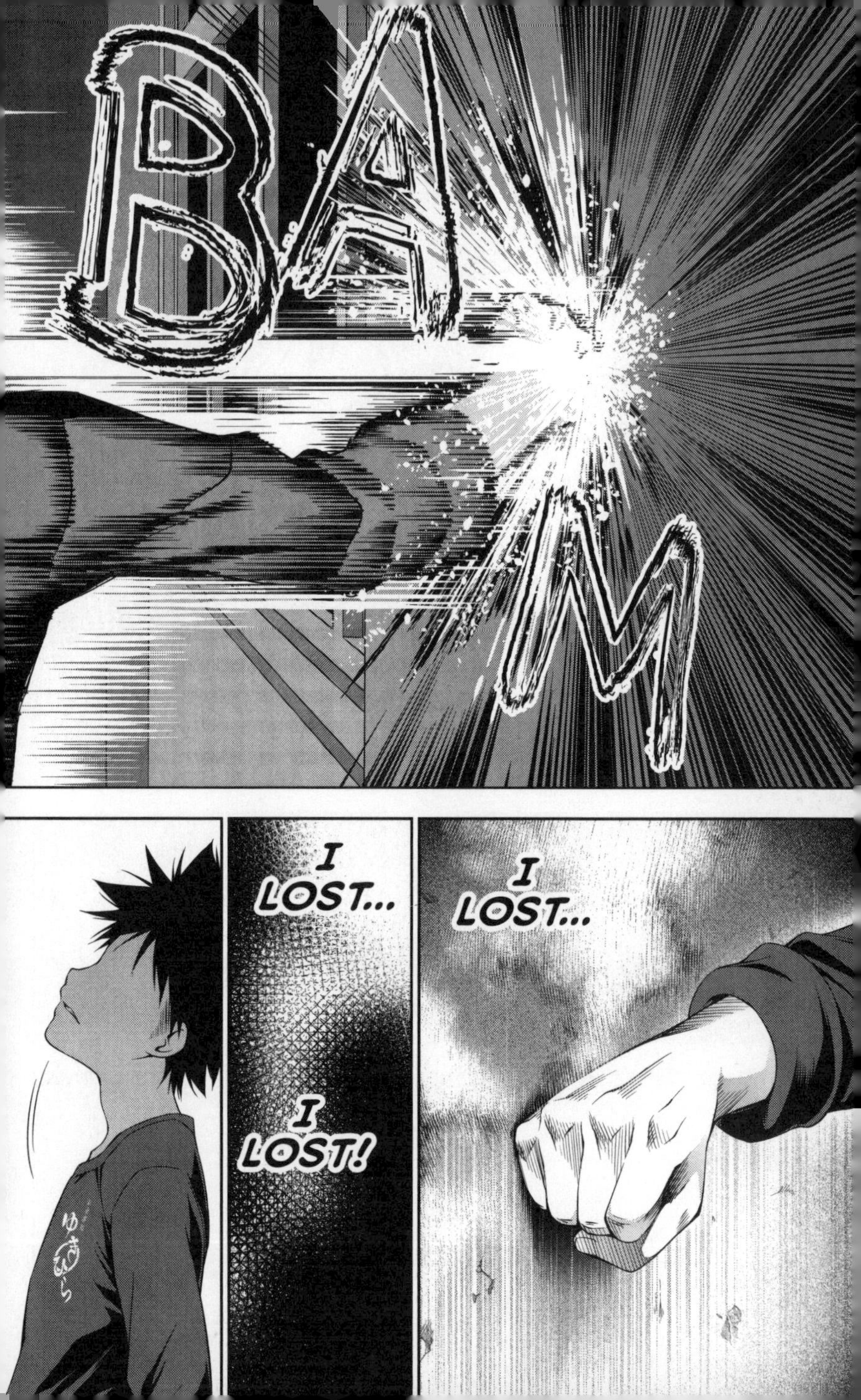
BAM
I LOST...
I LOST...
I LOST!
ゆきひら

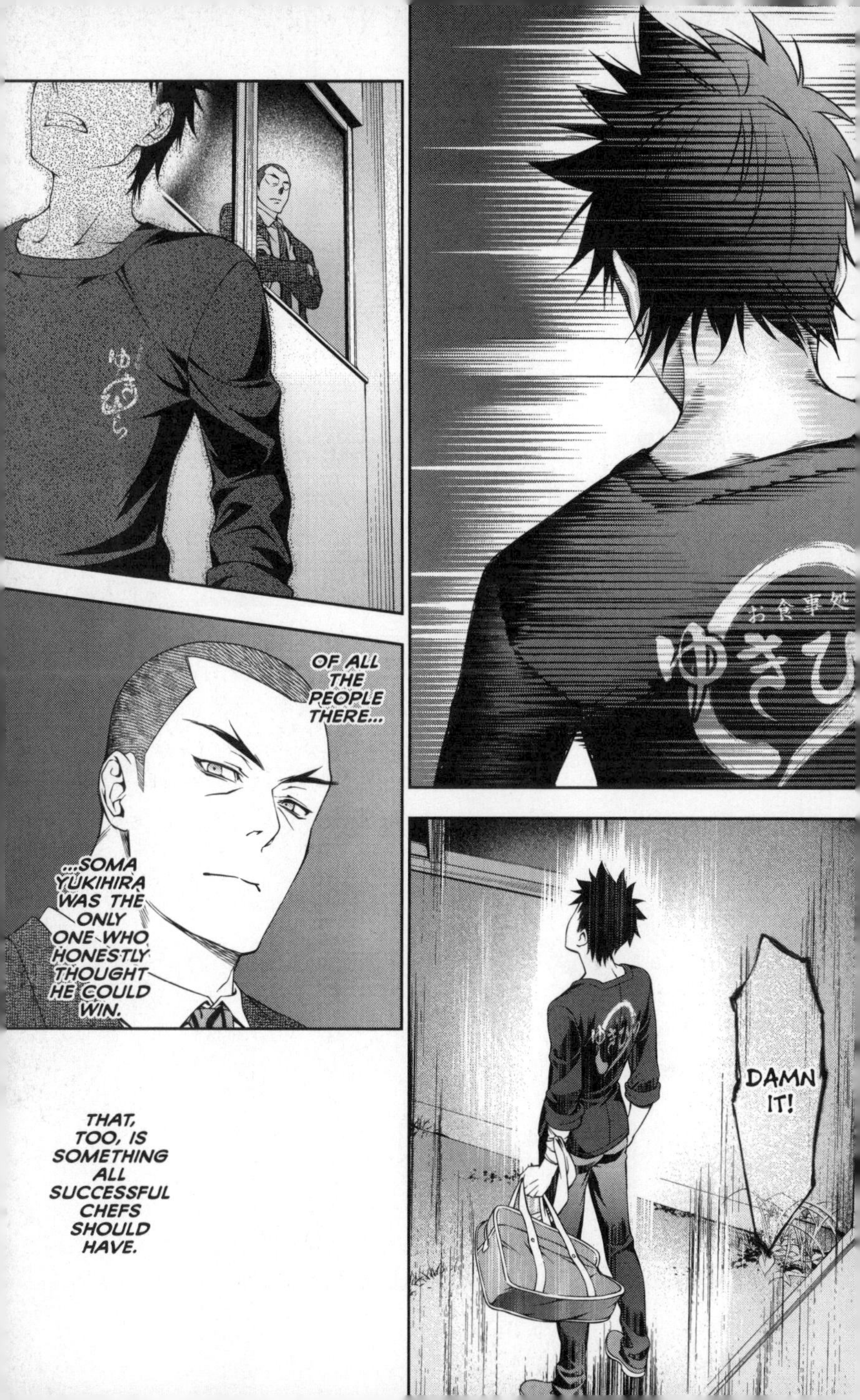
お食事処
DAMN IT!
OF ALL THE PEOPLE THERE...
...SOMA YUKIHIRA WAS THE ONLY ONE WHO HONESTLY THOUGHT HE COULD WIN.
THAT, TOO, IS SOMETHING ALL SUCCESSFUL CHEFS SHOULD HAVE.

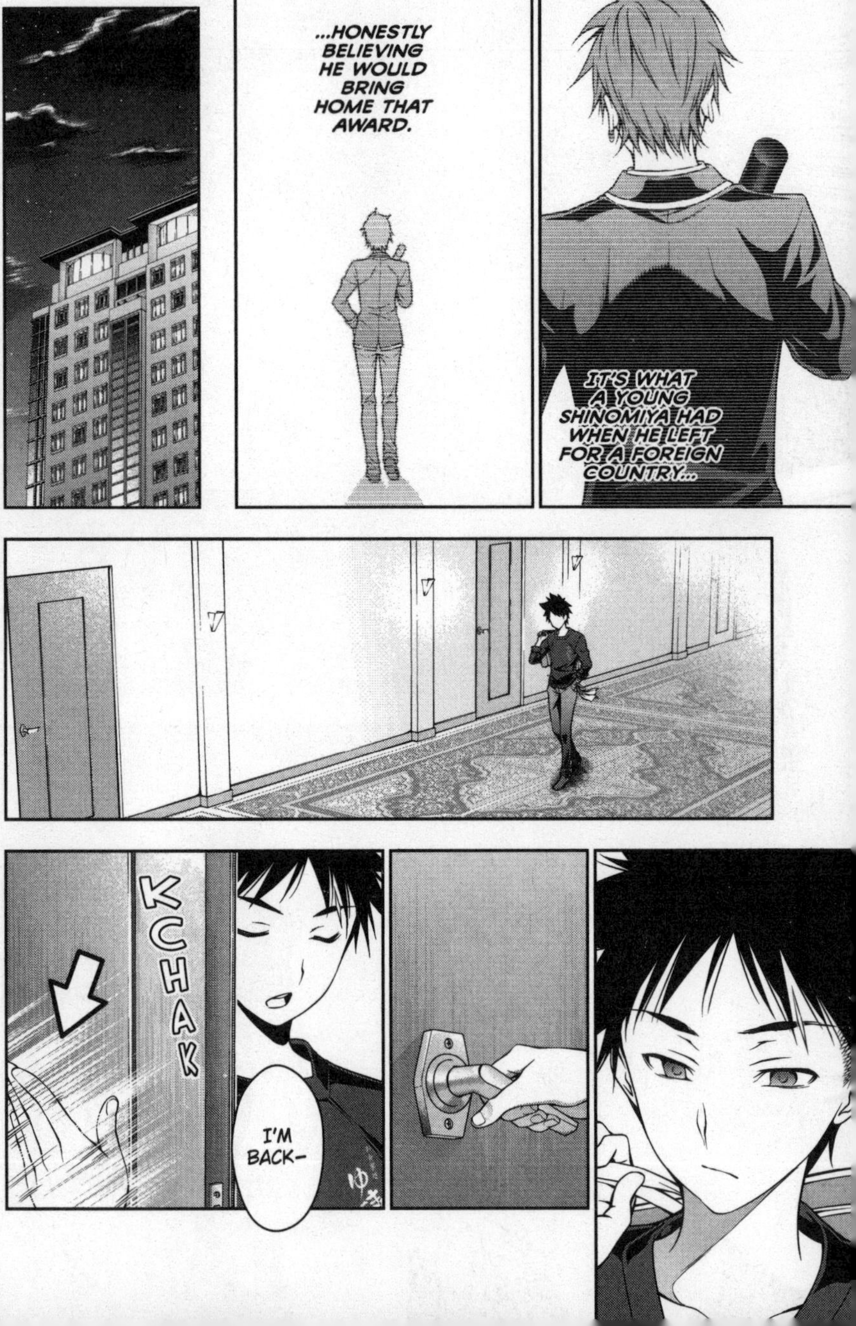
IT'S WHAT A YOUNG SHINOMIYA HAD WHEN HE LEFT FOR A FOREIGN COUNTRY...
...HONESTLY BELIEVING HE WOULD BRING HOME THAT AWARD.
I'M BACK-
KCHAK

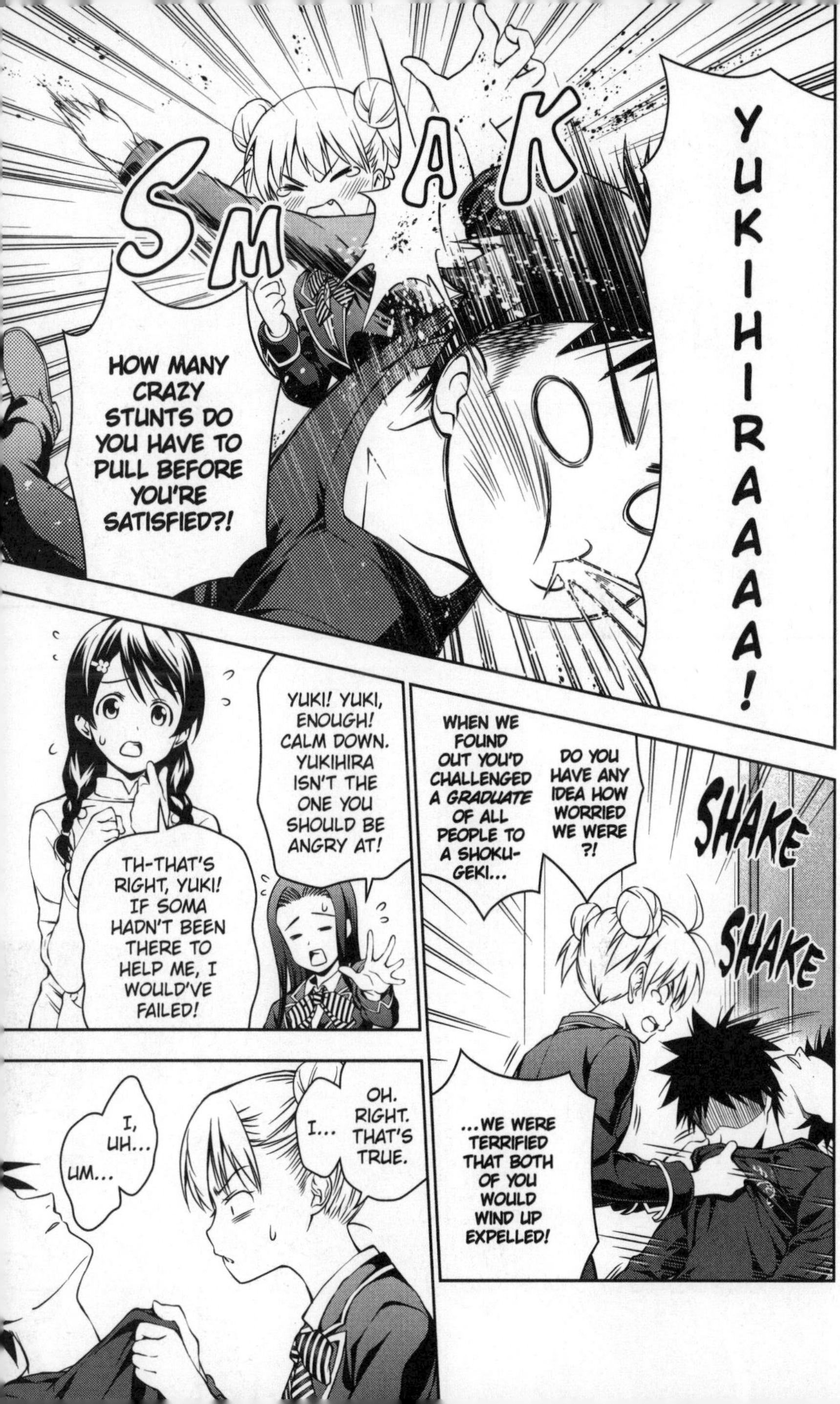
YUKIHIRAAAAA!
SMAK
HOW MANY CRAZY STUNTS DO YOU HAVE TO PULL BEFORE YOU'RE SATISFIED?!
DO YOU HAVE ANY IDEA HOW WORRIED WE WERE ?!
WHEN WE FOUND OUT YOU'D CHALLENGED A *GRADUATE* OF ALL PEOPLE TO A SHOKU-GEKI...
SHAKE
SHAKE
...WE WERE TERRIFIED THAT BOTH OF YOU WOULD WIND UP EXPELLED!
YUKI! YUKI, ENOUGH! CALM DOWN. YUKIHIRA ISN'T THE ONE YOU SHOULD BE ANGRY AT!
TH-THAT'S RIGHT, YUKI! IF SOMA HADN'T BEEN THERE TO HELP ME, I WOULD'VE FAILED!
OH. RIGHT. THAT'S TRUE.
I...
I, UH...
UM...

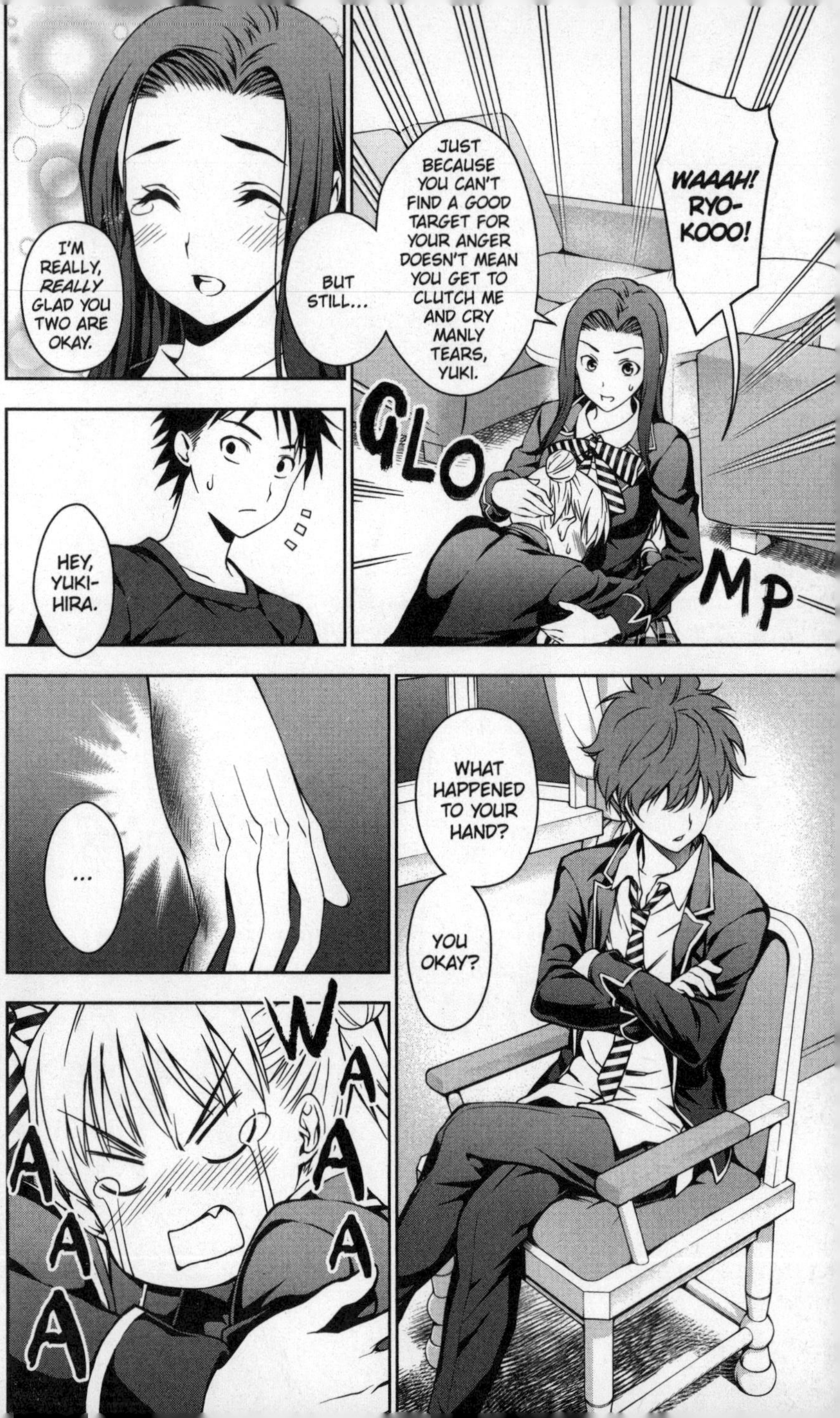
WAAAH! RYO-KOOO!
JUST BECAUSE YOU CAN'T FIND A GOOD TARGET FOR YOUR ANGER DOESN'T MEAN YOU GET TO CLUTCH ME AND CRY MANLY TEARS, YUKI.
GLOMP
BUT STILL...
I'M REALLY, *REALLY* GLAD YOU TWO ARE OKAY.
HEY, YUKI-HIRA.
WHAT HAPPENED TO YOUR HAND?
YOU OKAY?
...
WAAAAAA

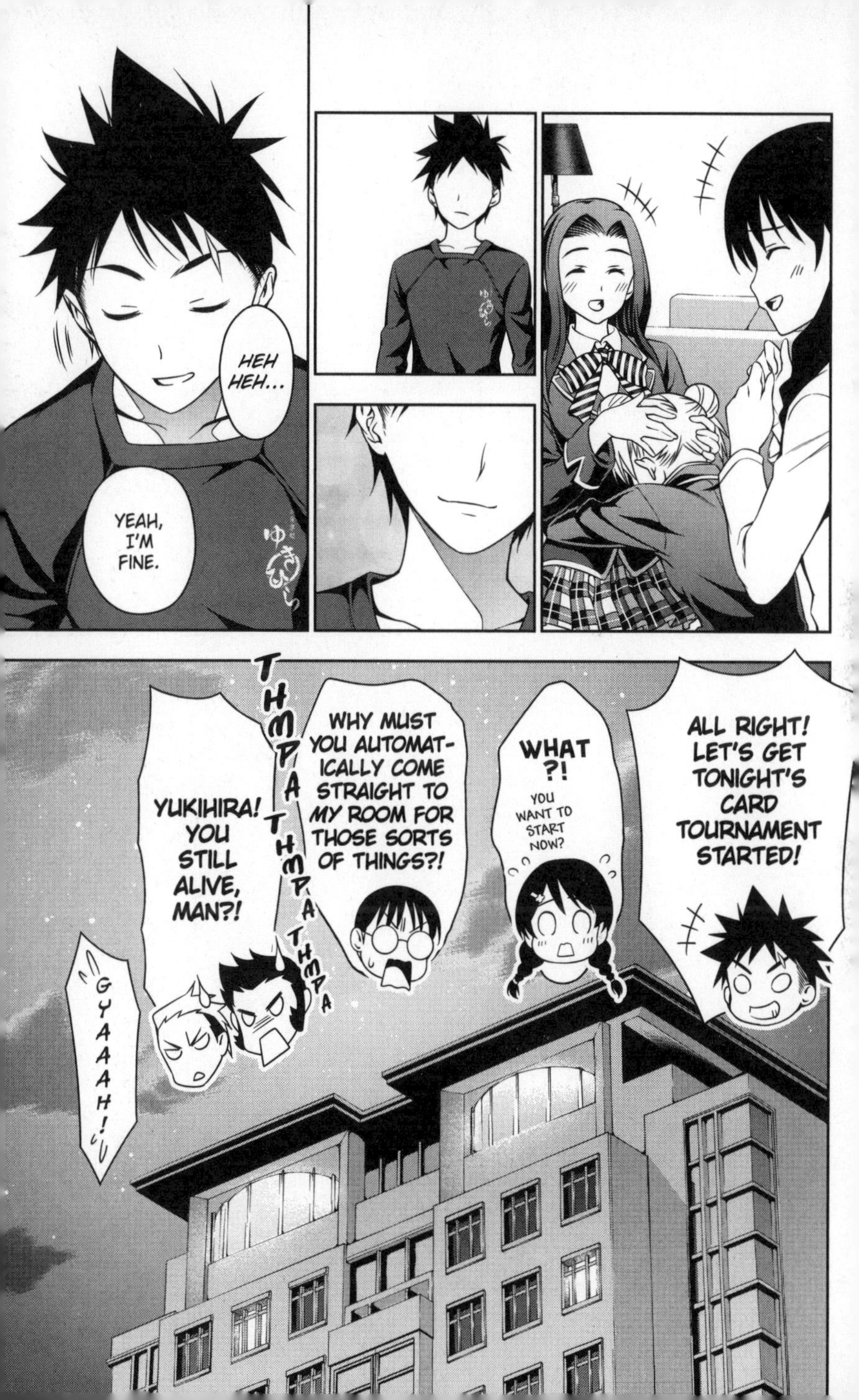
HEH HEH...
YEAH, I'M FINE.
ALL RIGHT! LET'S GET TONIGHT'S CARD TOURNAMENT STARTED!
WHAT?!
YOU WANT TO START NOW?
WHY MUST YOU AUTOMATICALLY COME STRAIGHT TO MY ROOM FOR THOSE SORTS OF THINGS?!
THMPA THMPA THMPA
YUKIHIRA! YOU STILL ALIVE, MAN?!
GYAAAAH!!

28 NO TIME FOR SLEEP

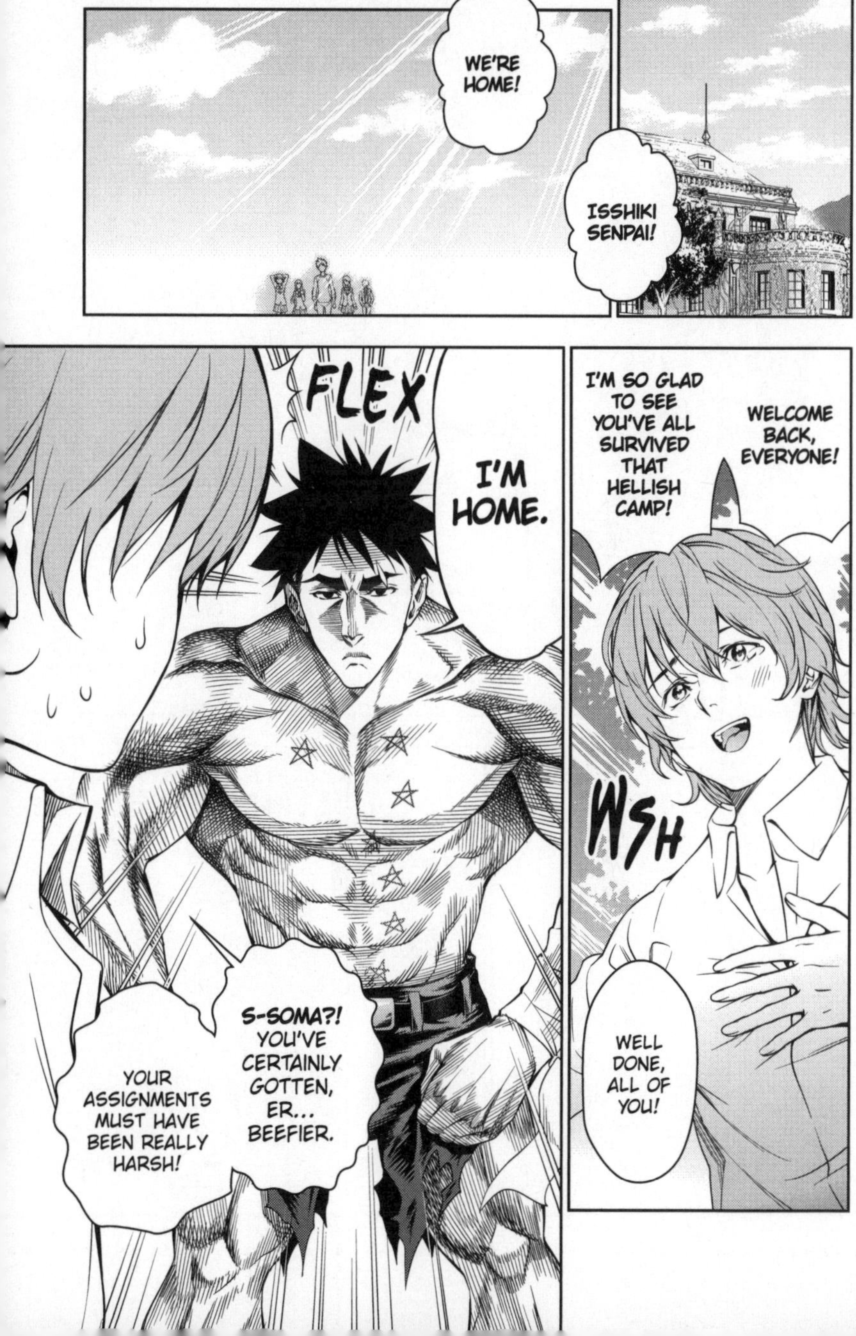
ISSHIKI SENPAI!
WE'RE HOME!
WELCOME BACK, EVERYONE!
I'M SO GLAD TO SEE YOU'VE ALL SURVIVED THAT HELLISH CAMP!
WSH
WELL DONE, ALL OF YOU!
FLEX
I'M HOME.
S-SOMA?! YOU'VE CERTAINLY GOTTEN, ER... BEEFIER.
YOUR ASSIGNMENTS MUST HAVE BEEN REALLY HARSH!

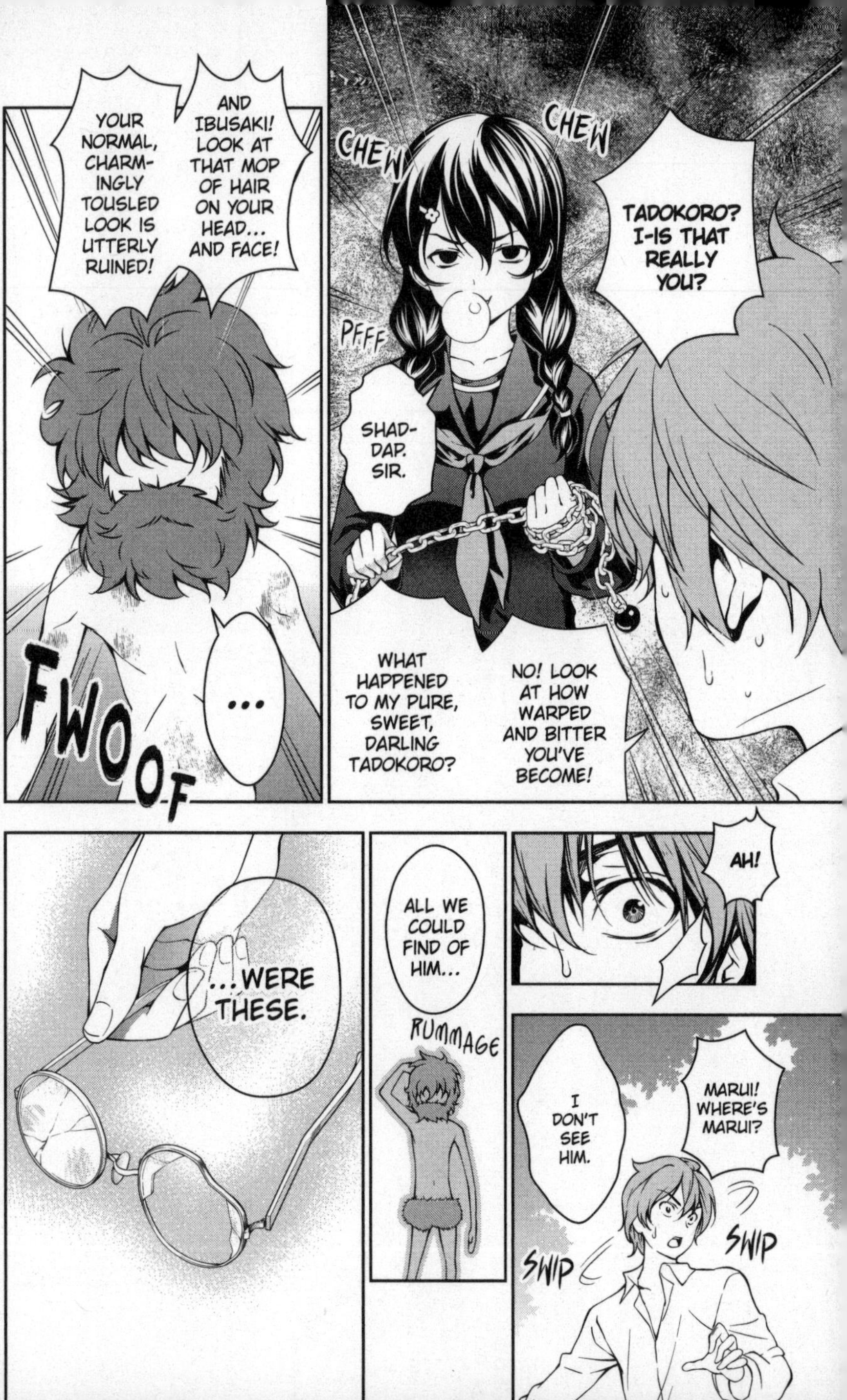
CHEW
CHEW
TADOKORO? I-IS THAT REALLY YOU?
PFFF
SHAD-DAP. SIR.
NO! LOOK AT HOW WARPED AND BITTER YOU'VE BECOME!
WHAT HAPPENED TO MY PURE, SWEET, DARLING TADOKORO?
AND IBUSAKI! LOOK AT THAT MOP OF HAIR ON YOUR HEAD... AND FACE!
YOUR NORMAL, CHARM-INGLY TOUSLED LOOK IS UTTERLY RUINED!
FWOOF
...
AH!
MARUI! WHERE'S MARUI?
I DON'T SEE HIM.
SWIP
SWIP
ALL WE COULD FIND OF HIM...
RUMMAGE
...WERE THESE.

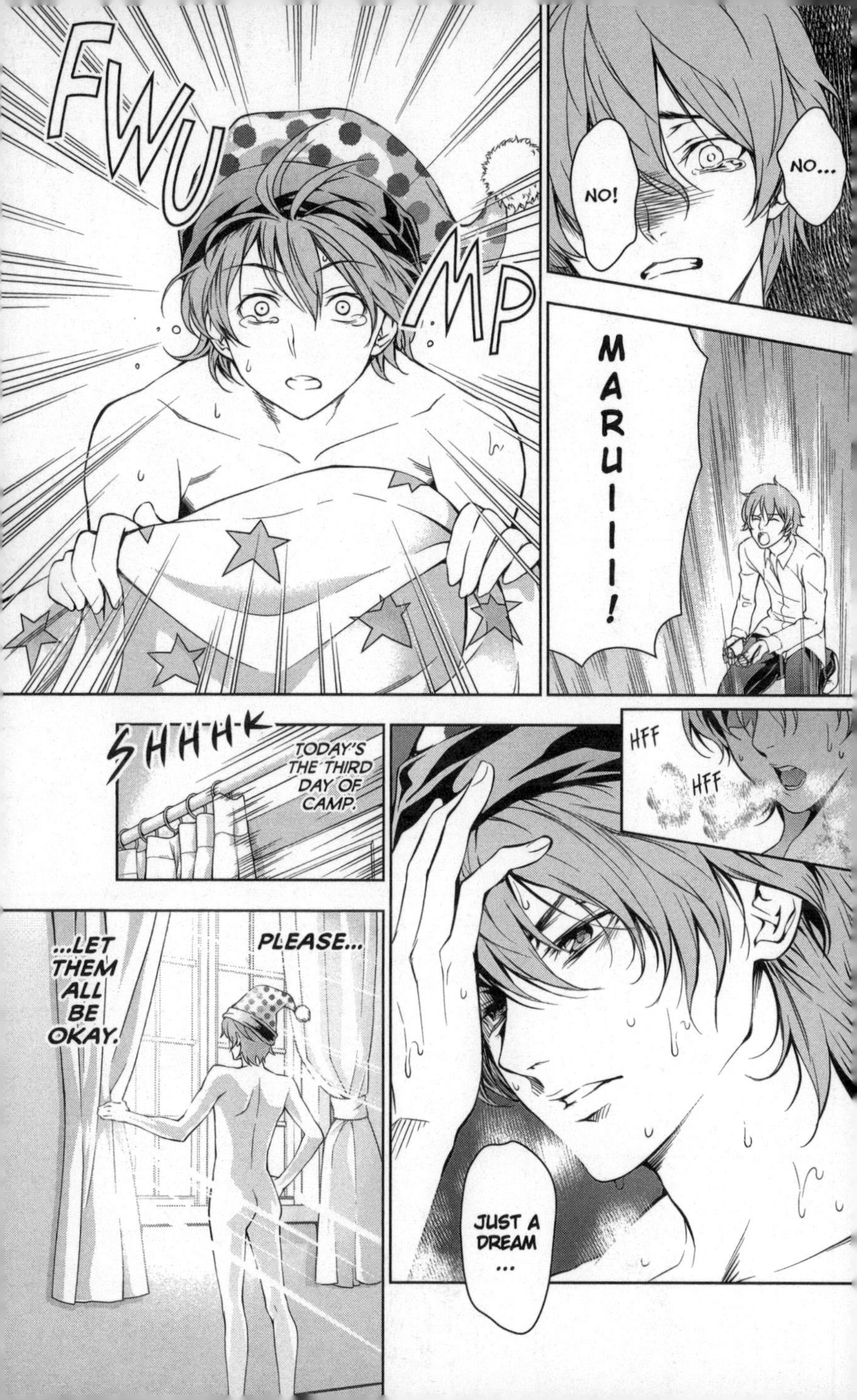
NO...
NO!
MARUIII!
FWUMP
HFF
HFF
JUST A DREAM...
SHHHK
TODAY'S THE THIRD DAY OF CAMP.
PLEASE...
...LET THEM ALL BE OKAY.

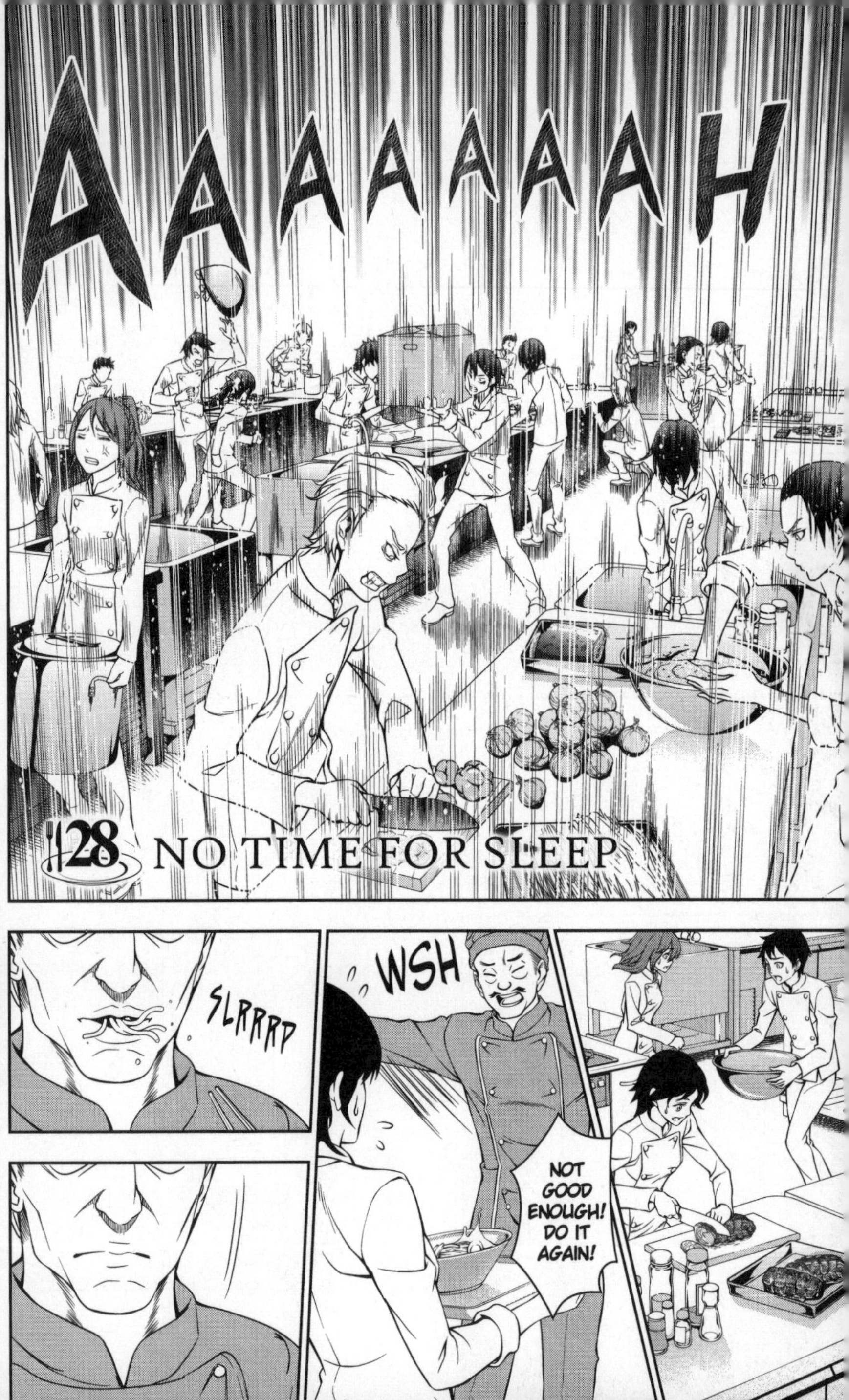
AAAAAAH
28 NO TIME FOR SLEEP
WSH
NOT GOOD ENOUGH! DO IT AGAIN!
SLRRRP

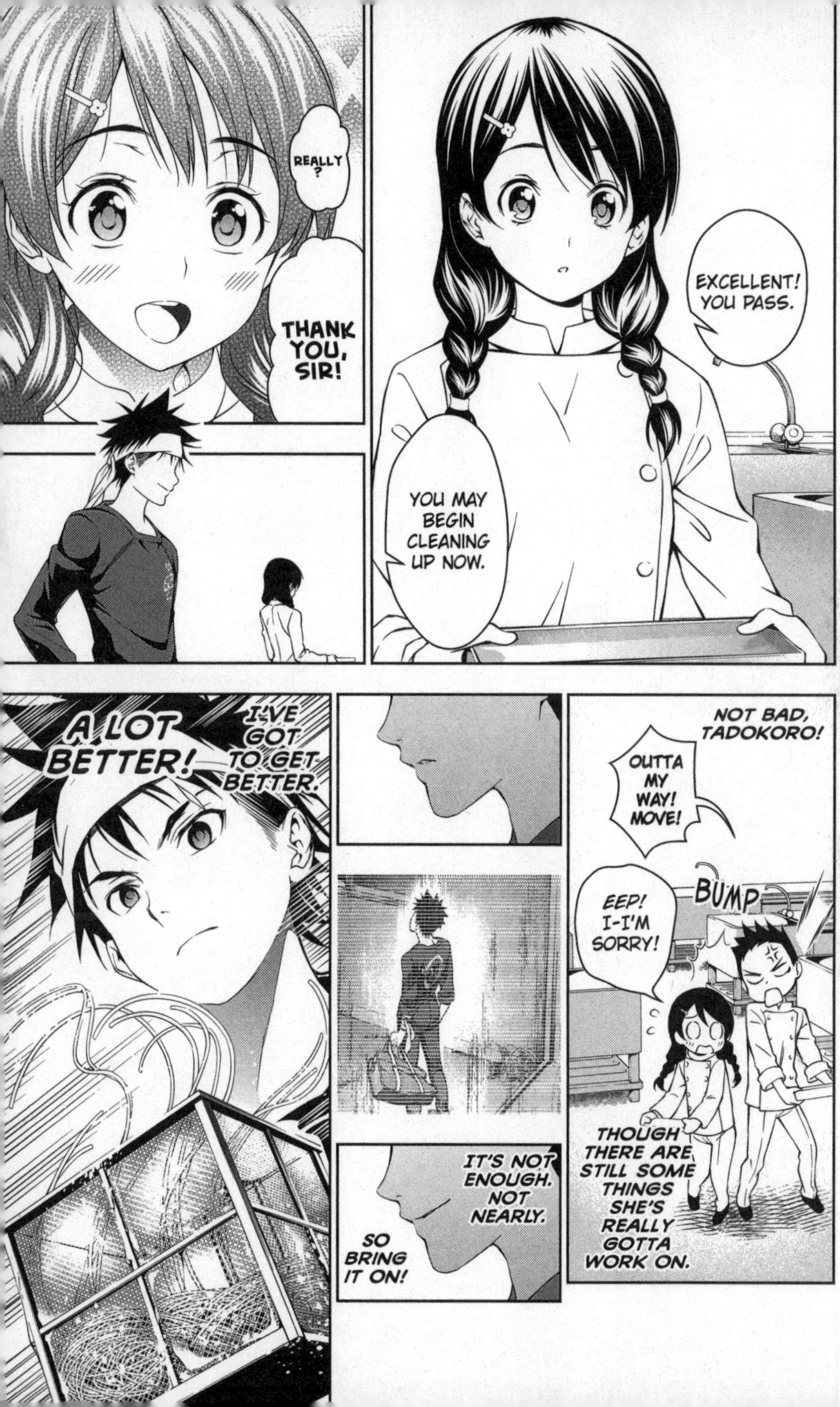
EXCELLENT! YOU PASS.
YOU MAY BEGIN CLEANING UP NOW.
REALLY?
THANK YOU, SIR!
NOT BAD, TADOKORO!
OUTTA MY WAY! MOVE!
BUMP
EEP! I-I'M SORRY!
THOUGH THERE ARE STILL SOME THINGS SHE'S REALLY GOTTA WORK ON.
IT'S NOT ENOUGH. NOT NEARLY.
SO BRING IT ON!
I'VE GOT TO GET BETTER.
A LOT BETTER!

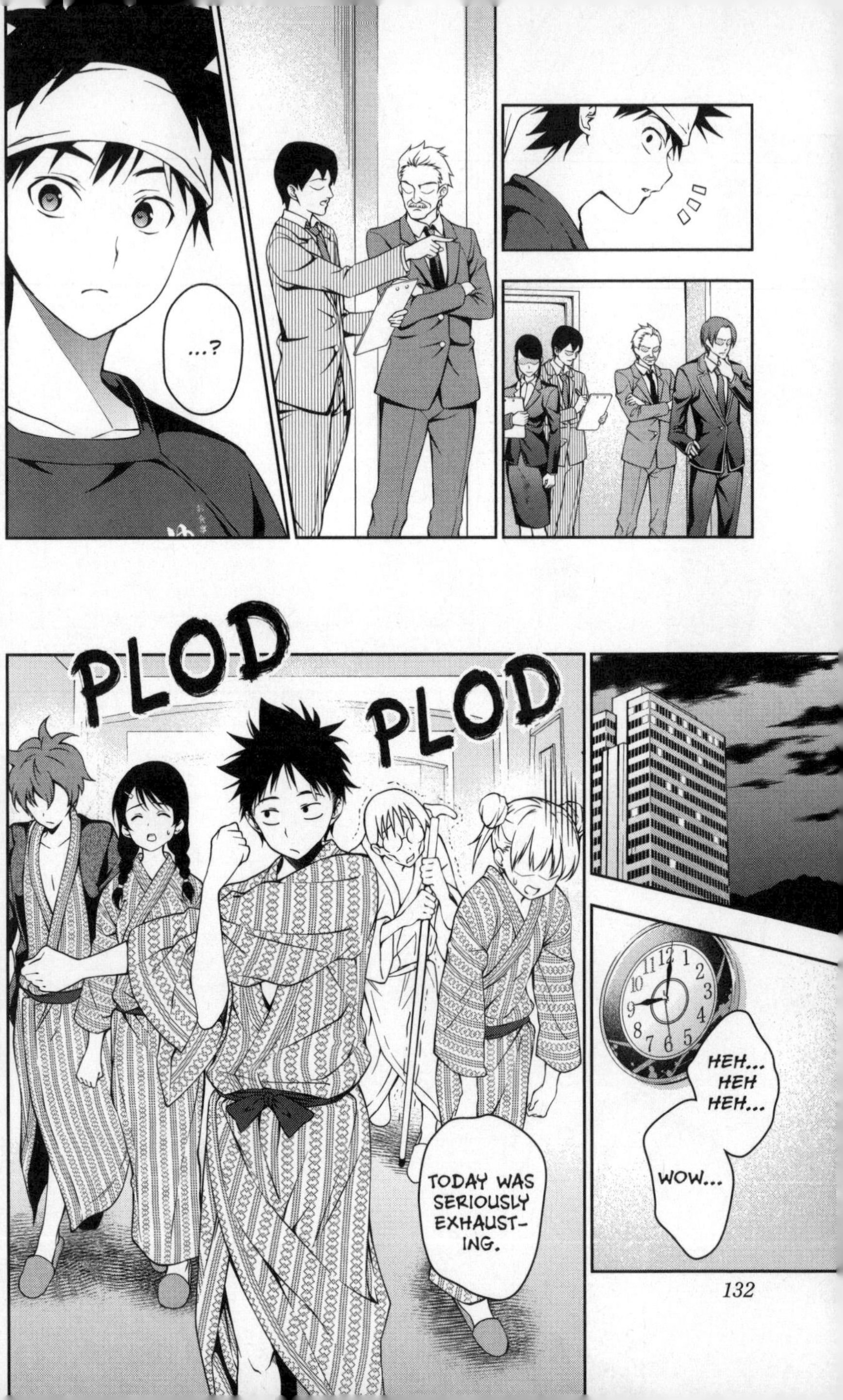
...?
HEH... HEH HEH...
WOW...
PLOD
PLOD
TODAY WAS SERIOUSLY EXHAUST-ING.

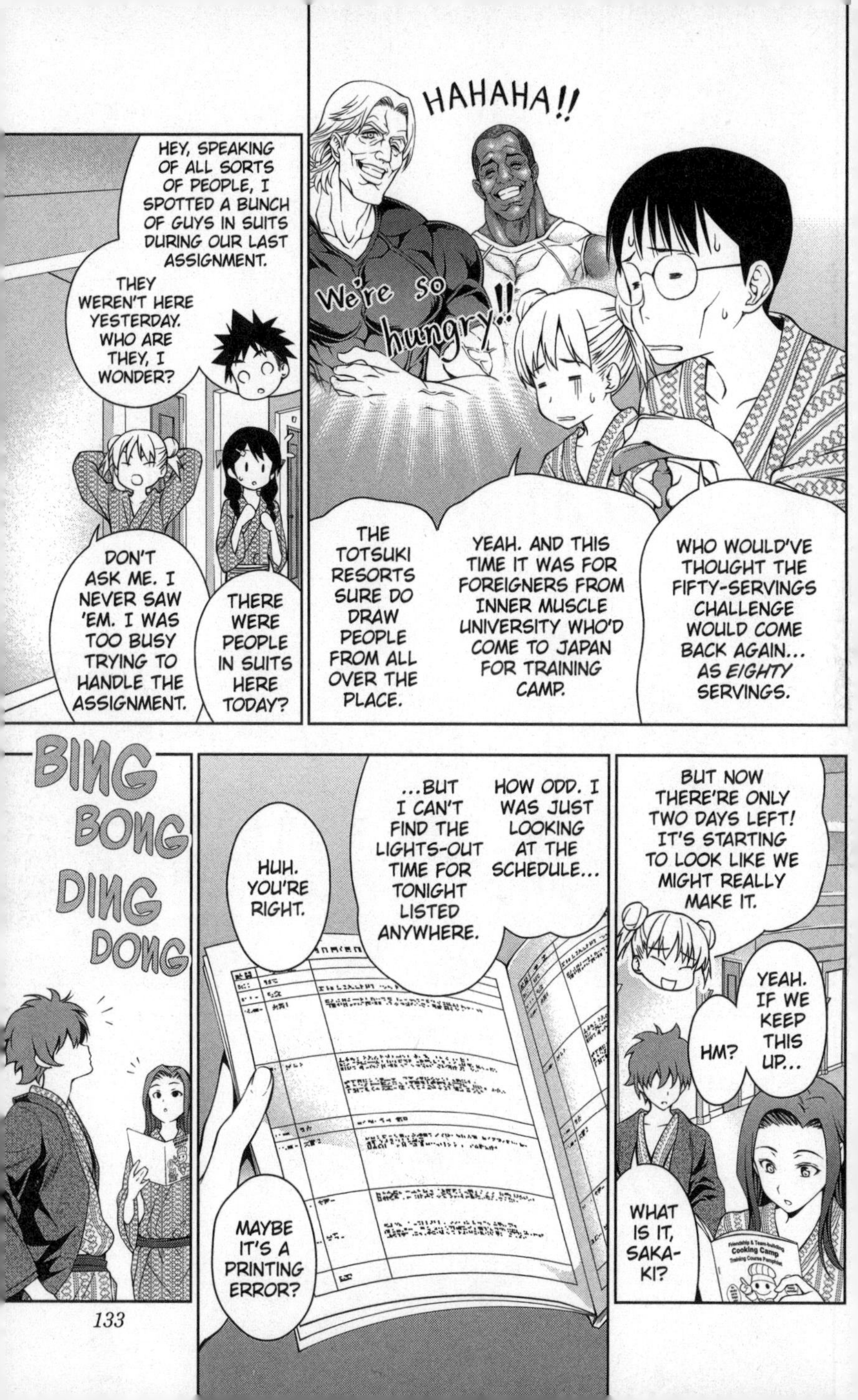

HAHAHA!!
We're so hungry!!
WHO WOULD'VE THOUGHT THE FIFTY-SERVINGS CHALLENGE WOULD COME BACK AGAIN... AS *EIGHTY* SERVINGS.
YEAH. AND THIS TIME IT WAS FOR FOREIGNERS FROM INNER MUSCLE UNIVERSITY WHO'D COME TO JAPAN FOR TRAINING CAMP.
THE TOTSUKI RESORTS SURE DO DRAW PEOPLE FROM ALL OVER THE PLACE.
HEY, SPEAKING OF ALL SORTS OF PEOPLE, I SPOTTED A BUNCH OF GUYS IN SUITS DURING OUR LAST ASSIGNMENT.
THEY WEREN'T HERE YESTERDAY. WHO ARE THEY, I WONDER?
THERE WERE PEOPLE IN SUITS HERE TODAY?
DON'T ASK ME. I NEVER SAW 'EM. I WAS TOO BUSY TRYING TO HANDLE THE ASSIGNMENT.
BUT NOW THERE'RE ONLY TWO DAYS LEFT! IT'S STARTING TO LOOK LIKE WE MIGHT REALLY MAKE IT.
YEAH. IF WE KEEP THIS UP...
HM?
WHAT IS IT, SAKAKI?
HOW ODD. I WAS JUST LOOKING AT THE SCHEDULE...
...BUT I CAN'T FIND THE LIGHTS-OUT TIME FOR TONIGHT LISTED ANYWHERE.
HUH. YOU'RE RIGHT.
MAYBE IT'S A PRINTING ERROR?
BING BONG
DING DONG

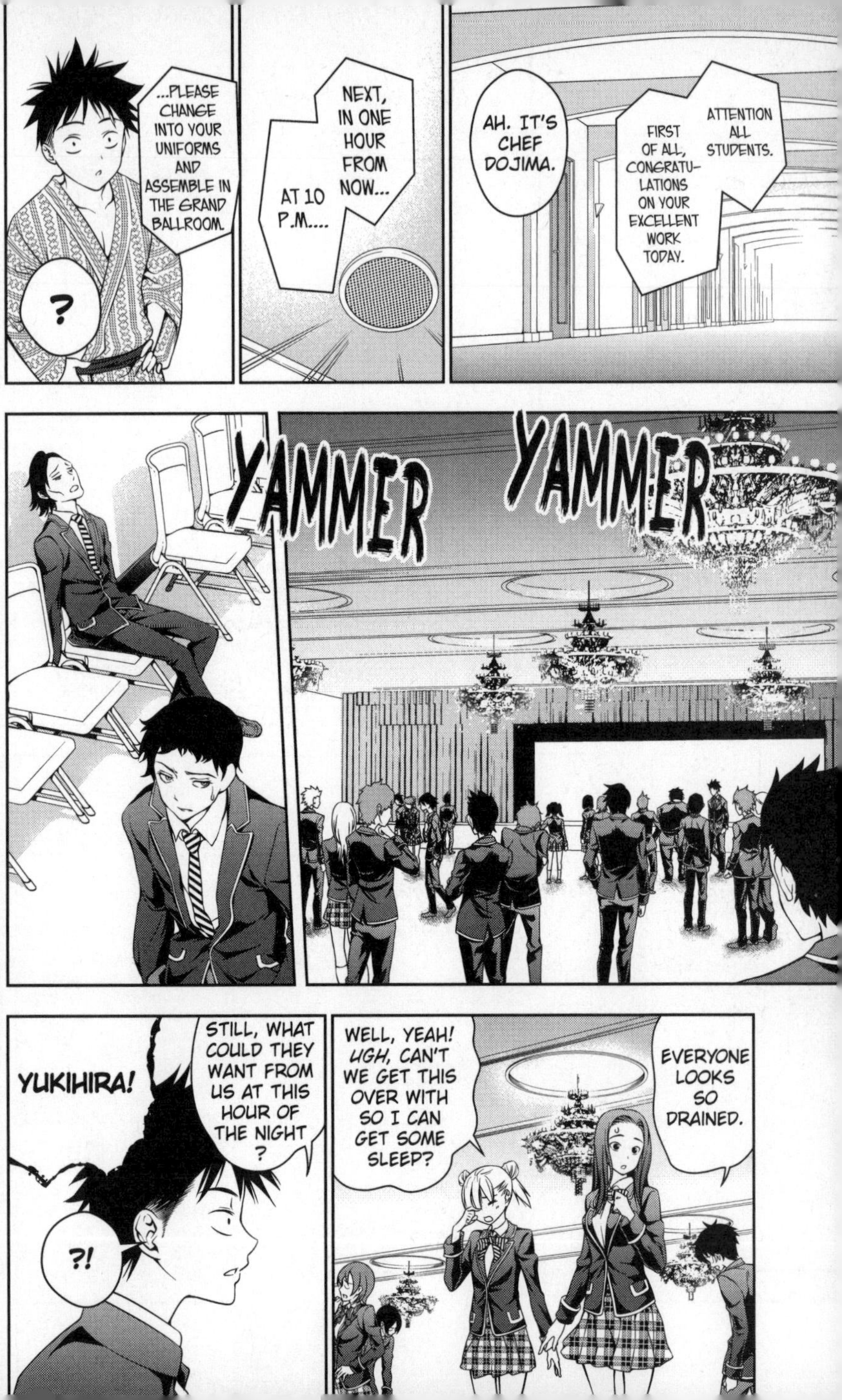
ATTENTION ALL STUDENTS.
FIRST OF ALL, CONGRATULATIONS ON YOUR EXCELLENT WORK TODAY.
AH. IT'S CHEF DOJIMA.
NEXT, IN ONE HOUR FROM NOW...
AT 10 P.M....
...PLEASE CHANGE INTO YOUR UNIFORMS AND ASSEMBLE IN THE GRAND BALLROOM.
?
YAMMER
YAMMER
EVERYONE LOOKS SO DRAINED.
WELL, YEAH! *UGH*, CAN'T WE GET THIS OVER WITH SO I CAN GET SOME SLEEP?
STILL, WHAT COULD THEY WANT FROM US AT THIS HOUR OF THE NIGHT?
YUKIHIRA!
?!

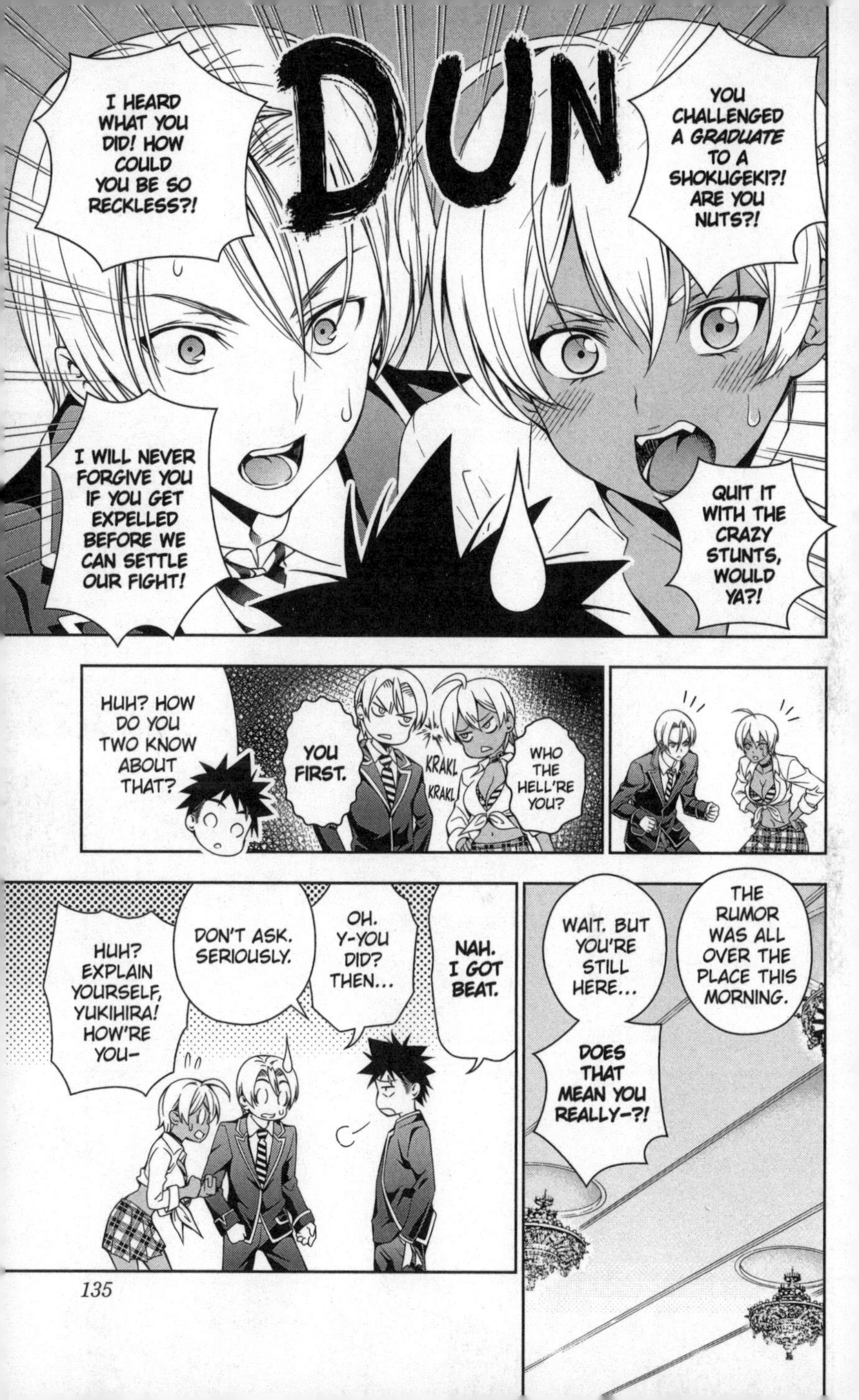
YOU CHALLENGED A GRADUATE TO A SHOKUGEKI?! ARE YOU NUTS?!
DUN
I HEARD WHAT YOU DID! HOW COULD YOU BE SO RECKLESS?!
QUIT IT WITH THE CRAZY STUNTS, WOULD YA?!
I WILL NEVER FORGIVE YOU IF YOU GET EXPELLED BEFORE WE CAN SETTLE OUR FIGHT!
HUH? HOW DO YOU TWO KNOW ABOUT THAT?
WHO THE HELL'RE YOU?
KRAKL KRAKL
YOU FIRST.
THE RUMOR WAS ALL OVER THE PLACE THIS MORNING.
WAIT. BUT YOU'RE STILL HERE...
DOES THAT MEAN YOU REALLY-?!
NAH. I GOT BEAT.
OH. Y-YOU DID? THEN...
HUH? EXPLAIN YOURSELF, YUKIHIRA! HOW'RE YOU-
DON'T ASK. SERIOUSLY.

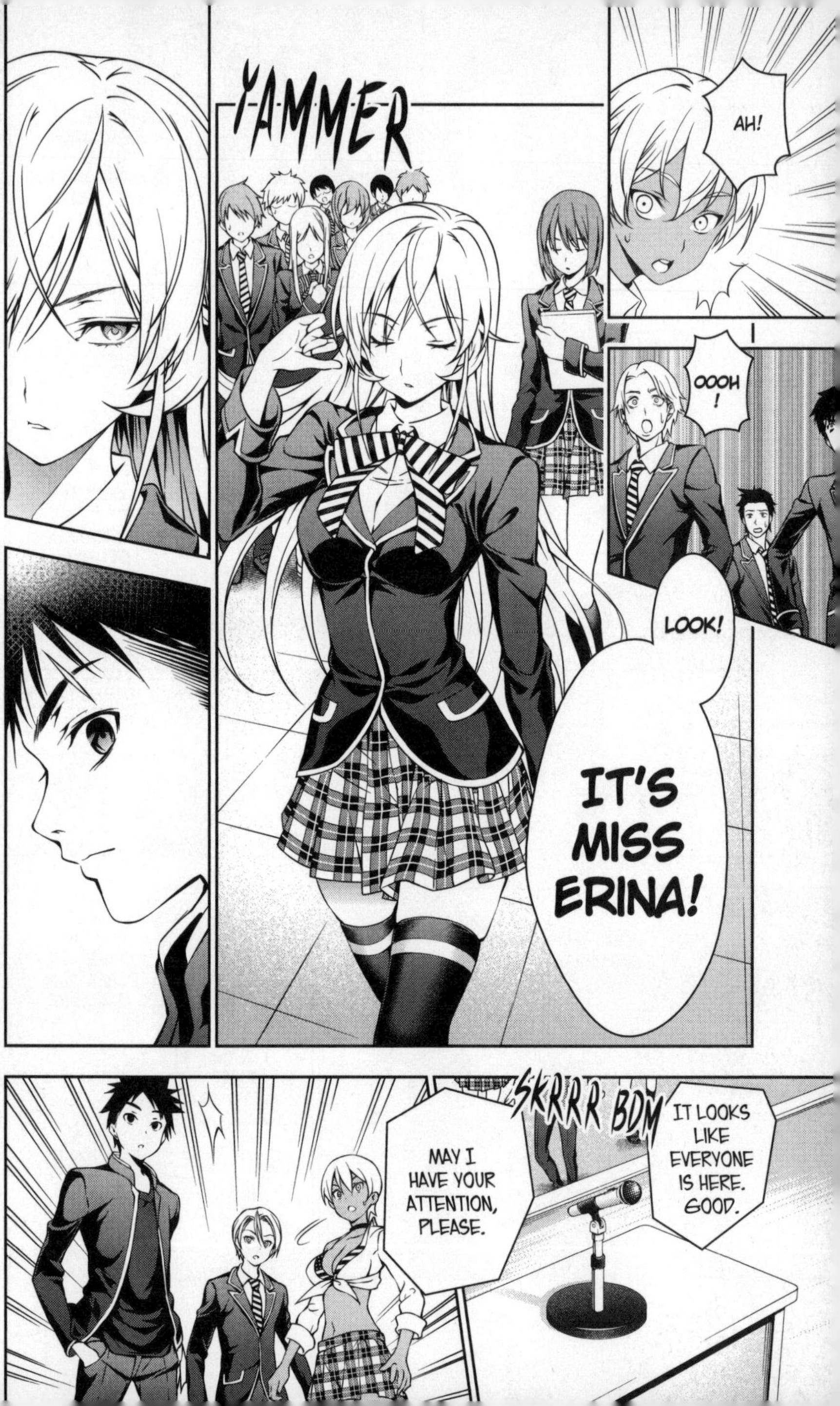
AH!
OOOH!
YAMMER
LOOK!
IT'S MISS ERINA!
SKRRR BDM
IT LOOKS LIKE EVERYONE IS HERE. GOOD.
MAY I HAVE YOUR ATTENTION, PLEASE.

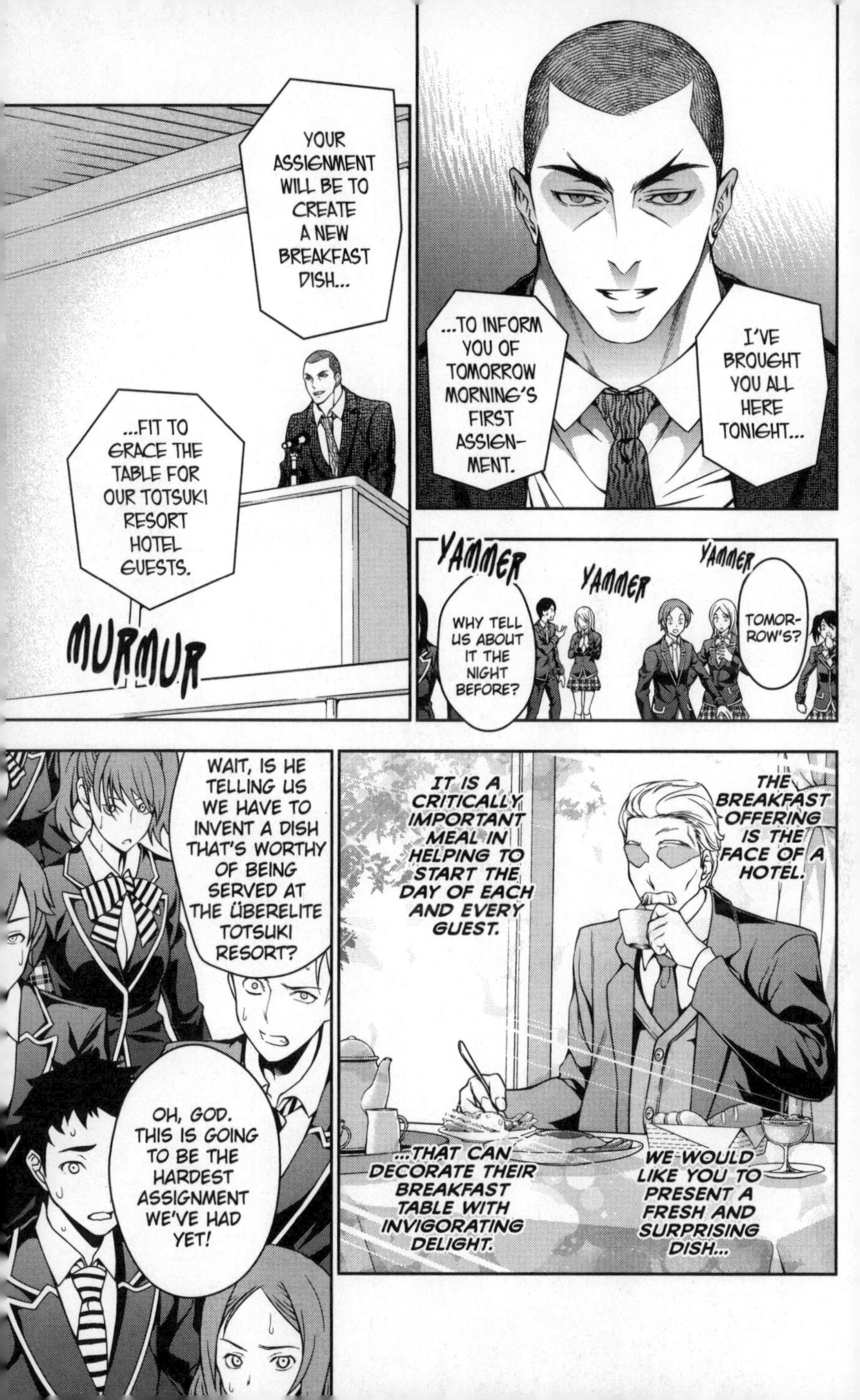

I'VE BROUGHT YOU ALL HERE TONIGHT...
...TO INFORM YOU OF TOMORROW MORNING'S FIRST ASSIGNMENT.
YAMMER
TOMORROW'S?
YAMMER
YAMMER
WHY TELL US ABOUT IT THE NIGHT BEFORE?
YOUR ASSIGNMENT WILL BE TO CREATE A NEW BREAKFAST DISH...
...FIT TO GRACE THE TABLE FOR OUR TOTSUKI RESORT HOTEL GUESTS.
MURMUR
THE BREAKFAST OFFERING IS THE FACE OF A HOTEL.
IT IS A CRITICALLY IMPORTANT MEAL IN HELPING TO START THE DAY OF EACH AND EVERY GUEST.
WE WOULD LIKE YOU TO PRESENT A FRESH AND SURPRISING DISH...
...THAT CAN DECORATE THEIR BREAKFAST TABLE WITH INVIGORATING DELIGHT.
WAIT, IS HE TELLING US WE HAVE TO INVENT A DISH THAT'S WORTHY OF BEING SERVED AT THE ÜBERELITE TOTSUKI RESORT?
OH, GOD. THIS IS GOING TO BE THE HARDEST ASSIGNMENT WE'VE HAD YET!

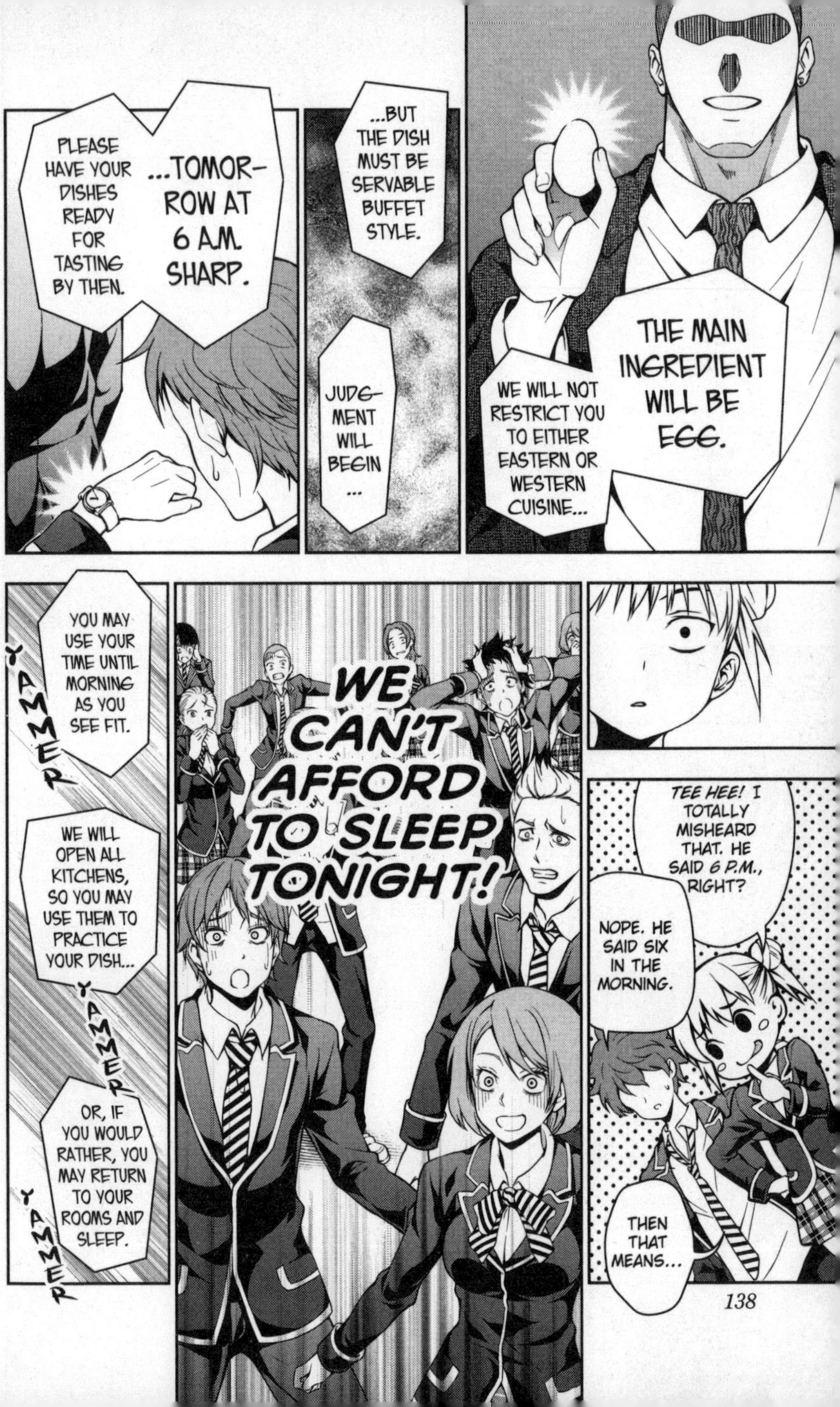
THE MAIN INGREDIENT WILL BE EGG.
WE WILL NOT RESTRICT YOU TO EITHER EASTERN OR WESTERN CUISINE...
...BUT THE DISH MUST BE SERVABLE BUFFET STYLE.
JUDGMENT WILL BEGIN ...
...TOMORROW AT 6 A.M. SHARP.
PLEASE HAVE YOUR DISHES READY FOR TASTING BY THEN.
TEE HEE! I TOTALLY MISHEARD THAT. HE SAID 6 P.M., RIGHT?
NOPE. HE SAID SIX IN THE MORNING.
THEN THAT MEANS...
WE CAN'T AFFORD TO SLEEP TONIGHT!
YOU MAY USE YOUR TIME UNTIL MORNING AS YOU SEE FIT.
YAMMER
WE WILL OPEN ALL KITCHENS, SO YOU MAY USE THEM TO PRACTICE YOUR DISH...
YAMMER
OR, IF YOU WOULD RATHER, YOU MAY RETURN TO YOUR ROOMS AND SLEEP.
YAMMER

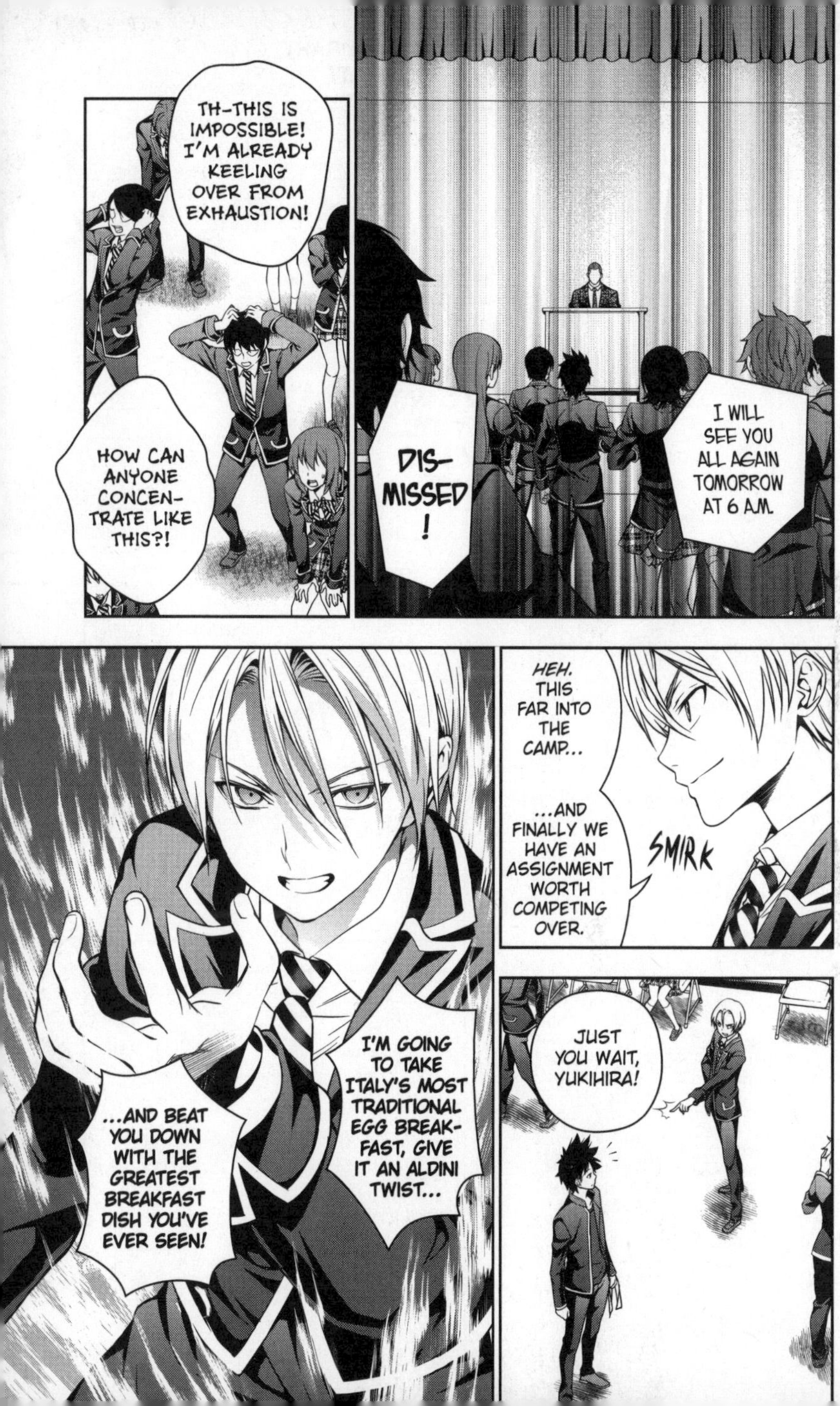
I WILL SEE YOU ALL AGAIN TOMORROW AT 6 A.M.
DIS-MISSED!
TH-THIS IS IMPOSSIBLE! I'M ALREADY KEELING OVER FROM EXHAUSTION!
HOW CAN ANYONE CONCEN-TRATE LIKE THIS?!
HEH. THIS FAR INTO THE CAMP...
...AND FINALLY WE HAVE AN ASSIGNMENT WORTH COMPETING OVER.
SMIRK
JUST YOU WAIT, YUKIHIRA!
I'M GOING TO TAKE ITALY'S MOST TRADITIONAL EGG BREAK-FAST, GIVE IT AN ALDINI TWIST...
...AND BEAT YOU DOWN WITH THE GREATEST BREAKFAST DISH YOU'VE EVER SEEN!

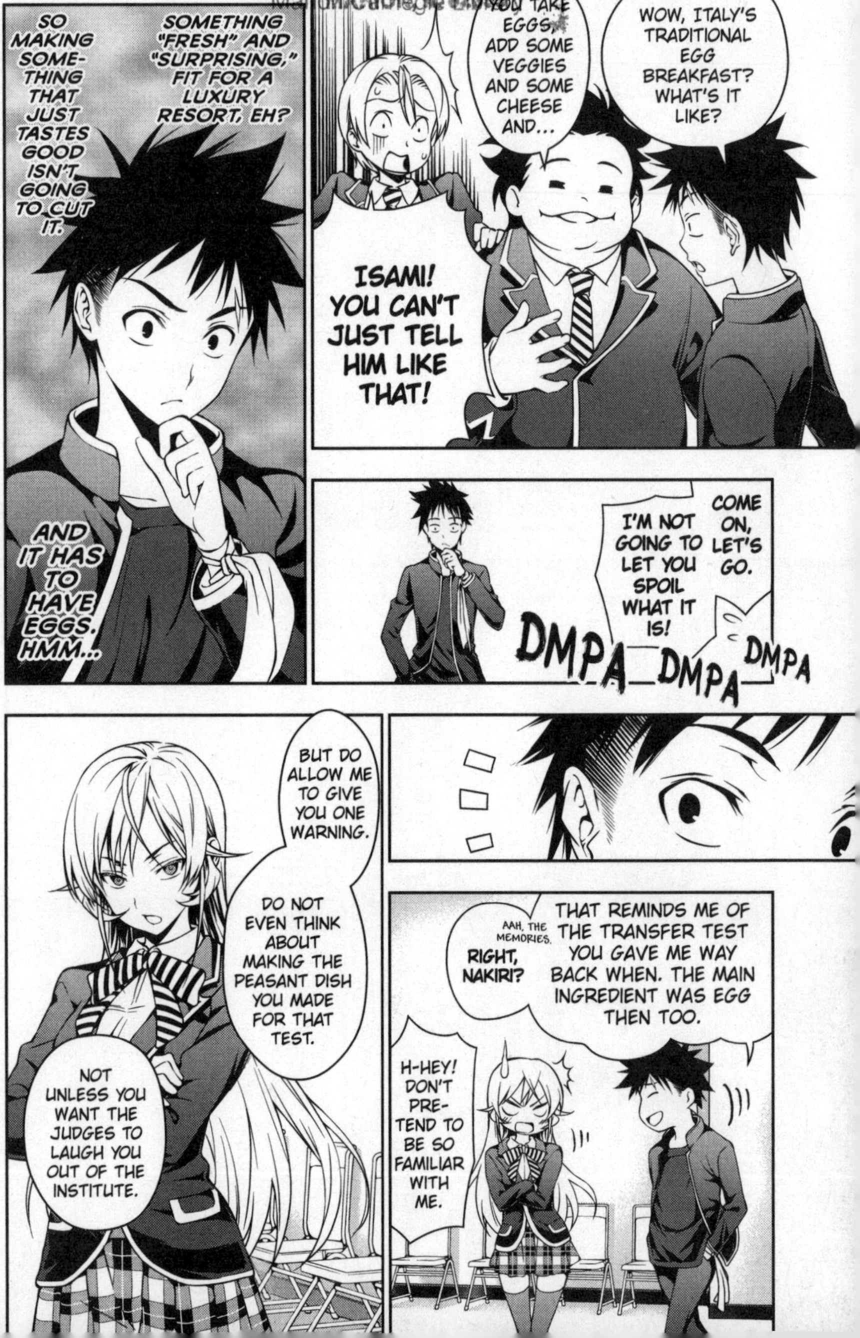
WOW, ITALY'S TRADITIONAL EGG BREAKFAST? WHAT'S IT LIKE?
YOU TAKE EGGS, ADD SOME VEGGIES AND SOME CHEESE AND...
ISAMI! YOU CAN'T JUST TELL HIM LIKE THAT!
COME ON, LET'S GO.
I'M NOT GOING TO LET YOU SPOIL WHAT IT IS!
DMPA DMPA DMPA
SOMETHING "FRESH" AND "SURPRISING," FIT FOR A LUXURY RESORT, EH?
SO MAKING SOME-THING THAT JUST TASTES GOOD ISN'T GOING TO CUT IT.
AND IT HAS TO HAVE EGGS. HMM...
THAT REMINDS ME OF THE TRANSFER TEST YOU GAVE ME WAY BACK WHEN. THE MAIN INGREDIENT WAS EGG THEN TOO.
AAH, THE MEMORIES.
RIGHT, NAKIRI?
H-HEY! DON'T PRE-TEND TO BE SO FAMILIAR WITH ME.
BUT DO ALLOW ME TO GIVE YOU ONE WARNING.
DO NOT EVEN THINK ABOUT MAKING THE PEASANT DISH YOU MADE FOR THAT TEST.
NOT UNLESS YOU WANT THE JUDGES TO LAUGH YOU OUT OF THE INSTITUTE.

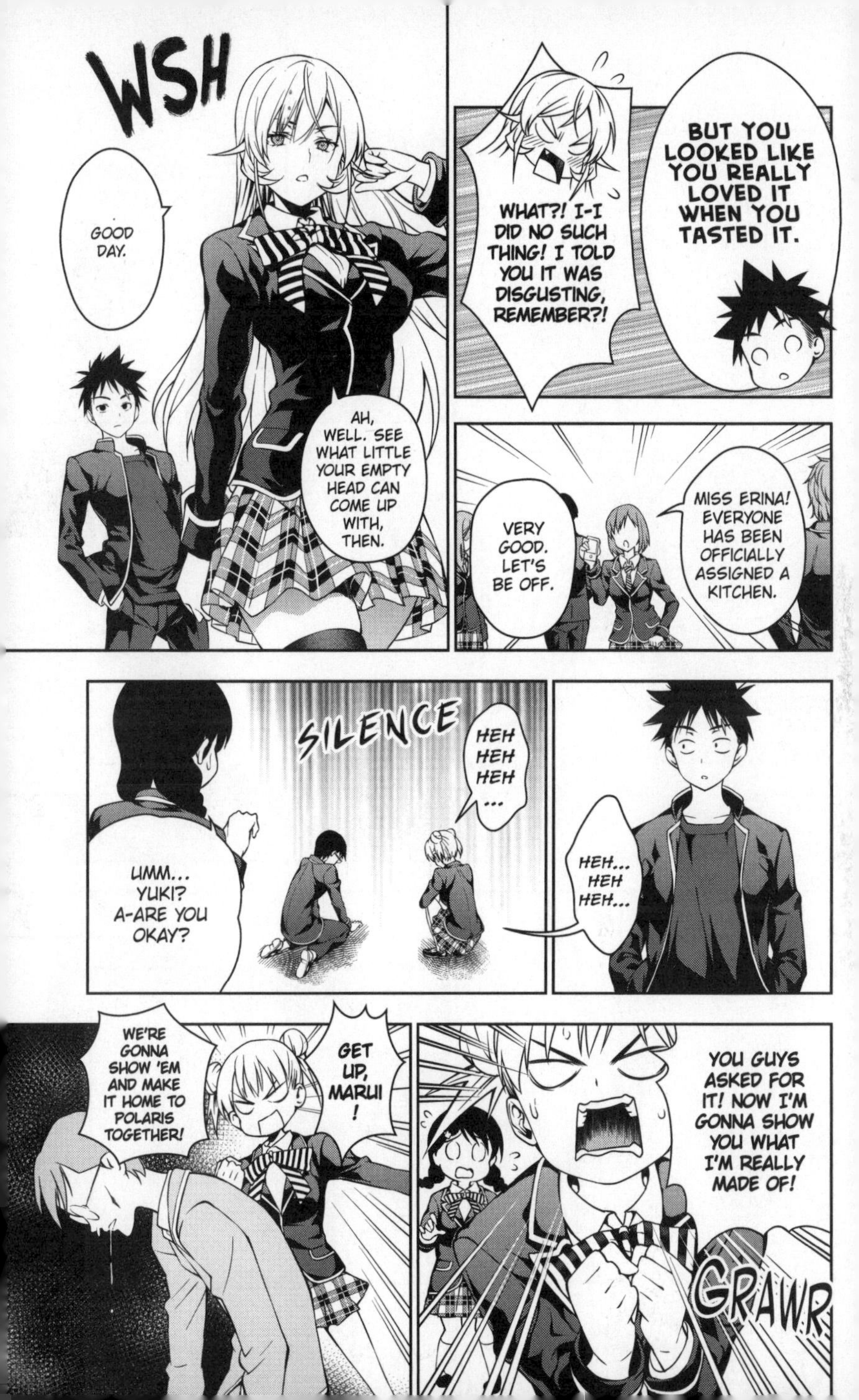
BUT YOU LOOKED LIKE YOU REALLY LOVED IT WHEN YOU TASTED IT.
WHAT?! I-I DID NO SUCH THING! I TOLD YOU IT WAS DISGUSTING, REMEMBER?!
MISS ERINA! EVERYONE HAS BEEN OFFICIALLY ASSIGNED A KITCHEN.
VERY GOOD. LET'S BE OFF.
AH, WELL. SEE WHAT LITTLE YOUR EMPTY HEAD CAN COME UP WITH, THEN.
WSH
GOOD DAY.
HEH... HEH HEH...
HEH HEH HEH ...
SILENCE
UMM... YUKI? A-ARE YOU OKAY?
YOU GUYS ASKED FOR IT! NOW I'M GONNA SHOW YOU WHAT I'M REALLY MADE OF!
GRAWR
GET UP, MARUI!
WE'RE GONNA SHOW 'EM AND MAKE IT HOME TO POLARIS TOGETHER!

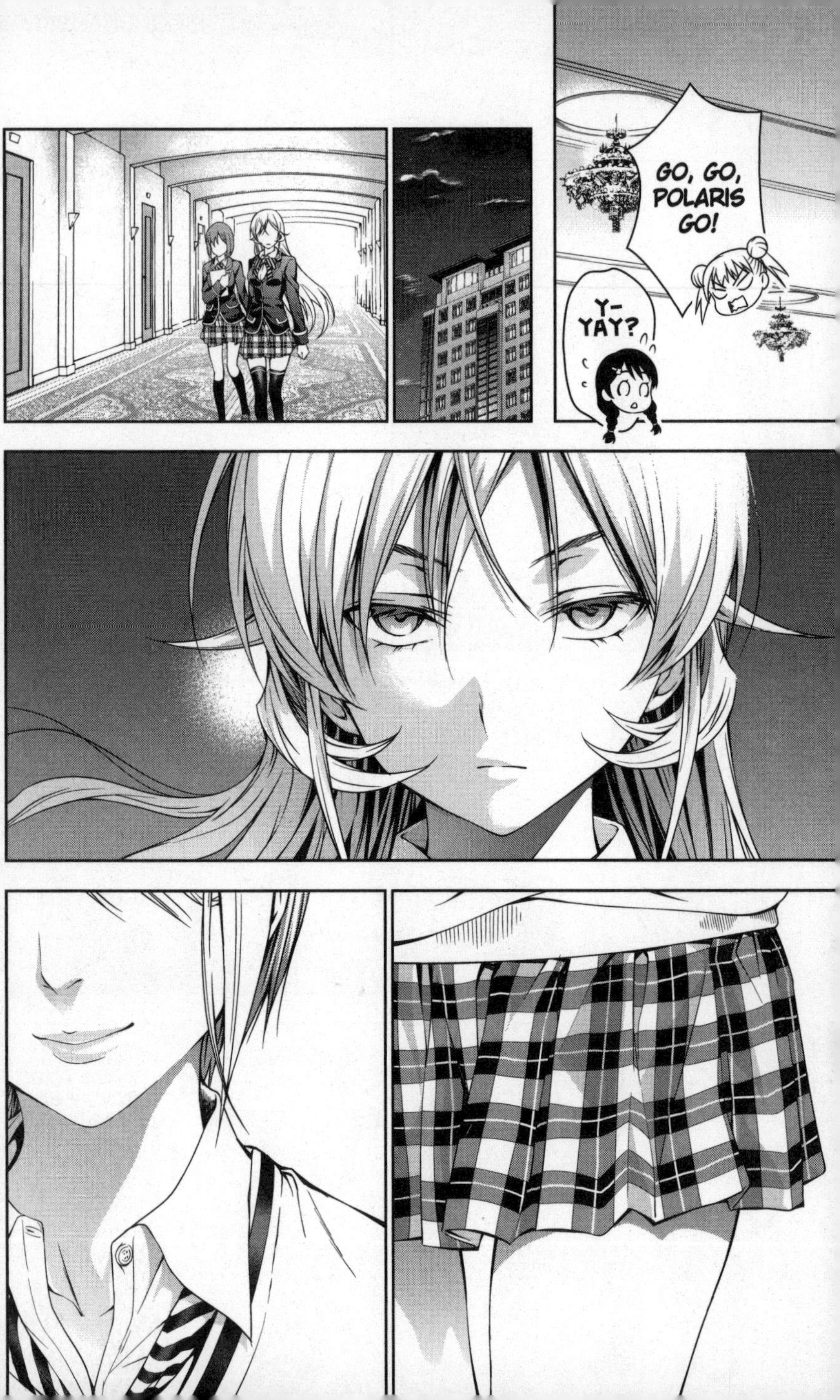
GO, GO, POLARIS GO!
Y- YAY?

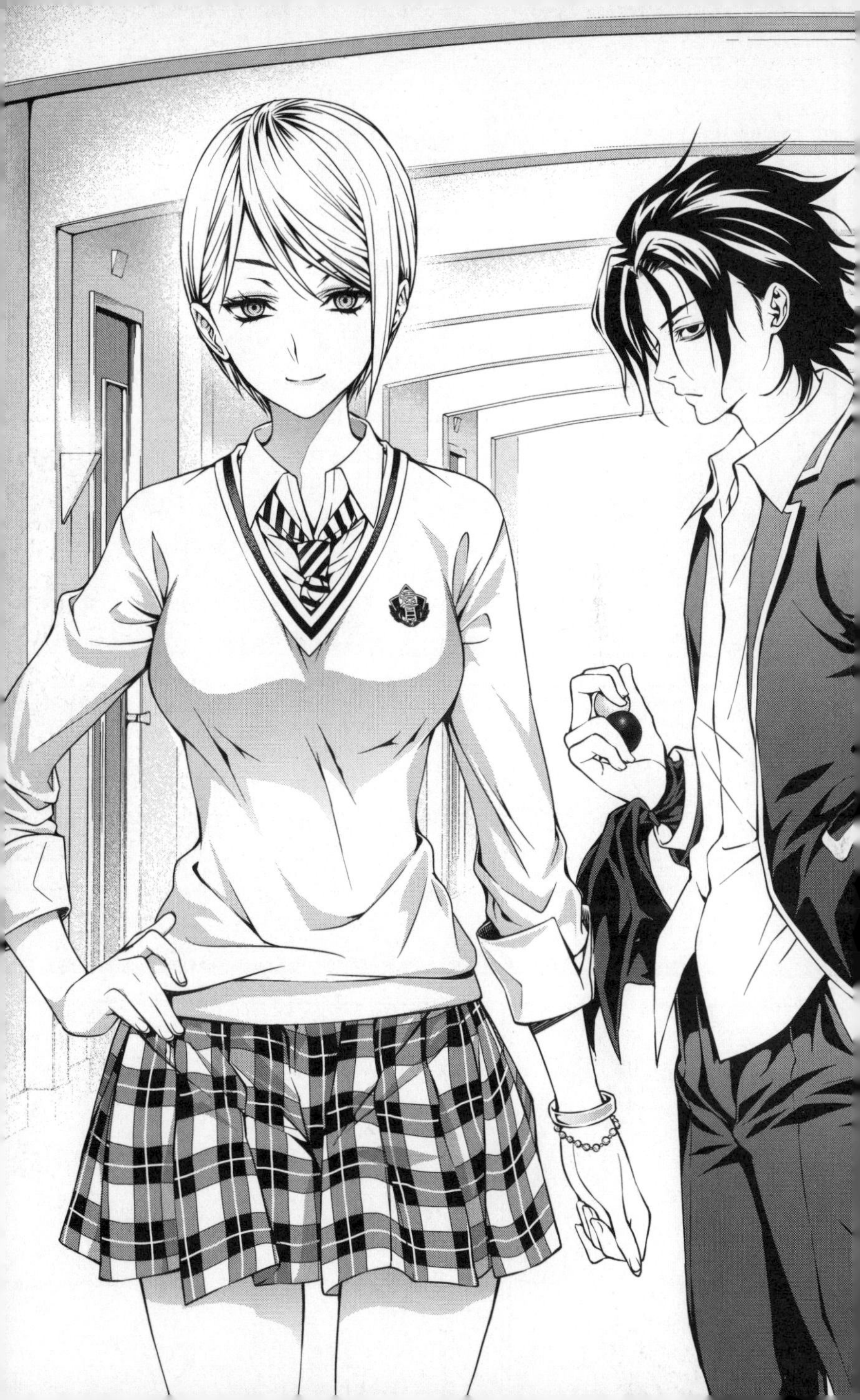

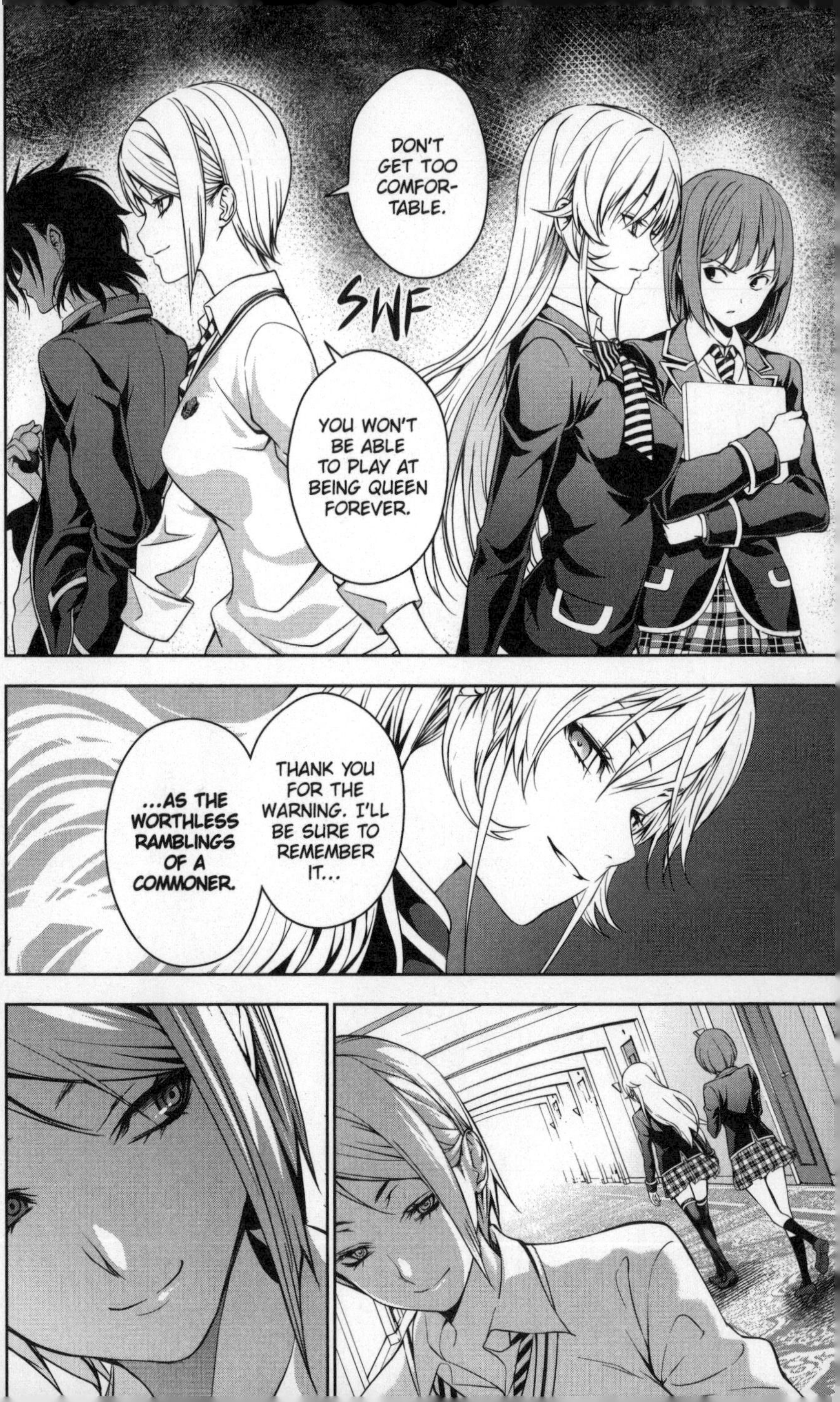
DON'T GET TOO COMFORTABLE.
SWF
YOU WON'T BE ABLE TO PLAY AT BEING QUEEN FOREVER.
THANK YOU FOR THE WARNING. I'LL BE SURE TO REMEMBER IT...
...AS THE WORTHLESS RAMBLINGS OF A COMMONER.

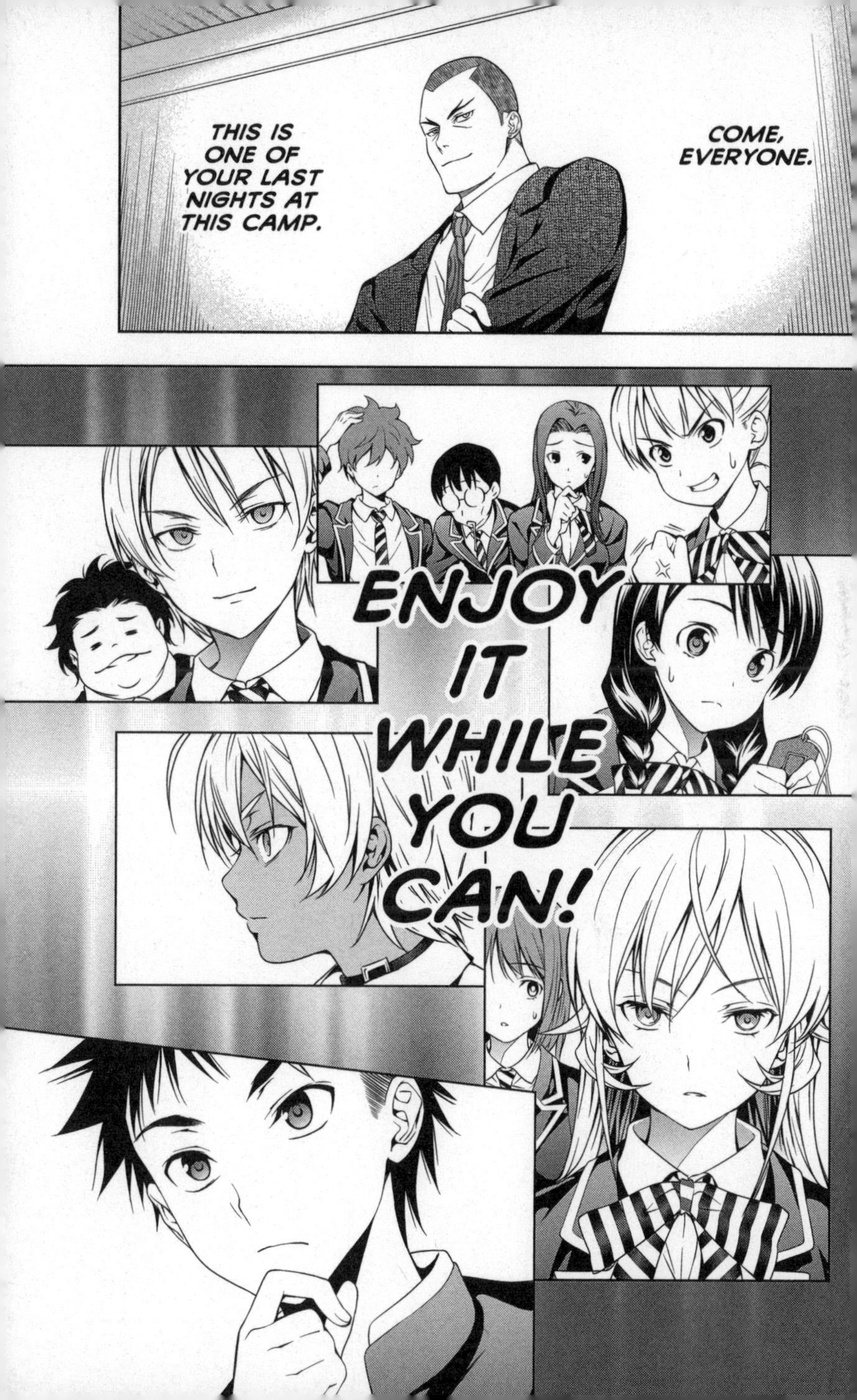
COME, EVERYONE.
THIS IS ONE OF YOUR LAST NIGHTS AT THIS CAMP.
ENJOY IT WHILE YOU CAN!

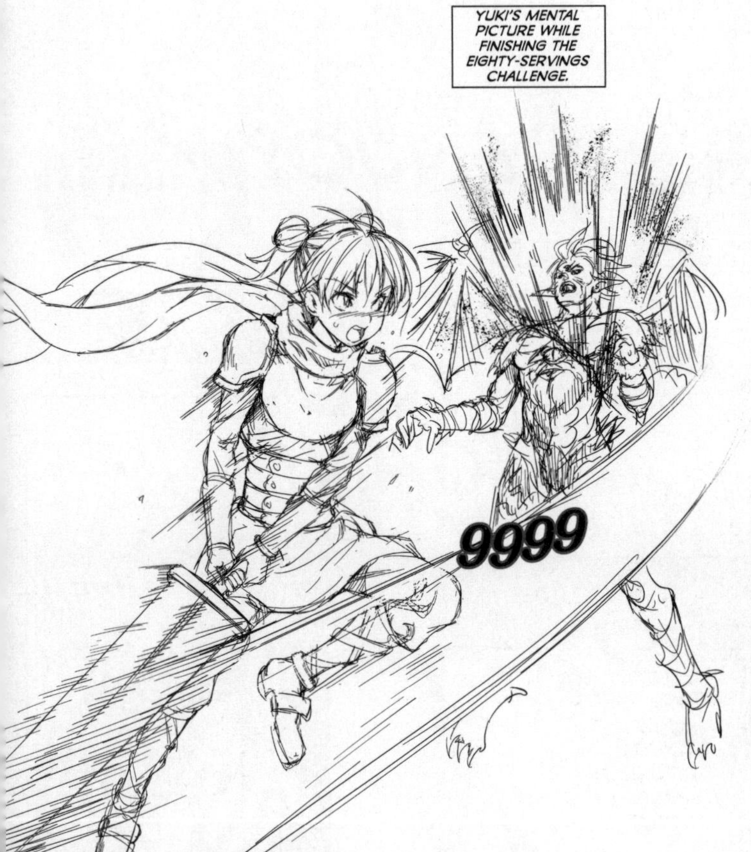
YUKI'S MENTAL PICTURE WHILE FINISHING THE EIGHTY-SERVINGS CHALLENGE.
9999

29 EGGS BEFORE DAWN

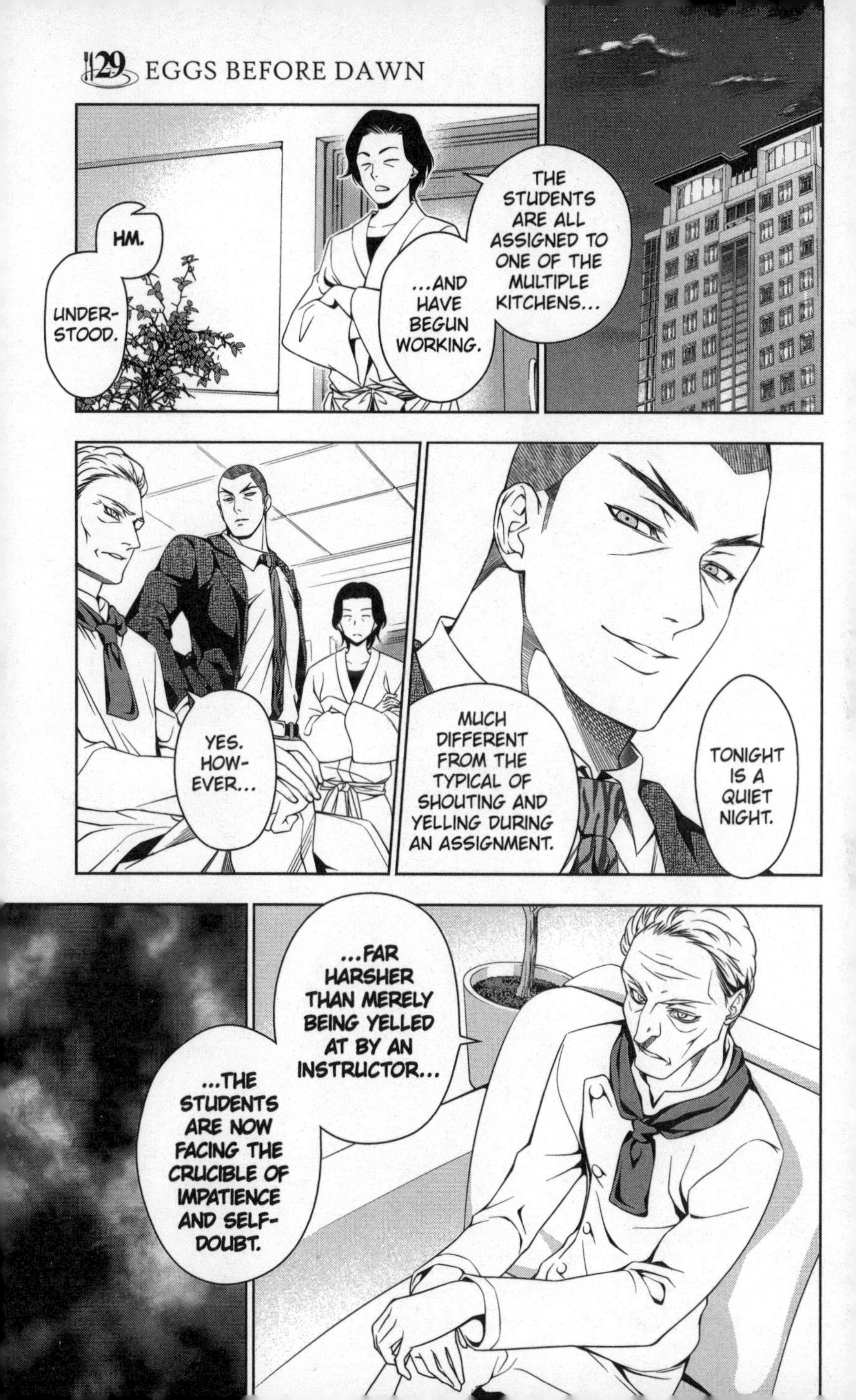
THE STUDENTS ARE ALL ASSIGNED TO ONE OF THE MULTIPLE KITCHENS...
...AND HAVE BEGUN WORKING.
HM. UNDERSTOOD.
TONIGHT IS A QUIET NIGHT.
MUCH DIFFERENT FROM THE TYPICAL OF SHOUTING AND YELLING DURING AN ASSIGNMENT.
YES. HOWEVER...
...FAR HARSHER THAN MERELY BEING YELLED AT BY AN INSTRUCTOR...
...THE STUDENTS ARE NOW FACING THE CRUCIBLE OF IMPATIENCE AND SELF-DOUBT.

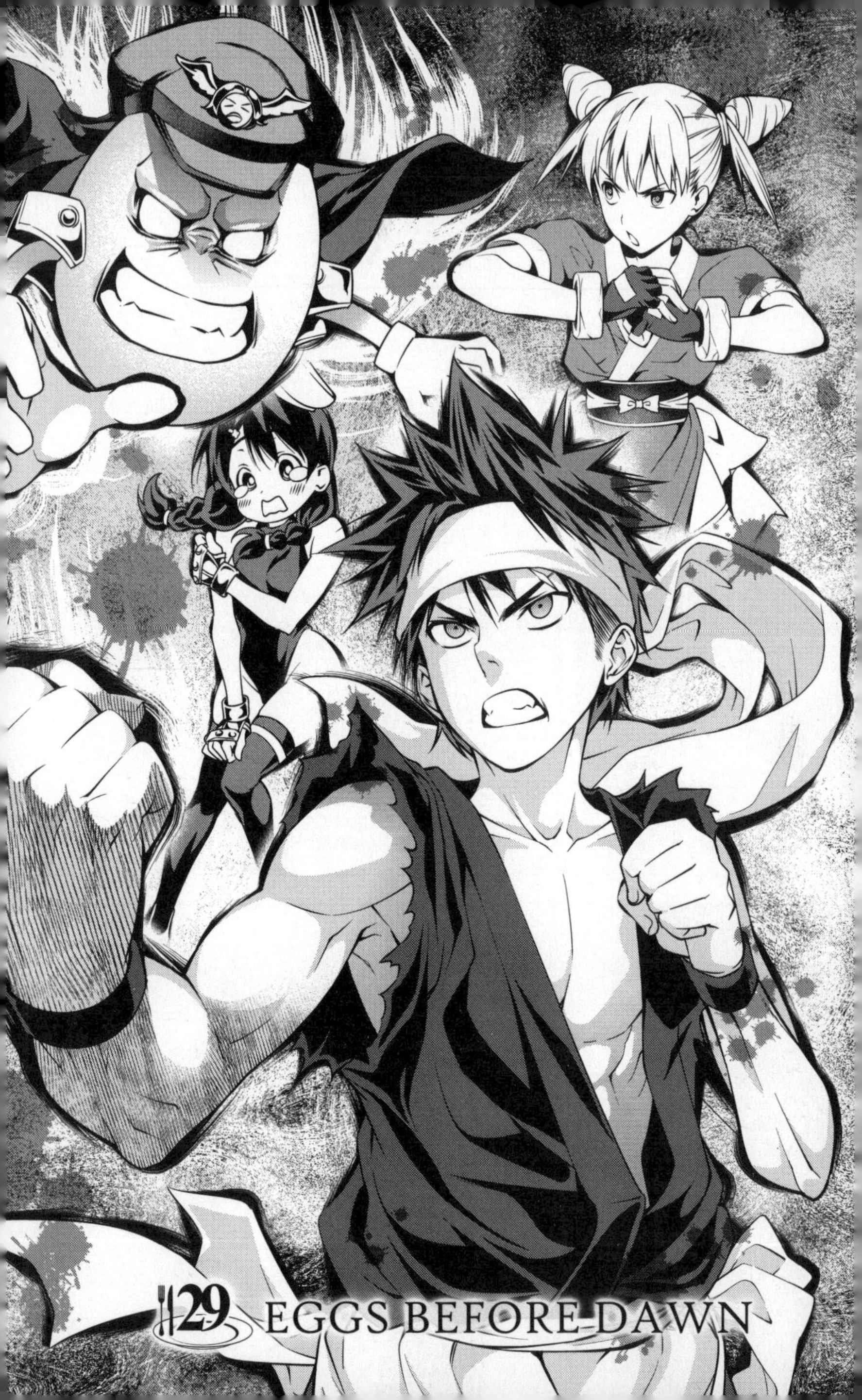
29
EGGS BEFORE DAWN

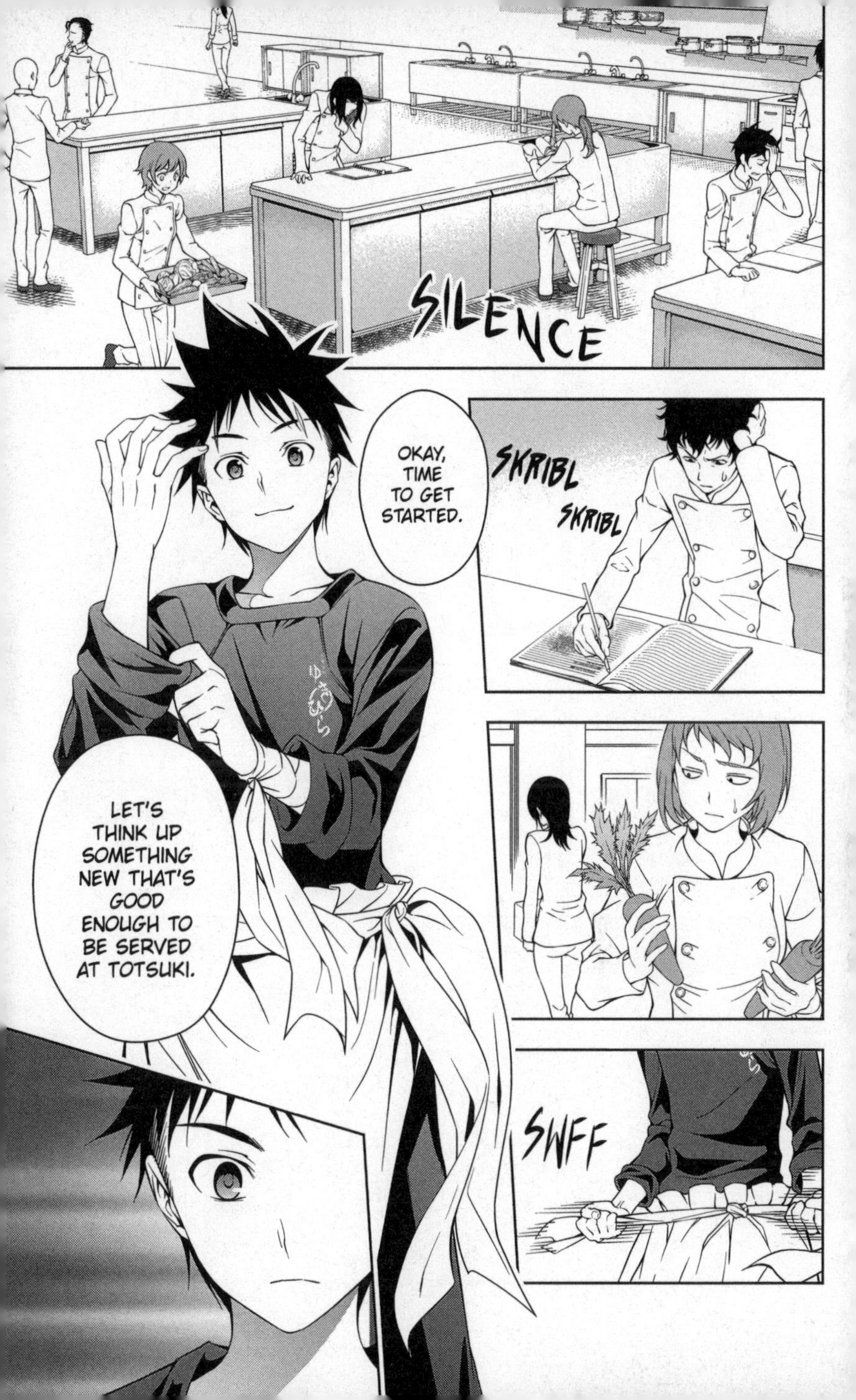
SILENCE
SKRIBL
SKRIBL
SWFF
OKAY, TIME TO GET STARTED.
LET'S THINK UP SOMETHING NEW THAT'S GOOD ENOUGH TO BE SERVED AT TOTSUKI.

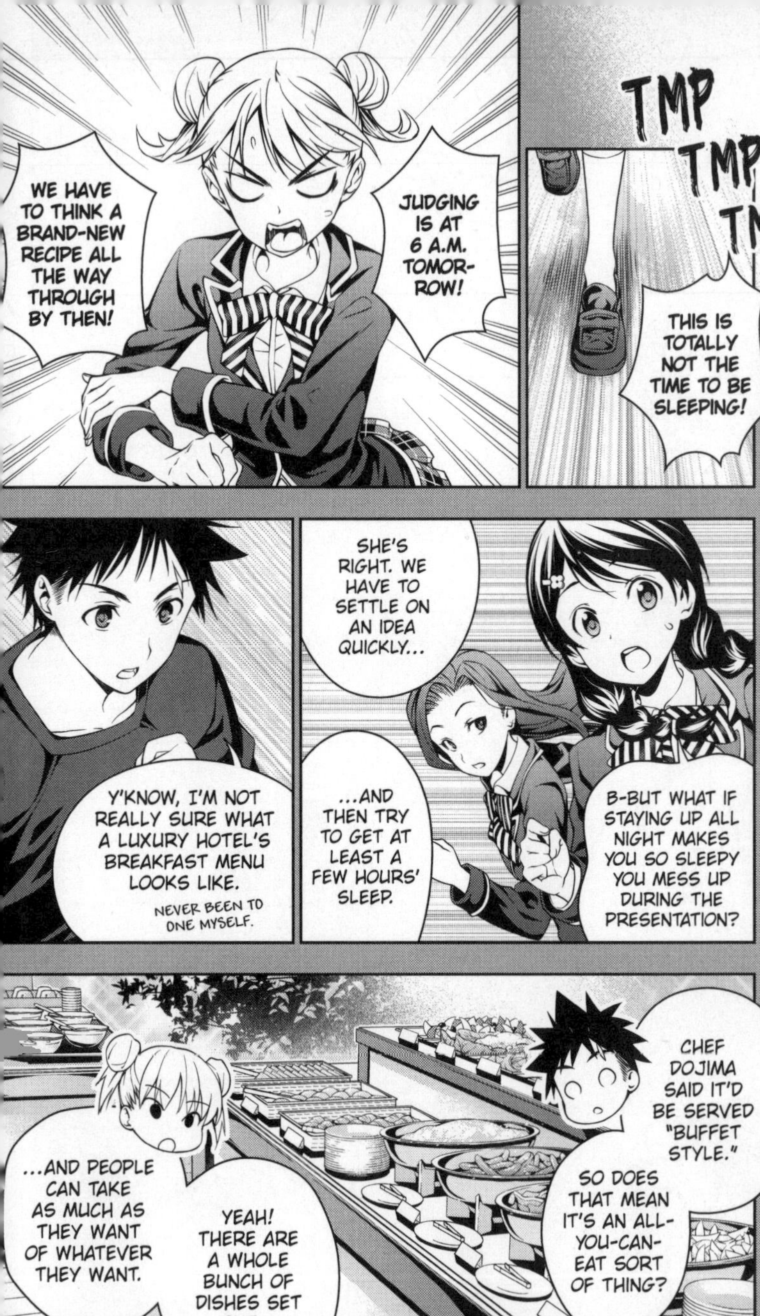
TMP TMP TMP
THIS IS TOTALLY NOT THE TIME TO BE SLEEPING!
JUDGING IS AT 6 A.M. TOMORROW!
WE HAVE TO THINK A BRAND-NEW RECIPE ALL THE WAY THROUGH BY THEN!
SHE'S RIGHT. WE HAVE TO SETTLE ON AN IDEA QUICKLY...
...AND THEN TRY TO GET AT LEAST A FEW HOURS' SLEEP.
B-BUT WHAT IF STAYING UP ALL NIGHT MAKES YOU SO SLEEPY YOU MESS UP DURING THE PRESENTATION?
Y'KNOW, I'M NOT REALLY SURE WHAT A LUXURY HOTEL'S BREAKFAST MENU LOOKS LIKE.
NEVER BEEN TO ONE MYSELF.
CHEF DOJIMA SAID IT'D BE SERVED "BUFFET STYLE."
SO DOES THAT MEAN IT'S AN ALL-YOU-CAN-EAT SORT OF THING?
YEAH! THERE ARE A WHOLE BUNCH OF DISHES SET OUT...
...AND PEOPLE CAN TAKE AS MUCH AS THEY WANT OF WHATEVER THEY WANT.

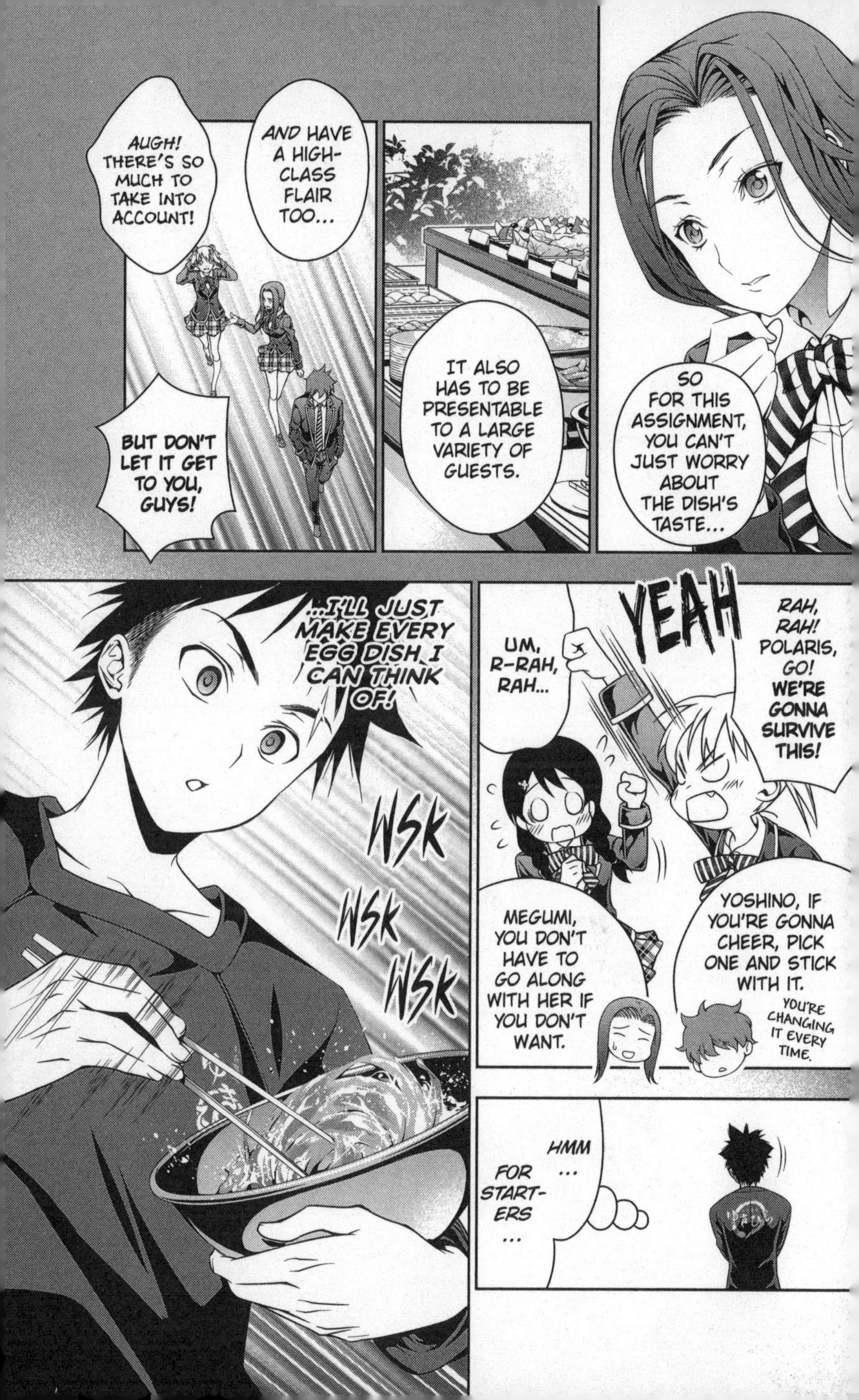
SO FOR THIS ASSIGNMENT, YOU CAN'T JUST WORRY ABOUT THE DISH'S TASTE...
IT ALSO HAS TO BE PRESENTABLE TO A LARGE VARIETY OF GUESTS.
AND HAVE A HIGH-CLASS FLAIR TOO...
AUGH! THERE'S SO MUCH TO TAKE INTO ACCOUNT!
BUT DON'T LET IT GET TO YOU, GUYS!
RAH, RAH! POLARIS, GO! WE'RE GONNA SURVIVE THIS!
YEAH
UM, R-RAH, RAH...
YOSHINO, IF YOU'RE GONNA CHEER, PICK ONE AND STICK WITH IT.
YOU'RE CHANGING IT EVERY TIME.
MEGUMI, YOU DON'T HAVE TO GO ALONG WITH HER IF YOU DON'T WANT.
HMM...
FOR STARTERS...
...I'LL JUST MAKE EVERY EGG DISH I CAN THINK OF!
WSK
WSK
WSK

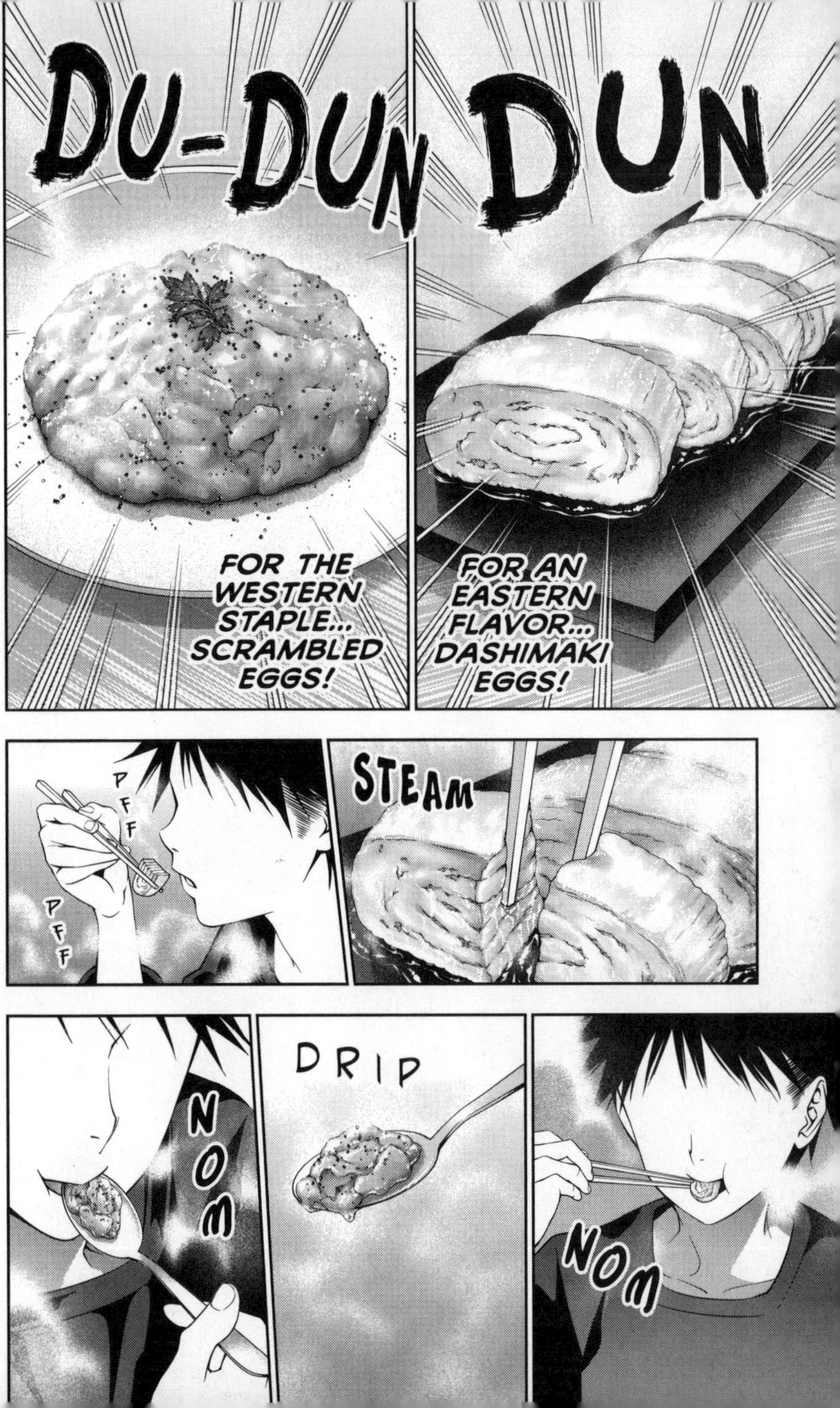
DU-DUN DUN
FOR AN EASTERN FLAVOR... DASHIMAKI EGGS!
FOR THE WESTERN STAPLE... SCRAMBLED EGGS!
STEAM
PFF
PFF
NOM
DRIP
NOM

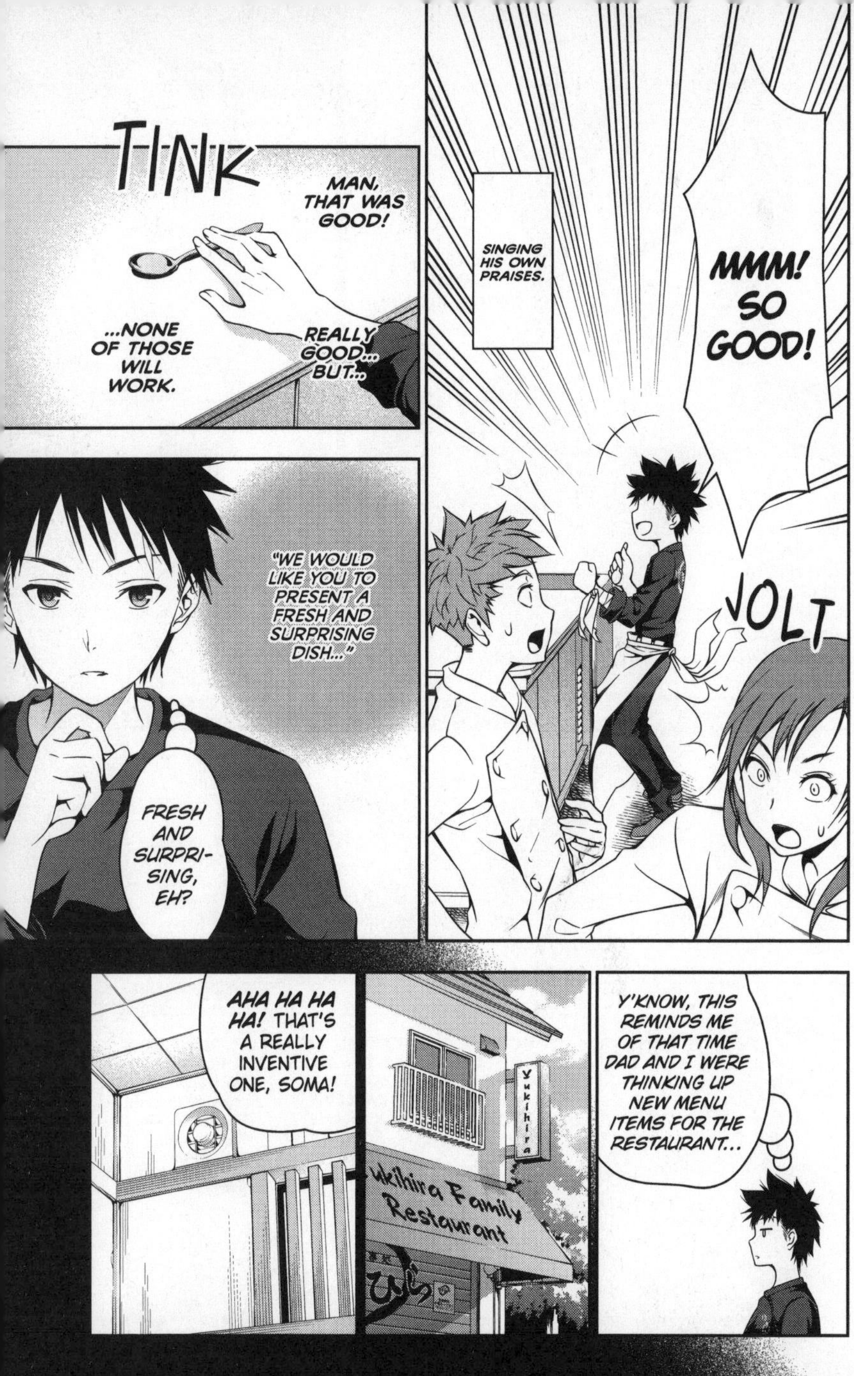
MMM! SO GOOD!
SINGING HIS OWN PRAISES.
JOLT
TINK
MAN, THAT WAS GOOD!
REALLY GOOD... BUT...
...NONE OF THOSE WILL WORK.
"WE WOULD LIKE YOU TO PRESENT A FRESH AND SURPRISING DISH..."
FRESH AND SURPRI-SING, EH?
Y'KNOW, THIS REMINDS ME OF THAT TIME DAD AND I WERE THINKING UP NEW MENU ITEMS FOR THE RESTAURANT...
Yukihira
Yukihira Family Restaurant
AHA HA HA HA! THAT'S A REALLY INVENTIVE ONE, SOMA!

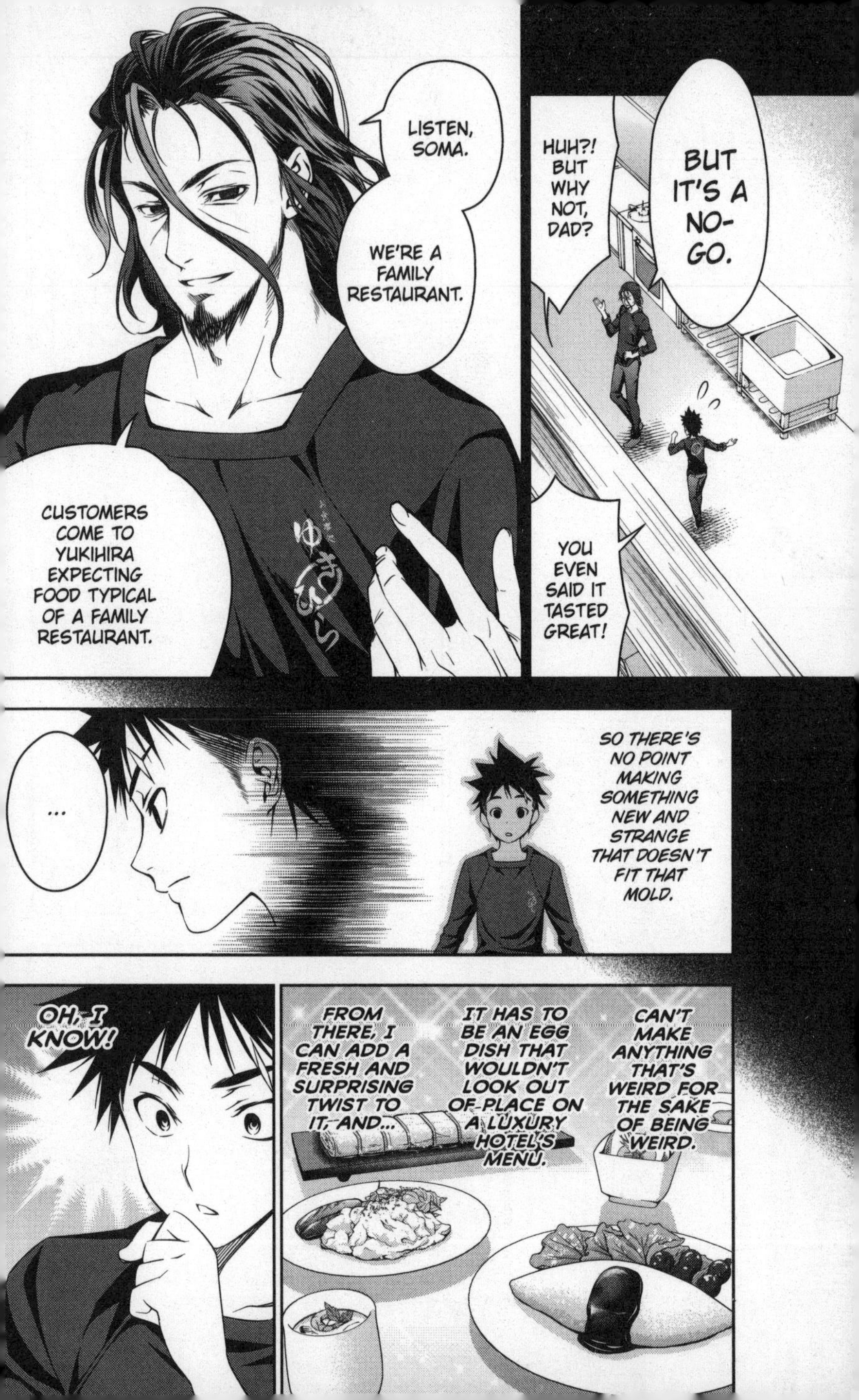
BUT IT'S A NO-GO.
HUH?! BUT WHY NOT, DAD?
YOU EVEN SAID IT TASTED GREAT!
LISTEN, SOMA.
WE'RE A FAMILY RESTAURANT.
CUSTOMERS COME TO YUKIHIRA EXPECTING FOOD TYPICAL OF A FAMILY RESTAURANT.
SO THERE'S NO POINT MAKING SOMETHING NEW AND STRANGE THAT DOESN'T FIT THAT MOLD.
...
CAN'T MAKE ANYTHING THAT'S WEIRD FOR THE SAKE OF BEING WEIRD.
IT HAS TO BE AN EGG DISH THAT WOULDN'T LOOK OUT OF PLACE ON A LUXURY HOTEL'S MENU.
FROM THERE, I CAN ADD A FRESH AND SURPRISING TWIST TO IT, AND...
OH, I KNOW!

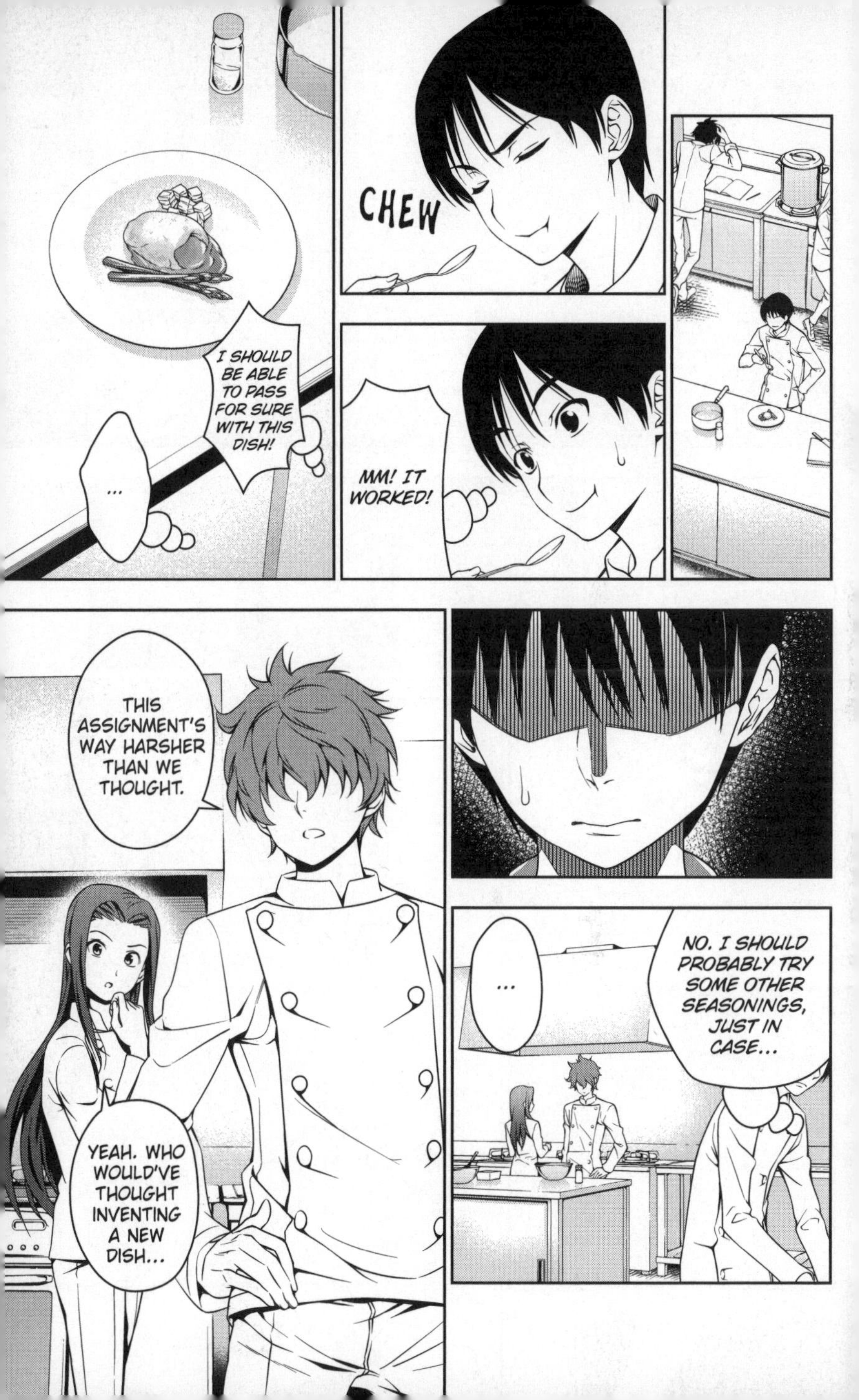
CHEW
MM! IT WORKED!
I SHOULD BE ABLE TO PASS FOR SURE WITH THIS DISH!
...
NO. I SHOULD PROBABLY TRY SOME OTHER SEASONINGS, JUST IN CASE...
...
THIS ASSIGNMENT'S WAY HARSHER THAN WE THOUGHT.
YEAH. WHO WOULD'VE THOUGHT INVENTING A NEW DISH...

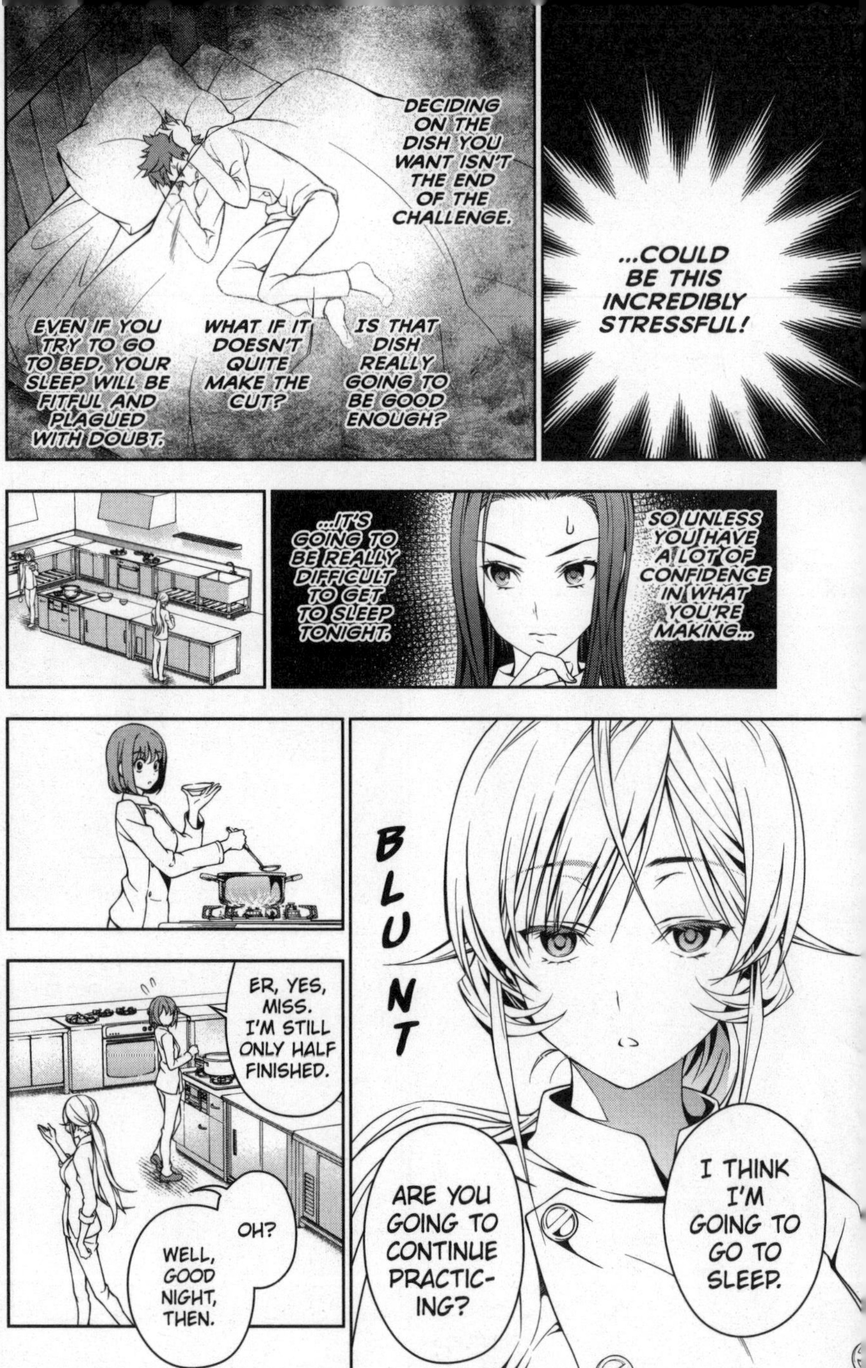
...COULD BE THIS INCREDIBLY STRESSFUL!
DECIDING ON THE DISH YOU WANT ISN'T THE END OF THE CHALLENGE.
IS THAT DISH REALLY GOING TO BE GOOD ENOUGH?
WHAT IF IT DOESN'T QUITE MAKE THE CUT?
EVEN IF YOU TRY TO GO TO BED, YOUR SLEEP WILL BE FITFUL AND PLAGUED WITH DOUBT.
SO UNLESS YOU HAVE A LOT OF CONFIDENCE IN WHAT YOU'RE MAKING...
...IT'S GOING TO BE REALLY DIFFICULT TO GET TO SLEEP TONIGHT.
BLUNT
I THINK I'M GOING TO GO TO SLEEP.
ARE YOU GOING TO CONTINUE PRACTIC-ING?
ER, YES, MISS. I'M STILL ONLY HALF FINISHED.
OH?
WELL, GOOD NIGHT, THEN.

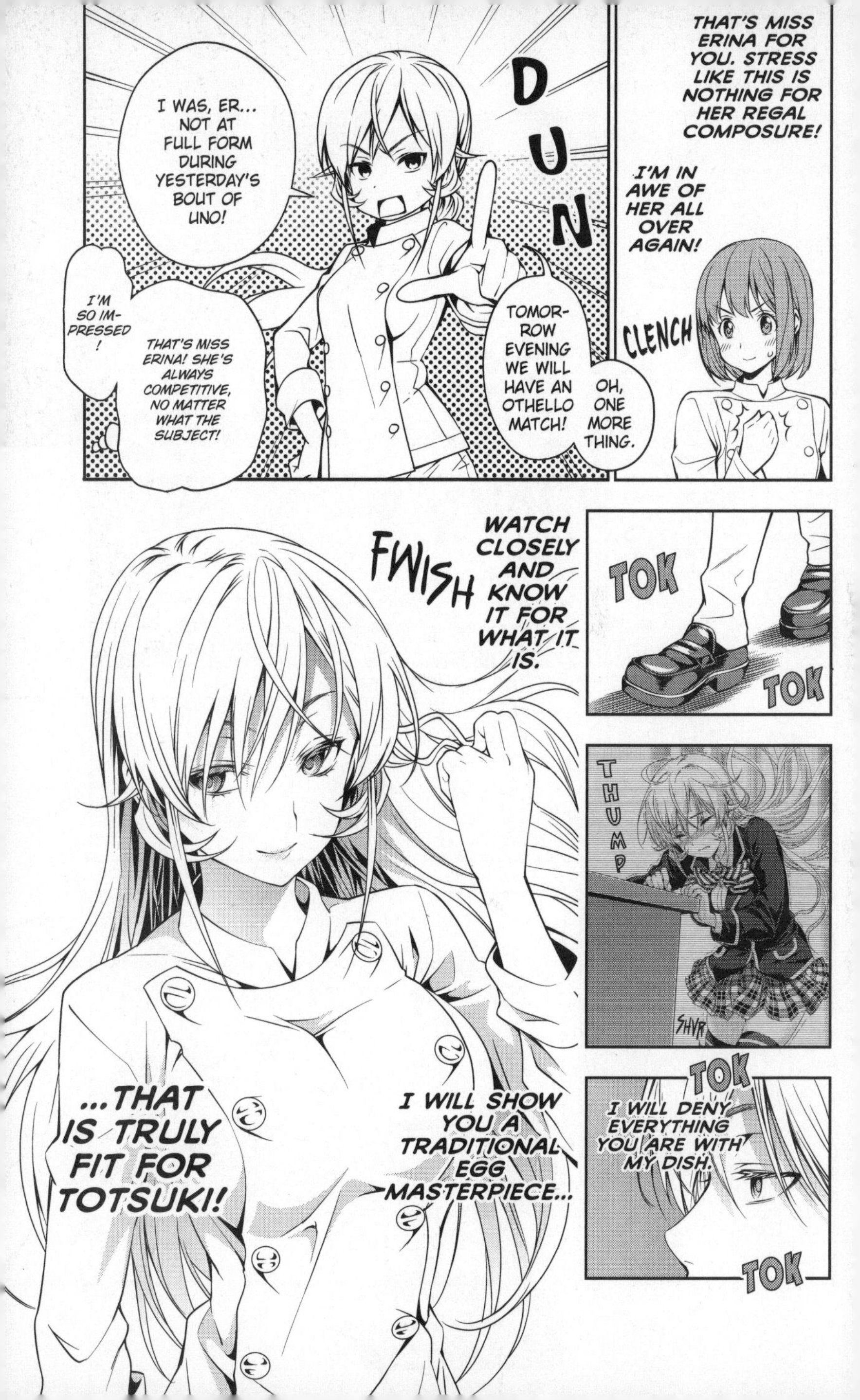
THAT'S MISS ERINA FOR YOU. STRESS LIKE THIS IS NOTHING FOR HER REGAL COMPOSURE!
I'M IN AWE OF HER ALL OVER AGAIN!
CLENCH
DUN
I WAS, ER... NOT AT FULL FORM DURING YESTERDAY'S BOUT OF UNO!
OH, ONE MORE THING.
TOMORROW EVENING WE WILL HAVE AN OTHELLO MATCH!
I'M SO IMPRESSED!
THAT'S MISS ERINA! SHE'S ALWAYS COMPETITIVE, NO MATTER WHAT THE SUBJECT!
TOK
TOK
THUMP
SHVR
TOK
I WILL DENY EVERYTHING YOU ARE WITH MY DISH.
TOK
FWISH
WATCH CLOSELY AND KNOW IT FOR WHAT IT IS.
I WILL SHOW YOU A TRADITIONAL EGG MASTERPIECE...
...THAT IS TRULY FIT FOR TOTSUKI!

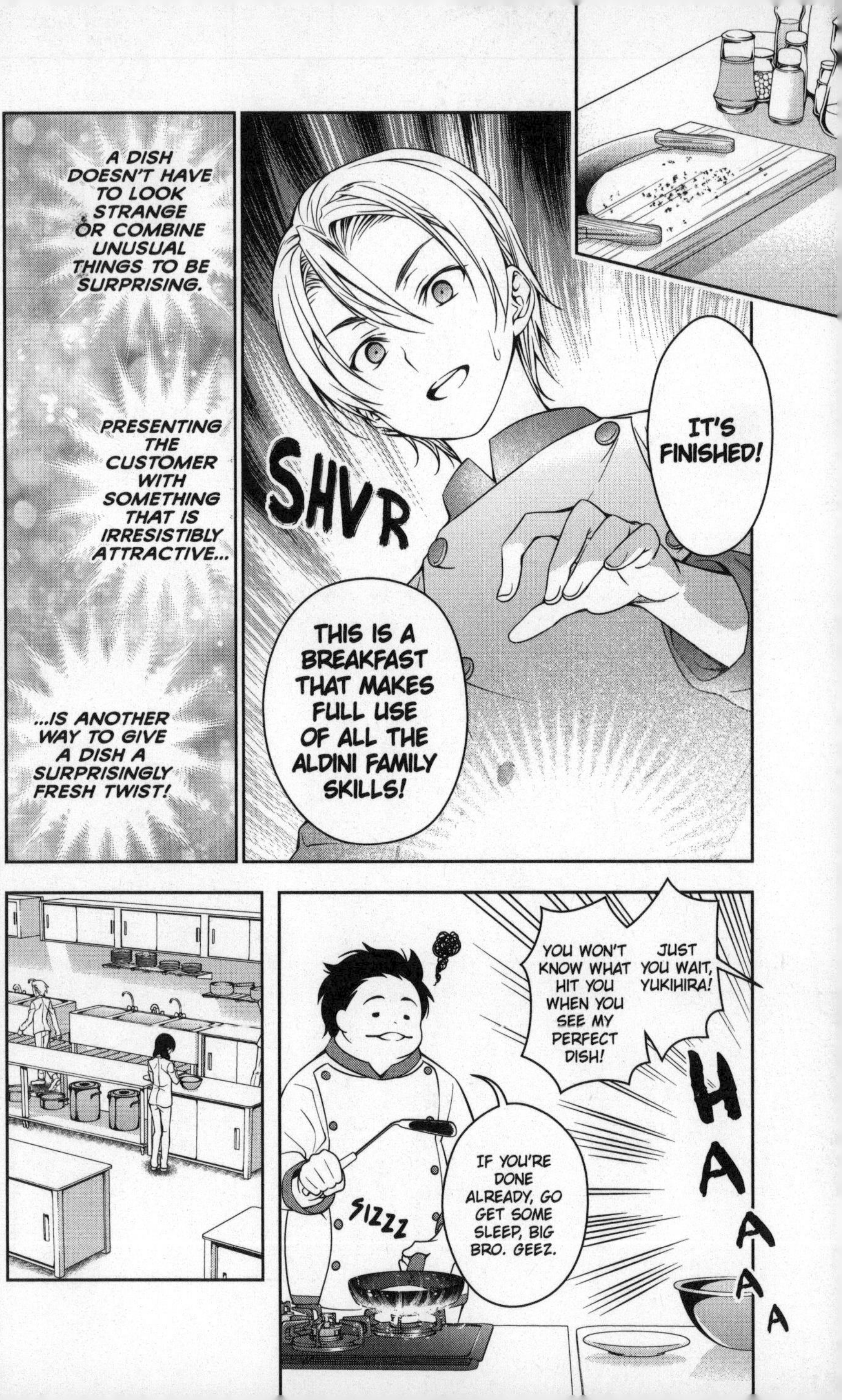
IT'S FINISHED!
SHVR
THIS IS A BREAKFAST THAT MAKES FULL USE OF ALL THE ALDINI FAMILY SKILLS!
A DISH DOESN'T HAVE TO LOOK STRANGE OR COMBINE UNUSUAL THINGS TO BE SURPRISING.
PRESENTING THE CUSTOMER WITH SOMETHING THAT IS IRRESISTIBLY ATTRACTIVE...
...IS ANOTHER WAY TO GIVE A DISH A SURPRISINGLY FRESH TWIST!
JUST YOU WAIT, YUKIHIRA!
YOU WON'T KNOW WHAT HIT YOU WHEN YOU SEE MY PERFECT DISH!
HAAAAA
IF YOU'RE DONE ALREADY, GO GET SOME SLEEP, BIG BRO. GEEZ.
SIZZZ

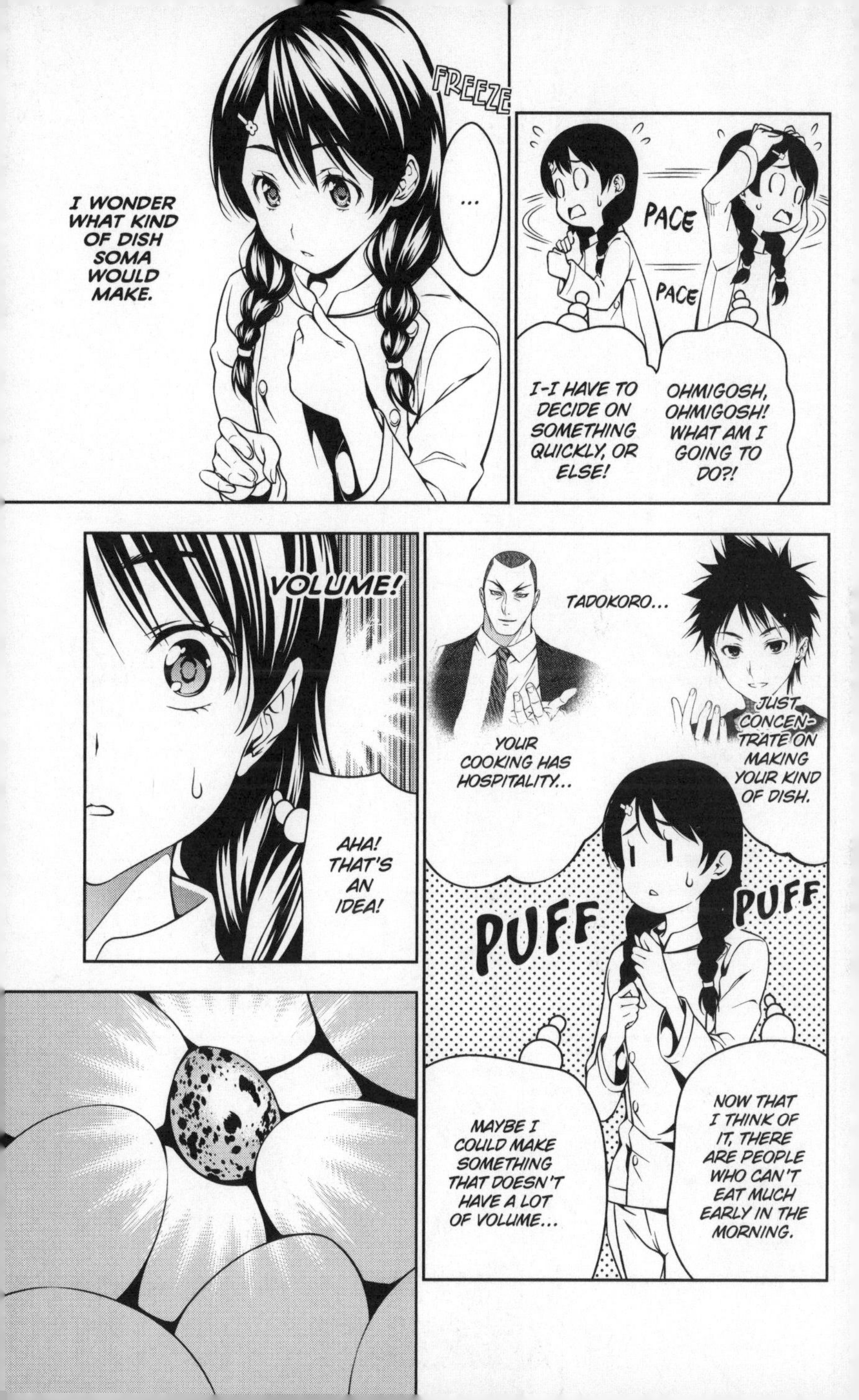
PACE
PACE
OHMIGOSH, OHMIGOSH! WHAT AM I GOING TO DO?!
I-I HAVE TO DECIDE ON SOMETHING QUICKLY, OR ELSE!
FREEZE
...
I WONDER WHAT KIND OF DISH SOMA WOULD MAKE.
JUST CONCENTRATE ON MAKING YOUR KIND OF DISH.
TADOKORO...
YOUR COOKING HAS HOSPITALITY...
PUFF
PUFF
NOW THAT I THINK OF IT, THERE ARE PEOPLE WHO CAN'T EAT MUCH EARLY IN THE MORNING.
MAYBE I COULD MAKE SOMETHING THAT DOESN'T HAVE A LOT OF VOLUME...
VOLUME!
AHA! THAT'S AN IDEA!

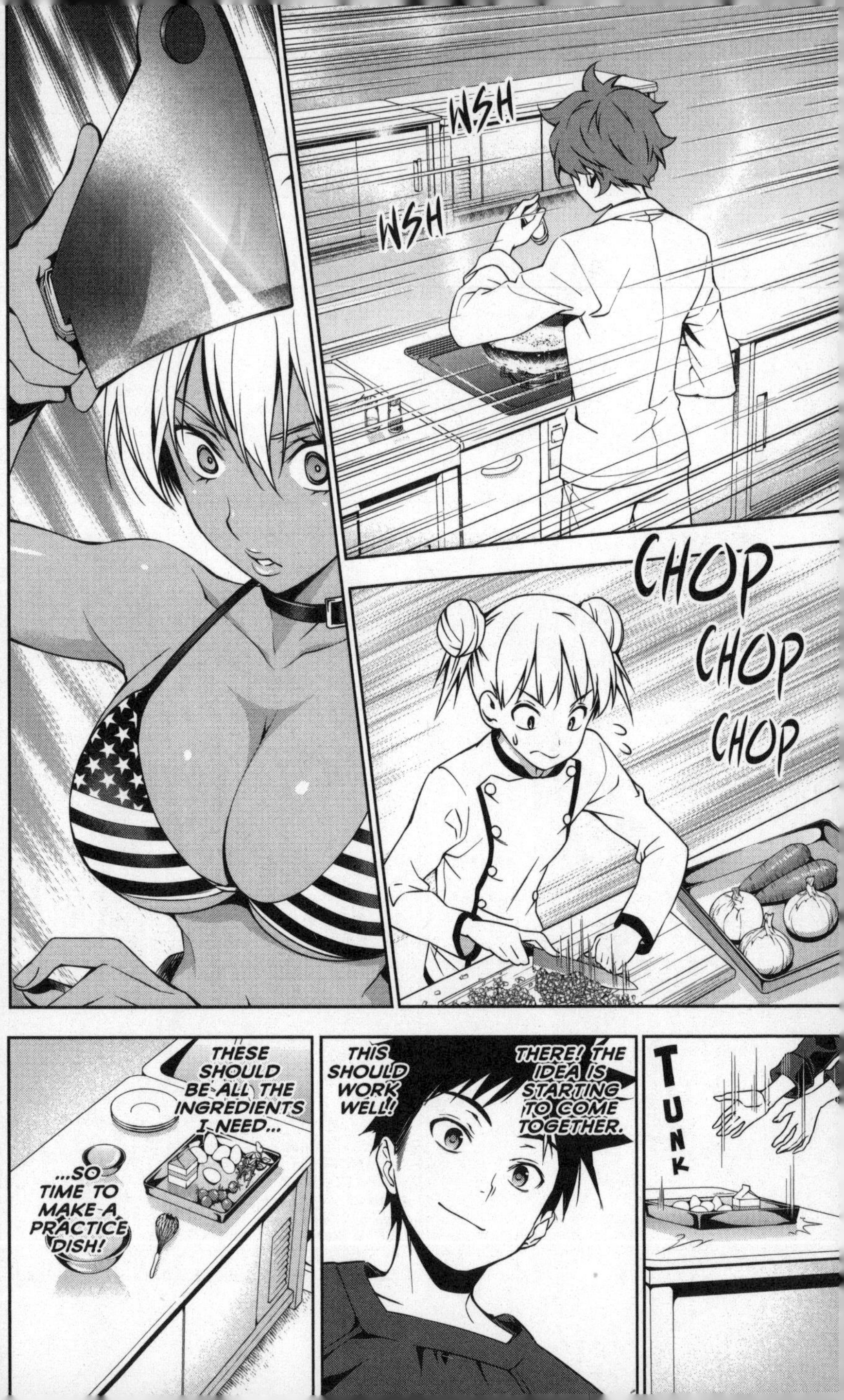
WSH
WSH
CHOP CHOP CHOP
TUNK
THERE! THE IDEA IS STARTING TO COME TOGETHER.
THIS SHOULD WORK WELL!!
THESE SHOULD BE ALL THE INGREDIENTS I NEED...
...SO TIME TO MAKE A PRACTICE DISH!

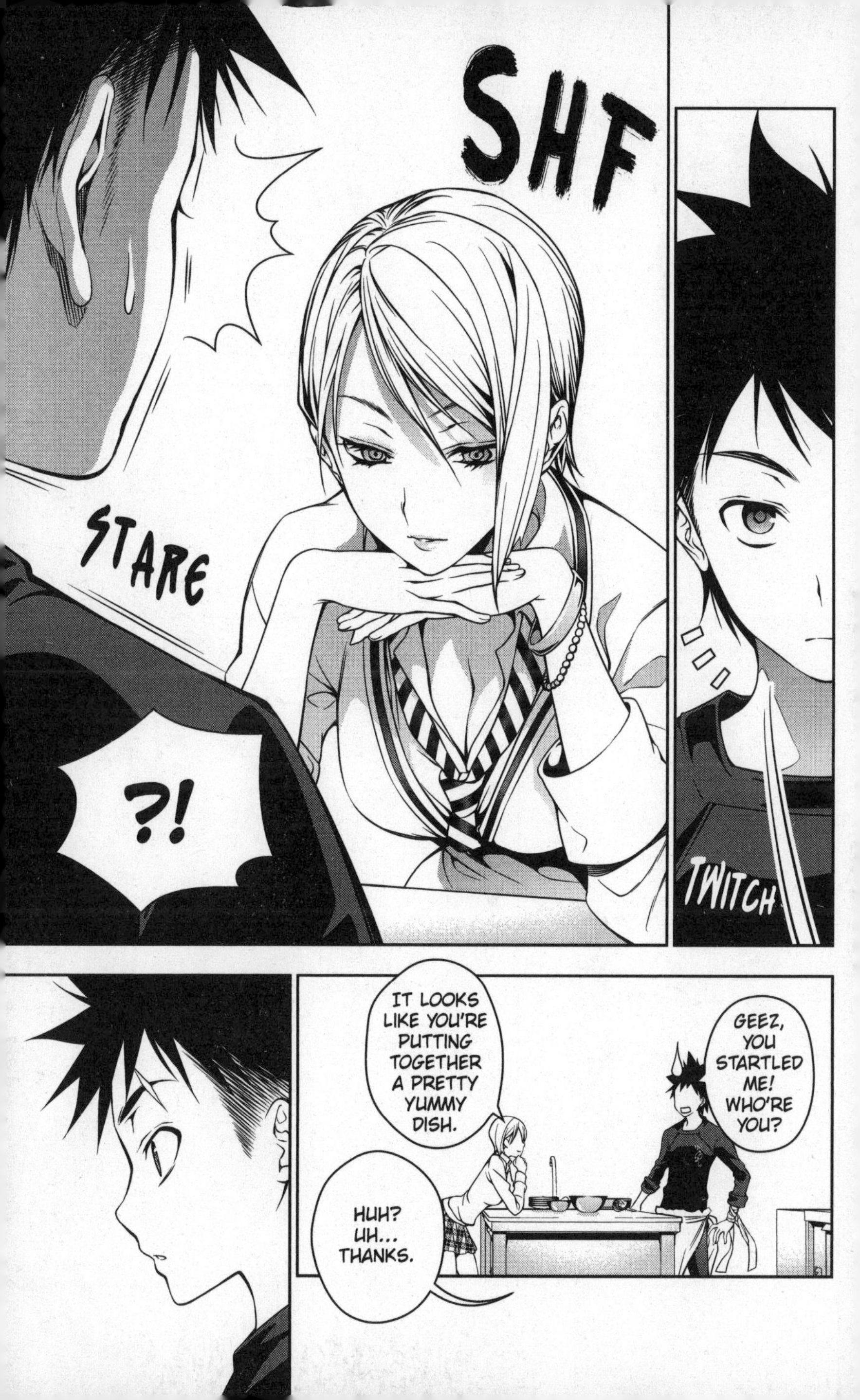
TWITCH
SHF
STARE
?!
GEEZ, YOU STARTLED ME! WHO'RE YOU?
IT LOOKS LIKE YOU'RE PUTTING TOGETHER A PRETTY YUMMY DISH.
HUH? UH... THANKS.

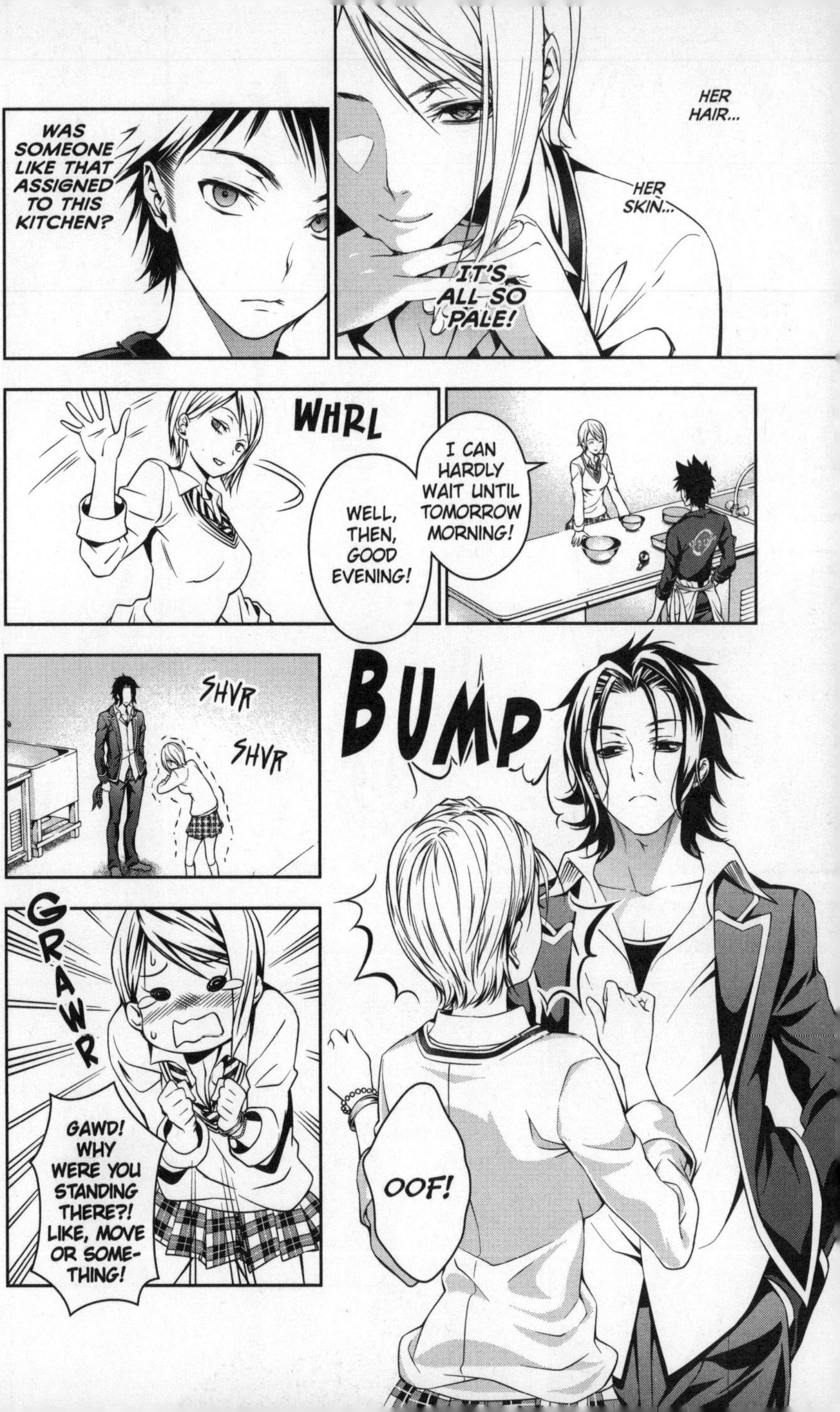
HER HAIR...
HER SKIN...
IT'S ALL SO PALE!
WAS SOMEONE LIKE THAT ASSIGNED TO THIS KITCHEN?
I CAN HARDLY WAIT UNTIL TOMORROW MORNING!
WELL, THEN, GOOD EVENING!
WHRL
BUMP
OOF!
SHVR
SHVR
GRAWR
GAWD! WHY WERE YOU STANDING THERE?! LIKE, MOVE OR SOME-THING!

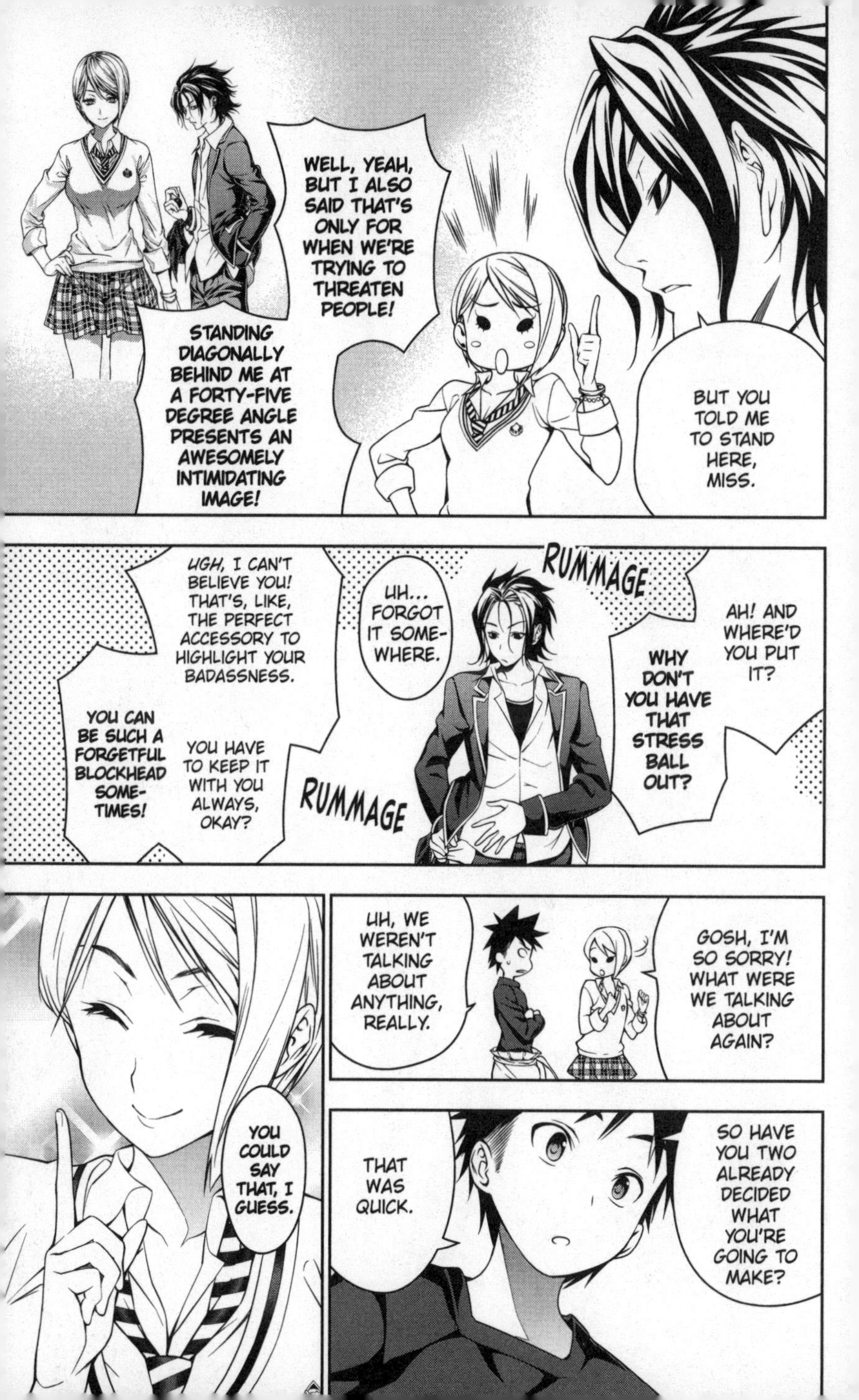
BUT YOU TOLD ME TO STAND HERE, MISS.
WELL, YEAH, BUT I ALSO SAID THAT'S ONLY FOR WHEN WE'RE TRYING TO THREATEN PEOPLE!
STANDING DIAGONALLY BEHIND ME AT A FORTY-FIVE DEGREE ANGLE PRESENTS AN AWESOMELY INTIMIDATING IMAGE!
AH! AND WHERE'D YOU PUT IT?
WHY DON'T YOU HAVE THAT STRESS BALL OUT?
RUMMAGE
UH... FORGOT IT SOME-WHERE.
RUMMAGE
UGH, I CAN'T BELIEVE YOU! THAT'S, LIKE, THE PERFECT ACCESSORY TO HIGHLIGHT YOUR BADASSNESS.
YOU HAVE TO KEEP IT WITH YOU ALWAYS, OKAY?
YOU CAN BE SUCH A FORGETFUL BLOCKHEAD SOME-TIMES!
GOSH, I'M SO SORRY! WHAT WERE WE TALKING ABOUT AGAIN?
UH, WE WEREN'T TALKING ABOUT ANYTHING, REALLY.
SO HAVE YOU TWO ALREADY DECIDED WHAT YOU'RE GOING TO MAKE?
THAT WAS QUICK.
YOU COULD SAY THAT, I GUESS.

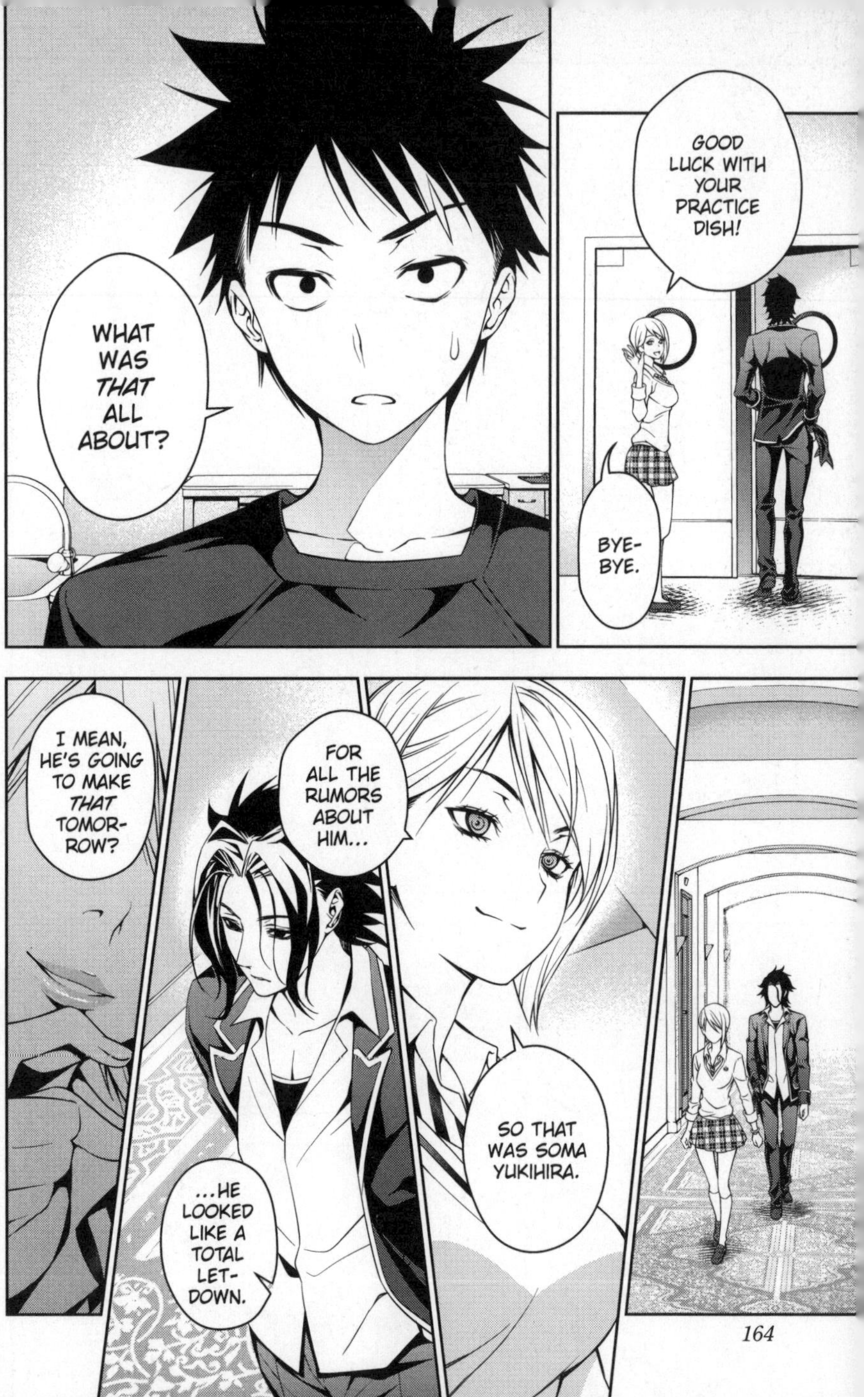
GOOD LUCK WITH YOUR PRACTICE DISH!
BYE-BYE.
WHAT WAS THAT ALL ABOUT?
SO THAT WAS SOMA YUKIHIRA.
FOR ALL THE RUMORS ABOUT HIM...
...HE LOOKED LIKE A TOTAL LET-DOWN.
I MEAN, HE'S GOING TO MAKE THAT TOMOR-ROW?

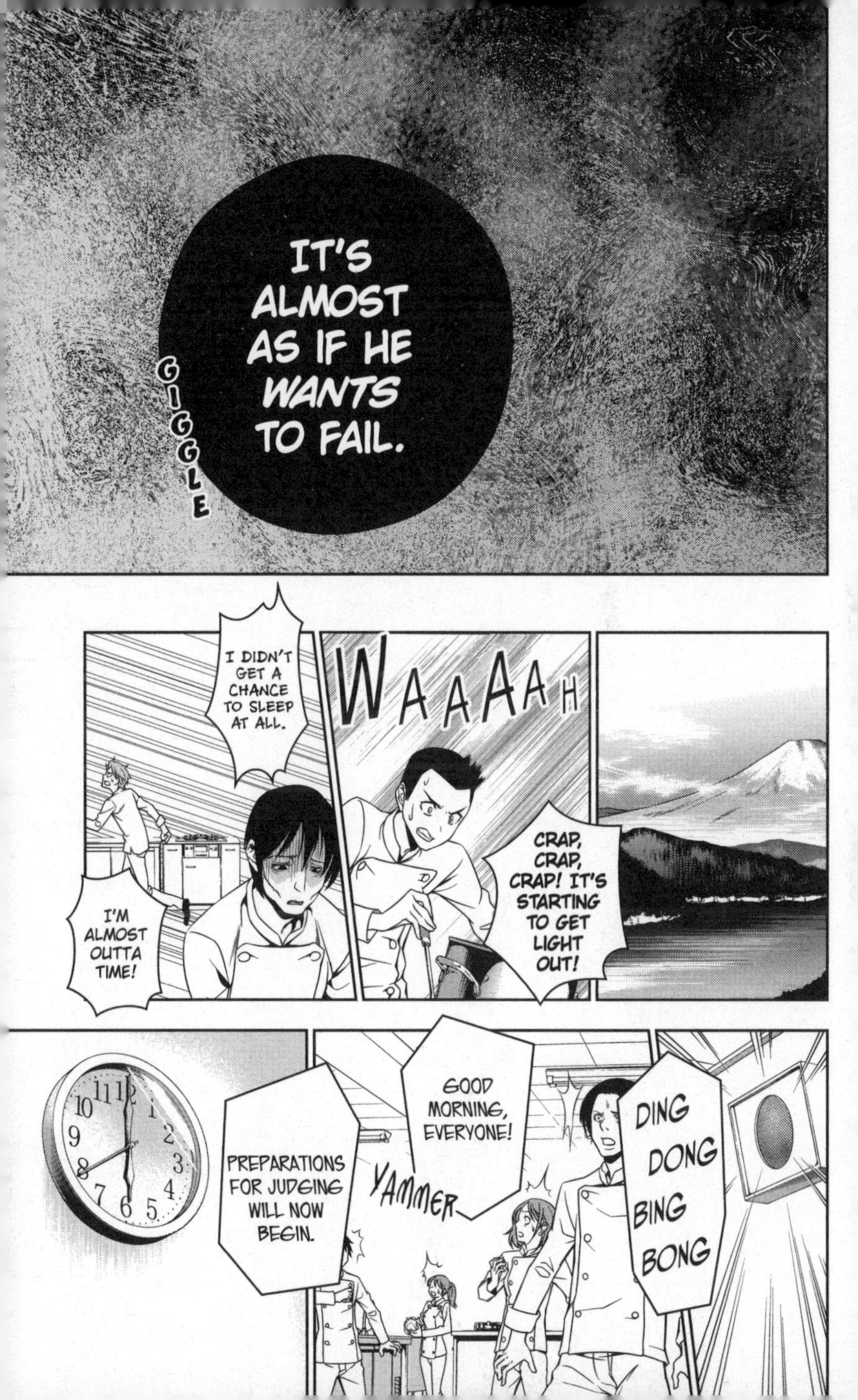
IT'S ALMOST AS IF HE *WANTS* TO FAIL.
GIGGLE
CRAP, CRAP, CRAP! IT'S STARTING TO GET LIGHT OUT!
WAAAAH
I DIDN'T GET A CHANCE TO SLEEP AT ALL.
I'M ALMOST OUTTA TIME!
DING DONG BING BONG
GOOD MORNING, EVERYONE!
PREPARATIONS FOR JUDGING WILL NOW BEGIN.
YAMMER

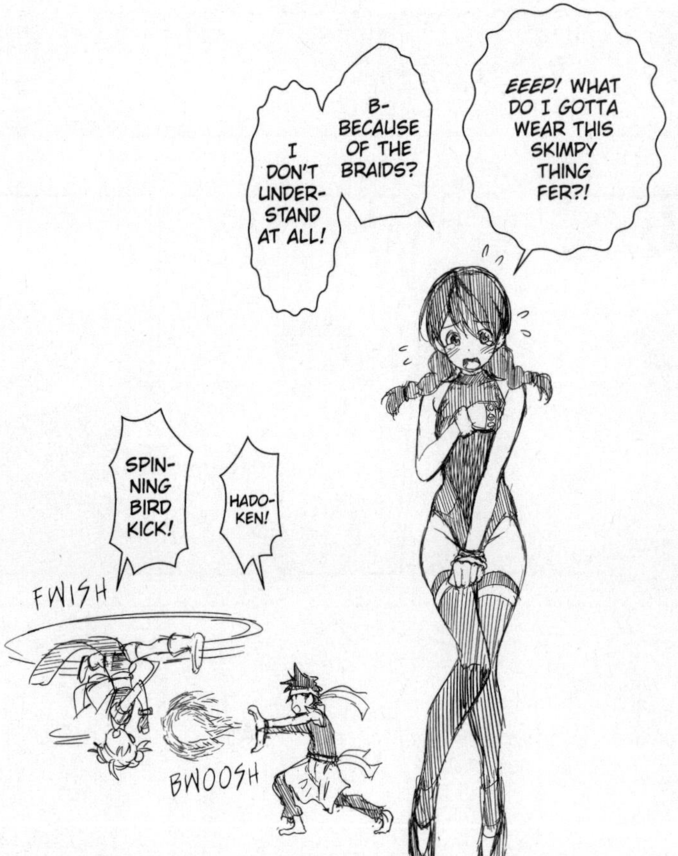
EEEP! WHAT DO I GOTTA WEAR THIS SKIMPY THING FER?!
B-BECAUSE OF THE BRAIDS?
I DON'T UNDER-STAND AT ALL!
HADO-KEN!
SPIN-NING BIRD KICK!
FWISH
BWOOSH

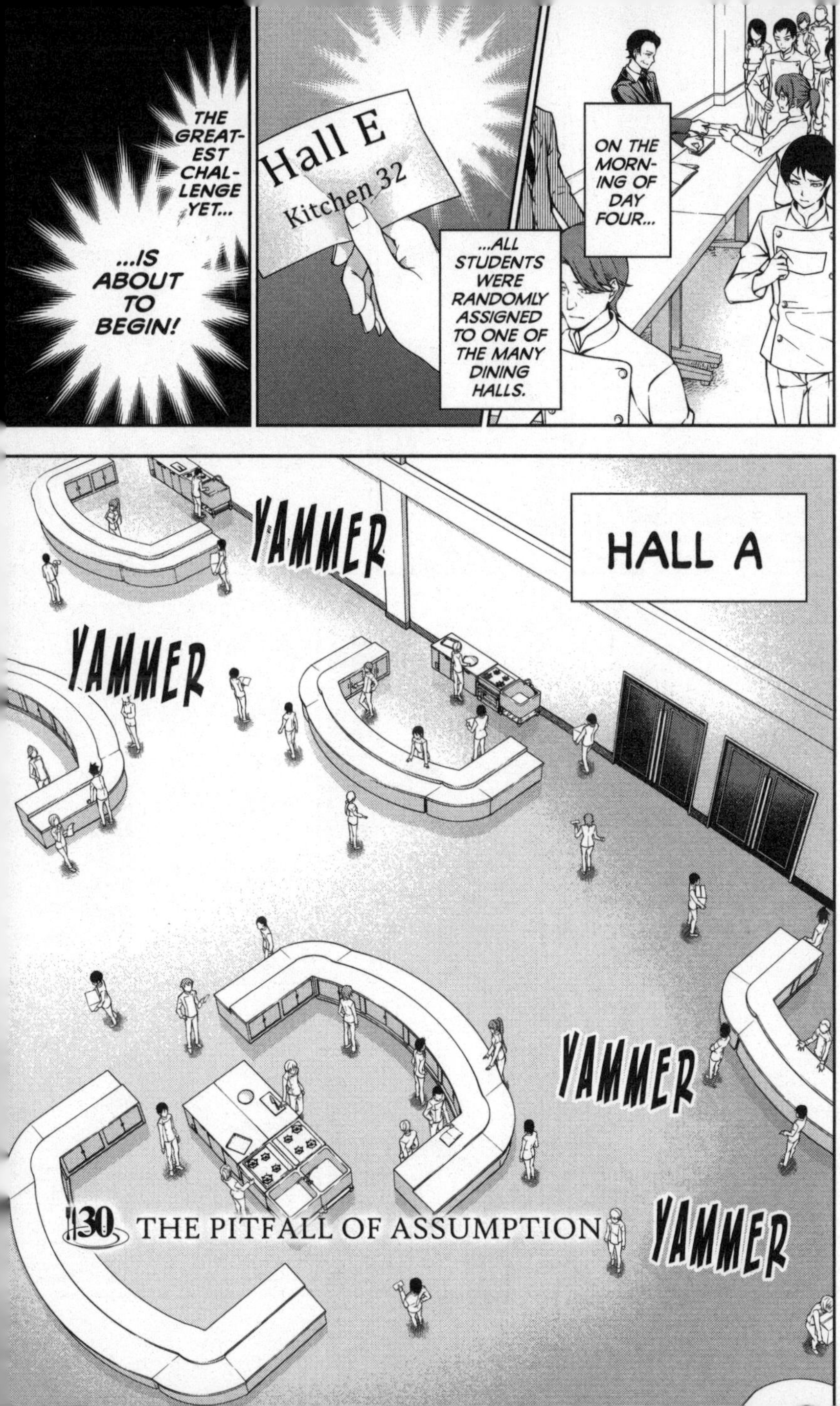
ON THE MORNING OF DAY FOUR...
...ALL STUDENTS WERE RANDOMLY ASSIGNED TO ONE OF THE MANY DINING HALLS.
Hall E
Kitchen 32
THE GREATEST CHALLENGE YET...
...IS ABOUT TO BEGIN!
HALL A
YAMMER
YAMMER
YAMMER
YAMMER
130 THE PITFALL OF ASSUMPTION

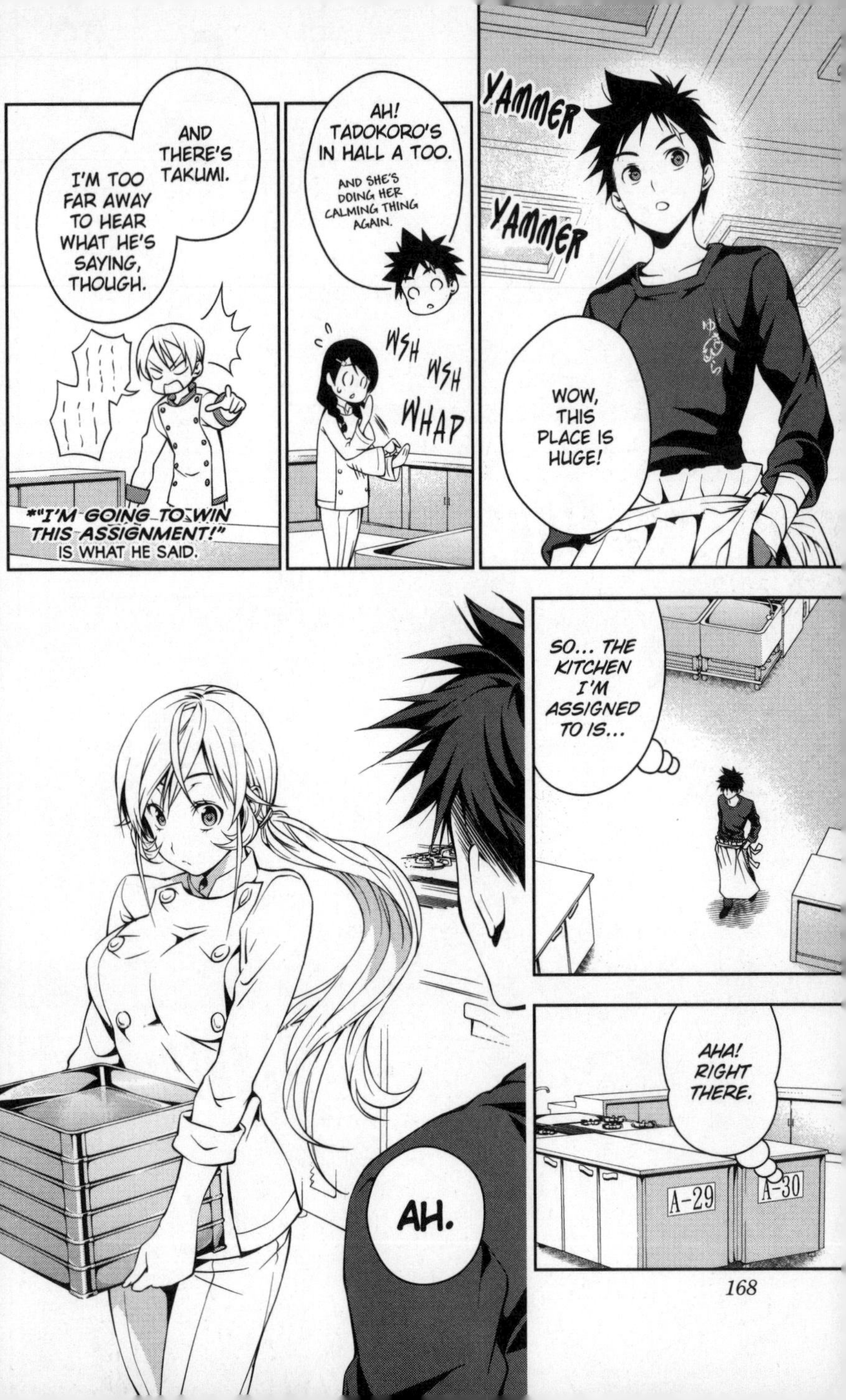
YAMMER
YAMMER
WOW, THIS PLACE IS HUGE!
AH! TADOKORO'S IN HALL A TOO.
AND SHE'S DOING HER CALMING THING AGAIN.
WSH
WSH
WHAP
AND THERE'S TAKUMI.
I'M TOO FAR AWAY TO HEAR WHAT HE'S SAYING, THOUGH.
*"I'M GOING TO WIN THIS ASSIGNMENT!" IS WHAT HE SAID.
SO... THE KITCHEN I'M ASSIGNED TO IS...
AHA! RIGHT THERE.
A-29
A-30
AH.

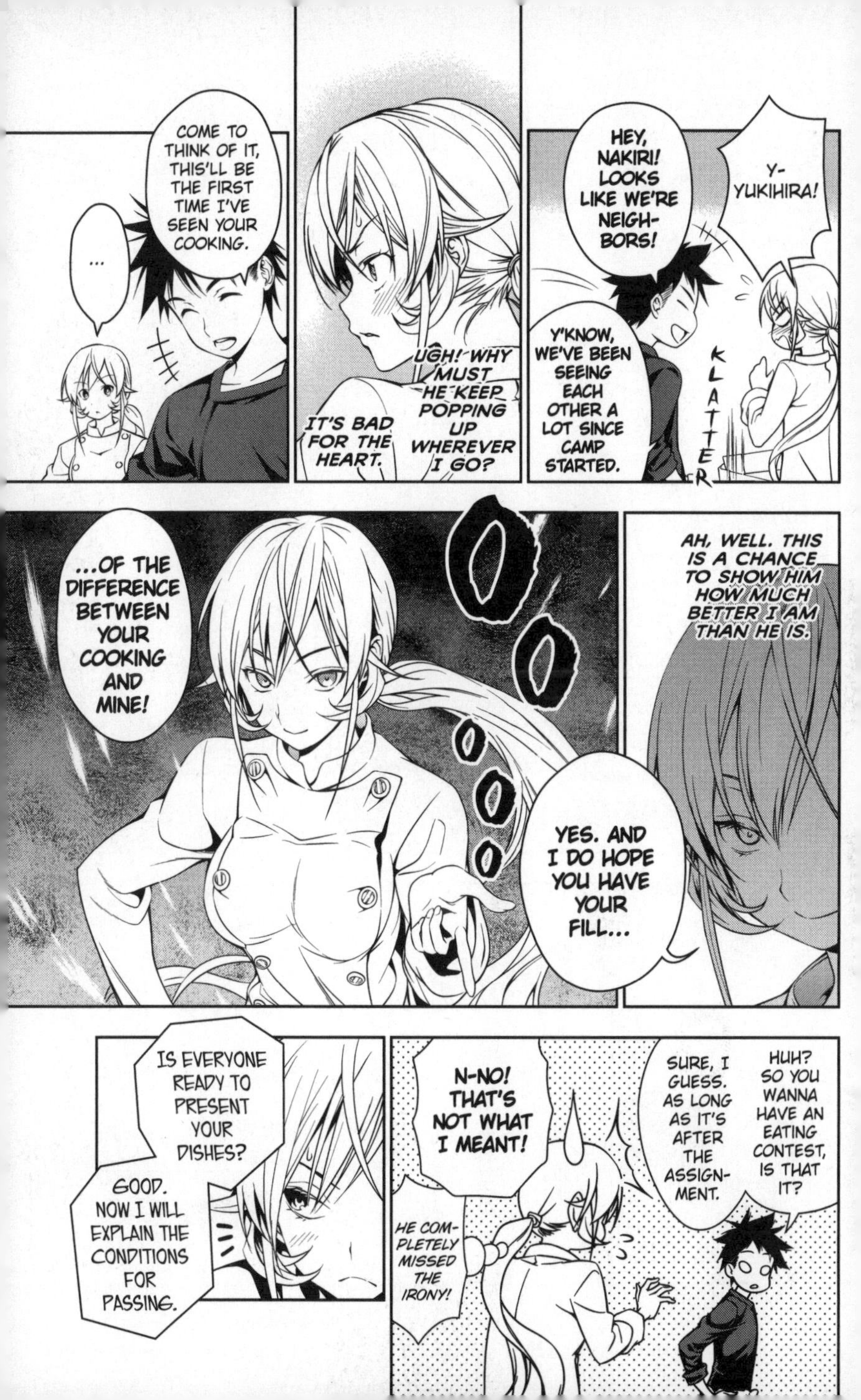
Y-YUKIHIRA!
KLATTER
HEY, NAKIRI! LOOKS LIKE WE'RE NEIGHBORS!
Y'KNOW, WE'VE BEEN SEEING EACH OTHER A LOT SINCE CAMP STARTED.
UGH! WHY MUST HE KEEP POPPING UP WHEREVER I GO?
IT'S BAD FOR THE HEART.
COME TO THINK OF IT, THIS'LL BE THE FIRST TIME I'VE SEEN YOUR COOKING.
...
AH, WELL. THIS IS A CHANCE TO SHOW HIM HOW MUCH BETTER I AM THAN HE IS.
YES. AND I DO HOPE YOU HAVE YOUR FILL...
...OF THE DIFFERENCE BETWEEN YOUR COOKING AND MINE!
HUH? SO YOU WANNA HAVE AN EATING CONTEST, IS THAT IT?
SURE, I GUESS. AS LONG AS IT'S AFTER THE ASSIGNMENT.
N-NO! THAT'S NOT WHAT I MEANT!
HE COMPLETELY MISSED THE IRONY!
IS EVERYONE READY TO PRESENT YOUR DISHES?
GOOD. NOW I WILL EXPLAIN THE CONDITIONS FOR PASSING.

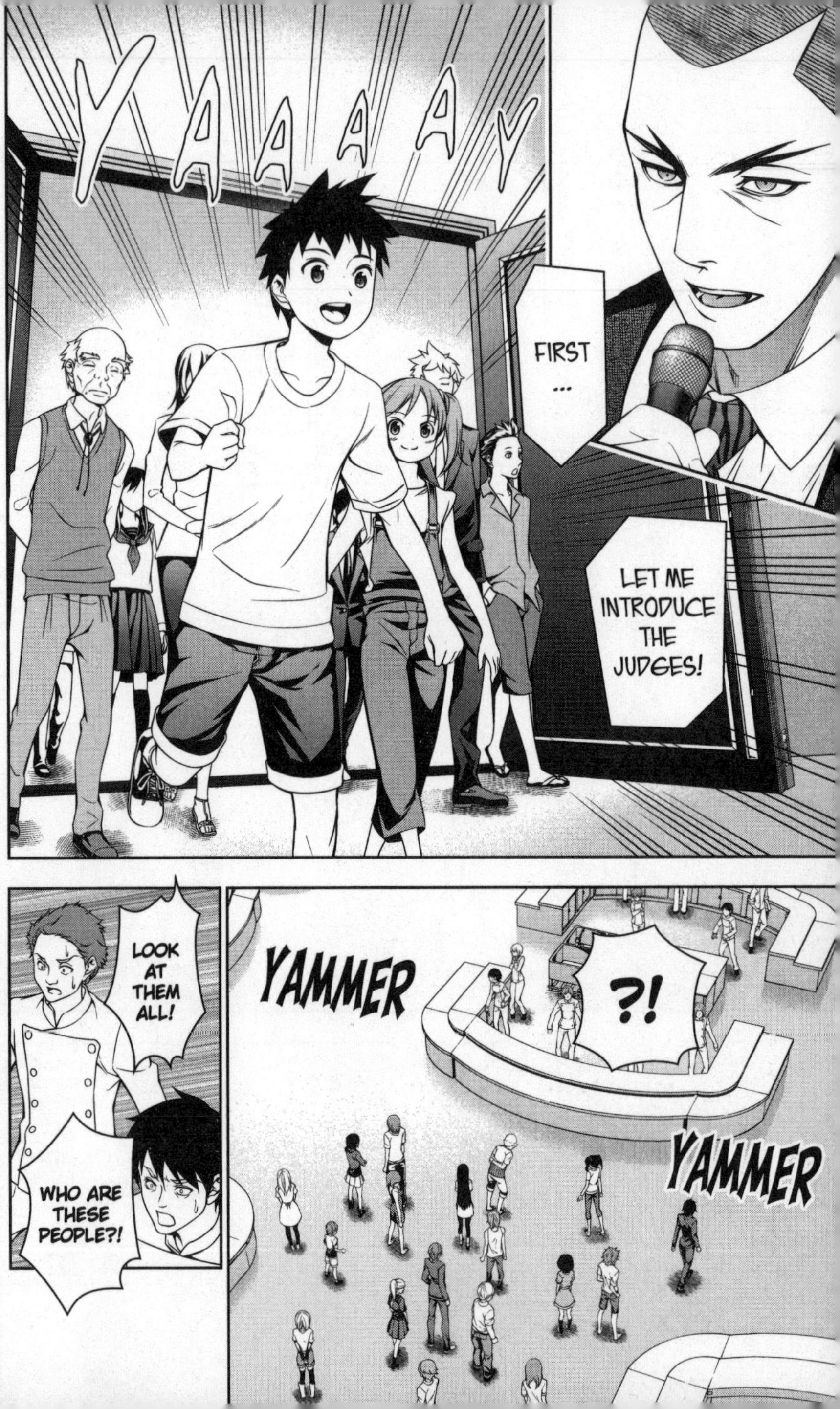
FIRST ...
LET ME INTRODUCE THE JUDGES!
YAAAAAY
?!
YAMMER
YAMMER
LOOK AT THEM ALL!
WHO ARE THESE PEOPLE?!

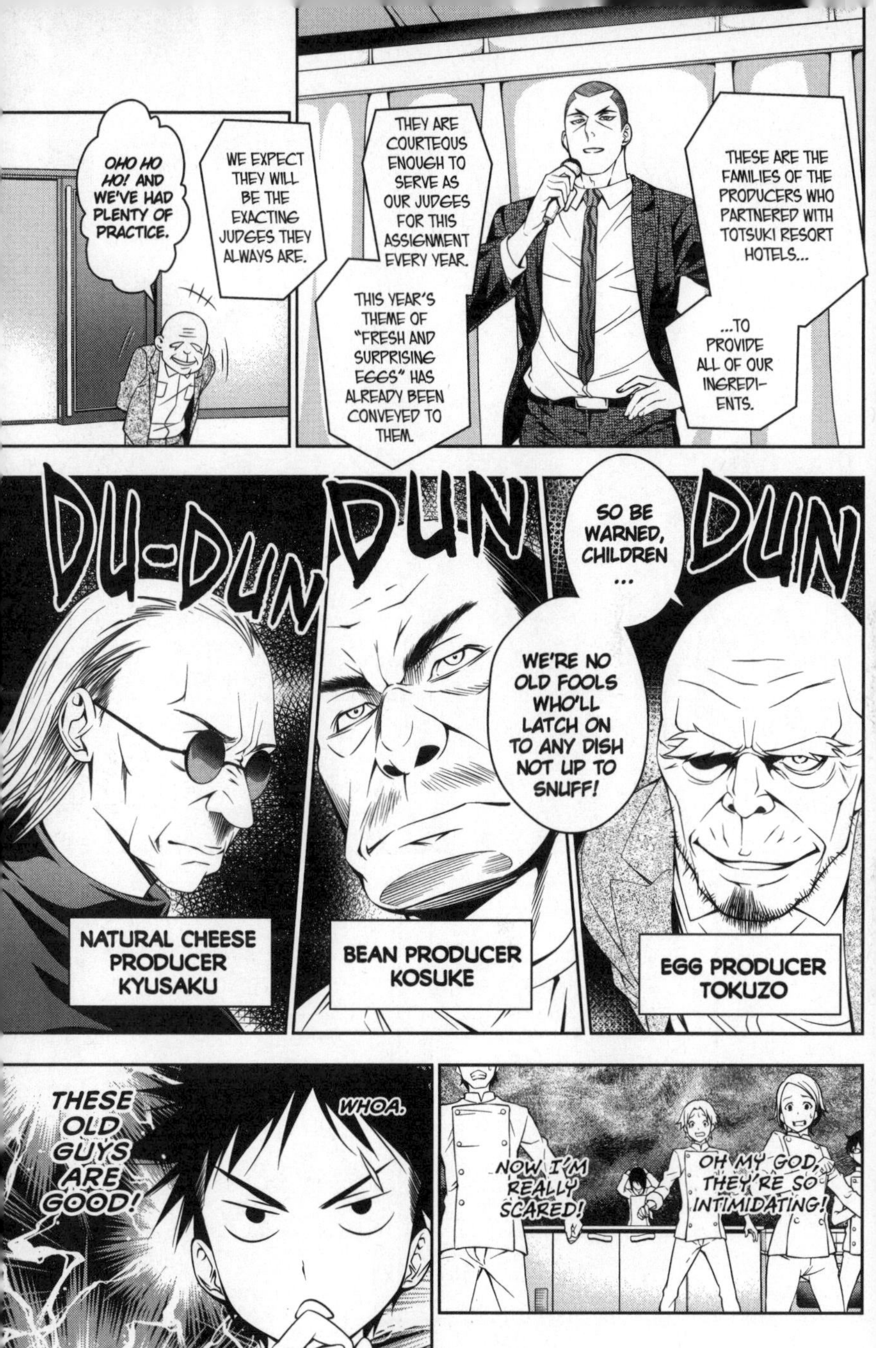
THESE ARE THE FAMILIES OF THE PRODUCERS WHO PARTNERED WITH TOTSUKI RESORT HOTELS...
...TO PROVIDE ALL OF OUR INGREDIENTS.
THEY ARE COURTEOUS ENOUGH TO SERVE AS OUR JUDGES FOR THIS ASSIGNMENT EVERY YEAR.
THIS YEAR'S THEME OF "FRESH AND SURPRISING EGGS" HAS ALREADY BEEN CONVEYED TO THEM.
WE EXPECT THEY WILL BE THE EXACTING JUDGES THEY ALWAYS ARE.
OHO HO HO! AND WE'VE HAD PLENTY OF PRACTICE.
DUN
SO BE WARNED, CHILDREN...
WE'RE NO OLD FOOLS WHO'LL LATCH ON TO ANY DISH NOT UP TO SNUFF!
EGG PRODUCER TOKUZO
DUN
BEAN PRODUCER KOSUKE
DU-DUN
NATURAL CHEESE PRODUCER KYUSAKU
OH MY GOD, THEY'RE SO INTIMIDATING!
NOW I'M REALLY SCARED!
WHOA.
THESE OLD GUYS ARE GOOD!

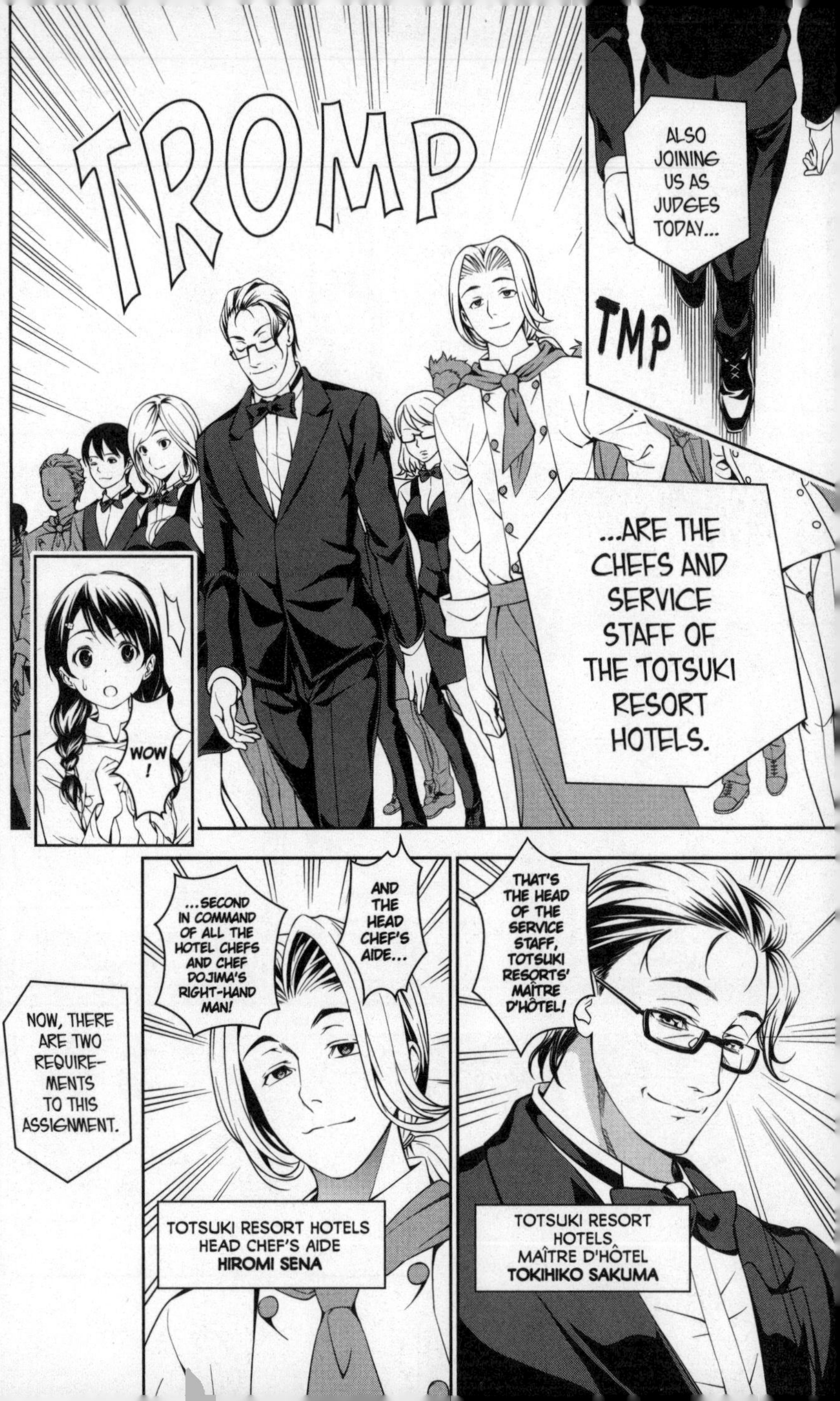
ALSO JOINING US AS JUDGES TODAY...
TMP
TROMP
...ARE THE CHEFS AND SERVICE STAFF OF THE TOTSUKI RESORT HOTELS.
WOW!
THAT'S THE HEAD OF THE SERVICE STAFF, TOTSUKI RESORTS' MAÎTRE D'HÔTEL!
TOTSUKI RESORT HOTELS MAÎTRE D'HÔTEL TOKIHIKO SAKUMA
AND THE HEAD CHEF'S AIDE...
...SECOND IN COMMAND OF ALL THE HOTEL CHEFS AND CHEF DOJIMA'S RIGHT-HAND MAN!
TOTSUKI RESORT HOTELS HEAD CHEF'S AIDE HIROMI SENA
NOW, THERE ARE TWO REQUIREMENTS TO THIS ASSIGNMENT.

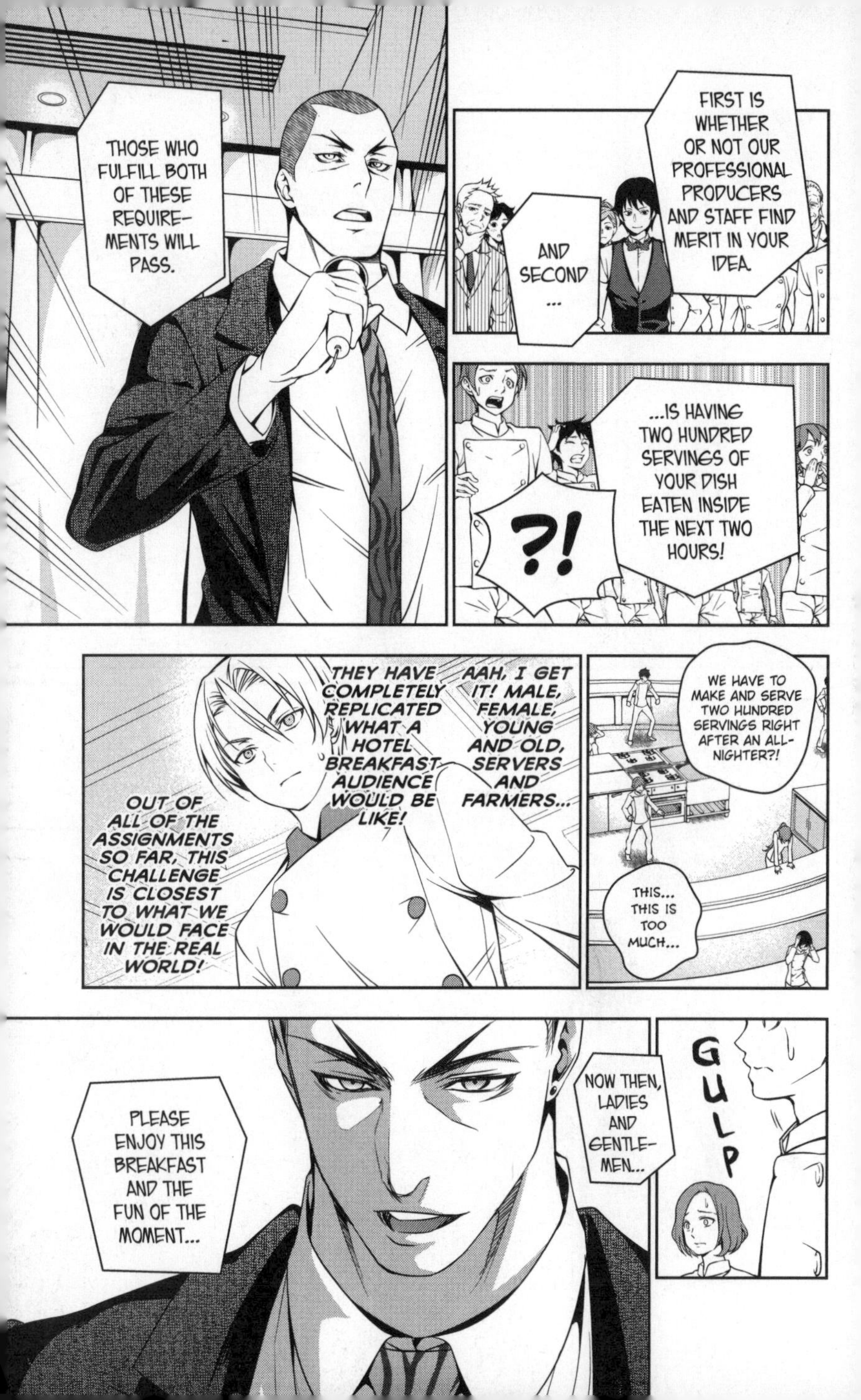
FIRST IS WHETHER OR NOT OUR PROFESSIONAL PRODUCERS AND STAFF FIND MERIT IN YOUR IDEA.
AND SECOND ...
...IS HAVING TWO HUNDRED SERVINGS OF YOUR DISH EATEN INSIDE THE NEXT TWO HOURS!
?!
THOSE WHO FULFILL BOTH OF THESE REQUIRE-MENTS WILL PASS.
WE HAVE TO MAKE AND SERVE TWO HUNDRED SERVINGS RIGHT AFTER AN ALL-NIGHTER?!
THIS... THIS IS TOO MUCH...
AAH, I GET IT! MALE, FEMALE, YOUNG AND OLD, SERVERS AND FARMERS...
THEY HAVE COMPLETELY REPLICATED WHAT A HOTEL BREAKFAST AUDIENCE WOULD BE LIKE!
OUT OF ALL OF THE ASSIGNMENTS SO FAR, THIS CHALLENGE IS CLOSEST TO WHAT WE WOULD FACE IN THE REAL WORLD!
GULP
NOW THEN, LADIES AND GENTLE-MEN...
PLEASE ENJOY THIS BREAKFAST AND THE FUN OF THE MOMENT...

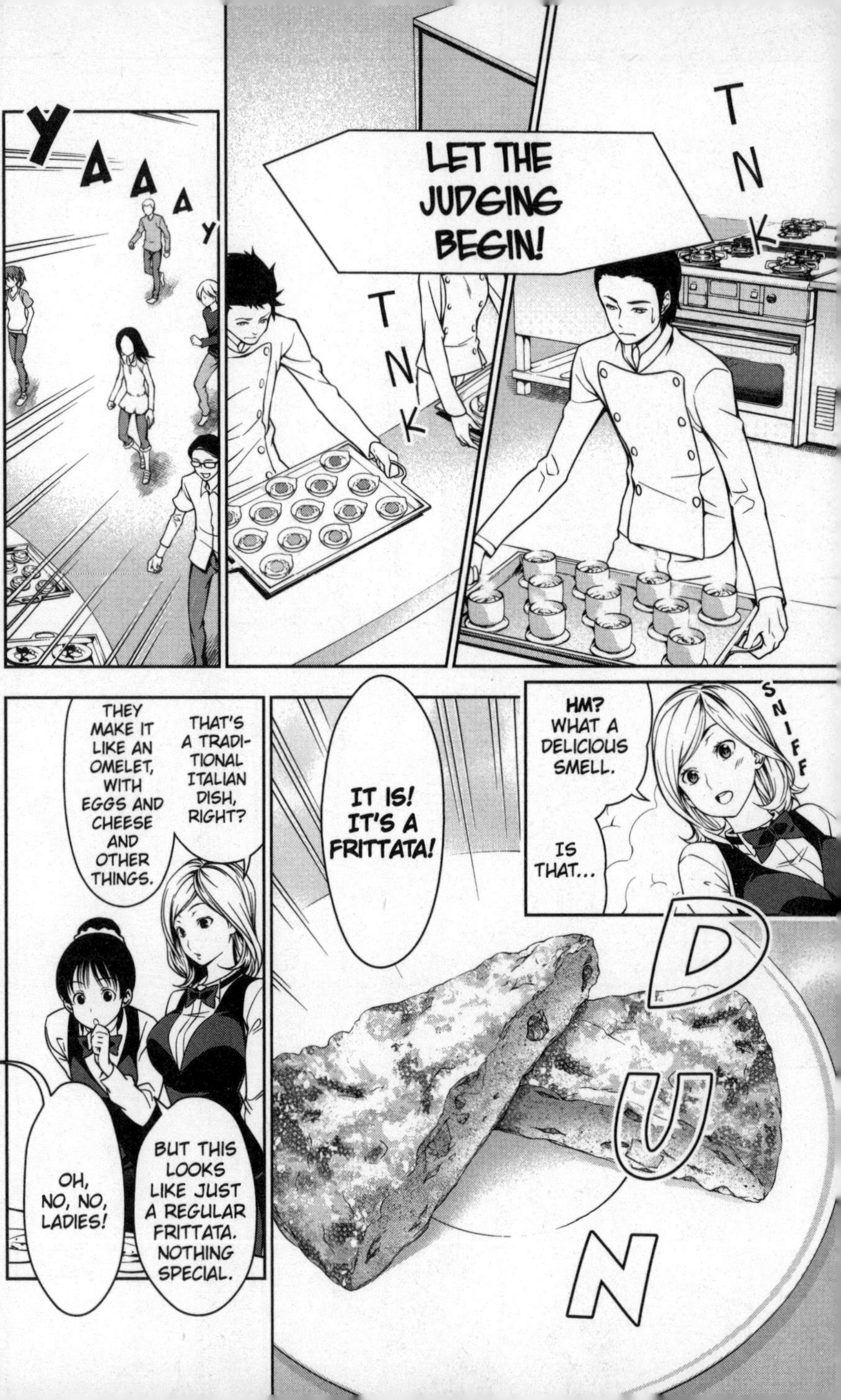
TNK
LET THE JUDGING BEGIN!
TNK
YAAAAY
SNIFF
HM? WHAT A DELICIOUS SMELL.
IS THAT...
IT IS! IT'S A FRITTATA!
DUN
THAT'S A TRADI-TIONAL ITALIAN DISH, RIGHT?
THEY MAKE IT LIKE AN OMELET, WITH EGGS AND CHEESE AND OTHER THINGS.
BUT THIS LOOKS LIKE JUST A REGULAR FRITTATA. NOTHING SPECIAL.
OH, NO, NO, LADIES!

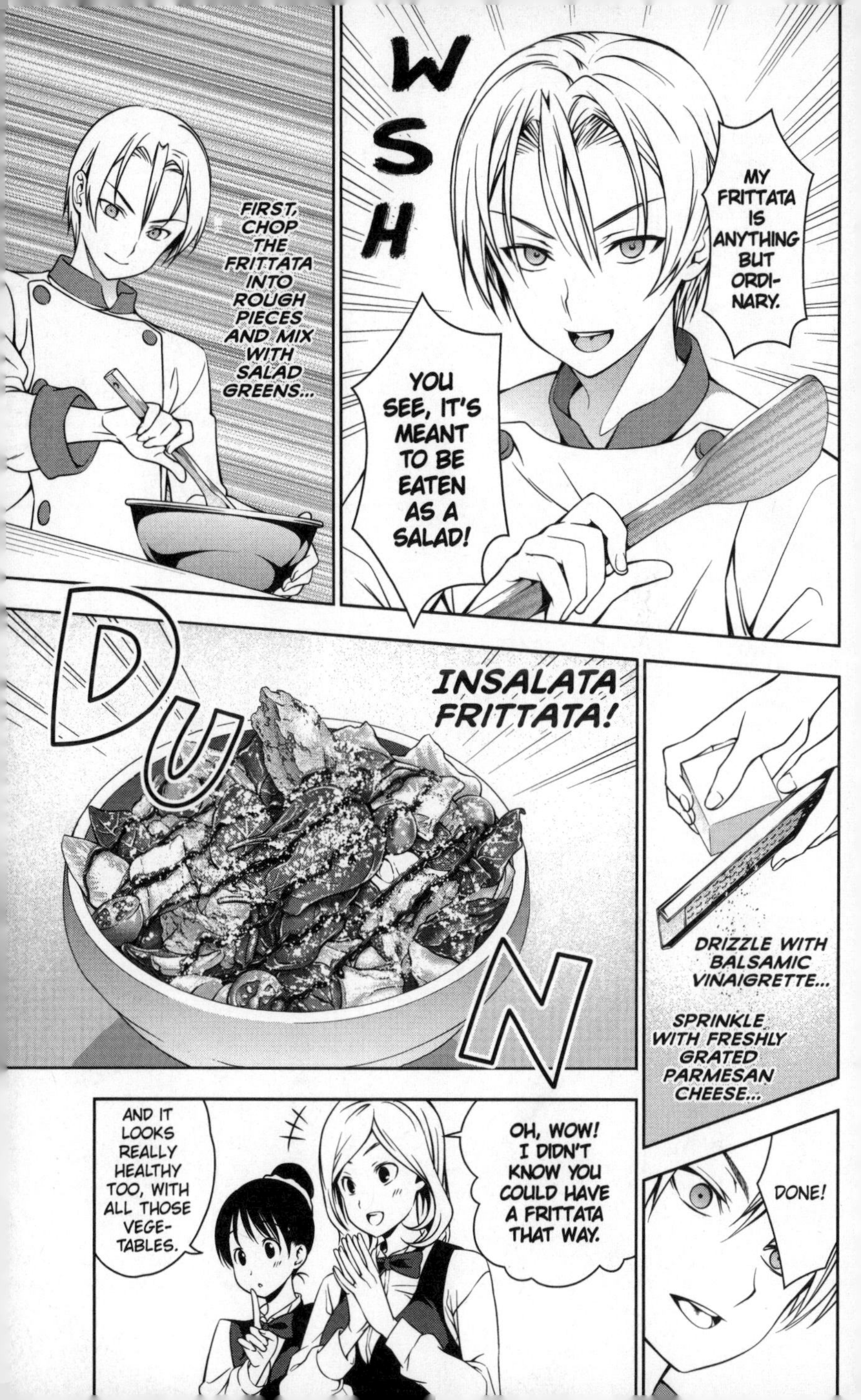

WSH
MY FRITTATA IS ANYTHING BUT ORDINARY.
YOU SEE, IT'S MEANT TO BE EATEN AS A SALAD!
FIRST, CHOP THE FRITTATA INTO ROUGH PIECES AND MIX WITH SALAD GREENS...
DRIZZLE WITH BALSAMIC VINAIGRETTE...
SPRINKLE WITH FRESHLY GRATED PARMESAN CHEESE...
DUN
INSALATA FRITTATA!
DONE!
OH, WOW! I DIDN'T KNOW YOU COULD HAVE A FRITTATA THAT WAY.
AND IT LOOKS REALLY HEALTHY TOO, WITH ALL THOSE VEGE-TABLES.

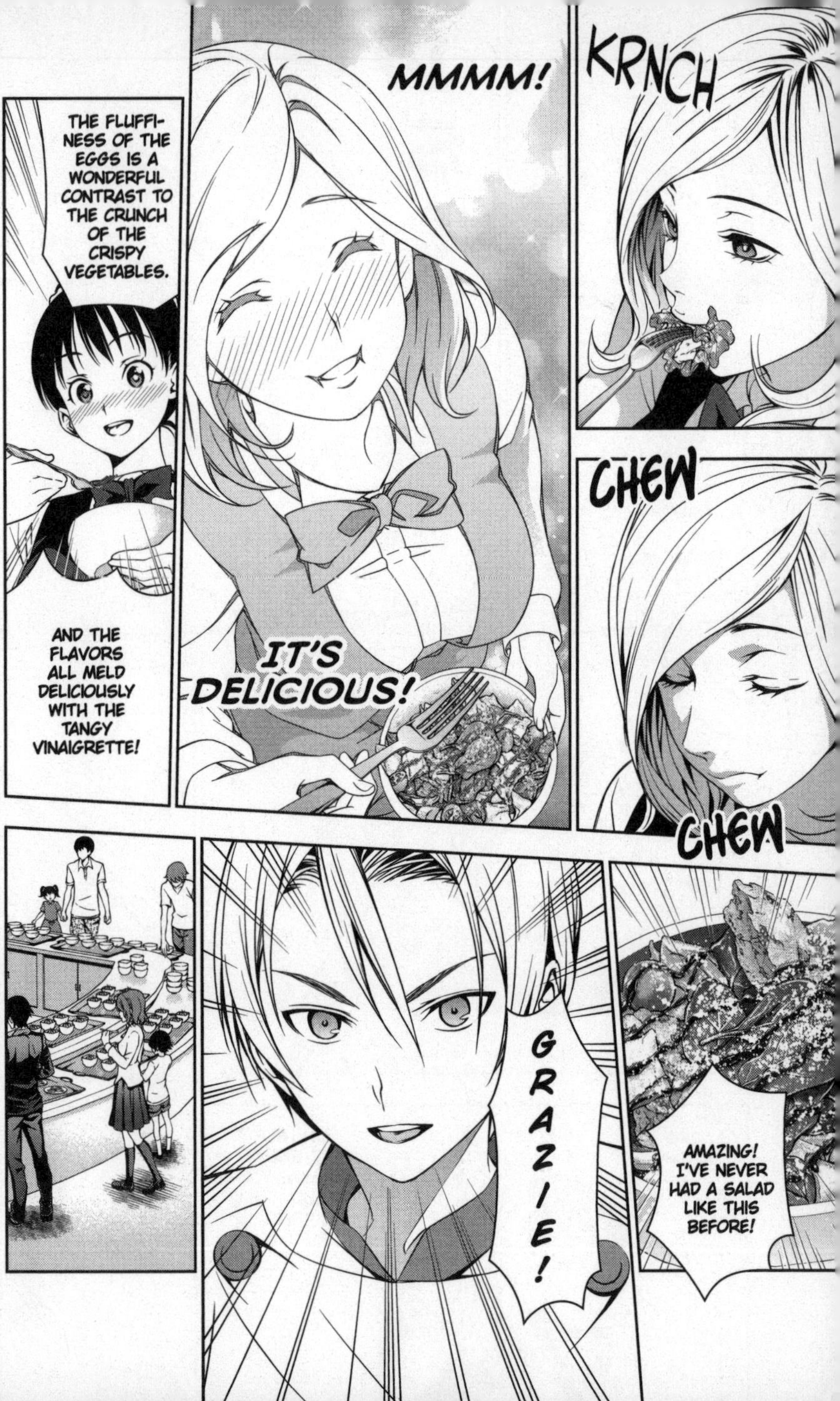
KRNCH
CHEW
CHEW
MMMM!
IT'S DELICIOUS!
THE FLUFFINESS OF THE EGGS IS A WONDERFUL CONTRAST TO THE CRUNCH OF THE CRISPY VEGETABLES.
AND THE FLAVORS ALL MELD DELICIOUSLY WITH THE TANGY VINAIGRETTE!
AMAZING! I'VE NEVER HAD A SALAD LIKE THIS BEFORE!
GRAZIE!

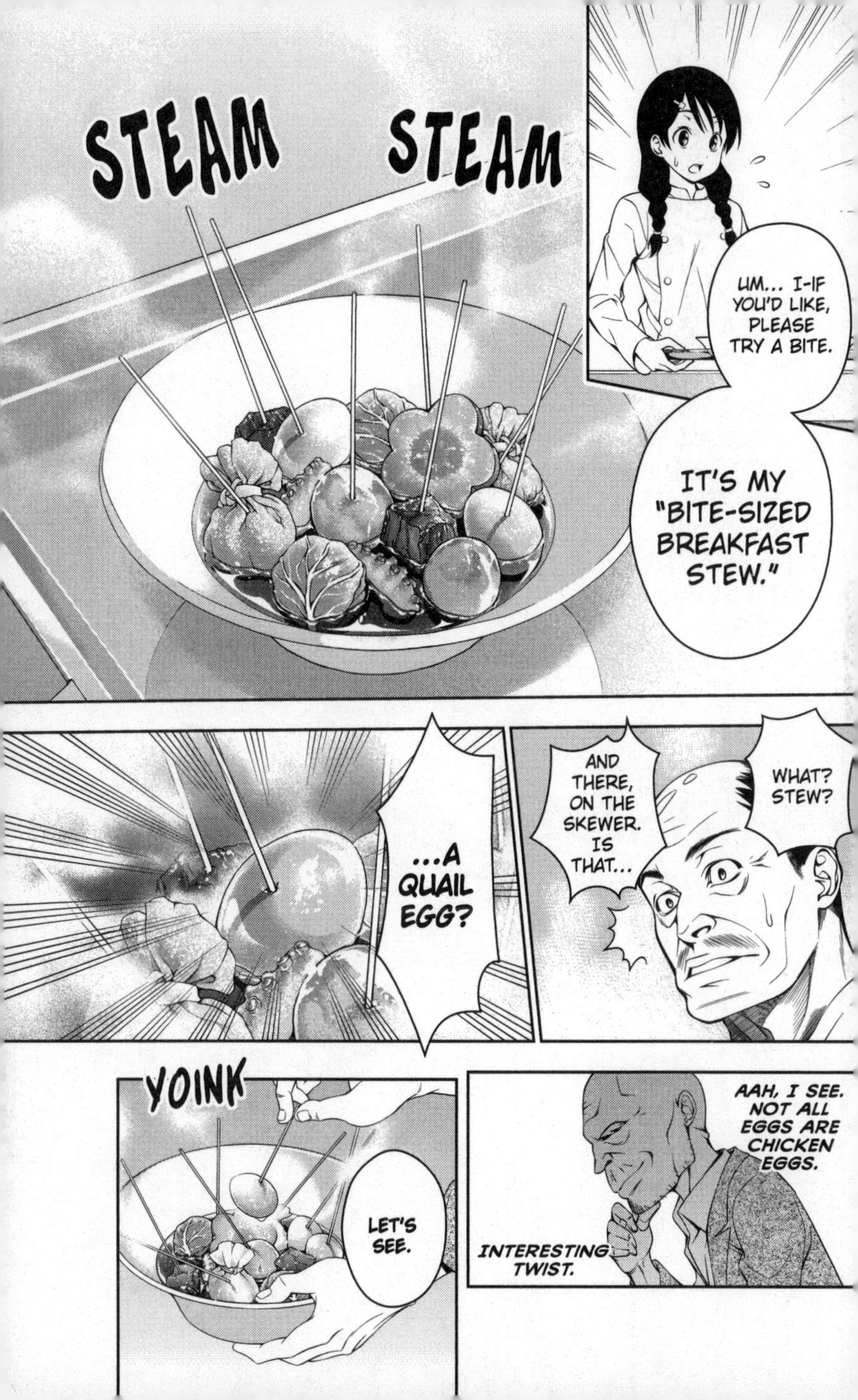
UM... I-IF YOU'D LIKE, PLEASE TRY A BITE.
IT'S MY "BITE-SIZED BREAKFAST STEW."
STEAM
STEAM
WHAT? STEW?
AND THERE, ON THE SKEWER. IS THAT...
...A QUAIL EGG?
AAH, I SEE. NOT ALL EGGS ARE CHICKEN EGGS.
INTERESTING TWIST.
YOINK
LET'S SEE.

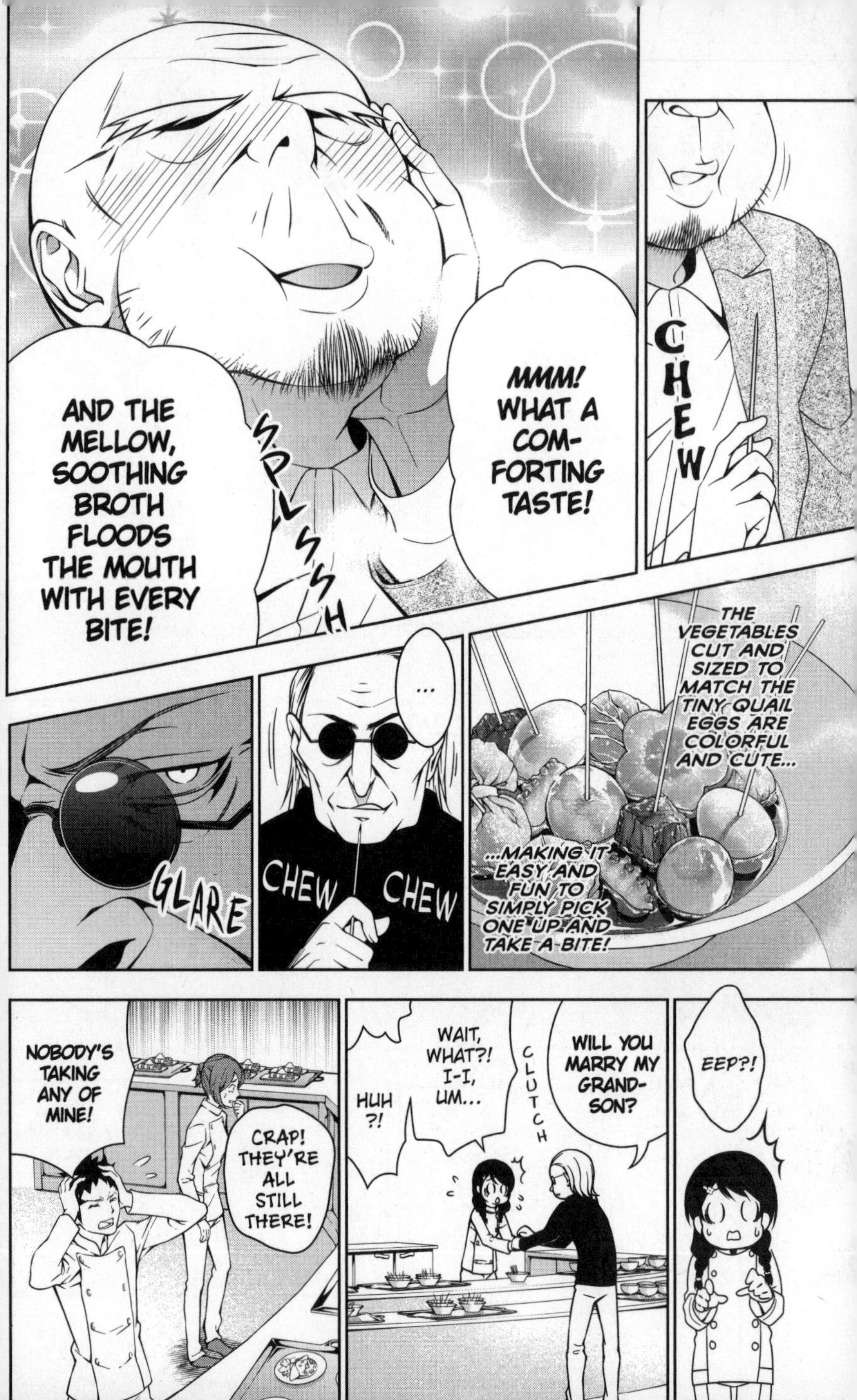
CHEW
MMM! WHAT A COM-FORTING TASTE!
AND THE MELLOW, SOOTHING BROTH FLOODS THE MOUTH WITH EVERY BITE!
SPLSSSH
THE VEGETABLES CUT AND SIZED TO MATCH THE TINY QUAIL EGGS ARE COLORFUL AND CUTE...
...MAKING IT EASY AND FUN TO SIMPLY PICK ONE UP AND TAKE A BITE!
...
CHEW CHEW
GLARE
EEP?!
WILL YOU MARRY MY GRAND-SON?
CLUTCH
WAIT, WHAT?! I-I, UM...
HUH ?!
NOBODY'S TAKING ANY OF MINE!
CRAP! THEY'RE ALL STILL THERE!

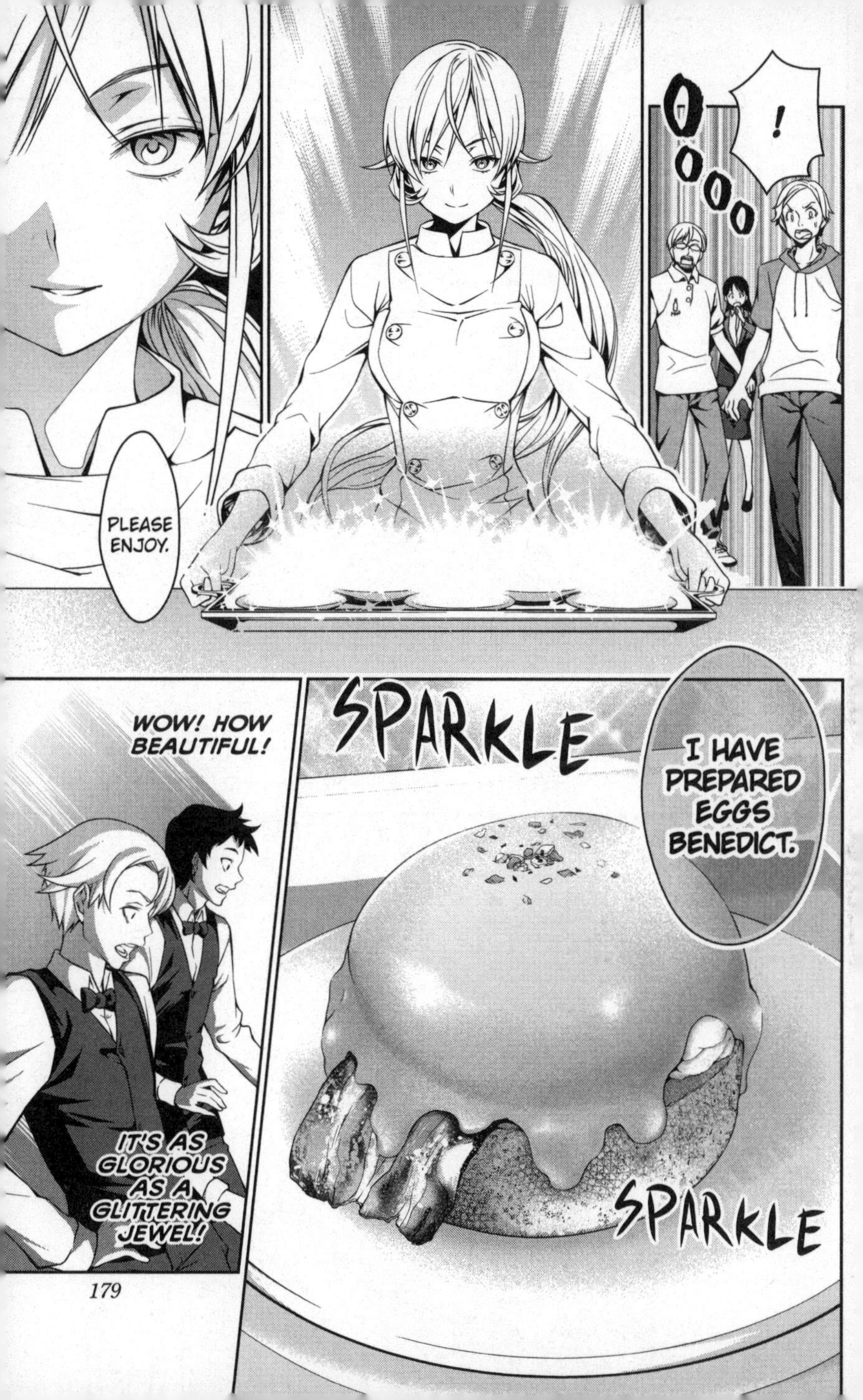
!
OOOO
PLEASE ENJOY.
SPARKLE
I HAVE PREPARED EGGS BENEDICT.
SPARKLE
WOW! HOW BEAUTIFUL!
IT'S AS GLORIOUS AS A GLITTERING JEWEL!

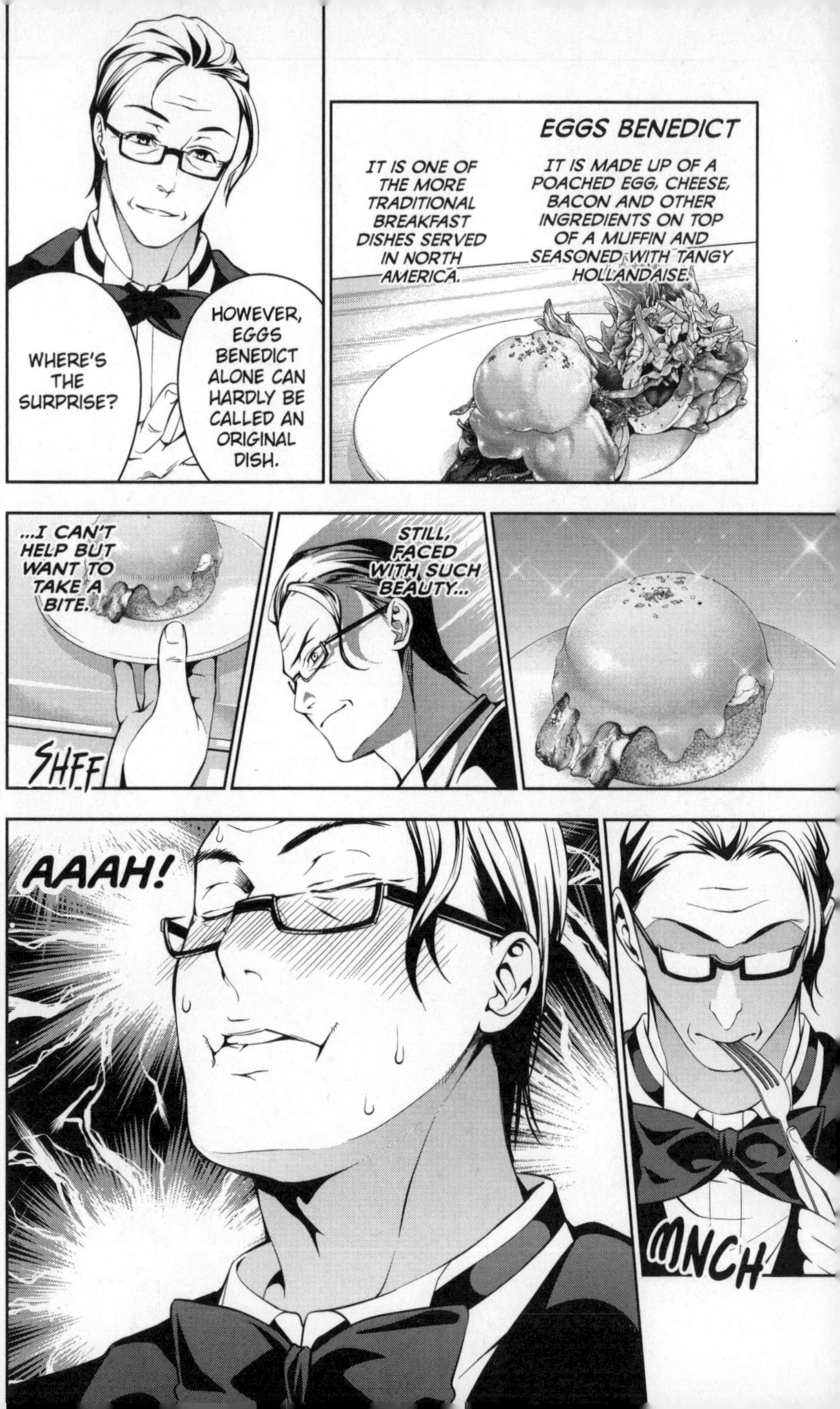
EGGS BENEDICT
IT IS MADE UP OF A POACHED EGG, CHEESE, BACON AND OTHER INGREDIENTS ON TOP OF A MUFFIN AND SEASONED WITH TANGY HOLLANDAISE.
IT IS ONE OF THE MORE TRADITIONAL BREAKFAST DISHES SERVED IN NORTH AMERICA.
HOWEVER, EGGS BENEDICT ALONE CAN HARDLY BE CALLED AN ORIGINAL DISH.
WHERE'S THE SURPRISE?
STILL, FACED WITH SUCH BEAUTY...
...I CAN'T HELP BUT WANT TO TAKE A BITE.
SHFF
MUNCH
AAAH!

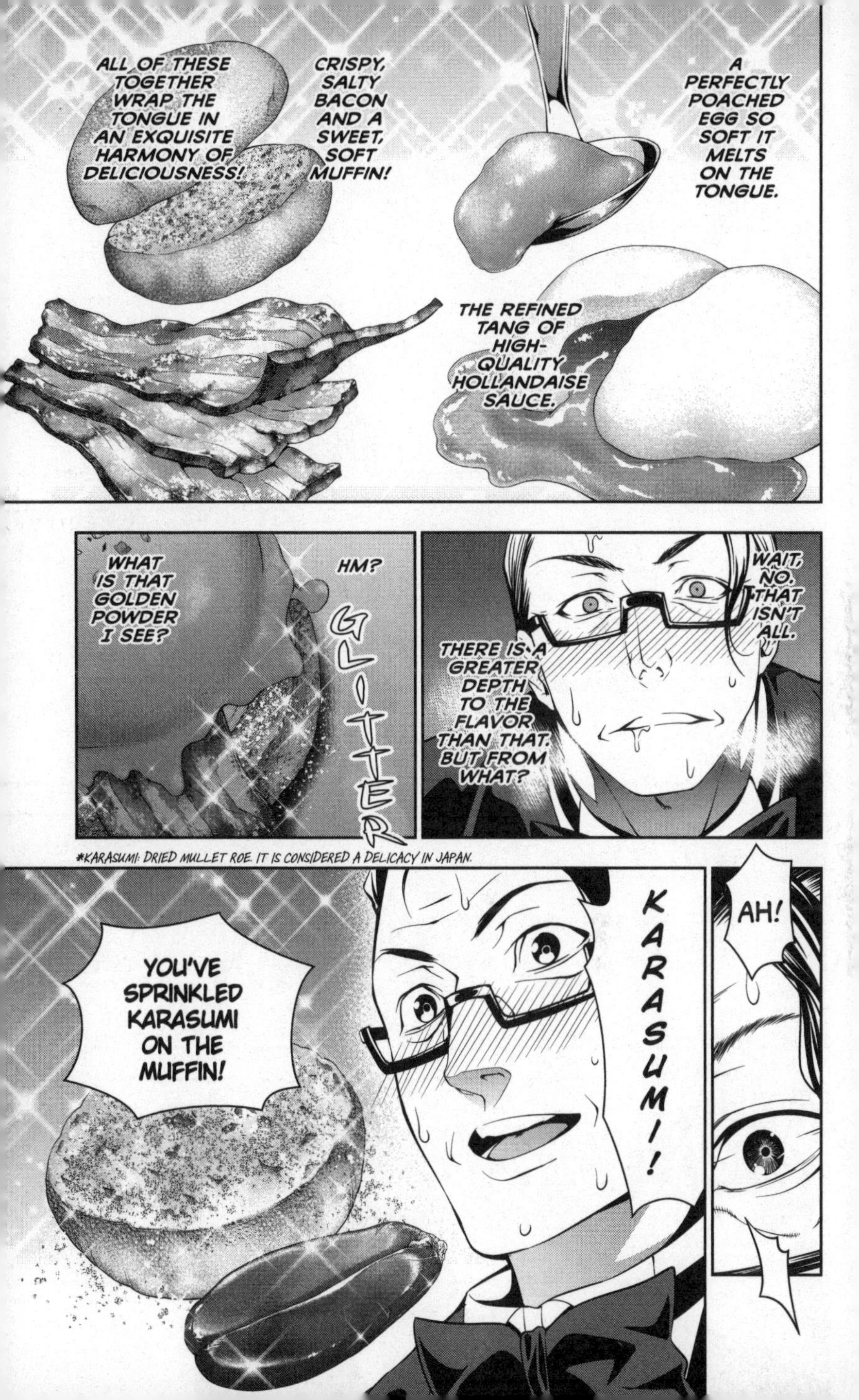
A PERFECTLY POACHED EGG SO SOFT IT MELTS ON THE TONGUE.
THE REFINED TANG OF HIGH-QUALITY HOLLANDAISE SAUCE.
CRISPY, SALTY BACON AND A SWEET, SOFT MUFFIN!
ALL OF THESE TOGETHER WRAP THE TONGUE IN AN EXQUISITE HARMONY OF DELICIOUSNESS!
WAIT, NO. THAT ISN'T ALL.
THERE IS A GREATER DEPTH TO THE FLAVOR THAN THAT. BUT FROM WHAT?
HM?
GLITTER
WHAT IS THAT GOLDEN POWDER I SEE?
AH!
KARASUMI!
YOU'VE SPRINKLED KARASUMI ON THE MUFFIN!
*KARASUMI: DRIED MULLET ROE. IT IS CONSIDERED A DELICACY IN JAPAN.

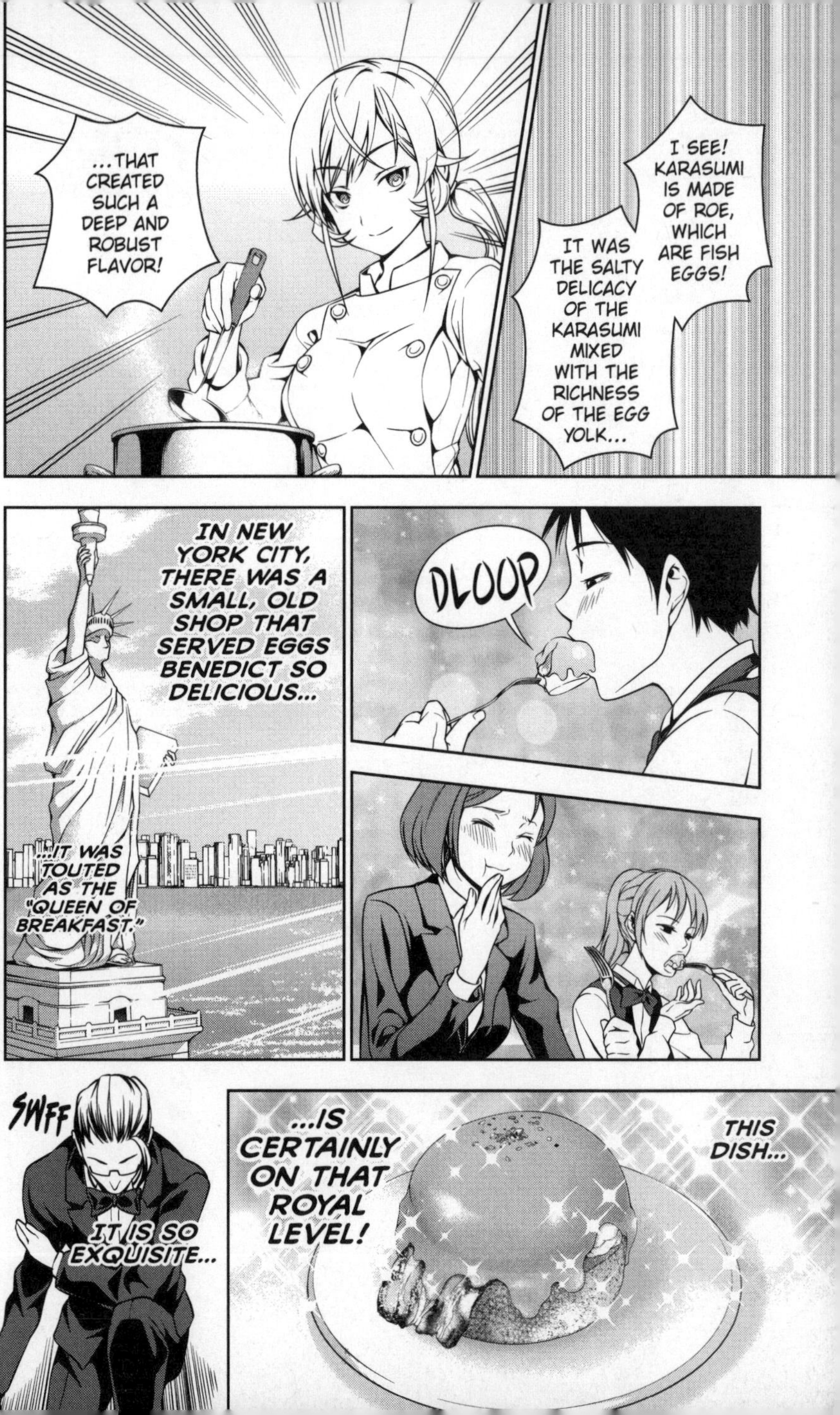
I SEE! KARASUMI IS MADE OF ROE, WHICH ARE FISH EGGS!
IT WAS THE SALTY DELICACY OF THE KARASUMI MIXED WITH THE RICHNESS OF THE EGG YOLK...
...THAT CREATED SUCH A DEEP AND ROBUST FLAVOR!
DLOOP
IN NEW YORK CITY, THERE WAS A SMALL, OLD SHOP THAT SERVED EGGS BENEDICT SO DELICIOUS...
...IT WAS TOUTED AS THE "QUEEN OF BREAKFAST."
THIS DISH...
...IS CERTAINLY ON THAT ROYAL LEVEL!
SWFF
IT IS SO EXQUISITE...

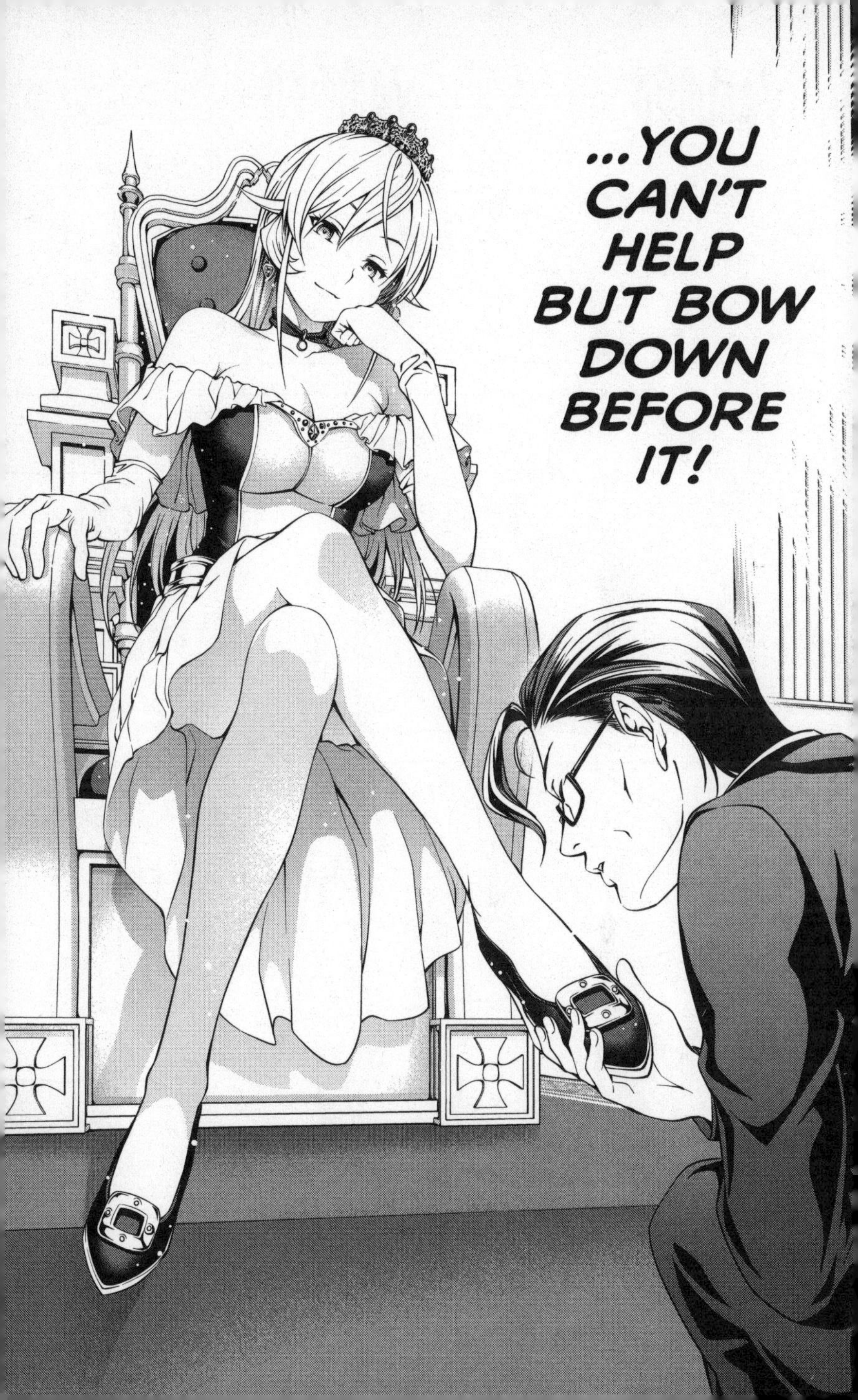
...YOU CAN'T HELP BUT BOW DOWN BEFORE IT!

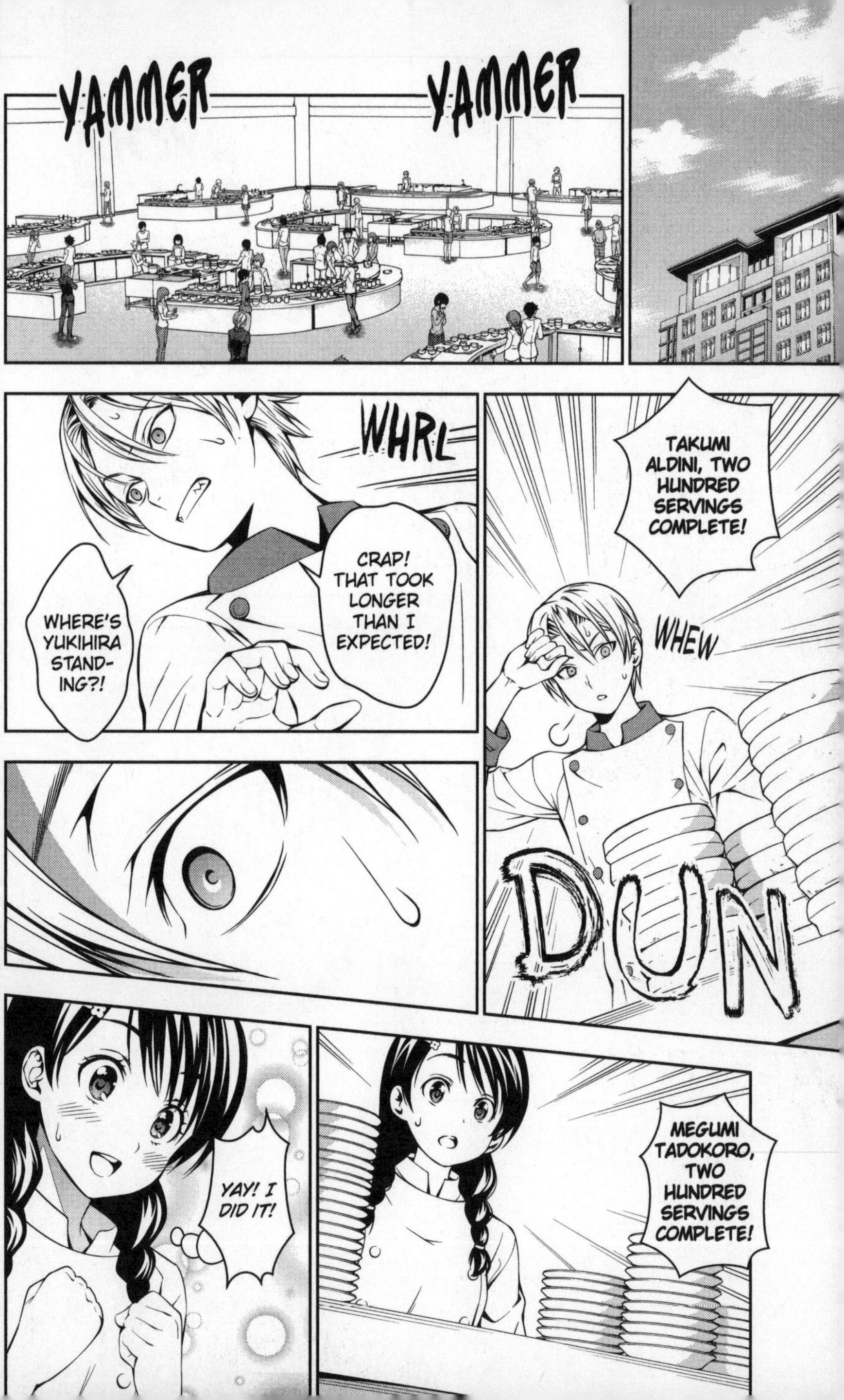
YAMMER
YAMMER
TAKUMI ALDINI, TWO HUNDRED SERVINGS COMPLETE!
WHEW
DUN
WHRL
CRAP! THAT TOOK LONGER THAN I EXPECTED!
WHERE'S YUKIHIRA STAND-ING?!
MEGUMI TADOKORO, TWO HUNDRED SERVINGS COMPLETE!
YAY! I DID IT!

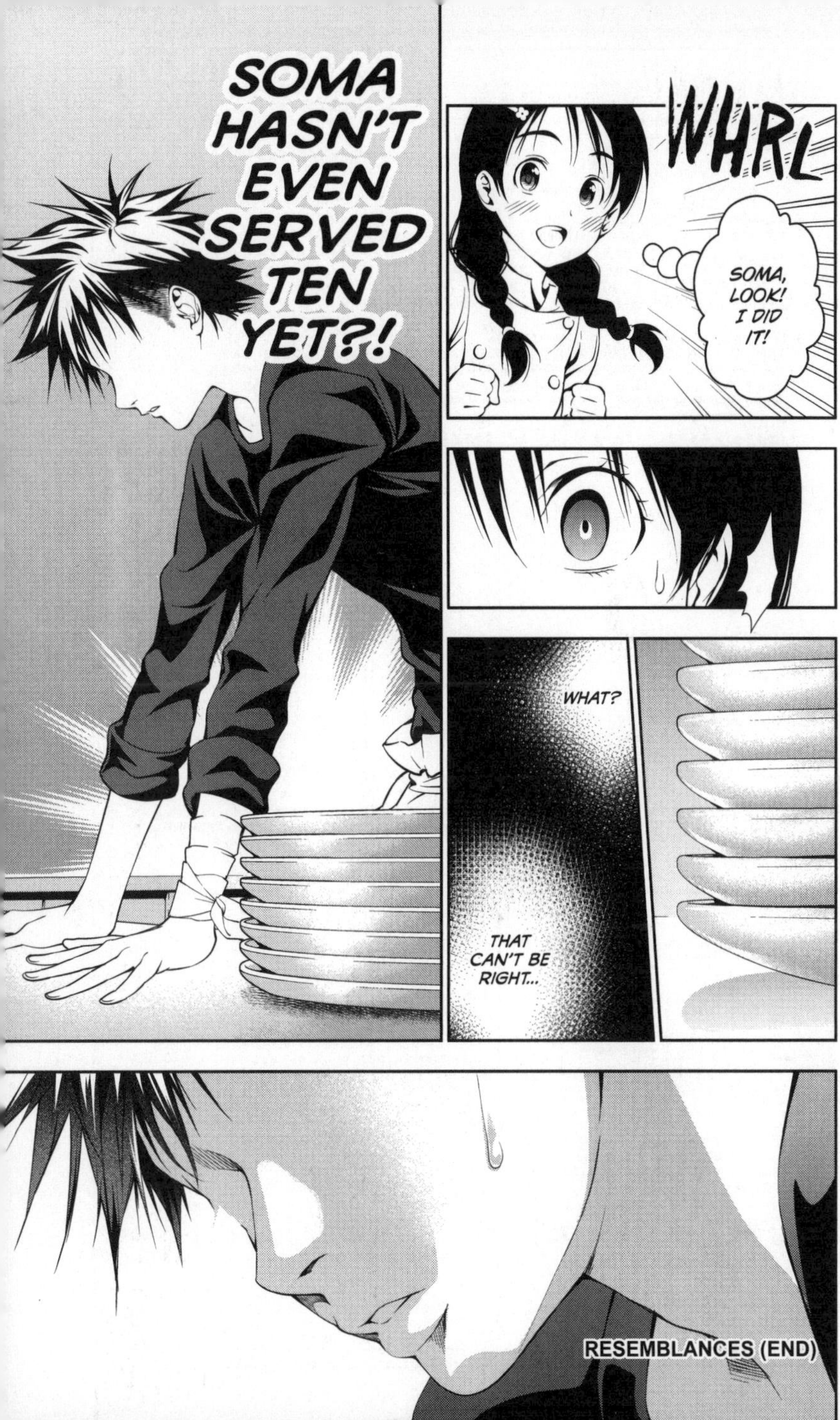
WHRL
SOMA, LOOK! I DID IT!
WHAT?
THAT CAN'T BE RIGHT...
SOMA HASN'T EVEN SERVED TEN YET?!
RESEMBLANCES (END)

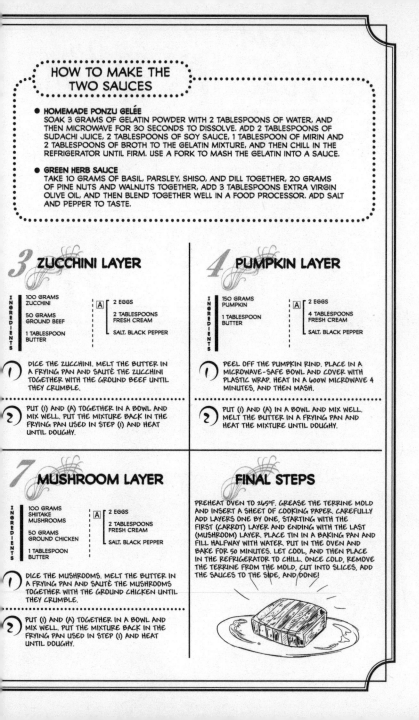

HOW TO MAKE THE TWO SAUCES

● **HOMEMADE PONZU GELÉE**
SOAK 3 GRAMS OF GELATIN POWDER WITH 2 TABLESPOONS OF WATER, AND THEN MICROWAVE FOR 30 SECONDS TO DISSOLVE. ADD 2 TABLESPOONS OF SUDACHI JUICE, 2 TABLESPOONS OF SOY SAUCE, 1 TABLESPOON OF MIRIN AND 2 TABLESPOONS OF BROTH TO THE GELATIN MIXTURE, AND THEN CHILL IN THE REFRIGERATOR UNTIL FIRM. USE A FORK TO MASH THE GELATIN INTO A SAUCE.

● **GREEN HERB SAUCE**
TAKE 10 GRAMS OF BASIL, PARSLEY, SHISO, AND DILL TOGETHER, 20 GRAMS OF PINE NUTS AND WALNUTS TOGETHER, ADD 3 TABLESPOONS EXTRA VIRGIN OLIVE OIL, AND THEN BLEND TOGETHER WELL IN A FOOD PROCESSOR. ADD SALT AND PEPPER TO TASTE.

3 ZUCCHINI LAYER

INGREDIENTS

100 GRAMS ZUCCHINI

50 GRAMS GROUND BEEF

1 TABLESPOON BUTTER

A
2 EGGS
2 TABLESPOONS FRESH CREAM
SALT, BLACK PEPPER

① DICE THE ZUCCHINI. MELT THE BUTTER IN A FRYING PAN AND SAUTÉ THE ZUCCHINI TOGETHER WITH THE GROUND BEEF UNTIL THEY CRUMBLE.

② PUT (1) AND (A) TOGETHER IN A BOWL AND MIX WELL. PUT THE MIXTURE BACK IN THE FRYING PAN USED IN STEP (1) AND HEAT UNTIL DOUGHY.

4 PUMPKIN LAYER

INGREDIENTS

150 GRAMS PUMPKIN

1 TABLESPOON BUTTER

A
2 EGGS
4 TABLESPOONS FRESH CREAM
SALT, BLACK PEPPER

① PEEL OFF THE PUMPKIN RIND. PLACE IN A MICROWAVE-SAFE BOWL AND COVER WITH PLASTIC WRAP. HEAT IN A 600W MICROWAVE 4 MINUTES, AND THEN MASH.

② PUT (1) AND (A) IN A BOWL AND MIX WELL. MELT THE BUTTER IN A FRYING PAN AND HEAT THE MIXTURE UNTIL DOUGHY.

7 MUSHROOM LAYER

INGREDIENTS

100 GRAMS SHIITAKE MUSHROOMS

50 GRAMS GROUND CHICKEN

1 TABLESPOON BUTTER

A
2 EGGS
2 TABLESPOONS FRESH CREAM
SALT, BLACK PEPPER

① DICE THE MUSHROOMS. MELT THE BUTTER IN A FRYING PAN AND SAUTÉ THE MUSHROOMS TOGETHER WITH THE GROUND CHICKEN UNTIL THEY CRUMBLE.

② PUT (1) AND (A) TOGETHER IN A BOWL AND MIX WELL. PUT THE MIXTURE BACK IN THE FRYING PAN USED IN STEP (1) AND HEAT UNTIL DOUGHY.

FINAL STEPS

PREHEAT OVEN TO 265°F. GREASE THE TERRINE MOLD AND INSERT A SHEET OF COOKING PAPER. CAREFULLY ADD LAYERS ONE BY ONE, STARTING WITH THE FIRST (CARROT) LAYER AND ENDING WITH THE LAST (MUSHROOM) LAYER. PLACE TIN IN A BAKING PAN AND FILL HALFWAY WITH WATER. PUT IN THE OVEN AND BAKE FOR 50 MINUTES. LET COOL, AND THEN PLACE IN THE REFRIGERATOR TO CHILL. ONCE COLD, REMOVE THE TERRINE FROM THE MOLD, CUT INTO SLICES, ADD THE SAUCES TO THE SIDE, AND DONE!

PRACTICAL RECIPE #2

VOLUME 4
SPECIAL SUPPLEMENT!

RAINBOW TERRINE

WHOA! THIS RECIPE IS TWO PAGES LONG!
I TRADED OUT SOME OF THE HARD-TO-GET INGREDIENTS WITH EASIER ONES.

ARTIST: YUTO TSUKUDA

NECESSARY ITEMS (ONE 35 CM TERRINE MOLD)

FIRST WE'LL MAKE THE SEVEN LAYERS AND THEN BAKE THEM IN THE OVEN.

1 CARROT LAYER

INGREDIENTS

- 100 GRAMS CARROTS
- 50 GRAMS GROUND CHICKEN
- 1 TABLESPOON BUTTER

A
- 2 EGGS
- 2 TABLESPOONS FRESH CREAM
- SALT, BLACK PEPPER

(1) DICE THE CARROTS. MELT THE BUTTER IN A FRYING PAN AND SAUTÉ THE CARROTS TOGETHER WITH THE GROUND CHICKEN UNTIL THEY CRUMBLE.

(2) PUT (1) AND (A) TOGETHER IN A BOWL AND MIX WELL. PUT THE MIXTURE BACK IN THE FRYING PAN USED IN STEP ONE (1) AND HEAT UNTIL DOUGHY.

2 SPINACH LAYER

INGREDIENTS

- 100 GRAMS SPINACH
- 1 TABLESPOON BUTTER

A
- 2 EGGS
- 2 TABLESPOONS CANNED TUNA
- 2 TABLESPOONS FRESH CREAM
- SALT, BLACK PEPPER

(1) BOIL THE SPINACH, THEN MINCE.

(2) PUT (1) AND (A) IN A BOWL AND MIX WELL. MELT THE BUTTER IN A FRYING PAN AND HEAT THE MIXTURE UNTIL DOUGHY.

5 POTATO LAYER

INGREDIENTS

- 120 GRAMS POTATOES
- 1 TABLESPOON BUTTER

A
- 2 EGGS
- 4 TABLESPOONS FRESH CREAM
- SALT, BLACK PEPPER

(1) PEEL THE POTATOES. PLACE IN A MICROWAVE-SAFE BOWL AND COVER WITH PLASTIC WRAP. HEAT IN A 600W MICROWAVE 4 MINUTES, THEN MASH.

(2) PUT (1) AND (A) IN A BOWL AND MIX WELL. MELT THE BUTTER IN A FRYING PAN AND HEAT THE MIXTURE UNTIL DOUGHY.

6 TOMATO LAYER

INGREDIENTS

- 50 GRAMS SEMI-DRIED TOMATOES
- 1 TABLESPOON BUTTER

A
- 2 TABLESPOONS TOMATO PASTE
- 2 EGGS
- 2 TABLESPOONS FRESH CREAM
- SALT, BLACK PEPPER

(1) CHOP THE SEMI-DRIED TOMATOES INTO SEMI-LARGE CHUNKS.

(2) PUT (1) AND (A) IN A BOWL AND MIX WELL. MELT THE BUTTER IN A FRYING PAN AND HEAT THE MIXTURE UNTIL DOUGHY.

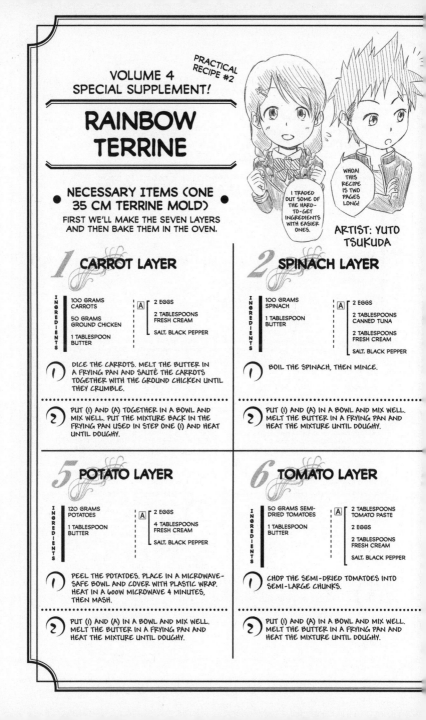

PRACTICAL RECIPE #3

VOLUME 4
SPECIAL SUPPLEMENT!

INSALATA FRITTATA ~ALDINI STYLE~

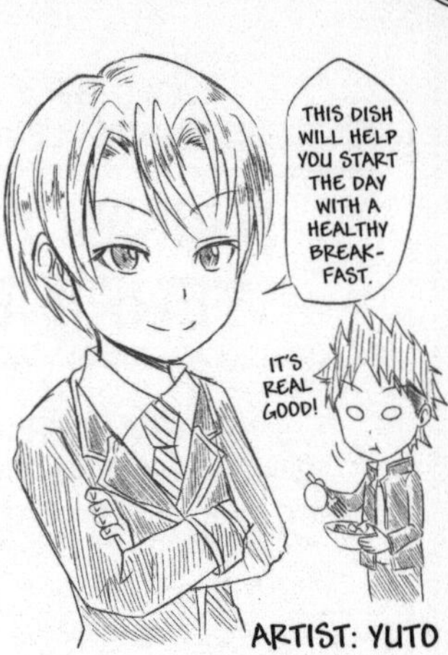
THIS DISH WILL HELP YOU START THE DAY WITH A HEALTHY BREAK-FAST.
IT'S REAL GOOD!

ARTIST: YUTO TSUKUDA

INGREDIENTS

- 4 EGGS
- 1/2 ONION
- 1 RED BELL PEPPER
- 2 PIECES BACON
- 100 GRAMS MOZZARELLA CHEESE
- 1 CUCUMBER
- 1 TOMATO
- SALT, PEPPER
- 2 TABLESPOONS OLIVE OIL
- MESCLUN, RED-LEAF LETTUCE, PARMESAN CHEESE, HAM

[A]
- 2 TABLESPOONS BALSAMIC VINEGAR
- 4 TABLESPOONS EXTRA VIRGIN OLIVE OIL
- 1 TEASPOON EACH MUSTARD POWDER AND HONEY

1. FINELY CHOP THE ONION. DICE THE BACON, BELL PEPPER AND MOZZARELLA CHEESE.

2. HEAT 1 TABLESPOON OLIVE OIL IN A FRYING PAN. SAUTÉ THE BACON TOGETHER WITH THE ONIONS AND BELL PEPPERS UNTIL TENDER. REMOVE FROM THE PAN.

3. SCRAMBLE THE EGGS IN A BOWL, AND THEN ADD IN (1) AND THE MOZZARELLA CHEESE. SPRINKLE WITH SALT AND PEPPER.

4. HEAT THE REMAINING OLIVE OIL IN A FRYING PAN. POUR IN (3) WHILE STIRRING, AND THEN NEATEN INTO SHAPE. COVER AND COOK ABOUT 5 MINUTES, OR UNTIL THE EGGS ARE HALFWAY COOKED. FLIP OVER AND COOK THE OTHER SIDE ANOTHER 5 MINUTES.

5. SLICE THE CUCUMBER. CUT THE TOMATO INTO WEDGES. RIP THE LETTUCE INTO BITE-SIZED PIECES BY HAND. PLACE INTO A BOWL WITH THE MESCLUN AND HAM.

6. MAKE THE DRESSING. PUT (A) IN A BOWL AND WHISK THOROUGHLY UNTIL OIL AND VINEGAR ARE EVENLY MIXED. SEASON WITH SALT AND PEPPER TO TASTE.

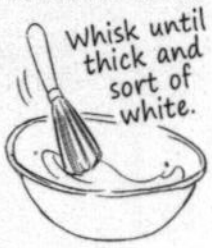
Whisk until thick and sort of white.

7. RIGHT BEFORE EATING, PLACE (4) IN (5). CHOP (4) INTO ROUGH CHUNKS AND MIX WELL WITH (5). DRIZZLE WITH (6), SPRINKLE WITH FRESHLY GRATED PARMESAN CHEESE, AND DONE!

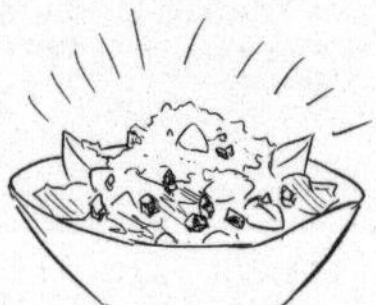

PRACTICAL RECIPE #4

VOLUME 4 SPECIAL SUPPLEMENT!

MEGUMI TADOKORO'S BITE-SIZED BREAKFAST STEW

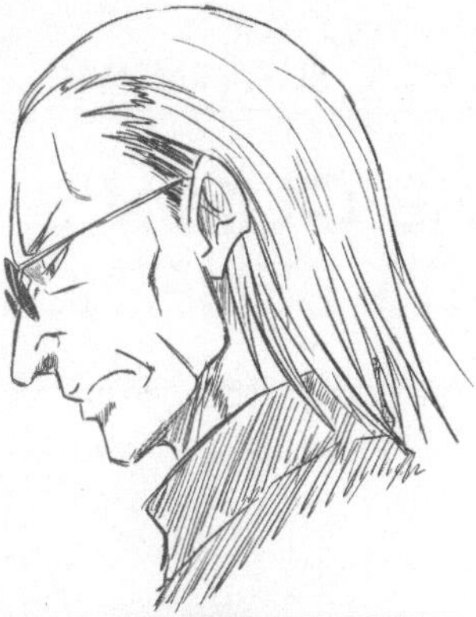

NATURAL CHEESE PRODUCER KYUSAKU
HOBBY: COLLECTING JAZZ RECORDS

ARTIST: YUTO TSUKUDA

INGREDIENTS

- 300 GRAMS DAIKON RADISH
- 1 CARROT
- 8 MINI CABBAGES
- 8 HARD-BOILED QUAIL EGGS
- 1 PIECE KONYAKU
- 2 PIECES SATSUMA AGE
- 1 PIECE HANPEN
- 2 CHIKUWA
- SALT, MUSTARD PASTE
- BAMBOO SKEWERS

★ MINI MOCHI KINCHAKU

- 4 PIECES MINI ABURAAGE
- 4 QUAIL EGGS
- 1 KIRIMOCHI CAKE
- GARLIC CHIVES

[A]

- 1 LITER BROTH
- 1 TABLESPOON EACH SUGAR, SAKE, MIRIN
- 1 TABLESPOON SOY SAUCE

1

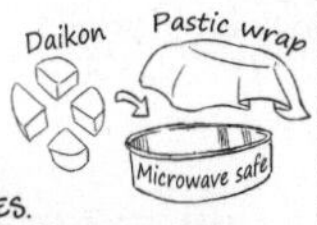
Daikon
Pastic wrap
Microwave safe

PEEL THE DAIKON RADISH, CUT INTO 3 CM. THICK SLICES, AND THEN QUARTER THE SLICES. PLACE IN A MICROWAVE-SAFE BOWL, COVER WITH PLASTIC WRAP AND HEAT FOR 6 MINUTES IN A 600W MICROWAVE. PEEL THE CARROT AND CUT INTO FLOWER SHAPES WITH A COOKIE CUTTER.

2

CUT THE KONYAKU INTO BITE-SIZED PIECES AND BOIL. WASH SATSUMA AGE IN HOT WATER TO REMOVE OILINESS. CUT THE HANPEN AND CHIKUWA INTO BITE-SIZED PIECES.

3

CUT THE MINI ABURAAGE PIECES IN HALF DIAGONALLY. USING YOUR HANDS, OPEN THE MIDDLE OF EACH TO FORM A POCKET. AND THEN WASH WITH HOT WATER TO REMOVE OILINESS. BOIL THE GARLIC CHIVES, AND THEN DRY. CUT THE KIRIMOCHI CAKE INTO 8 EQUAL PIECES.

4

PUT A KIRIMOCHI PIECE AND A HARD-BOILED QUAIL EGG INTO EACH ABURAAGE POCKET. GATHER THE ABURAAGE ENDS TOGETHER INTO A POUCH AND TIE TIGHTLY CLOSED WITH A GARLIC CHIVE.

5

PUT (A) INTO A POT AND ADD ALL REMAINING INGREDIENTS EXCEPT THE HANPEN. PUT A DROP-LID ON THE POT, HEAT TO A BOIL, AND THEN REDUCE HEAT AND SIMMER FOR APPROXIMATELY 1 HOUR. ADD THE HANPEN DIRECTLY BEFORE EATING AND BOIL FOR ONLY A FEW MINUTES. POUR INTO A BOWL, STICK WITH BAMBOO SKEWERS, PLACE MUSTARD PASTE TO THE SIDE, AND DONE!

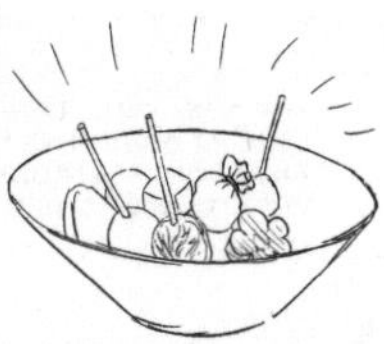

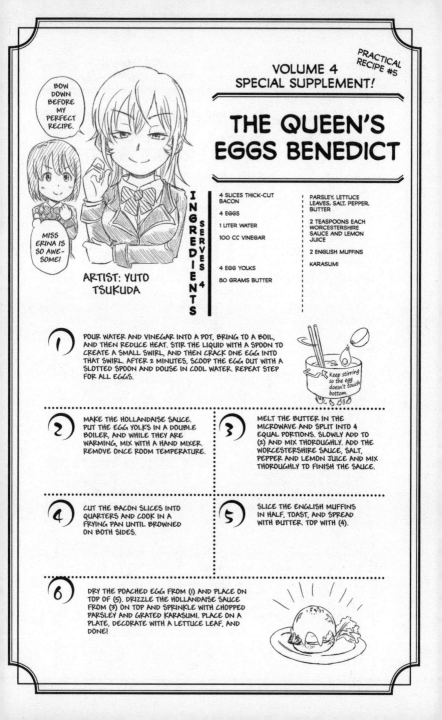

VOLUME 4
SPECIAL SUPPLEMENT!

THE QUEEN'S EGGS BENEDICT

BOW DOWN BEFORE MY PERFECT RECIPE.

MISS ERINA IS SO AWESOME!

ARTIST: YUTO TSUKUDA

INGREDIENTS — SERVES 4

4 SLICES THICK-CUT BACON

4 EGGS

1 LITER WATER

100 CC VINEGAR

4 EGG YOLKS

80 GRAMS BUTTER

PARSLEY, LETTUCE LEAVES, SALT, PEPPER, BUTTER

2 TEASPOONS EACH WORCESTERSHIRE SAUCE AND LEMON JUICE

2 ENGLISH MUFFINS

KARASUMI

1 POUR WATER AND VINEGAR INTO A POT, BRING TO A BOIL, AND THEN REDUCE HEAT. STIR THE LIQUID WITH A SPOON TO CREATE A SMALL SWIRL, AND THEN CRACK ONE EGG INTO THAT SWIRL. AFTER 2 MINUTES, SCOOP THE EGG OUT WITH A SLOTTED SPOON AND DOUSE IN COOL WATER. REPEAT STEP FOR ALL EGGS.

Keep stirring so the egg doesn't touch bottom.

2 MAKE THE HOLLANDAISE SAUCE. PUT THE EGG YOLKS IN A DOUBLE BOILER, AND WHILE THEY ARE WARMING, MIX WITH A HAND MIXER. REMOVE ONCE ROOM TEMPERATURE.

3 MELT THE BUTTER IN THE MICROWAVE AND SPLIT INTO 4 EQUAL PORTIONS. SLOWLY ADD TO (2) AND MIX THOROUGHLY. ADD THE WORCESTERSHIRE SAUCE, SALT, PEPPER AND LEMON JUICE AND MIX THOROUGHLY TO FINISH THE SAUCE.

4 CUT THE BACON SLICES INTO QUARTERS AND COOK IN A FRYING PAN UNTIL BROWNED ON BOTH SIDES.

5 SLICE THE ENGLISH MUFFINS IN HALF, TOAST, AND SPREAD WITH BUTTER. TOP WITH (4).

6 DRY THE POACHED EGG FROM (1) AND PLACE ON TOP OF (5). DRIZZLE THE HOLLANDAISE SAUCE FROM (3) ON TOP AND SPRINKLE WITH CHOPPED PARSLEY AND GRATED KARASUMI. PLACE ON A PLATE, DECORATE WITH A LETTUCE LEAF, AND DONE!

I GO TO MEET
THE ONE WHO
IS A BETTER
CHEF THAN I.

You're Reading in the Wrong Direction!!

1
2
3
1
2
3
4
5
6

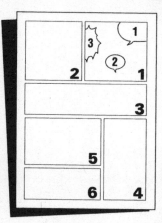

Whoops! Guess what? You're starting at the wrong end of the comic!

...It's true! In keeping with the original Japanese format, **Food Wars!** is meant to be read from right to left, starting in the upper-right corner.

Unlike English, which is read from left to right, Japanese is read from right to left, meaning that action, sound effects and word-balloon order are completely reversed... something which can make readers unfamiliar with Japanese feel pretty backwards themselves. For this reason, manga or Japanese comics published in the U.S. in English have sometimes been published "flopped"—that is, printed in exact reverse order, as though seen from the other side of a mirror.

By flopping pages, U.S. publishers can avoid confusing readers, but the compromise is not without its downside. For one thing, a character in a flopped manga series who once wore in the original Japanese version a T-shirt emblazoned with "M A Y" (as in "the merry month of") now wears one which reads "Y A M"! Additionally, many manga creators in Japan are themselves unhappy with the process, as some feel the mirror-imaging of their art skews their original intentions.

We are proud to bring you Yuto Tsukuda and Shun Saeki's **Food Wars!** in the original unflopped format.

For now, though, turn to the other side of the book and let the adventure begin...!

—Editor

AHA HA HA HA HA HA!
AHA HA! YOU'RE SOOO COOL, SHINOMIYA! AHA HA HA!
SHORTLY THEREAFTER, SHE WAS SMACKED.